Second Growth

Sean Markey, John T. Pierce,
Kelly Vodden, and Mark Roseland

Second Growth:
Community Economic Development
in Rural British Columbia

UBCPress · Vancouver · Toronto

15 14 13 12 11 10 09 08 07 06 05   5 4 3 2 1

Printed in Canada on acid-free paper that is 100% post-consumer recycled, processed chlorine-free, and printed with vegetable-based, low-VOC inks.

Library and Archives Canada Cataloguing in Publication

Second growth : community economic development in rural British Columbia / Sean Markey ... [et al.].

Includes bibliographical references and index.
ISBN 0-7748-1058-0 (bound); ISBN 0-7748-1059-9 (pbk.)

1. Rural development – British Columbia. 2. British Columbia – Economic conditions. 3. British Columbia – Rural conditions. 4. Community development – British Columbia. I. Markey, Sean Patrick, 1970-

HC117.B8S42 2005   338.9711'09173'4   C2004-906097-X

Canadä

UBC Press gratefully acknowledges the financial support for our publishing program of the Government of Canada through the Book Publishing Industry Development Program (BPIDP), and of the Canada Council for the Arts, and the British Columbia Arts Council.

This book has been published with the help of a grant from the Canadian Federation for the Humanities and Social Sciences, through the Aid to Scholarly Publications Programme, using funds provided by the Social Sciences and Humanities Research Council of Canada.

UBC Press
The University of British Columbia
2029 West Mall
Vancouver, BC V6T 1Z2
604-822-5959 / Fax: 604-822-6083
www.ubcpress.ca

Contents

Maps, Figures, and Tables

Foreword

The origin of the Community Economic Development Centre at Simon Fraser University goes back to the early 1980s, when, on a lecture tour for the Vanier Institute of the Family, I had the good fortune to meet and make friends with David Ross and Peter Usher. David, an economist, and Peter, a geographer, had just been commissioned by the Vanier Institute to write a book on community economic development (CED). The book, entitled *From the Roots Up: Economic Development as if Community Mattered* (Canadian Council on Social Development 1986), is now a classic, one of the best sequels to E.F. Schumacher's *Small Is Beautiful*. In 1994 David was appointed executive director of the Canadian Council on Social Development. A few years earlier, he and I had been asked by the Institute for the Humanities at Simon Fraser University to undertake a feasibility study for a centre for community economic development at the university. The centre was started in 1989 and this book embodies its first major research project.

In the meantime, the forces that threaten the very existence of local economies in both rich and poor countries have been gathering strength. Globalization, spurred on by the operations of big business and the political pressures they exert, and by the World Bank and the World Trade Organization, is consolidating the market power of giant corporations that are responsible to no governments, and certainly not to any local communities anywhere. In Britain, in this respect probably typical of other industrial countries, the consequences are summed up by the New Economics Foundation as "Ghost Town Britain," where 30,000 shops and services – retail stores, grocers, banks, post offices, pubs – have disappeared in the five years up to 2000.[1] This trend continues, in spite of government programs aimed at arresting the decline of local economies. During the past ten years, we have had City Task Forces and Action Teams, Urban Development Corporations, City Challenge, Regeneration Budgets, and, going back a bit further, support to worker-owned firms and cooperatives. There has been some emphasis on community involvement, generally hampered by excessive bureaucracy, while funds from the European Union targeted at deprived areas are limited by the byzantine complexity of securing them. The 1997 Labour government introduced New Deal Communities aimed at better community involvement, but this has proved to be a bureaucratic nightmare. The verdict on the past ten years: of course, some successes, but Ghost Town Britain still predominates. And so far there is no coherent approach to reviving local communities.

That is, of course, also true of other Western countries, including Canada. The starting point of this book is the question "What can CED contribute to the prosperity and sustainability of rural areas?" Thus, the book is concerned with the ways in which communities can use CED to adapt to changes driven by the political and economic restructuring imposed by globalization. How do communities cope with rapid technological changes and job losses, increased competition, and overexploitation of resources? Everywhere the diversity of local economies and the quality of peoples' lives are diminishing or are under threat.

The aim of the research upon which this book is based was to work with forest communities in British Columbia to identify strategies and actions to strengthen local economic capacity. More precisely, the research team was guided by five main questions:

- How can forest-based communities become more self-reliant?
- How can communities assess their current capacity to develop CED initiatives?
- What do communities need to know about themselves and about various potential CED initiatives to proceed with confidence?
- How can communities increase that capacity?
- How can one community's experience with CED be usefully shared with other communities?

The research was participatory, with researchers and communities being drawn together on an equal footing to agree on objectives and action. Community workshops helped the research/community teams to work together and assess progress.

The book is built around three themes: dependency, transition, and resilience. Dependency deals with the history and present condition of rural resource-based communities. Transition describes the changing social, economic, and environmental conditions of life at community, regional, and national levels: the impact of globalization broadly considered. Resilience enables communities to adapt, to inform themselves, and to organize, and is the quality that gets things done to improve their lives and ensure their survival.

These themes are elaborated by the authors in masterly fashion, as they give a lucid account of much of Canada's development and also illustrate the potential of CED in the nation's future. The conclusions spell out some guiding principles for increasing the impact of CED in forest-based and non-metropolitan communities: a community charter for revitalization. It is recognized that "when so many important factors in community life depend on decisions made by senior governments and large, distant corporations, the notion of seeking more local control over the economy may appear to be unrealistic," but there is "a growing body of evidence that demonstrates that deliberate community action can and does influence the local economy and is capable of improving the quality of life for local residents." I would add that there is also a growing body of opinion in both rich and poor countries that globalization is on a collision course with people and the environment, a social and economic disaster. What is needed now is not globalization but localization,[2] and *Second Growth* is a decisive step in that direction.

George McRobie
Former director, Centre for Intermediate Technology
Author, *Small Is Possible*

Acknowledgments

The authors would like to thank the many individuals in our partner communities for their courage and willingness to participate in the project upon which this book is based. Their dedication of time and energy, over and above ongoing and demanding efforts to sustain and develop their communities, added tremendously to the quality and depth of our research. In particular, we would like to thank Norman Dale, Larry Casper, Bob McKay, and Nigel Hemingway for their lead roles in facilitating the project at the community level.

We would like to thank the many research assistants who dedicated their time and enthusiasm to the project and to the communities: Jennifer Gunter, Ross Smith, Andy Mills, John Terry, Rhonda Carriere, Shawn Jodway, Jamie Wood, and Sheldon Leong.

We would like to thank Stephen Ameyaw, Research Associate, Simon Fraser University Community Economic Development Centre, for his outstanding community development efforts and guidance throughout the entire course of the project. Thanks also to Larry Trunkey for his critical work in the early stages of the project.

We would like to thank Christina Lai and Penny Simpson for their administrative and Web-based assistance.

Finally, we would like to thank our peer reviewers for their insightful suggestions, and the people at UBC Press, particularly Randy Schmidt, for their guidance and support in bringing this book to fruition.

Disclaimer
At the request of the Aboriginal communities participating in this project, the Community Economic Development Centre has included the following notice of disclaimer with regard to all information about the communities in this book:

"Any information provided by Aboriginal peoples relates to the particular project under consideration, and cannot be used by governments or others in consideration of other projects in the future, without the express written consent of the Aboriginal peoples."

Abbreviations

AAC	annual allowable cut
ACOA	Atlantic Canada Opportunities Agency
BCENTS	Business and Community Employer Network Technology System
CDC	community development corporation
CED	community economic development
CEDO	community-based economic development organization
CRD	Capital Region District
CRM	community-based natural resource management
CSRD	Columbia-Shuswap Regional District
DIA	Downtown Improvement Association
EBM	ecosystem-based management
EDO	economic development officer
FL	Forest Licence
FPC	Forest Practices Code
FRBC	Forest Renewal BC
GDP	gross domestic product
GNP	gross national product
GVRD	Greater Vancouver Regional District
HRDC	Human Resources Development Canada
LED	local economic development
LQ	location quotient
LRMP	Land and Resource Management Planning
LRSY	long-run sustained yield
LTC	Lillooet Tribal Council
LTHL	long-term harvest level
NGO	nongovernmental organization
OD	organizational development
OECD	Organisation for Economic Co-operation and Development
SAEDC	Salmon Arm Economic Development Corporation

SCIP	Shuswap Construction Industry Program
SMZ	Special Management Zone
TFL	Tree Farm Licence
TSA	Timber Supply Area
WD	Western Diversification

Second Growth

1
Approaching Rural and Small-Town Communities

A struggle is taking place in the minds of Canadians over the image of rural and small-town communities. On the one hand, our historical roots conjure up images of a fiercely independent rural culture, carving out a nation from the rugged and plentiful resources that formed and continue to play a large role in our national economy and society. On the other hand, more recent political and economic changes, which coincide with the urbanization of the Canadian population, shift common perceptions of rural areas from being independent to being dependent on provincial and federal governments for their survival. The perceptual dichotomy of rural areas prompts the following questions: are rural and small-town communities the backbone of the Canadian economy, supplying the resources that drive urban and new economy growth? Or are our rural areas being propped up by the wealth generated in urban areas?

The debate over the viability of rural areas in British Columbia and across Canada is due, in part, to the fact that for the past quarter-century, rural communities and regions across Canada have struggled to cope with powerful forces of change. Changes in the economy have radically altered the relationship between corporations and communities. Governments, driven by budgetary restrictions and ideological commitments, have attempted to reduce their responsibilities to manage and to maintain the condition and parity of rural areas. Finally, resource scarcity and changes in our understanding of both ecological functioning and biodiversity have challenged traditional environmental standards and the exploitative practices of past economic activity. These forces have dramatically shaken conventional understandings of the social and economic nature of rural and small-town areas.

The debate between the *independence* and *dependence* of rural areas is also, to some extent, a false generalization. Change and variability in rural areas betray convenient interpretations of a homogeneous "rural" portrayed in the media and in political and policy representations. Nevertheless, our interest as Canadians in the future of rural areas is clear, whether that interest is stimulated by discussions of land use and resource scarcity, tax dollar distribution, corporate restructuring, population losses or gains, heritage, or the resolution of long-standing Aboriginal claims to title and treaty.

This book offers a different perspective on the state of rural debate. We outline certain economic dependencies in rural communities and regions, but we are primarily interested in exploring what rural and small-town communities are doing, and can do, to diversify their local economies and become more viable and more resilient to change. We will characterize these locally based development efforts as community economic development (CED).

In the absence of traditional sources of economic and social certainty in rural areas, communities and governments at all levels are increasingly turning to CED to make a contribution to the economy and to the society of hinterland areas (Bryant and Joseph 2001). As will become clear over the course of this book, numerous challenges confront locally based approaches to development. Nevertheless, communities across British Columbia (and Canada) continue to forge ahead with their own economic development visions and plans, gradually and subtly altering the rural economic landscape and becoming themselves another force of change.

In this volume, we explore these issues in the context of four forest-based communities in British Columbia. Like many other jurisdictions, these communities are seeking ways to cope with change and hopefully to thrive, despite economic downturns, restructuring in the forest and other resource sectors, forest fires, international disputes over tariffs on softwood lumber, and a host of other issues that are beyond their control.

A three-year participatory research project, the Forest Communities project, facilitated our relationship as university researchers with the four case communities. We designed the project to explore the ways in which rural and small-town communities may use a CED approach to increase economic opportunities at the local level. This volume recounts our project experience and seeks to answer critical questions relevant to other communities surrounding the use of and prospects for CED.

"CED" is a term used to describe a participatory, bottom-up approach to development. The definition of CED that we used to guide the project was as follows: "CED is a process by which communities can initiate and generate their own solutions to their common economic problems and thereby build long-term community capacity and foster the integration of economic, social, and environmental objectives" (Ross and McRobie 1989). As such, CED is an approach for generating economic opportunity and addressing social and ecological issues at the local level. CED is gaining increasing attention from governments and development practitioners, and in academic circles, to describe locally based development and to generate locally appropriate economic development strategies. As we will see throughout this book, CED was a particularly useful approach for facilitating both development action and our research objectives.

Purpose

Despite the practical affiliations and origins of CED, the purpose of this volume is to reflect on our project experiences and to view the conditions and changes taking place at the community level from a broader perspective. Specifically, we are interested in how our project experience is able to provide insight into the apparent conflict between the economic imperative and fluidity of capital versus the lived worlds of rural and small-town places. This conflict is responsible for much of the uncertainty that rural and small-town areas face on a daily basis. The mediation of this conflict will ultimately determine the relative success or failure of the development prospects for rural and small-town communities. More specifically still, we investigate the capacity of CED to be a contributing force to the successful transformation and/or continued prosperity of rural areas. We ask whether CED is capable of fostering local initiatives that will help create a more sustainable economic future for rural and small-town communities. Or will CED exist on the margins of economic development – a localized and palliative strategy for the spatially, economically, and socially marginalized? Answers to these questions are important if we are to move forward in finding meaningful solutions, economically and politically, to the intractability of uneven development.

Objectives

Our inquiry into CED is driven by two overall objectives: (1) to provide theoretical substance to an investigation of CED, and (2) to provide a systematic case study of CED linking inquiry, practice, and policy making. These two objectives are drawn from a realization that despite a strong record of localist or community-based research in Canada, understanding of the local, or CED, process is relatively limited. This is particularly true in terms of the mediating functions of local development processes and structures relative to economic change in an emerging global/local context. In general, local development, and CED as a form of local development, is often characterized as an "unruly" or random process that suffers from the lack of a more systematic approach. In addition, the contextual diversity (the real-world "messiness") that defines the use of CED, and the limited amount of relevant systematic inquiry into CED, leads some to conclude that our present conceptualizations of local development also lack theoretical sophistication (Nutter and McKnight 1994; Filion 1998; Savoie 2000; Hayter 2000): "Forest towns have varied in their commitment to, and organization of, local diversification. In this context, unruly implies a broad definition of entrepreneurialism, connoting a patchwork of bottom-up, entrepreneurial developments, only loosely coordinated, if at all, by broader planning frameworks" (Hayter 2000, 319).

The combination of the practical and conceptual limitations of our understandings of CED ultimately hinders the advancement of CED as a coherent policy response to economic change. Despite the conceptual growing pains of CED, however, increasing evidence suggests that communities and regions across Canada are actively engaging in self-directed development efforts that seek to diversify and strengthen their communities and local economies.

CED is action-oriented, but from a research and policy perspective, there are a variety of advantages to enhancing the theoretical relevance of CED. First, a better understanding of theory will enhance the relevance of a CED research agenda. Theoretical foundations provide CED researchers with the opportunity to build knowledge in a more systematic fashion. Theory provides common conceptual frameworks and common terms that will help to avoid repetition and researcher isolation.

Second, theoretical rigour improves practice. The opportunity to reflect on the dynamics of local development practice, to extrapolate "best practices," and to narrow our understanding of the relationships between different contextual circumstances and local development implementation will provide practitioners with useful information and examples.

Finally, better theorization will lead to better policy. Theory necessarily facilitates generalizations drawn from experience. Over time, an increasing amount of research may lead to a sense of predictability and certainty regarding CED processes. Greater certainty is a necessary ingredient in the policy process, enabling policy makers to embrace a community-based approach to development and to construct appropriate standards for local accountability.

Themes
Three broad themes provide a conceptual foundation for our objectives. First, we use the concept of *dependency* to highlight the economic development lineage and, to a certain extent, the present condition of rural, resource-based communities. Dependency adequately captures the critical features and relationships between resource-based communities, governments, and corporations. We use dependency to uncover the roots of the changes rural communities are currently facing and to help to explain why change is so difficult for many communities and regions in the rural, resource-dependent environment.

Second, we employ the term *transition* to describe the changing social, economic, and environmental circumstances, at all levels, that are clearly evident across the rural landscape. Identifying the characteristics of change is again critical to understanding the challenges and opportunities that communities face in pursuing more sustainable economic futures. Finally, as British Columbia adapts to new economic realities, the *resilience* of communities is important in terms of their ability to adapt, generate information, organize, and implement meaningful action.

Literature Comparisons and Contributions

A number of existing texts help to frame the specific contributions of this volume relative to our understanding of economic development and change in the rural environment. Pierce and Dale (1999) provide an overview of the state of community development and sustainability across Canada. Hayter (2000) provides an industrial and political perspective on the restructuring of the forest industry in BC. Cashore et al. (2001) concentrate on the policy process associated with the "search for sustainability" in BC forests. Each of these books, among others, makes an excellent contribution to building an understanding of the economic, political, and environmental changes currently influencing communities in BC and across Canada.

Our volume seeks to build on the above works by contributing and refining a *local development* perspective to our understanding of rural development issues, expressed here as community economic development (CED). Here again, though, we are building on the works of other researchers in Canada who have been steadily documenting and refining our understanding of the role and practices of CED (Coffey and Polese 1985; Bryant and Preston 1989; Barnes and Hayter 1994; Douglas 1994; Savoie 2000; Roseland 1998; Lloyd 1996). The Forest Communities project gained valuable insights from this literature, and this text seeks to address and advance many of the concerns and observations expressed by previous authors.

We must also mention the broader contributions of geography to our understanding of local development. Geography is well suited to inquiry into matters of local development. As Barnes and Hayter state (1997, 198): "Community development is highly sensitive to where a place is located (its situation), and the resources found there (its site)." Geographic inquiry contributes two distinctive ideas to this work. First, recent geographic research has paid particular attention to the role of the local and the importance of context in the development process. As a result, Massey (1995) states that we need a better understanding of local and global relations. In furthering her point, Massey provides five reasons to calm fears that a focus on local research will cause geography to drift into idiographic obscurity (1995, 324):

- The world is endlessly unique.
- An understanding of difference depends upon an understanding of broader structures.
- The comprehension of difference is one of the raisons d'être of the human sciences.

- Intervening in the world requires an appreciation of its differences.
- It is the understanding of how the local and the global interact that is the next challenge.

Recent Canadian geographic research has responded to the challenge, broadly speaking, of greater inquiry into local development. First, of particular interest to this work are those studies that focus on rural and resource-based communities. These works have substantially contributed to the origins and design of this volume. For example, Barnes and Hayter (1994) provide an analysis of the impacts of the restructuring process in the BC forest products industry upon resource communities. Gill and Reed (1997) explore the role and impact of local and extra-local coalitions in bringing about policies and land-use decisions in a post-productivist landscape. Reed (1995a, 1995b) explores the role of local and national governments in promoting sustainable development. Clapp (1999) welcomes the role of local agency in resource management, advocating that industrialization be scaled back in favour of ecological, social, and cultural sustainability. Finally, Barnes et al. (2000) underscore the importance of local geographies and histories to the study of Canadian economic geography.

Second, the rural geographic literature has played an important role in outlining and guiding the inquiry for this work. Randall and Ironside (1996) highlight the continued importance of rural resource-based communities in defining Canada's global economic role. Their research is also important in challenging stereotypical perceptions of resource-based communities and revealing a greater degree of social and economic diversity, which will be critical to local development processes and to the continued survival and prosperity of rural communities. Troughton (1995) identifies a need to explore rural maintenance through models of sustainable rural development. He states that a laissez-faire political economic approach has left communities vulnerable to technological and economic changes. He contends that it is a priority for rural geography to redefine the entire rural system by focusing on the integration of its parts from the bottom up: "Rural geography is eminently suited to engage in a community-based approach" (Troughton 1995, 302). Pierce (1998) echoes Troughton's concerns, stating that the true diversity of rural environments has not received adequate attention in rural geography. Pierce specifically calls for more attention to locality and sustainable rural development in terms of improving our understanding of policies for sustainability and scale sensitivity.

In general, as Massey envisaged, there has been an increasing focus on the role of the local relative to global economic and state restructuring. Processes of development and the formation and mediation of uneven development become much more dynamic and contextually complex in a scale-flux environment. Hayter appropriately captures the situation from the local perspective (2000, 392): "The wider global 'space' economy offers opportunities and threats to 'places,' with the result that the place-space relation is dynamic and subject to tension ... The ability of local populations to cope with these processes is highly varied and defines the substance and meaning of local models." This volume seeks to explore and enhance our understanding of these "local models."

Research Design

As stated earlier, the overall purpose of the Forest Communities project was to work with forest-based communities in BC to identify strategies and tools for strengthening local economic capacity. Forest Renewal BC (FRBC), a now defunct provincial Crown corporation, sponsored the research. The mandate of FRBC was to improve the well-being of BC's forests, forest industry, and forest communities through the reinvestment of funds drawn from fees and royalties charged to forest companies for the right to harvest timber on Crown lands. The Forest Communities project qualified for funding due to the extent to which communities require diversification and stabilization strategies as a response to dealing with economic downturns and broader forces of restructuring in the province's forest industry.

To guide the project, the Community Economic Development Centre (now the Centre for Sustainable Community Development) at Simon Fraser University outlined five overall research questions in advance:

- How can forest-based communities become more self-reliant?
- How can communities assess their current capacity to develop CED initiatives?
- What do communities need to know about themselves and about various potential CED initiatives to proceed with confidence?
- How can communities increase that capacity?
- How can one community's experience with CED be usefully shared with other communities?

The selection of communities for the project was extremely important given its scope and participatory intent. We identified four communities through a multi-stage process. First, the CED Centre listed a call for "expressions of interest" through e-mail discussion lists (listservs). Researchers from the centre also made a number of personal inquiries to ensure that specific communities or regions not represented on the listserv were made aware of the project. Second, a number of communities responded to the initial scan and provided the centre with letters of support for the funding proposal. Third, upon receipt of the funding, the research team at the CED Centre conducted a brief survey questionnaire with interested communities. The survey gathered the following information:

- diversity of the local economy and the level of forest dependency
- history of development and planning initiatives
- extent of public involvement in these initiatives
- demonstrated interest in the research and willingness to commit resources to the project

The survey helped to determine the conditions of the responding communities (for example, level of forest dependency, planning and CED experience, and socio-economic conditions) and whether they would be likely to benefit from and fully participate in the research project. All communities had to exhibit a moderate degree of forest dependency and a willingness to contribute meaningfully to the project. The research team was also interested in working with a variety of circumstances in terms of economic diversity and levels of CED capacity. Finally, the research team expressed an interest in working with four specific communities, and each community invited us to meet with them to develop appropriate terms of reference. Research assistants organized a workshop in each community to devise a research workplan and to determine the specific development objectives for each community through a participatory process.

The above discussion briefly outlines the delicate balancing act required between funding institutions, researchers, and communities when seeking to adopt a participatory research model. In its purest form, the form of participatory research adopted by the project, "action research," demands that researchers and communities or organizations be drawn together on an equal footing to negotiate and determine project objectives pertaining to research and action. The Forest Communities project design deviates from the purity of the participatory model. Our funder required a detailed proposal before releasing funds, that is, the CED Centre could not engage with the communities in any significant detail before receiving funding, and so the main proposal design did not involve the project communities. In an attempt to preserve collaborative respect with its potential research partners, the CED Centre used the above techniques to meet the demands of the funding body for predetermined research objectives while also maintaining directional flexibility with the communities. The culmination of the selection process, being a community-based workshop in each community, enabled the Centre and its new community partners to learn from one another and to reorient the research and action process to fit more closely with community conditions and objectives (see Chapter 9 for more details on the community/university relationship).

Project Methods
The negotiation of research relationships and the underlying intentions of the research process are important factors when selecting research methods.

This section highlights the methods used to facilitate the participatory research process. In doing so, this chapter responds in part to Reason's (1994) observation that methodological descriptions of participatory research processes are lacking in the literature.

Participatory research is a collaborative process that links researchers with practitioners in the joint pursuit of better theory *and* practice. The reasons for selecting a participatory methodology for the project will be explained in greater detail later, but there are two main reasons for using participatory research: (1) participatory research and CED share many of the same principles and goals, including participation, collaboration, and self-reliance; and (2) the project communities were interested in the process because they were motivated to create change, and not simply be the passive recipients of yet another research or consultant report.

Participatory research provided us with the means through which we could achieve both research and practical objectives within the same project. Combining theory and practice offers many research advantages, but it also raises challenging questions about both the validity of research and the utility of practice.   •

We will outline our reflections on the research process in Chapter 9. In brief, however, the participatory research process united community working groups and the CED Centre research team at each major stage of the project, including:

- setting the research parameters and deciding the agenda
- collecting research data
- conducting analysis and drawing conclusions
- planning and implementing CED initiatives
- evaluating progress and responding to the results of such evaluations

Decisions about methods that we used and who was primarily responsible for implementing specific project details were the result of a negotiated process, and were dependent upon the skills, resources, and time available to either the community or the university research team. A negotiated research process and the division of project-related labour accurately describes the form of participation demonstrated in the project. Research partners were not "joined at the hip," collaborating on every nuance in the research and development process. Instead, project partners designed a research strategy that balanced efficiency with self-determination in order to meet both research and development (that is, action) objectives. Community workshops provided the research partners with an opportunity for collective reflection in assessing the progress and contributions of the project.

We relied upon a variety of methods to facilitate the negotiated participatory research process. First, as stated earlier, the research team at the CED

Centre and community-based working groups facilitated the university/ community partnership. Second, the research design stipulated that we assign research assistants to each of the communities to act as resource people for the working groups and to serve as liaisons between the university-based research team and the communities. Third, in addition to the specific community-based research activities of the research assistants, the project workplan scheduled four main workshops in each community throughout the three-year project, to serve as benchmarks for evaluating activities and for planning future activities. Fourth, the research team hired interns during the summers to work directly with the project communities. Both local residents and nonlocal undergraduate students from the CED Centre held intern positions. The research team and each community-based working group jointly determined internship job descriptions. Finally, the project relied upon a variety of data sources to inform research findings and to guide development decisions, including:

- community profiles
- surveys
- document analysis
- community workshops
- participant observation

Table 1.1 summarizes the relationship between the main data sources and the important themes identified for project reporting.

The participatory research relationship between the research team and the working groups offered a number of benefits to the project. First, the participatory research process facilitated a division of labour between mutually agreed upon tasks. Each community had experienced unsatisfactory external research and consulting relationships in the past. Consequently, the communities did not immediately grasp the action research process.

Table 1.1

Data matrix showing the relationship between the main data sources and the important themes identified for project reporting

	Data source			
Project component	Community profiles	Surveys	Community workshops	Participant observation
CED process			×	×
Capacity assessment	×	×	×	×
Capacity building	×	×	×	×
CED strategies	×	×	×	×

The project required several months of relationship building before there was a clear understanding that the university research team was not simply a quasi-consulting resource, solely intent on delivering a research report. For example, one community's inability to assign tangible resources to the project prevented any significant project development at the community level for the entire first year of the project.

Second, creating an organizational structure at the community level (working groups) created the necessary community-based resources to conduct the project. Finally, we designed the project to enhance, rather than to duplicate, previous or ongoing development processes and initiatives. The negotiated participatory research relationship ensured that the project did not supersede or duplicate existing group activities.

Defining "Rural"
Throughout this chapter and in the rest of the text, we employ the term "rural" to describe the case communities. We use this term for two reasons. First, residents in the case communities define their communities as "rural," and speak of a desire to maintain their "rural" quality of life while also pursuing new economic opportunities. Second, despite the many technical definitions of rural, the term "degrees of rurality" is perhaps the most useful concept for consolidating the differences in rural definitions *and* the similar socio-economic characteristics that may be attributed to rural areas (Du Plessis et al. 2002). We are aware of and sensitive to technical rural differences, but, particularly in the "heartland"/"hinterland" dichotomy of British Columbia, we use the term "rural" in more general non-metropolitan terms. We will continue a discussion of the meaning of "rural" and the status of rural areas in BC and Canada in Chapter 2.

Organization
In order to investigate the three themes outlined earlier – dependency, transition, and resilience – this book is divided into nine remaining chapters. In Chapter 2 we provide an overview of the BC provincial economy and profiles of the four project communities. The chapter will provide readers with an opportunity to understand the broader provincial and specific community conditions under which the project operated. The relatively poor performance of the BC economy, combined with community-based concerns regarding the extent of forest and public sector dependency, created conditions in which the project communities were looking for new ideas and approaches to facilitating economic development.

Chapter 3 introduces the first part of the conceptual framework used to guide the analysis of research findings: dependency. The concept of dependency is drawn from the legacy of staples development in BC and across Canada described by staples theory. Staples theory describes Canadian economic development in terms of the successive exploitation of resources (Innis 1933; Watkins 1981, 1982). We use staples theory for its seminal contribution to understanding the unique character of economic development in Canada and for revealing the historical conditions that contribute to the traditional social and economic dependency of resource-based communities. Staples theory is also relevant to the project research because of its ability to describe dimensions of the current condition of Canadian economic development (Barnes 1996; Britton 1996; Hutton 1994). The legacy of staples development and the marginalization of First Nations communities will provide a contextually based account of the origins of community dependency and help to explain some of the many challenges associated with implementing CED.

Chapter 4 introduces the second component of our conceptual framework: transition. Specifically, this chapter outlines the process and impacts of economic restructuring in BC. We discuss restructuring in the forest sector specifically from a local development perspective. In addition to describing change in the forest sector, we briefly review other forces of social and economic change in BC, including the environmental movement, First Nations activism, economic diversification, government policy, and community action.

In Chapter 5, we introduce the final part of our conceptual framework: resilience. This chapter provides a more detailed discussion of the origins and meaning of CED. We associate the origins of CED with the lessons learned from and frustrations associated with market failure and other approaches to local and regional development. This experience-based description of CED builds a case for the use of CED beyond promoting matters of social equity and environmental justice. The CED approach is soundly based upon lessons learned in the past about how to promote successful local (and sustainable) development.

In Chapter 6, we present findings drawn from an extensive literature review that identifies important success factors associated with community and regional development around the world. The chapter presents a "success factor framework" that we used to assess the conditions and capacity of the case communities for engaging in CED planning. Community practitioners and researchers may use the assessment process and the community indicators attached to the framework to identify strategic opportunities and monitor the CED process at the local level. This chapter contributes to an ongoing dialogue within BC and across Canada concerning best practices for community-based development and the challenges associated with how to measure the impacts of various CED activities.

Chapter 7 reviews the components of strategic planning that we used to facilitate the CED process in the project communities. This chapter builds on the success factor framework presented in Chapter 6 to outline the specifics of the CED process; in other words, how do you implement CED? The chapter reviews lessons drawn from the project on how to prepare for CED planning, how to manage the CED planning process once it is operating, and how to sustain the CED process beyond an initial start-up phase.

Chapter 8 provides a systematic review of various CED strategies used by the case communities in an effort to diversify their local economies – the story of development. We divide our observations of the various CED strategies into the following sections: business development; arts, culture, and heritage development; community resource management; tourism promotion and development; and networks and community relations. This chapter illustrates the great diversity of CED strategies available to communities and discusses different challenges and opportunities associated with a shift in development focus from external to internal.

In Chapter 9, we reflect on the utility and challenges of the participatory research process. Participatory research is an effective tool for navigating between the dual objectives of research and action in the project. However, the figurative and literal distance between the university and the communities presents numerous opportunities to discuss the dynamics of the research process. As universities seek to enhance their overall relevance to society, participatory research (which offers an opportunity to maintain the integrity of the research process while also delivering tangible benefits to community research partners) will be an increasingly valuable, although controversial, tool for constructing university/community relationships.

Finally, Chapter 10 provides a synthesis of major findings. The chapter outlines lessons and challenges facing practitioners, researchers, and policy makers concerning the viability and resilience of forest communities. The chapter discusses specific challenges associated with enhancing the scope and scale of CED activity, and highlights elements of a continuing research agenda to enhance our understanding of the potential and limitations of CED. The chapter ends with a discussion of a theoretically and practically based "community charter," consisting of a series of guiding principles, for increasing the leverage and capacity of CED in forest-based and rural, non-metropolitan communities and regions. We hope that this community charter will contribute to the revitalization, or second growth, of resource communities in the coming years.

Throughout the book, we have included specific "community voice" contributions. A number of community-based individuals associated with the project provide written contributions with an insider look at the workings and dynamics of CED in their communities. These individuals represent a cross-section of different community development organizations, local governments, and working group members from each community.

Conclusion

When so many important factors in community life depend on decisions made by senior governments and large, distant corporations, the notion of seeking more local control over the economy may appear to be unrealistic. We acknowledge that the challenges communities face are significant, and that even with increased diversification and flexibility, a prosperous and sustainable future for many communities may continue to be elusive. However, we are motivated to look for local or community solutions due to a growing body of evidence that demonstrates that deliberate community action can and does influence the local economy and is capable of improving the quality of life for local residents. While the prospects for CED are constrained and impacted by many external factors, the choices communities make on their own can be important in determining their future.

As the following chapters will illustrate, local initiative has always played an important role in the development of rural communities across Canada. However, the present pace and dynamic nature of change creates both immense challenges and great opportunities for locally based development to play an even more *structurally* significant role in the economic health and sustainability of rural communities. This book seeks to increase our level of understanding about how CED can be implemented effectively and how CED efforts fit within the context of other forces of change across the political, economic, environmental, and social landscape.

2
Context and Communities

Two clashing cultures cause most of the discord that characterizes our country. Until we reconcile the two, large parts of our economy will continue as cripples, large parts of our environment will continue to be destroyed, and regional movements – some of them separatist – will threaten to tear us apart.

These incompatible cultures are not English v. French Canada, not Central Canada v. the West and other regions, not whites v. coloured immigrants. The clash is between a largely expansive free market urban economy that generates most of Canada's wealth and a largely protectionist government-run rural economy that nurses grievances and demands ever-greater subsidies from the rest of the country. (Solomon 2003)

Accompanying metropolitan areas' increasing share of the province's population has been an increasing demand for a larger share of federal and provincial tax revenue for their governments. In the extreme, arguments are now made that these "city states" and their "new economies" are the engines of economic growth.

Before accepting that they are either the engines of growth or deserving of a greater share of taxes, it is necessary to determine how much metropolitan regions actually contribute to the provincial and national economic base. Such analysis indicates that, in reality, metropolitan regions in British Columbia make a below average per capita contribution, and hence are dependent on international export revenue from commodities originating in non-metropolitan regions of the province. (Baxter and Ramlo 2002, 3)

The two opinions presented in the above quotations encapsulate an ongoing debate within Canada over the state of rural areas. In the first quote, by Solomon (2003), the perception of rural areas as dependent, demanding, and backward is a common theme running through Canadian politics and policy making in the postwar period. The second quote, by Baxter and Ramlo (2002), highlights a connection between provincial and national resource-dependent economies and the actual source of those resources, which are in rural, non-metropolitan areas. The latter argument counters perceptions of rural dependency and characterizes rural areas as the fuel for so-called urban growth engines.

The easiest way to resolve these perceptual and statistical differences between urban and rural is to note that the regional diversity in Canada and across British Columbia makes both opinions correct under certain circumstances. That said, regardless of whether rural or urban areas are given credit for provincial economic performance, rural areas generally underperform in major socio-economic indicators when compared with their metropolitan neighbours. In addition, rural areas face particular economic challenges and have been experiencing a period of decline relative to the growth and expansion of urban areas.

In order to provide some contextual substance to the rural debate, we have two overall purposes in this chapter. First, we will provide a general overview of the state of the BC economy. Reviewing broad economic conditions in the province provides a backdrop that helps to explain the specific conditions and motivations for development present in the case communities. Second, we will narrow our contextual lens and provide basic socio-economic profile information about the project communities and present, in their own words, their reasons for wishing to participate in the project.

Context and Timing

Understanding the general social and economic context in BC and across Canada is important for framing the conditions of the project communities. The project, beginning in 1998, coincided with the start of a particularly severe and prolonged downturn in the forest sector and in the economic health of BC more generally. From a project perspective, the economic downturn created the conceptual "space" for community leaders to consider other approaches to generating economic development. The late 1990s in BC also marked a turning point when a critical mass of observers from a variety of sectors began to seriously question the economic make-up of the province and the extent to which our economic past has created certain obstacles to dealing with economic transition within a "new economy."

The BC Context

Canada is a rich periphery when the economic relationships and conditions of the global economy are considered (Hayter 2000). Within Canada, British Columbia is a rich periphery. As will be discussed in Chapters 3 and 4, a staples-based economy provided and continues to provide BC with

Table 2.1

Contribution of forest, mineral, and energy exports to total exports and GDP in Canada, 1996

Jurisdiction	Forest, mineral, and energy exports	
	% of total exports	% of GDP
British Columbia	71.0	19.7
Alberta	64.2	19.9
Saskatchewan	41.3	13.8
Manitoba	18.4	4.4
Ontario	5.3	2.1
Quebec	20.4	5.8
New Brunswick	62.7	17.9
Nova Scotia	29.9	5.3
Prince Edward Island	2.5	0.4
Newfoundland	75.7	19.6
Canada	24.6	8.0

Source: BC Stats 2001b.

tremendous wealth and well-diversified metropolitan regions. However, the peripheral regions of BC maintain substantial influence in terms of defining BC's overall economy – within Canada and at a global level. The continued reliance of the BC economy on resource production significantly shapes the internal economic characteristics of the province and the way in which the province is viewed by the global economy (Randall and Ironside 1996). BC is Canada's second highest exporter of natural resource products, which represent a significant part of the provincial GDP (see Table 2.1).

In terms of broadening and updating our understanding of the characteristics of a staples economy, Hutton describes the state of the BC economy as "a mature, advanced export-oriented staple economy in transition" (1994, 4). A mature, advanced staples economy displays the following characteristics:

- substantial depletion of resource endowments following extensive period of resource extraction
- well-established export markets for its principal staple commodities
- increasingly capital- and technology-intensive resource extraction processes
- increasing competition from lower-cost staple regions
- over time, an evolution of development paths from a "pure" extraction mode to more refining and secondary processing of resource commodities
- increasing diversification of the industrial structure of settlements and zones
- evolution of settlement patterns over time

- increasing pressure from environmental groups, the community at large, and (largely as a consequence) politicians

Certainly, as will be made clear throughout the next two chapters, BC exhibits many of the above characteristics. It is important to note, however, that the concept of transition used by Hutton does not apply equally to all communities and regions of the province. Some areas may experience transition, with varying levels of hardship and/or economic opportunity (positive or negative transition experiences), while other areas may simply not have anything to "transition to," or may remain within an older staples paradigm.

The most simplistic point of distinction to make within the BC economy is to speak of two BC economies: the key metropolitan areas of the Lower Mainland and the Capital Region District (Vancouver and Victoria), and the "rest of the province" (Davis and Hutton 1992). Vancouver and Victoria have larger populations and more diversified economies than the peripheral areas of the province, although the Okanagan region and Prince George represent emerging metropolitan regions that arguably make the "two economies" concept outdated.

Hayter (2000) notes the extent to which Fordism in the forest sector created strong core/periphery contrasts between Vancouver and the hinterlands of BC.[1] Vancouver has always been "the centre of the forest industry in terms of manufacturing, distribution, and forward, backward, and final demand linkage effects" (63). Such core/periphery contrasts hold for the economy as a whole. For example, Hutton (1994) indicates that between 1975 and 1981, the non-metropolitan areas of the province expanded more quickly than the large urban areas. However, the recession of 1982-84 marked a significant turning point in the economic fortunes of hinterland regions and communities. The resource-dominated hinterland was most seriously affected. Since 1983, trends have increasingly favoured metropolitan areas. The BC Progress Board notes that between 1981 and 1991, 360,000 net new jobs were created in BC, and all but 1,000 of these were located in the Lower Mainland (de Wolf 2002).

The disparity between the metropolitan and rural regions of the province has continued to expand since the early 1980s. In the early 1980s, BC's economy, on a per capita basis, was second only to Alberta within Canada. By 1998, however, the performance of the BC economy had slipped to below the Canadian average. Finally, in an event with as much symbolic as economic significance, BC officially lost its "have" status – a term that denotes whether a province contributes ("have") to national wealth redistribution as opposed to receiving federal assistance ("have-not") – within Canada in 2002. Such a striking fall within two decades prompts the following question: "How on earth, wonders anyone reared on the old image of

British Columbia, did a province blessed with so much natural wealth tumble so far, so fast?" (Little 2002).

BC: From "Have" to "Have-Not"

BC's equalization cheque on the way: Canada's newest have-not province will receive its first payments from federal government since 1962. (McInnes 2002)

Researchers generally attribute the relative economic decline in BC to a variety of external and internal factors. Externally, perhaps the most significant factor is associated with the long-term decline in the prices of commodities, such as forest products, minerals, and fish. These products have traditionally provided the foundation for wealth in the province (Pierce 2000). Increasing global competition in a variety of resource sectors exacerbates price decline (Marchak et al. 1999). Other, more recent external factors include the impacts associated with the Asian financial crisis beginning in 1997. The crisis in Asia undermined a significant economic asset of BC, its position on the Pacific Rim. Finally, the imposition of duties by the US on Canadian softwood lumber in May 2002 negatively impacted the BC economy, particularly in resource-dependent rural areas.

Despite the significance of external forces affecting the BC economy, provincial economy watchers are paying increasing attention to home-grown problems due to the length and severity of the economic crisis and the extent to which BC politics are characterized by sharp polarization. First, BC has fallen behind the rest of Canada in terms of investment. An 8 percent investment growth rate since 1992 is weaker than in any other region in Canada except the Yukon. Nationally, business and government spending on fixed capital has risen by 29 percent (BC Stats 1999b). Below-average increases in business and government investment in structures and machinery represent a critical economic weakness in BC.

During the 1990s, much of the blame for the decline in investment focused on the "visceral" relationship between the business community and the NDP government, which held power for a decade starting in 1991 (Little 2002). The perception that the NDP was anti-business coincided with very pro-business governments in other parts of the country, notably Alberta and Ontario. As Little (2002) indicates, however, such politically sensitive interpretations of decline must also consider the fact that the growth rate in BC was slow and below the Canadian average during the 1980s, when a business-friendly Social Credit government was in power.

Second, land-base uncertainty surrounding the settlement of First Nations treaties represents an internal source of uncertainty that is particularly relevant to rural communities. The treaty process is discussed in more detail later, but First Nations activism and court decisions related to title and treaty issues crested in the 1980s and 1990s (Blomely 1996). The BC Treaty Commission was established in 1992, but lengthy delays in the treaty process have exacerbated land-use tensions in the province and undermined investment confidence in both Aboriginal and non-Aboriginal communities.

Third, the BC economy remains highly dependent on natural resources:

> The core of British Columbia's dwindling economic fortunes lies in a deeper, more gradual shift that is rarely acknowledged in a province where the politics is polarized and public discourse is often limited to finger-pointing. Slowly, BC has been torn away from its easy-money roots as an exploiter of resources in a world that desperately wanted them; increasingly, it is a province that has to scramble to earn a living in a world whose needs and wants are much different. (Little 2002)

The more gradual and root cause of resource dependency and decline has moved from the academic literature to the mainstream, as illustrated by the recent comments of Jock Finlayson, vice president of the BC Business Council: "We grew rich off resources. Now we are in genteel decline. We created a political and institutional environment in which we didn't seek other ways to make a living" (Little 2002).

The extent of resource decline in the province exacerbates the problem of economic dependency on natural resources. Select fish populations in BC have declined, reaching endangered levels similar to those that caused the collapse of the cod fisheries on the East Coast; the mining industry has declined as mining companies have directed investment to other parts of the world; old-growth forests are threatened, and there is a substantial gap facing certain regions of the province regarding the availability of second-growth forests to meet volume demands. Hutton (1994) extends the problems associated with resource decline to include an overall "sustainability deficit" facing the province. The sustainability deficit refers to the erosion of the capital stocks of natural resources at rates "which both jeopardize the integrity of the stock, and impair the welfare of future generations" (Hutton 1994, 21).

Forestry in particular represents a critical component of the provincial economy. The importance of forest products exports in the province has changed little in the past fifty years. In 1956 lumber and pulp represented 49 percent of provincial exports; in 1996, the figure was 43 percent (BC Stats 1998). The degree of dependency on the forest sector is heightened in non-metropolitan areas. Table 2.2 presents income dependency figures for the non-metropolitan areas of BC, highlighting the significance of the forest sector and the public sector to rural-area economies.

Table 2.2

British Columbia income dependencies by region (percent), 1996

	Vancouver Island/ Coast	Mainland/ Southwest average*	Thompson Okanagan	Kootenay	Cariboo	North Coast	Nechako	Northeast
Forestry	21	13	16	16	37	29	32	24
Mining	1	1	4	12	1	6	5	19
Fishing/trapping	5	0.3	0	0	0	5	0	0
Agriculture	1	4	4.5	2	3	0	4	3
Tourism	7	9	7	7	6	7	6	7
High tech	0	1	0.5	0	1	0	0	0
Public sector	24	25	21	21	20	30	30	18
Construction	7	10	7	7	7	4	5	8
Other basic	4	9	8	4	4	5	2	7
Transfer payment	17	17	20	19	14	10	11	10
Other non-employment	13	10	12	12	7	4	5	4
Total	100	100	100	100	100	100	100	100

* Excluding Greater Vancouver Regional District and Victoria.
Source: Horne 1999.

The importance of the forest sector to BC and to BC's hinterland economies provides relevant context for broader discussions concerning rural local development in the province and the impacts of restructuring. A report
by the Urban Futures Institute underscores the importance of the forest
economy and the economic contribution of the non-metropolitan areas of
BC to the provincial economy:

> Out of the total provincial annual average of $33.8 billion in international
> exports, $24.0 (71%) came from non-metropolitan areas and $9.8 billion
> (29%) came from metropolitan areas. Of the average annual international
> exports of $7.1 billion in services, $4.4 billion (61%) came from metropoli-
> tan areas and $2.7 billion (39%) came from non-metropolitan areas. Of the
> average annual international export of goods of $26.7 billion, $21.3 billion
> (80%) originated in non-metropolitan regions and $5.5 billion (20%) came
> from metropolitan regions. (Baxter and Ramlo 2002, 3)

> With the provincial average annual international exports of $8,659 per capita
> (2001 population), the value of exports from non-metropolitan regions was
> $14,290 per person, while that of the metropolitan regions was only $4,278,
> half the provincial, and 30% of the non-metropolitan average. The non-
> metropolitan areas' contribution to the international exports was $29,789
> per (1996) labour force participant, compared to the metropolitan region's
> $8,513 per labour force participant and the provincial average of $17,258.
> (Baxter and Ramlo 2002, 20)

Clearly, despite the many challenges facing the non-metropolitan areas
of BC, the importance of these areas to the provincial economy demands
that greater attention be paid to the social, economic, and environmental
health of rural communities.

Understanding Rural Canada

A good way to begin a general overview of rural or small-town BC is to
explore the various ways in which the literature defines and describes "rural." General characterizations of "rural," which have served to guide rural
research, tend to concentrate on a variety of factors: remoteness from major
metropolitan centres; a reliance on primary economic activity; conflicts
between preservation and a variety of economic interests; and the extent to
which rural areas are *not* urban, yet are often not differentiated from urban
areas in policy design and program implementation (Robinson 1990).

Hoggart and Buller (1987) review various treatments of "rural" in the literature and outline three possible lines of distinction:

- Socio-cultural – behavioural and attitudinal differences between rural and urban are stressed due to lower populations in rural communities, sense of community, and suspicion of change
- Occupational – reliance on primary industries
- Ecological – small areas separated by substantial zones of open countryside

Each definition alone is insufficient to capture the true diversity of rural environments and communities, but taken together they provide a method for analyzing different dimensions of the rural experience. As we describe later, however, rural areas are changing and these characteristics are now less common in some locales than others, further diversifying the rural milieu according to adaptation and change.

Other definitions of "rural" in the literature present a fluid interpretation in distinguishing between urban and rural. For example, Cloke (1977) provides a definition of "rural" as a settlement continuum with "rural" at one end and "urban" at the other. Also common among efforts to distinguish rurality are various population figures attached to different conceptualizations of "rural."

Definitions of "Rural" by Population and Space

There are several definitions of "rural" from a population and geographical perspective. In Canada, statistical tracking provided by Statistics Canada stresses distance from major centres and difference in population size as distinguishing features (see Table 2.3).

Table 2.3

Definitions of "rural"

Term	Definition
Census rural	Individuals living in the countryside outside centres of 1,000 or more
Rural and small town	Population living in towns and municipalities outside the commuting zone of larger urban centres (that is, outside the commuting zone of centres with populations of 10,000 or more)
Non-metropolitan regions	Refers to individuals living outside metropolitan regions with urban centres with populations of 50,000 or more
OECD rural	Individuals in communities with less than 150 persons per square kilometre

Source: Bollman 2001d.

Table 2.4

Rural population measures in Canada, 2001

| Jurisdiction | Total private household population (1996) | Private household population under alternative definitions of rural | | |
		Census rural	Rural and small town	Non-metropolitan regions
Newfoundland	545,825	236,215	304,245	297,845
Prince Edward Island	131,800	74,200	60,425	63,210
Nova Scotia	896,595	408,155	346,540	442,030
New Brunswick	727,365	374,400	353,120	331,210
Quebec	7,008,125	1,524,555	1,565,335	2,123,770
Ontario	10,605,055	1,777,580	1,573,650	1,566,295
Manitoba	1,087,145	303,615	358,845	477,720
Saskatchewan	970,175	354,555	418,055	524,275
Alberta	2,647,110	535,410	669,340	576,500
British Columbia	3,677,890	661,310	569,825	1,085,505
(%)		(18.0)	(15.5)	(29.5)
Yukon	30,000	11,835	8,485	30,000
Northwest Territories	38,835	18,890	21,685	38,840
Nunavut	24,760	17,630	24,755	24,755
Canada	28,390,685	6,298,350	6,274,320	7,581,970
(%)		(22.2)	(22.1)	(26.7)

Source: Bollman 2001d.

These differences in classification matter to rural development because of the relationship between political significance, the allocation of resources, and the size or influence of a particular sector/group (Fairbairn 1998). The size of Canada's rural population varies depending upon the definition used. For example, if the "census rural" definition is used, 22 percent of Canada's total population is considered rural. However, if an OECD definition is used, the rural population figure jumps to 38 percent of the population, with variations between these two definitions (see Table 2.4).

Rural population figures over time are also informative when considering the political significance of rural areas. In 1931, just over 50 percent of Canada's population was classified as urban. Sixty-five years later, Canada's urban population is more than three-quarters of the national total. The slide in rural population relative to the growth of urban areas leads some researchers to speculate on its significance for rural policy: "The *perception* of rural decline has quite likely led many urban people, and many government officials, to regard rural problems as marginal: questions of adjustment, that will go away in time" (Fairbairn 1998, 3).

The Forest Communities project worked with a combination of census rural and rural and small-town communities. Despite the population differences in the project communities, the following chapters will illustrate that they exhibited a variety of similarities in terms of economic opportunities and barriers. The similarities are causally related not only to population but also to factors of geography, economic make-up, government structure, and rural policy – hence the term "degrees of rurality" used in Chapter 1 (Du Plessis et al. 2002).

In addition, we gain from a definition of "rural" an introduction to the importance of rural economic development issues. Despite common perceptions of rural decline, we recognize that we are speaking about an issue that continues to affect over one-third of the population in BC and across Canada. In the following chapter, we will continue this argument of why does rural matter by investigating the economic significance of rural areas.

Besides population figures, a major reason for addressing rural development issues is that rural areas throughout BC and Canada tend to underperform on critical socio-economic indicators. One reason for the rural/urban disparity is the fact that rural Canada is undergoing significant and fast-paced changes in its industrial structure (Bollman 2001b). These changes mirror a number of trends affecting other industrialized nations as well, including the following:

- Resource processing favours urban areas.
- Capital intensification displaces labour.
- Foreign competition depresses prices and shifts markets.
- Resource depletion raises costs and decreases available supply.

In general, we are witnessing a period of reduced employment associated with primary industries and increasing levels of employment in the service sector (a trend that, in general, places rural areas at a disadvantage in terms of attracting investment and employment in the new economy). The following section outlines a variety of standard indicators used to assess the health of rural economies and regions (Table 2.5). Narrowly interpreted, these same indicators have contributed to top-down, symptomatic responses from governments. Therefore, the limitations of the indicators in capturing a more sophisticated and dynamic picture of rural Canada must be taken into consideration.

First, income levels are lower in rural areas. For example, BC has the highest Canadian average rural incomes, but rural family incomes are between 10 and 15 percent lower than family incomes in areas with a population of 100,000 or more (Bollman 2001b). On the positive side, rural areas show a lower degree of income inequality. Second, employment participation rates are lower. A greater reliance on resource sectors and less

Table 2.5

Socio-economic indicators for rural Canada, 2001

Indicator	Census rural	Rural and small town	Non-metropolitan regions	Canada total
Employment rate, ages 25-54 (%)	74.9	73.7	74.2	76.7
Average income of economic families ($)	50,424	47,002	47,989	55,986
Incidence of low income (%)	13.1	15.7	16.5	19.7
Persons ages 25-54 with some postsecondary education (%)	52.8	51.1	52.6	61.8

Source: Bollman 2001a.

economic diversification generally contributes to greater employment instability. Third, overall educational levels in rural areas are lower than in urban settings.

In terms of employment by sector, not surprisingly the primary sector is overrepresented in rural areas. Bollman (2001e) measures a high location quotient (LQ) in the primary sector (between 307 and 330) in rural economies between 1987 and 1994.[2] An overreliance on the primary sector poses a particular set of development challenges to rural Canada for a variety of reasons linked with staples theory (see Chapter 3). Primary sector dependency may produce significant local wealth, but a variety of supportive development policies are necessary to transform primary sector *growth* into local and regional *development*.

In terms of government support, transfer payments make a substantial contribution to the stability of rural economies (Vodden 1999). In general, rural residents receive more in social transfers and pay relatively less in taxes than the average urban resident. A variety of factors contribute to this disparity: unemployment rates are higher in rural areas, there is a higher proportion of children in rural areas (and thus residents receive more in child tax credit), and a higher proportion of retired people (receiving Canada and Quebec Pension Plan benefits) live in rural areas (Bollman 2001a).

The issue of transfer payments is highly subject to confusion and misrepresentation. For example, a recent rural survey indicates that rural residents feel that the tax system does not reflect the higher costs of servicing, and in some ways living, in rural communities (Canadian Rural Secretariat 1998). However, cuts to rural services and a more direct and universal interpretation of the relationship between cost and service delivery is clearly undermining past regional development policy approaches, which tended to stress equity and universal access as guiding principles (Cummings 1989). Government transfer payments serve as an example where we must support narrow statistical evidence with additional evidence and contextual explanation in order to provide a clear picture of rural conditions and policy efficacy.

The Project Communities

In this section, we move from the national/provincial level to the community level in order to provide some basic historical, statistical, and local assessment information about the project communities (see Map 2.1). We used standard socio-economic data in the early project stages to determine the condition of each community. Community interns created community profiles in the first year of the project in cooperation with community-based working groups. As stated in Chapter 1, we purposely selected the

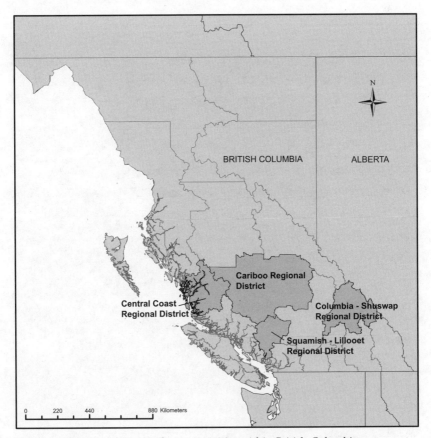

Map 2.1 Location of case study communities within British Columbia

communities to represent a diversity of issues, conditions, and stages in the local development planning process.

As we will see in later chapters, the use of community information in the community economic development (CED) process is critical for identifying and implementing appropriate projects, that is, projects that are well suited to the values, resources, and needs of the particular community. Too often in community planning, projects are identified on the basis of sweeping generalizations or inappropriate comparisons with other communities or regions. Gathering meaningful community-based information is critical to project success. Quality information is also useful for being able to determine whether projects are succeeding in their stated objectives.

Salmon Arm

Salmon Arm is a community of approximately 16,000 people. The community is located on the southwest arm of Shuswap Lake in the Southern Inte-

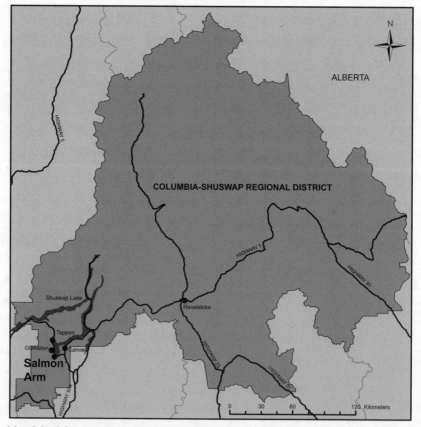

Map 2.2   Salmon Arm and region

rior of British Columbia, approximately halfway between Vancouver and Calgary on the Trans-Canada Highway (Map 2.2).

The history of the region mirrors the development trajectory of other rural communities with regard to the exploitation of staples in the west-ward expansion of the Canadian economy. Prior to contact with fur traders in the nineteenth century, the Secwepemc Nation inhabited the region. The Secwepemc Nation consists of four bands: the Adams Lake Band, the Neskonlith Band, the Spallumcheen Band, and the Little Shuswap Band. Despite early fur trade contact in 1811, the first wave of settlers followed some fifty years later, with the discovery of gold in the creeks flowing into Shuswap Lake. The gold rush in the area was short-lived, however, as the focus of mining in the province shifted to other, more productive regions in BC around 1865.

Following fur and gold, the region experienced growth in agriculture, principally dairy farming and fruit growing. More permanent and expan-sive settlement occurred in the area following the construction of the Cana-dian Pacific Railway, which provided access to the Canadian market. Lumber production increased following the expansion of the railroad, later becom-ing the centrepiece of the regional economy (IMPAX 1996).

Salmon Arm is a "hub community" for the Shuswap region, meaning that it is a major service provider for outlying peoples and smaller towns. Within a 125-kilometre radius of the community, there is a population of over 585,000 people. The following sections outline some of the key socio-economic features of Salmon Arm and the surrounding region.

On the basis of its geography and economy, the Salmon Arm area is an extension of the Okanagan Valley to the south. Transportation improve-ments and industrial incentives programs combined to initiate rapid eco-nomic and population growth throughout the Okanagan-Shuswap country during the 1960-1980 period. Considerable diversification of the economy has been achieved, but the forest industries remain by far the most impor-tant resource sector, followed by agriculture and tourism. Expansion of the tertiary sector has been strong, and trade and services have accounted for the largest number of new jobs. Future economic expansion is expected to be broadly based, with growing emphasis on tourism and the retirement industry (BC Stats 2003c).

Labour Force

As can be seen from Table 2.6, Salmon Arm has a well-diversified local economy. Its regional hub status, central transportation advantages, and proximity to

Table 2.6

Salmon Arm and the Columbia-Shuswap Regional District (CSRD) labour force by industry, 2001

Type of industry	Experienced labour force		% distribution*		
	Salmon Arm	CSRD	Municipal	District	Province
All industries	7,385	23,805	100	100	100
Agriculture, food, and beverage	270	835	3.7	3.5	3.0
Fishing and fish processing	0	30	0	0.1	0.5
Logging and forestry manufacturing	445	2,605	6.0	10.9	4.7
Mining, oil, gas extraction and processing	90	335	1.2	1.4	2.0
Non-resource–based manufacturing	485	960	6.6	4.0	3.9
Construction	505	1,965	6.8	8.3	5.9
Transportation, storage, and utilities	260	1,795	3.5	7.5	6.2
Business, professional, related services	635	1,765	8.6	7.4	10.9
Information, entertainment, other services	620	2,180	8.4	9.2	10.3
Wholesale and retail trade	1,135	3,185	15.4	13.4	15.7
Finance, insurance, real estate	395	970	5.3	4.1	6.1
Accommodation and food services	890	3,105	12.1	13.0	8.3
Education, health, public administration	1,670	4,070	22.6	17.1	22.5

*   % distribution between municipal, district, and province economies where each column
    adds up to 100%.
Source: BC Stats 2001.

the growing Okanagan Valley region provide a solid foundation for economic development.

Local Area Income Dependency

Again, income dependency figures confirm the relative diversity of the Salmon Arm economy (Table 2.7). As the project application from Salmon Arm indicates, however, community residents recognize that the diversity of their economy is relatively fragile and vulnerable to changing economic circumstances (particularly in the forest sector) or government cutbacks. While the unemployment level in the community has not fluctuated a great deal in recent years, the regional unemployment rate is higher than in metropolitan areas. There is also a local concern that the jobs being lost or replaced are "good jobs" and the new job opportunities are of a lower quality (lower paying and seasonal); a Salmon Arm resident stated: "Three new hotels have been built which has provided a positive boost to the community, but they don't replace forest jobs."

SALMON ARM PROJECT APPLICATION

Salmon Arm is at a critical point of its economic development. Former lack of economic direction, objectives, and strategies combined with recent Government cutbacks, both Provincial and Federal, have left Salmon Arm in a very tenuous position.

With a heavy economic reliance on existing core industries (forestry, tourism, retirement) and the subsequent downsizing, redistribution of, and new Government controls affecting these core industries, there is now an urgent, critical need for development of a decisive and shared industrial economic direction and appropriate initiative for Salmon Arm.

Proactive economic planning and initiatives will determine the short term and long term future prosperity of Salmon Arm. Lifestyle, employment and social planning can only be attained by economic vitality.

In view of our current economic position, it is judged imperative that we focus on the next three years, identifying issues and engaging positive initiatives that encourage/revitalize economic development in the greater Salmon Arm area. We must quickly become one of the most "Pro Business" communities in the province, if we hope to achieve our willed future. To that extent, we have already established an Economic Development Steering Committee chaired by the Mayor. This committee is made up of all community agencies, the district of Salmon Arm, key business and cultural groups, and leaders from the local Native Bands.

The key is that we cannot fail the community. We are one of the highest unemployment areas in the interior of British Columbia, whose sole economy is primarily based on forestry and forestry related jobs. Salmon Arm is in essence a "one product line community." This is a very tenuous and dangerous position to be in especially for a "hub" city. If the economy of Salmon Arm fails due to its dependency on forestry, all communities around Salmon Arm will be adversely affected. On the other hand, if we prosper, so will the communities around us.

Table 2.7

Salmon Arm income dependency (percent), 1996

	Salmon Arm	Thompson Okanagan	BC (excluding GVRD)
Forestry	12	16	21
Mining	1	4	4
Fishing/trapping	0	0	2
Agriculture	4	4.5	3
Tourism	4	7	7
High tech	3	0.5	–
Public sector	19	21	23
Construction	10	7	7
Other basic	4	8	6
Transfer payment	24	20	17
Other non-employment	19	12	10
Total	100	100	100

Source: Horne 1999.

Lillooet Tribal Council

The Lillooet Tribal Council (LTC) is a representative body of the six bands of the Upper St'at'imc Nation. The St'at'imc have occupied their territory, some 11,000 square miles extending from Pavilion in the north to Port Douglas in the south, for thousands of years. The St'at'imc language is part of the Interior Salish branch of the Salishan language family. The six bands of the Upper St'at'imc Nation are located approximately 300 kilometres northeast of Vancouver in the Southern Interior, within the Chilcotin Range of the Coast Mountains (Map 2.3). Archeological evidence indicates that the area has experienced human occupation for approximately 7,000 years. From the period from 3500 to 200 BP, there is evidence of a sedentary way of life based upon the harvesting of salmon, which is characteristic of the St'at'imc people today (Deva Heritage Consulting 1998).

The current population of the Upper St'at'imc is approximately 2,137 people, with 1,269 people living on reserve. The population of the nation before the smallpox epidemics of 1862 is estimated to have been approximately 4,000 people. The first Aboriginal-European contact occurred in 1808, when Simon Fraser camped overnight in Lillooet on his way down what would become the Fraser River. European settlement of Lillooet did not occur until fifty years later, with the advent of the Fraser River gold rush, which caused the population of the Lillooet area to swell to a peak of 16,000 people. The history of contact for the St'at'imc people resembles the pattern of exploitation experienced by other First Nations across British

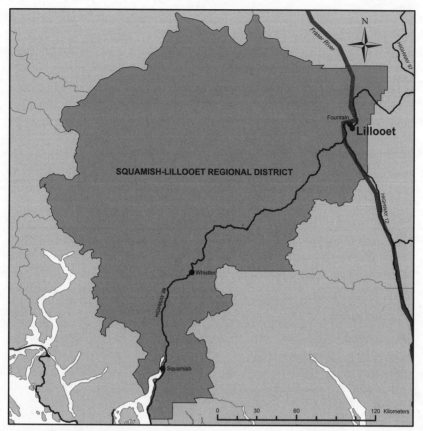

Map 2.3 Lillooet and region

Columbia, including a smallpox epidemic, residential schooling, and the imposition of the reserve system.

Economic opportunity was a principal driving force motivating the settlement and exploration of the St'at'imc territory by settlers. The history of settlement in the area again follows the general staples dynamic, with salmon harvesting following the gold rush, to be supplanted by industrial mining, hydro development, and forestry, which by the middle of the twentieth century had become the dominant economic activity in the region.

Currently the LTC and the bands of the Upper St'at'imc Nation are engaged in a variety of efforts designed to reclaim greater degrees of cultural, economic, and territorial self-reliance for the St'at'imc people. The following socio-economic information covers the Upper St'at'imc communities and the Lillooet region in general (see Table 2.8).

Table 2.8

Population of the Upper St'at'imc Nation, 1999

Band	Total population	On reserve
Shalath (Seton Lake)	453	325
Sekw'elw'as (Cayoosh Creek)	136	62
Tl'itl'kit (Lillooet)	215	125
Ts'kw'aylaxw (Pavilion)	322	225
Xaxl'ip (Fountain)	715	440
Xwisten (Bridge River)	296	92
Total	2,137	1,269

Source: Lillooet Tribal Council 1999.

Table 2.9

Lillooet municipality and the Squamish-Lillooet Regional District (SLRD) labour force by industry, 2001

| Type of industry | Experienced labour force | | % distribution* | | |
	Lillooet	SLRD	Municipal	District	Province
All industries	1,480	20,200	100	100	100
Agriculture, food, and beverage	45	255	3.0	1.3	3.0
Fishing and fish processing	10	35	0.7	0.2	0.5
Logging and forestry manufacturing	250	1,395	16.9	6.9	4.7
Mining, oil, gas extraction and processing	0	165	0	0.8	2.0
Non-resource–based manufacturing	15	180	1.0	.09	3.9
Construction	75	1,800	5.1	8.9	5.9
Transportation, storage, and utilities	155	1,365	10.5	6.8	6.2
Business, professional, related services	95	1,900	6.4	9.4	10.9
Information, entertainment, other services	60	2,330	4.1	11.5	10.3
Wholesale and retail trade	195	2,210	13.2	10.9	15.7
Finance, insurance, real estate	35	885	2.4	4.4	6.1
Accommodation and food services	135	4,060	9.1	20.1	8.3
Education, health, public administration	420	3,605	28.4	17.8	22.5

* % distribution between municipal, district, and province economies where each column adds up to 100%.
Source: BC Stats 2001.

Labour Force

Statistical information for First Nations communities in British Columbia continues to be poor. Tables 2.9 and 2.10 provide labour force information for the municipality of Lillooet and rough figures for three of the Upper St'at'imc bands. The municipal figures provide insight into the shape of the local economy and the economic characteristics of the region, although regional figures are badly skewed by the inclusion of Squamish and the Resort Municipality of Whistler, which have significantly different and larger economies than those found in the Lillooet area.

Table 2.10

Labour force by industry: Lillooet Reserve, Fountain Reserve, and Bridge River Reserve, 2001

Type of industry	Lillooet 1 Reserve	Fountain Reserve	Bridge River Reserve
All industries	90	80	70
Agriculture and other resource-based industries	10	15	15
Manufacturing and construction	20	15	15
Wholesale and retail trade	10	10	10
Finance and real estate	0	0	0
Health and education	15	15	0
Business services	10	0	10
Other services	30	20	25

Source: Statistics Canada 2001.

Historically, [in the Lillooet area] mining was the leading economic activity, but the gold mines at Bralorne were gradually phased out and the industry at present is confined to exploration work, although a renewal of mining at Bralorne (on a smaller scale) is proposed. The forest industries, cattle ranching, the BC Railway, BC Hydro generation plants, and First Nations communities currently provide the foundation for the local economy, but tourism and ginseng farming are seen as the most promising growth areas. Lillooet serves as the main trade and service centre for the surrounding district. Upgrading of the road link to the coast via Pemberton has presented Lillooet and environs with new development opportunities, as reflected by the recent rapid growth. A future possibility is completion of a Pemberton-Bralorne all-weather link that would bring the recreational assets surrounding the latter community within easier reach of the Vancouver market and stimulate local growth (BC Stats 2003c).

Local Area Income Dependency

Income dependency figures for Lillooet illustrate a substantial dependency on the forest and public sectors, making the community particularly vulnerable to restructuring (Table 2.11). As noted in the application by the Lillooet Tribal Council, however, the local Aboriginal population does not play a significant role in the existing forest economy, although forestry, by virtue of resources and economic alternatives, is a critical focal point for Upper St'at'imc economic development planning.

Table 2.11

Lillooet income dependency (percent), 1996

	Lillooet	Mainland/ Southwest average	BC (excluding GVRD)
Forestry	29	13	21
Mining	0	1	4
Fishing/trapping	0	0.3	2
Agriculture	2	4	3
Tourism	7	9	7
High tech	0	1	–
Public sector	30	25	23
Construction	5	10	7
Other basic	7	9	6
Transfer payment	14	17	17
Other non-employment	7	10	10
Total	100	100	100

Source: Horne 1999.

LILLOOET TRIBAL COUNCIL PROJECT APPLICATION

The five Upper St'at'imc communities of the Lillooet Tribal Council (LTC) have always maintained a traditional and historical relationship to the forest and its resources. While some practices (such as burning to promote growth of berry producing bushes, root gathering, harvesting wood or taking strips of cedar for house construction) have diminished or disappeared, others continue to flourish, i.e., hunting, food and medicine gathering. The balanced or holistic view of the environment, land, forest and its resources extends far past the singular monetary value of the timber market.

In the modern sense, however, with approximately 50% of the total population within the Lillooet Timber Supply Area (TSA), the St'at'imc community members are certainly affected by economic cycles of good and bad times.

Previously, greater numbers of St'at'imc people were involved in the local forestry industry. However, the move towards mechanization and central- ization displaced local employment in the logging/log hauling business. With little else offered in the way of large-scale manufacturing or employ- ment, forestry remains a key focus in the LTC community's present and future economic plans. This is especially so given the abundance of the forest resource (on and off reserve) and the perceived opportunities yet to be realized, particularly in the technical, contracting/business, tenure and management sectors of the forest industry.

The LTC has engaged in a variety of planning exercises related to eco- nomic development, including:

- Leadership in community planning
- Community survey to determine the level and the quality of education in the Lillooet School District
- Land use planning workshops

Through a partnership with SFU, the LTC, including the Natural Resources Coordinator and Forest Renewal Coordinator, Band staff and economic de- velopment committees would have assistance in promoting, implementing and maintaining current and future planning. This may include:

- CED strategy for LTC and community(s)
- St'at'imc land use planning, including natural resource/wildlife
- Forest sector economic plan
- St'at'imc cultural heritage strategy

South Cariboo

The South Cariboo is situated in the Central Interior of British Columbia. The South Cariboo area extends from Lac La Hache in the north to 70 Mile House in the south (east of the Coast Mountains between the Fraser Basin and the Thompson Plateau). The District of 100 Mile House is situated on Highway 97, BC's main arterial north-south route. The town lies northeast of Vancouver and south of Prince George (Map 2.4).

The post-contact historical roots of the South Cariboo begin with the fur trade. More permanent settlement did not occur until 1860, with the ar- rival of thousands of gold seekers. Between 1862 and 1870, over 100,000 people travelled the Cariboo Wagon Road from Lillooet, making their way north into Cariboo country. Throughout this time of gold fever, certain roadhouses, because of their favourable locations along the Cariboo Wagon Road from Lillooet to Soda Creek, grew to become supply points for the gold seekers and the surrounding district. 100 Mile House, the South Cariboo's dominant community, was originally one of these stopping points along the

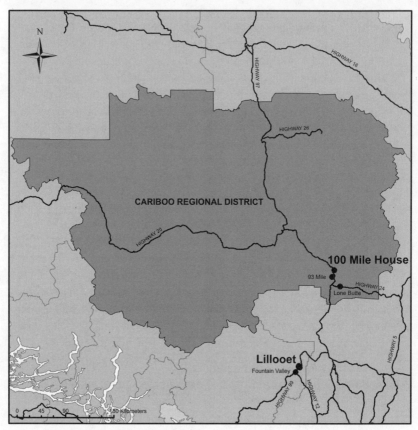

Map 2.4   100 Mile House and South Cariboo region

gold rush trail. 100 Mile House was so named because it was located 100 miles from Lillooet (mile 0 of the Cariboo Wagon Road). As the gold rush subsided, ranchers supplanted miners as the primary settlers in the region.

In 1912, a British nobleman, the Marquis of Exeter, purchased the land around 100 Mile House. His son, Lord Martin Cecil, arrived in the South Cariboo in 1930 to look after his family's holdings. The population of the settlement was approximately twelve people at this time. However, abundant stands of timber throughout the South Cariboo drew dozens of portable sawmill owners in the late 1940s and 1950s, building a foundation for the modern economy of the region.

Lord Martin Cecil arranged lease settlements in the area. The lease agreement grew and eventually included what is now the District of 100 Mile House. The leasing plan remained in place until the town of 100 Mile House was incorporated in 1965, when the lease property was bought by the tenants of the estate.

Currently, the South Cariboo consists of a number of small, unincorporated communities in the outlying area surrounding 100 Mile House and has a population of approximately 20,000 people. The following socio-economic data cover 100 Mile House and the surrounding region.

Labour Force
The labour force of the South Cariboo is again extensively forest-dependent (Table 2.12). The forest sector is currently at maximum harvest limits and

Table 2.12

100 Mile House and Cariboo labour force by industry, 2001

| Type of industry | Experienced labour force | | % distribution* | | |
	100 Mile House	Cariboo	Municipal	District	Province
All industries	795	34,375	100	100	100
Agriculture, food, and beverage	10	1,625	1.3	4.7	3.0
Fishing and fish processing	0	15	0	0	0.5
Logging and forestry manufacturing	155	7,910	19.5	23.0	4.7
Mining, oil, gas extraction and processing	0	570	0	1.7	2.0
Non-resource–based manufacturing	0	340	0	1.0	3.9
Construction	45	2,070	5.7	6.0	5.9
Transportation, storage, and utilities	40	1,850	5.0	5.4	6.2
Business, professional, related services	30	1,980	3.8	5.8	10.9
Information, entertainment, other services	105	2,310	13.2	6.7	10.3
Wholesale and retail trade	120	4,595	15.1	13.4	15.7
Finance, insurance, real estate	40	1,050	5.0	3.1	6.1
Accommodation and food services	70	3,075	8.8	8.9	8.3
Education, health, public administration	190	6,965	23.9	20.3	22.5

* % distribution between municipal, district, and province economies where each column adds up to 100%.
Source: BC Stats 2001.

primary milling capacity is expected to decline. The region may experience economic growth through product upgrading and use of wood residues, however. The tertiary sector has expanded in recent years and there is potential for large mining projects in the region.

Local Area Income Dependency

As the income dependency figures in Table 2.13 and the project application indicate, forest dependency in the area has meant that local leaders have not seriously engaged in broader economic development planning.

Table 2.13

Williams Lake income dependency (percent), 1996

	Williams Lake area	BC (excluding GVRD)
Forestry	31	21
Mining	3	4
Fishing/trapping	0	2
Agriculture	4	3
Tourism	7	7
High tech	1	–
Public sector	22	23
Construction	7	7
Other basic	3	6
Transfer payment	14	17
Other non-employment	8	10
Total	100	100

Source: Horne 1999.

SOUTH CARIBOO PROJECT APPLICATION

We are enthused and feel that this project will go a long way to implementing a stable sustainable community for our citizens to live in. Having only just started on the road to economic development planning we feel a project such as this would be of great benefit.

Since the South Cariboo is predominately rural, local governments to date have not concentrated on community initiatives and economic planning exercises for the area. The focus has been on Zoning Bylaws and Official Community/Settlement plans. The Federal Government, Provincial Government and special interest groups have spearheaded most of the community economic initiatives that have been implemented.

This area has always felt very secure with a strong, vibrant, local based forest industry and, therefore, the need for long term economic planning and implementation was not realized. The first steps have now been taken by the formation of an economic development strategy, an economic development committee and the hiring of an economic development coordinator by the committee.

Historically, the initiatives within this area have been spearheaded by well meaning citizens and community groups. While these people have had the best intentions there was no overall coordination and cooperation. Recently local government has realized the need for an economic development strategy for the area.

The South Cariboo has a strong history of working together to support area objectives. The nature of the people who have chosen to live here has developed an attitude of community cooperation. The Economic Development team is enthused about this project and looks forward to participating in this research.

Bella Coola

Nestled between the mountains and deep fjords of the central Pacific coast about 560 kilometres northwest of Vancouver, the Bella Coola valley and surrounding area has been the home of the Nuxalk Nation for thousands of years (Map 2.5). The current membership of the Nuxalk Nation is 1,218 people. Approximately 900 Nuxalk reside on the reserve located in Bella Coola, although traditionally the Nuxalk population numbered in the thousands and lived in at least forty-five distinct villages located along the forested valleys and ocean shores of the region.

Travelling the Nuxalk-Carrier Grease Trail accompanied by Native guides, explorer Alexander Mackenzie encountered the Nuxalk in 1793, seven weeks after Captain George Vancouver's survey vessel charted the North Bentick Arm. Mackenzie's journals record the warm welcome he received from the Nuxalk at "Friendly Village" (Nutl'lhiiwx or Burnt Bridge Village) and the large settlement at "Great Village" (Nusq'lst or Noosgulch).

The established Native coastal-interior trade routes were integral to the success of the fur trade. Trading posts were established in the area by numerous interests: between 1800 and 1830 by the Spanish, in 1835 by three "Boston men" (Americans), and in 1867 by the Hudson's Bay Company at Bella Coola. The increasing non-Aboriginal population in the area during the mid-1800s brought the devastating smallpox epidemic, eliminating approximately one-third of the Aboriginal population.

In 1892, only sixteen non-Aboriginal residents had settled in the valley. Two years later, eighty-four Norwegians arrived from Minnesota, attracted

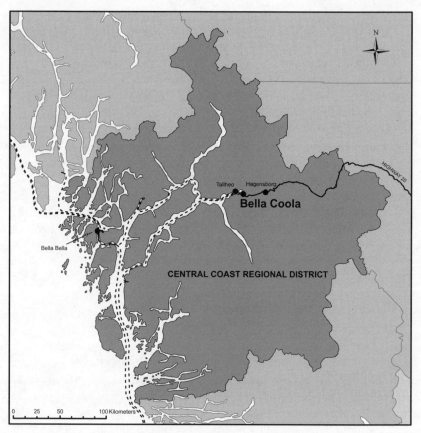

Map 2.5 Bella Coola and region

to a landscape that resembled the fjordlands. The Norwegians drew lots for land, cleared the trees, established farms, and founded the town of Hagensborg. Notably, the Norwegian settlement has a colourful history as one of the early "utopian experiments" of British Columbia (Scott 1997). The Nuxalk established their own thriving community, originally located on the north side of the river, adjacent to the non-Native settlement. In 1902 the government consolidated the remaining Nuxalk villages into reserves, with the principal reserve located at the mouth of the Bella Coola River.

Today, the Nuxalk Nation has seven reserves in the Bella Coola area that total approximately 2,025 hectares. Approximately 3,000 Aboriginal and non-Aboriginal people make their home in the Bella Coola valley. Forestry and fishing remain the economic mainstays of the region, although resources and resource-sector jobs faced downward pressures in the 1990s. Compared with the rest of the Central Coast region, however, Bella Coola's economy is considered relatively diversified. Although job losses in the resource sectors have had an impact on the community at large, the effect on the Nuxalk has been greater as they rely more heavily on the resource sector than does the non-Aboriginal population in the region. Joblessness for the Nuxalk has always been high, with local estimates stating that at least 80 percent of the community is considered unemployed.

The Bella Coola Valley supports some farming activity, mainly on a part-time basis, but forestry is the primary support for the local economy. The Area lacks a central trade and service core because of transportation problems between local communities. Access is also poor to points outside of the Area and this has restricted development.

Future economic change in part will be determined by decisions relating to the harvesting and utilization of local timber resources, and to the development of improved surface and air transportation. The community appears unlikely to retain its former size (BC Stats 2003c).

Labour Force

Besides a reliance on forestry and the public sector, as witnessed in the other project communities, Bella Coola and the Central Coast region display an added dependency on the fisheries. The participation of the Aboriginal population in the forest sector is minimal, and Aboriginal residents stated that recent restructuring in the fishing industry caused a loss of employment in that sector. Again, local residents state that statistical information about the reserve population is inaccurate. Nevertheless, area statistics provide a general picture of the economic activities in the area (Tables 2.14 and 2.15). At the time of the project, unemployment on the reserve was extremely high and there were no significant economic activities in operation or at the planning stage.

Table 2.14

Bella Coola Reserve labour force by industry, 2001

Industry	Total
All industries	320
Agriculture and other resource-based industries	70
Manufacturing and construction	40
Wholesale and retail trade	20
Finance and real estate	0
Health and education	95
Business services	20
Other services	75

Source: BC Stats 2001.

Table 2.15

Central Coast region labour force by industry, 2001

Type of industry	Experienced labour force	% distribution*	
		District	Province
All industries	1,875	100	100
Agriculture, food, and beverage	35	1.9	3.0
Fishing and fish processing	170	9.1	0.5
Logging and forestry manufacturing	220	11.7	4.7
Mining, oil, gas extraction and processing	0	0	2.0
Non-resource–based manufacturing	10	0.5	3.9
Construction	105	5.6	5.9
Transportation, storage, and utilities	120	6.4	6.2
Business, professional, related services	95	5.1	10.9
Information, entertainment, other services	90	4.8	10.3
Wholesale and retail trade	175	9.3	15.7
Finance, insurance, real estate	15	0.8	6.1
Accommodation and food services	115	6.1	8.3
Education, health, public administration	720	38.4	22.5

* % distribution between district and province economies where each column adds up to 100%.
Source: BC Stats 2001.

Local Area Income Dependency

Income dependencies for the area on the forest sector highlight a particular challenge facing the Bella Coola area and other rural regions throughout the province: the allocation of resources (Table 2.16). The project

Table 2.16

Central Coast region income dependency (percent), 1996

	Central Coast	BC (excluding GVRD)
Forestry	26	21
Mining	0	4
Fishing/trapping	8	2
Agriculture	1	3
Tourism	10	7
High tech	0	–
Public sector	37	23
Construction	5	7
Other basic	1	6
Transfer payment	8	17
Other non-employment	4	10
Total	100	100

Source: Horne 1999.

application by the Nuxalk speaks to their hopes and intentions regarding access to the forest resources. However, the Nuxalk are also clearly aware of the competing forces and complexities involved (both internal capacity issues and external corporate and government pressures) in creating economic opportunities for their community based upon the resources in the region.

BELLA COOLA PROJECT APPLICATION

As of 1995, the Nuxalk Nation had a total membership of 1166, out of which 761 lived on reserve. While the potential work force for forestry has been estimated at 200, at present 80% of the employable population have no paid work at all. Virtually all households rely to a very large extent on non-market economic activities which involve substantial forest dependency. These include traditional and continuing activities such as cutting trees for lumber used in the construction of homes and community buildings; harvesting for fuel wood; carving for artistic/ceremonial purposes; and gathering bark, leaves and herbaceous plants for medicinal purposes. Non-timber forest values including foodstuffs, deer, bear, and stream life reliant indirectly on the forest ecosystem are also highly significant to the Nuxalk household economies.

In terms of participation in the market-based forest sector, by the 1980s, employment in logging had plummeted to fewer than a dozen full time loggers and small scale Nuxalk entrepreneurs had virtually disappeared. But times once again are changing. The continuing success of First Nations in legal struggles for recognition of their land rights and jurisdictions have been a major factor in giving the Nuxalk a new foothold in forestry and other economic sectors. As a result, a new era may be beginning.

In recent years, the Nuxalk community has actively pursued a number of initiatives whose aims are consistent with the SFU Community Economic Development Centre's definition and vision of community-based forest development. We readily admit that the challenge in achieving this currently outstrips community capacity. We need to build partnerships with those who have the expertise generally to help communities diagnose their needs and act upon this assessment.

Over the past few years truly global forces and players have converged on our traditional forest lands. Corporate giants now court us relentlessly and we see possibilities for benefits – but only if the Nuxalk are very clear on our interests and how "partnering" with these companies fits into our unique vision of "good community." Non-aboriginal governments continue to hold-out short-term funding for all sorts of initiatives – provided that their basic control of the situation is maintained. Meanwhile our participation is sought in forest planning (e.g., Central Coast LRMP), again provided that the Province maintain a veto power over whatever is planned. International environmental organizations are now flocking to our homeland, renaming the territory, and assuring us (as generations of non-Nuxalk have done before them) that they know what is best for us and the lands we traditionally used and governed.

We need partners who do not act on self-interest but on shared goals and visions. The Nuxalk believe that SFU and the CED Centre may be such a partner.

Diversity and Vulnerability

Intuitively, we tend to associate a diverse local economy with a more stable and resilient local economy. The exception to this rule occurs when a single industry performs well and provides extensively to the local community. Over the long term, however, and as we will learn more in the following chapter, a diverse local economy helps to spread different external and internal shocks to the community economy over a broader range of activities. Therefore, if one sector faces a downturn, the overall economy of the community may continue to prosper by relying on other sectors that are performing adequately. This is the essence of diversity in strictly economic terms.

Forest Dependency and Economic Diversity

Two final pieces of statistical information help to illustrate the economic conditions of the project communities. First, with the exception of

Table 2.17

Vulnerability indices in the case communities, compared with other areas of BC

Area	Vulnerability index
Port Hardy	100
Quesnel	82
Prince George	47
Central Coast	42
Lillooet	42
Williams Lake	41
Salmon Arm	12
Trail-Rossland	6
Penticton	5
Kelowna	3

Source: Horne 1999.

Table 2.18

Diversity indices for the case areas, compared with other areas in BC

Area	Diversity index*	
Ashcroft	77	Most diversified
Peachland	76	areas in province
Fort St. John	75	
Salmon Arm	73	
Williams Lake	68	
Lillooet	64	
Central Coast	60	
Stikine	48	Least diversified
Port Hardy	52	areas in province
Quesnel	56	

* "The diversity index would be zero if the community were entirely dependent on one sector. At the other extreme, the diversity index would be 100 if a local area were equally dependent on each of the defined sectors" (Horne 1999, 41).
Source: Horne 1999.

Salmon Arm, which, because of its larger size and location, displays quasi-metropolitan characteristics, the project communities may be found in the middle-low range in terms of forest dependency and overall economic diversity compared with other communities in the province (see Table 2.18). We must also remember that on a strictly comparative basis, the Aboriginal communities in the project dramatically underperform on an indicator basis and are often simply not represented accurately in statistical terms. Second, "British Columbia is particularly dependent on the forest sector as a driver of local economies in many parts of the province. The Forest Vulnerability Index provides a number which indicates the vulnerability of each local area to potential down-turns in the forest sector (Table 2.17). The rationale behind it is that a community will be particularly vulnerable if its dependency on the forest sector is high and if its diversity is low" (Horne 1999, 44). As Horne states, "though a community with one strong industry may be better off than one with a number of weak ones, there is an intuitive appeal to the notion that a diversified economic base will provide more stability in volatile economic times."

Conclusion

As the brief community profile information provided above indicates, the four communities are quite diverse in terms of culture and economic conditions. Forest dependency was and remains an important, if not defining, feature of the community economies, along with the public sector. In the case of the Aboriginal communities, however, forest dependency better defines the surrounding economy, in which the Aboriginal populations are, for the moment, marginal participants. The Nuxalk Nation and the Lillooet Tribal Council see the commercial forest sector as a potential source of wealth for their communities, but at present they are more dependent on the forests for more traditional forms of sustenance and spiritual practice rather than for commercial activity.

The project communities are very much by-products of a national and provincial resource-led development process. Resource-based settlement patterns, the specialized economic base approach to development, and the exclusion of Aboriginal communities are all defining features of the evolution of the resource economy in Canada. As such, the story of the four communities may resonate with the conditions, challenges, and strategies being pursued by local actors and governments in other rural communities across BC and Canada.

The project engaged with the communities during what were and continue to be challenging times for rural and small-town communities in BC. Community reliance on the forest and public sectors has eroded confidence levels in the communities by local and outside investors alike, due to the extensive restructuring taking place in these two key sectors.

On a positive note, the combination of forces impacting local economies in the rural environment created the conceptual space for beginning the search for alternative forms of economic development and community cohesion. Each of the communities displayed a very high level of awareness about the state of its local economy and the variety of external forces affecting it. From this perspective, the conditions were right for an engagement with the university in the search for a more diverse and community-based approach to development.

In the following chapters, we take a step back from the immediate context of the project communities and our research experiences to outline the three basic components of our conceptual framework. The framework will help to enhance our overall understanding of how rural and small-town communities across BC developed, why they are experiencing difficulties, why the road to implementing CED is so challenging, and what CED means and how to implement it. Once these conceptual building blocks are in place, we will return to our project communities and relate (and reflect upon) their stories of development and change.

3
Forest Dependency and Local Development in British Columbia

In this chapter we seek to better understand some of the difficulties associated with economic change in British Columbia and across Canada. Many analyses of community economic development in Canada fail to address the role of historical forces in shaping patterns of development. This chapter presents us with an opportunity to take a step back from the here and now of economic change to better understand some of the origins of our economic development landscape.

To direct the review of our economic lineage, we introduce the first component of our conceptual framework, *dependency*. We will present dependency in economic terms through staples theory. Staples theory describes the economic development of Canada in terms of the successive exploitation of resources, driven by external sources of capital and technology (Innis 1933; Watkins 1981, 1982). The theory is useful for its foundational contribution towards understanding the unique characteristics of economic development in Canada. Staples theory provides a conceptual foundation from which to reveal the constraints and opportunities associated with current economic change.

Specifically, we will offer a renovation of staples theory from a local development perspective. In practical terms, we will illustrate how a staples-based approach to development imprinted itself on the landscape and on the communities of British Columbia. Forest-based communities and the forest sector serve as a particular focus for animating the concept of staples theory and to build a case for understanding the economic conditions in the project communities.

Despite its origins in the early to mid-twentieth century, staples theory continues to be useful for describing the current conditions of Canadian economic development (Barnes 1996; Britton 1996; Hutton 1994). In our treatment of staples theory, we will draw from a synthesis of modern staples literature to answer important questions, including:

- How did we get to where we are today?
- What are the historical and contextual factors that both enable and constrain efforts to build viable local development strategies in present-day British Columbia?

We will answer these questions in three sections. First, we will review staples theory and outline its relevance to inquiry into local development. Second, we will apply the concepts of staples theory to the case of the forest economy in British Columbia. This section presents specific policies that are, in part, responsible for fostering forest dependency in British Columbia. Finally, we will provide a statistical review of forest dependency and discuss the misleading concept of "community stability," which is often used in reference to economic development in forest-dependent communities.

Modernization and Staples Theory in Perspective

Two broad interpretations of the economic history and development of Canada tend to dominate debate. The first reading of Canadian economic development requires an appreciation for the lure of modernization. Earlier economic theories dictated that a society would pass through a series of linear stages en route to becoming an advanced, industrialized nation. These theories, drawn from the experiences of industrialized European nations, were very influential in directing the project of nation building in Canada.

The colonial ties of Canada made the adaptation of European development models relatively easy for Canadian officials. Rostow, building on the work of neoclassical economists, developed an often-cited modernist approach to achieving economic development that consists of a linear series of five developmental stages for a given society:

1) the traditional society:
   limited production functions; pre-Newtonian science; spiritual attitudes toward the physical world; agricultural; hierarchical social structure; little scope for social mobility.

2) the pre-take-off society:
   new production functions in agriculture and industry; education expanded; investment increases.

3) take-off:
   blockages to steady growth are overcome; technological advancement; favourable political contexts; increased investment; class of entrepreneurs expanded.

4) the road to maturity:
   growth outstrips any rise in population; sufficient entrepreneurial and technical skills to produce wide range of goods.

5) the mass consumption society:
   leading industrial sectors become durable goods and services; real incomes rise allowing consumption beyond need; may choose to allocate increased resources for social welfare and social security. (Rostow 1960, adapted from Peet 1997)

From a linear development perspective, the resource-intensive and heavy export focus of the Canadian economy was to be a temporary stage from which a more advanced and diversified economy would emerge. The pure simplicity of the model is appealing. It enables economists and politicians to view the growth and exploitation of natural resources within the context of nation building. The main proponent of this view in Canada was W.A. Mackintosh, who envisioned that Canada was on a trajectory, dictated by economic growth, that would propel an autonomous nation into the international economy (Drache 1976; Mackintosh 1969). The demand for resources was a precursor to mature industrialism.

In contrast to this linear approach, Harold Innis (1933) proposed a countertheory to universal, market-based theories of development. Innis argued that a foreign, market-based approach to understanding Canadian development was inappropriate and limited in its ability to capture the true dynamics of the Canadian economy. Instead, Innis offered a more contextually grounded approach to understanding Canadian economic history, staples theory. Staples theory concentrates on the explanatory powers provided by an understanding of geography, institutions, and technology: "At the core of Innis' staples framework is his belief that theorizing requires an acute sensitivity to geographical and historical context ... Ideas developed in one context cannot be readily applied to another one and, in particular, a theory of development articulated within and for old world conditions is not relevant to the new world" (Hayter and Barnes 1990, 157).

Staples theory characterizes the emergence of Canada as a modern state as the product of the spread of industrialism and capitalism (Innis 1933). Staples theory investigates the sequential exploitation of Canadian resources (cod, fur, lumber, gold, pulp, and wheat) and the development patterns associated with each resource. Staples theory highlights the effects of transporting raw materials over long distances (causing a weakness in other lines of development), dependency on external industrialized areas for markets and supplies of manufactured goods, and dependency on external sources of capital to cover the high costs of resource development. All of these factors cause national and local instability due to fluctuating external demands for resource products and a lack of indigenous, diversified industries in the staples-producing nation (Drache 1976; Innis 1956).

Innis recognized that Canada had become more diversified and economically powerful, but that the nation's dependent status as staples provider remained, causing deficiencies and stagnation in other areas of the economy. Due to the external focus of staples development and the market realities of the time, indigenous capitalists retained a primarily export focus. As a result, the development of Canadian industry became dominated by branch plants, again limiting the degree of Canadian control over the functions of innovation necessary to relinquish dependency status and to diversify the economy – a phenomenon known as the "staples trap" (Watkins 1963).

Why Staples Theory?

Both the market-oriented approach of the staged economic growth model and staples theory provide us with information that helps to contextualize our understanding of the challenges and conditions facing local development in Canada. The Rostowian model of linear growth tends to blame patterns of uneven development or underdevelopment on local and institutional factors – a "blame-the-local approach." A market deficiency perspective of local (under)development concentrates on factors such as local culture, lack of resources, geographical distance, and an unskilled workforce. This simplistic approach to understanding local barriers to development is consistent with the five-stage format for understanding growth and development in the first place.

In contrast, staples theory provides a more contextually rich analysis of development and enables us to probe various dimensions of national, provincial, and local development. The following sections will outline the usefulness of applying staples theory to our inquiry into local development processes and into the specific development context in BC. First, a review of staples-oriented research will illustrate the various dimensions of the staples thesis in Canada, highlighting its depth and resiliency. Second, we will link staples theory specifically to local development. Finally, given that two of the case studies in the Forest Communities project involve First Nations, we will use staples theory to provide insight into the economic exclusion and cultural harm experienced by Aboriginal peoples in Canada as a result of Canadian economic development.

Staples Theory and Dimensions of Development

The intellectual and contextual significance of Innis's staples theory provides a foundation for a wide range of inquiry into the economic development of Canada. First, Watkins (1982) elaborates on the "staple-trap," noting the lack of regional reinvestment that takes place in a staples-based economy. He argues that shareholders, not regional economies, have been the primary beneficiaries of the exploitation of Canadian resources. From this perspective, an overreliance on staples can create a "blockage" to diversified development, thereby creating underdevelopment (Watkins 1982).

Second, Levitt (1970) and Laxer (1989) link the staples thesis to issues of control over economic decision making. Levitt (1970) concentrates his analysis on the influence of large multinational corporations, describing Canada's industrial emergence as one of growth but not development. Development, Levitt asserts, occurs when control is exerted over decision making about economic and corporate planning. Levitt argues that the Canadian capitalist elite chose income over corporate control, and managerialism over entrepreneurialism, leaving mainly American-based corporations in charge of the Canadian economy. Laxer's thesis (1989) corroborates Levitt's interpretation by illustrating the branch-plant mentality of the emerging Canadian economy.

Third, Hayter and Barnes have together and in individual works researched many of the characteristics and implications of staples development in British Columbia and across Canada. For example, their work illustrates the relative lack of economic diversification in Canada compared with other industrialized nations, the large extent of foreign direct investment in Canada, and the continued high level of staples exports and low proportion of Canadian world exports in manufactured end products (Hayter 2000; Barnes 1996; Hayter and Barnes 1990): "The staples theory that Innis enunciated in the 1930s and 1940s to describe such peripheral resource economies as British Columbia remains, more or less, an accurate account of the way things are now" (Hayter and Barnes 1990). "In sum, from the perspective of Canadian political economy, there is a direct relationship between the type of trade in which Canada engages and its historic inability to become a fully industrialized nation. This connection is not one that traditional (neoclassical) economic theory would ever make" (Barnes 1996, 50).

Finally, Clapp (1998) adds an ecological economics perspective to staples theory, stating that all wild resources under industrial commercial use pass through a "resource cycle." Overexpansion, ecosystem disruption, and economic crisis define the parameters of the cycle of resource use. Clapp (1999) further clarifies his point by stating that the industrialization of renewable resources should be avoided wherever possible, and scaled back where it is already entrenched. Resource management defined by the scales and pressures of industrial use is inherently unsustainable. Clapp's observations reinforce Innis's earlier description of a cycle of exploitation, exhaustion, and expansion experienced in the fur trade and applied to the analysis of other staple products (Innis 1956).

Another important dimension of the resource cycle noted by Clapp (1998) is the close relationship that develops between governments and resource industries. Such political/industrial ties, referred to by Clapp as an attitude of "resourcism," means that politicians are reluctant to engage in sustainably oriented change due to their dependency on the revenues and investments of industrial resource sectors.

We can see from this brief review that staples theory offers a flexible and wide-reaching foundation from which to explore various patterns of development in the Canadian economy. In summary, the characteristics of a staples economy can be summarized as follows: lack of reinvestment, foreign control, lack of diversification, limited research and development, high staples exports, low levels of manufacturing, resource exhaustion, and resourcism. The following section seeks to contribute to the dialogue by illustrating the relevance of staples theory specifically to local development.

Local Development Link
Besides identifying the stultifying effects of staples theory on economic development in Canada, the above-mentioned researchers and others have also pointed to the need for resource communities to diversify their economies. Economic diversification is posited as a solution to the stifling effects of economic specialization or the ecological impacts associated with resource decline and degradation (Clapp 1998; Barnes and Hayter 1997; Hutton 1994; Britton 1996).

Local development represents one approach to devising an overall strategy for achieving economic diversification (Coffey and Polese 1985; Bryant and Preston 1989; Barnes and Hayter 1994; Douglas 1994; Pierce and Dale 1999). To date, however, our understanding of the role of local or community economic development in fostering economic diversification remains limited and overly descriptive.

In this section, we draw from staples research to address deficiencies in our understanding of economic development at the local level. Three staples-relevant themes outline the impacts of the staples economy on localized forms of development: economic impacts, government impacts, and attitudinal impacts (see Table 3.1). The factors in each of the categories build upon the observations of the staples-oriented authors noted above and provide generalizations of their findings with respect to the local development process.

From an economic perspective, the growth imperative driving the expansion-exhaustion cycle of resource use creates three negative consequences. First, the use of the economic-base approach for measuring the success of community and regional economies fundamentally confuses growth with development. The economic-base model dictates that income and employment, driven by exports, are the measures by which we assess the economic health of communities and regions. This approach fails to consider longer-term and holistic interpretations of development, both of which we now consider fundamental to the sustainable futures of communities. At a broader level, the export focus of the staples economy contributes to the comparative advantage impulse of Canadian economic development – trade – at the expense of community-based approaches (Hayter 2000).

Table 3.1

**Impacts of staples development on community
economic development capacity**

Type of impact	Specific impacts
Economic	Economic base
	Export focus
	Specialization
	Commodity production
	Environmental decline
Government	Corporate/government alliances
	Dependency
	Inertia with respect to change
	Megaproject scale
	Centralization
Attitudinal	Economic dependency
	Low entrepreneurial activity
	Limited planning
	Marginalization

Second, staples-led development causes intense economic specialization. Because of the bountiful resources available in Canada, economic specialization in resource sectors is capable of producing vast wealth. The long-term economic health of communities and regions, however, is largely associated with a diversified approach to development. Attention to diversification also creates opportunities for local initiatives to play a more recognized role in the health of community and regional economies.

Third, the commodity focus of resource industries contributes to the unsustainable use of Canadian resources (Clapp 1998, 1999). Reform in favour of local economies is impeded by the extent to which unsustainable resource extraction practices continue and the degree to which the inertia of past practices and relationships continue. The "resource cycle" leaves community-based development approaches with fewer and fewer economic opportunities. Policy makers and resource managers have generally excluded nonproductivist values and community-based approaches to resource use, both of which contribute to economic diversification.

Staples-oriented government barriers to community-based development are driven primarily by the extent to which close alliances are forged between industry and governments in the pursuit of economic growth and expansion. Historically, the task of nation or province building increased the government's affinity for foreign (and large-scale) capital, thereby facilitating the entrenchment of staples-based relationships.

Strong government/corporate alliances produced tremendous wealth and positive economic growth, but such alliances also present a variety of structural barriers to change and economic adaptation. First, government dependency on large industry curtails its ability to promote specifically national, provincial, or community interests: "The government, meanwhile, had difficulty reducing this external dependence because it has little bargaining leverage with the multinationals. Since these firms control savings, levels of employment and production, technology and investment, the government must either accept the terms offered or suffer the political consequences of an investment strike" (Weaver and Gunton 1982, 23). Close government/industry relationships also contribute to the inertia impeding the search for more sustainable and community-based forms of development (Clapp 1998). Wresting power from the status quo and sharing it with community-based institutions is not a simple process; nevertheless, it is a central tenet of CED (Frank and Smith 1999).

Second, management of the staples economy was and is highly centralized. Governments and corporations implemented development in a top-down fashion. Resource and economic development experts, drawing from economic development theory that was contextually blind and narrowly focused, were largely responsible for development decisions (Savoie 1992). The legacy of top-down planning tends to reduce levels of trust in local decision-making ability and foster local dependency on external planners.

The most obvious staples imprint on government planning is highlighted by a weakness for megaprojects. The megaproject approach to regional development dominated policy particularly in the 1980s (Savoie 1992). Megaprojects are popular because large-scale development schemes offer greater degrees of short-term political capital. It is more difficult for government to take direct credit for the decentralized, smaller-scale initiatives favoured by local development, which again inhibits the transition to, or recognition of, a more decentralized approach to development.

Finally, a number of researchers note various attitudinal impacts, at the community level, associated with the legacy of staples-led development. Freudenburg (1992) refers to a local "addiction" to resources. This addiction, in part, helps to explain lower rural educational levels, weak entrepreneurialism, and an overall resistance to change. Watkins's staples trap (1981) is relevant to the local level in terms of preventing movement towards economic diversification. Auty (1994, 1995) calls the phenomenon of stifled local development and diversification a resource curse afflicting the developing world. Finally, Clapp's resource cycle predicts similar dangers associated with an addiction or overadaptation to a specific economic sector: "Resource endowments often backfire by generating a regional overadaptation to a specific economic niche ... Both resource-led prosperity and stagnation tend to reinforce regional dependence and hinder the development of alternative economic activities" (Clapp 1998, 132).

In summary, local economic dependency in Canadian communities is associated with two phenomena: (1) economic specialization and (2) our past approaches to economic development planning. Researchers stress the degree to which a focus on large-scale industry inhibits entrepreneurial abilities in the Canadian regional context (Hayter 2000; Weaver and Gunton 1982; Fairbairn 1998). Similarly, communities and regions are passive, dependent players in policy and project development when development planning is coordinated from above, by external experts.

The following section continues to describe some of the negative development implications associated with staples theory. Besides emphasizing the dependency and economic specialization of European-settled hinterland communities, staples theory may also be used to explore features of underdevelopment in Aboriginal communities.

First Nations Exclusion
A recent review of Aboriginal peoples in Canadian geographical research claims that the way in which researchers apply staples theory to British Columbia ignores the colonial past that separated Aboriginal peoples and communities from the forest economy (Peters 2000). From a purely economic interpretation of the forest economy in BC, oversight of First Nations communities is to some extent justifiable, due to their intentional removal from any form of significant control over the forest economy, other than perhaps as consumers. As Claudia Notzke states (1994, 2): "With regard to natural resources, native people in Canada are looking back on a history of exclusion and denial of power."

In earlier manifestations of staples development in Canada, most notably the fur trade, Aboriginal peoples played a crucial role in facilitating the economic development of the nation. However, as economic activity advanced to staples that either required a settled population or facilitated settlement and fixed patterns of land use (such as lumber), Aboriginal peoples became increasingly economically isolated. Even when Aboriginal peoples did participate in the staples economy, primarily as a labour force, they were unable to control the benefits derived from resource exploitation (Peters 2000).

Within the staples literature, Innis associates the dependency and marginalization of Aboriginal peoples with a vortex of rapid technological advancement (1956, 388): "The new technology with its radical innovations brought about such a rapid shift in the prevailing Indian culture as to lead to whole-scale destruction of the peoples consumed by warfare and disease." Other more politically and economically inclined perspectives elaborate upon Innis's technological observations. These additional perspectives highlight the alienation and exploitation of First Nations' culture and territories. For example, Watkins (1981) summarizes the condition of First Nations by noting their almost complete exclusion from the factors of production, a removal accomplished through a number of intentional government policies.

In British Columbia, successive governments used the idea of "empty lands" to justify the social and economic marginalization of Aboriginal peoples. The "empty lands" thesis "legitimized the denial of Aboriginal title and sanctified the new white doctrine that all land in the colony was not only under British sovereignty but also directly owned by the Crown" (Tennant 1989, 41). It is well documented that Aboriginal peoples attach different values to the land base, thereby devaluing any legitimate indigenous ownership claim from a colonial perspective. As Howlett (2001) indicates, BC sanctioned this colonial argument by evading the original tenets of the Royal Proclamation of 1763. The Proclamation recognizes Indians as Nations, asserts that Indians are not to be interfered with, and acknowledges that Indians continue to own the lands that they use and occupy. The government of British Columbia persistently argued that Aboriginal title did not exist in the province because it was not part of the area covered by the original Proclamation. The *Calder* court decision[1] later overturned this argument, providing a major precursor to modern treaty making in British Columbia.

Until very recently, however, governments in British Columbia refused to recognize First Nations' title and implemented a number of strategies that ultimately marginalized Aboriginal peoples from their traditional territories and from any form of significant participation in the economy. Most notable among these strategies was the reserve system, which isolated communal groups on small, marginal areas of land that are generally insufficient to support existing or growing populations (Peters 2001). If reserve lands proved to be of economic value in later years (for example, following the discovery of minerals or hydro-electric power), lands were often simply reappropriated by the government with minimal compensation: "Whenever immigrants valued Aboriginal land, the state – depending on time and place, either the province or the dominion – took most of it and made it available in a variety of tenures. Such land, it was rationalized, had been a waste, used little if at all by savage peoples. Both the land and the people were to be improved, the land by being put to proper use, the people by being civilized" (Harris 2001, 200).

The economic marginalization of Aboriginal peoples, combined with other tools of assimilation, including the residential school system and the policy of denying traditional religious and political rituals, had devastating effects on Aboriginal populations throughout the province and across Canada. As

Tennant states (1989, 72), "within societies whose traditional beliefs and customs and leaders are incapable of controlling rapid change, especially change for the worse, it becomes an affliction of whole communities." As we will see in later chapters, however, those expecting to witness the gradual assimilation of Aboriginal peoples and cultures severely underestimated the role of the courts and the attachment to land, identity, and community of Aboriginal peoples themselves.

Staples theory provides a foundation for understanding the economic motivation that led to the isolation and marginalization of Aboriginal peoples at the hands of settlers and politicians. Staples theory also illuminates the extent to which Aboriginal economic isolation perpetuated other forms of discrimination towards First Nations populations. In combination with other approaches to understanding the social and political dimensions of the legacy of Aboriginal peoples in BC and Canada, staples theory adds an appreciation for the complexity and the difficult nature of the quest for justice, reconciliation, and development in Aboriginal communities and between Aboriginal and non-Aboriginal communities.

The Forest Economy in BC: Staples Theory in Action

With some theoretical backing now in place, we will now narrow the contextual lens of inquiry to the BC forest sector. The focus on BC will outline some of the conditions responsible for the patterns of development in the four case communities. More generally, we will illustrate some of the barriers and opportunities that communities throughout the province face in adopting local development strategies and in adapting to a changing economic environment.

In an effort to answer the question, "how is staples theory manifested in the BC context?" the following sections outline specific forest policies that facilitated the dominance of the forest sector in BC. To illustrate the significance of the forest sector in BC, we provide a snapshot of the modern forest industry. Together, this portrait of the forest sector and forest development policy provides a foundation for the following chapter. Chapter 4 uses a local development perspective to outline some of the negative implications associated with current economic conditions in BC.

Policies of Dependency

As Hayter (2000) observes, the forest sector in British Columbia developed in two distinct phases. The first phase took place between the 1880s and the 1940s and was characterized by an entrepreneurial model where ownership and control of the forest resource was highly decentralized and localized. The second phase, beginning in the 1940s, was characterized by the Fordist paradigm of large government involvement, large corporations, and large unions.

During the first phase, the forest industry consisted of thousands of small companies, and the government received few benefits from the cutting of timber on Crown lands (Drushka 1993). While the diversity of this first phase may have led to the development of an indigenous and competition-based forest industry in BC in later years, the entrepreneurial flare of this early period was accompanied by speculation, concerns about the conservation of the resource, and the need to link broader development objectives with the forest resource. Consequently, the system was overhauled through the recommendations of the Sloan Commission in 1945, which provided the foundation for the transition from a smaller-scale entrepreneurial model to industrial forestry.

The recommendations of the Sloan Commission are plentiful. From a local development perspective, *sustained yield* is a key policy instrument that sought to link the exploitation of the forest resource to the development objectives of the province. The policy of sustained yield provided a way to balance the immense harvesting capacity of the industry with regional development objectives. The policy also provided a scientific rationale for transforming and turning over the forest industry to the large-scale, largely foreign-owned model that dominates the sector today. As a result of the continuing legacy of the Sloan Commission, our analysis of forest policy and the forest sector in BC will focus on the postwar, Fordist period.

Sustained Yield and the Tenure System

The primary tenet of sustained yield is that trees should not be cut faster than new trees can grow. Sustained yield in BC is defined as a perpetual yield of wood of commercially useable quality from regional areas in yearly or periodic quantities of equal or increasing volume. Sustained yield is predicated on the orderly conversion of first-growth forests into even-aged managed timber crops to be harvested on periodic rotations (Forest Resources Commission 1991; BC Wild 1998). "The principle of sustained yield was guided, up until 1984, by the adoption of the 'Hanzlik formula,' which functions on the basis of the liquidation of old growth forests. The Hanzlik formula estimates the rate of cut by dividing the volume of mature timber by the average rotation age and adding the average growth rate from second growth stands. Rotation age is the age at which second growth forests will be logged, typically 70-120 years" (BC Wild 1998, 6).

By the 1940s, the BC government recognized the potential for forest liquidation. However, the adoption of sustained yield policies also appears to have been equally motivated by the desire to promote large-scale industrial development (Barnes and Hayter 1992). In order to facilitate the development process, policy makers in the 1940s and 1950s used the concept of sustained yield to justify the transfer of cutting rights from the multitude of small businesses to larger corporations.

Government facilitated the transfers through long-term area-based renew-able leases, now referred to as Tree Farm Licences (TFLs).[2] TFLs are a form of forest tenure in BC that provide exclusive timber-harvesting rights to the holder of the licence and impose certain forest management and develop-ment responsibilities over a designated area base and time period (Forest Resources Commission 1991). Tenure responsibilities include economic, social, and ecological priorities determined by the government. TFLs have a twenty-five-year term, renewable every ten years. The licence holder is obli-gated to cut between 90 and 110 percent of the volume determined by a five-year "cut control period." Failure to meet the imposed target can result in penalties and forfeit. The other main form of forest tenure in BC is the Forest Licence, which is a volume-based, rather than area-based, agreement set at fifteen-year terms.

The government believed that the standardization and government con-trol of the forest industry through sustained yield and the TFL system would yield certain benefits:

> The allocation or reserve of Crown timber for the units of industry would serve two purposes: First, it would enable the operator to maintain pro-duction from the cut of mature crown timber during the period necessary to restock his own land; secondly, the combined area of the private and Crown acreage should, on the second rotation, produce enough timber on a sustained-yield basis to maintain production of the unit in perpetuity – perhaps not at the peak capacity, but sufficient to ensure a profitable opera-tion with congruent benefit to those communities dependent upon the permanence of the industry. (Sloan 1945)

This quotation illustrates the interrelationships between community de-velopment objectives, sustained yield, the tenure system, and corporate control, which would prove to have deep-rooted and lasting implications for the development of the province. Community development objectives and the government's desire for revenue significantly influenced the ratio-nale for granting of tenure rights to larger corporations. Governments viewed larger companies as more reliable (less likely to close down in a recession), more responsible (their long-term interests would benefit the management of the resource and the stability of the labour force), and more profitable (the economies of scale offered by larger corporations generate higher re-turns) (Marchak 1983).

The general rule of development at the time was that bigger is better. That said, conservation measures were also a contributing factor to the rationale for government control of forest resources and for the development of the corporate-dominated tenure system. Government viewed the combination of scientific management offered by the formula for sustained yield, big business, and government control as the answer to responsible forest use, yielding appropriate conservation and production goals (Clogg 1999).

The adoption of sustained yield principles and the tenure system designed to implement them was the product of a variety of forces and objectives: expansionism, regional development and community stability, profit, government revenue generation, and the responsible management of the forest resource. As early as 1947, however, the gap between the intended objectives of the policies and the reality of their implementation was already showing. The immense industrial opportunities created by an assured timber supply were generally overlooked by the government of the day: "Whereas I had thought that, given the authority, we just might induce some public spirited and far sighted operator to take up a forest management license with all its attendant responsibilities, the fact turned to be that almost at once we were deluged with applications. Industry saw in an assured timber supply a capital gain that I had quite overlooked, and no one in government or Civil Service detected" (Sloan, quoted in Drushka et al. 1993, 155).

The provincial government formally incorporated sustained yield policies into the Forest Act in 1960 and strengthened them again in the Forest Act of 1978. The latter act encompassed the recommendations of a 1976 Royal Commission with some minor administrative revisions. While the 1976 Royal Commission made room for consultation with interests representing other forest values, the incorporation of the Forest Act also provided the Ministry of Forests with sweeping powers over the forest land base. Before the Forest Act of 1978, many ministries shared responsibility for the allocation, use, and management of forests. The exclusion of other ministries from forest management and the legal entrenchment of the powers of the Ministry of Forests resulted in an emphasis on the primacy of timber values and in the pursuit of community stability through forest dependency (Cashore et al. 2001).

M'Gonigle and Parfitt (1994) attribute a 600 percent increase in provincial logging levels in the immediate postwar period in part to the impact of policy decisions implemented at the time, policies that assured timber supply for large corporations and entrenched the legal protection of timber values. During the years between 1940 and the early 1970s, the forest industry was characterized by a rapid expansion in the timber processing industry that provided substantial wealth to the province and employed large numbers of people. Government policy forged the bond between community development and timber dependency in British Columbia during this period.

As we will see in the following sections, the policies adopted in the postwar period were highly successful in creating a large forest industry, an industry that generated tremendous wealth and created, for a time, stable

communities dependent upon the forest industry. It should be noted, however, as a precursor to our discussion in the next chapter on the impacts of
growth, that the policy of sustained yield has never been fully implemented
in BC. Although ecological concerns, in part, motivated the adoption of
sustained yield policies, the transfer of harvesting privileges to large corporations and the development of large industrial capacity ensured a continuation of the forest liquidation seen in the prewar period (Barnes and Hayter
1992). Following the implementation of sustained yield, it would be expected that the rate of cut would drop gradually to account for the transition from old growth to second growth; in fact, however, harvesting levels
increased steadily from 1947 until the late 1980s.

We see from Figure 3.1 that the roundwood harvest level in British Columbia finally peaked in 1987 at 90,591,000 cubic metres, approximately
40,000,000 cubic metres above current estimates of the long-term harvest
levels (LTHL). This gap indicates that successive governments never fully
implemented the policy of sustained yield in BC due to the ever-present
opportunity to exploit new territory and old-growth forests in the Central
and Northern Interior. Governments believed that natural regeneration was
sufficient to restock the forests (Barnes and Hayter 1997). The availability of
new forest lands, combined with the structural arrangements of the tenure
system, delayed the restocking of the forest land base (an obvious requirement of the sustained yield policy and a cornerstone of community stability under the system). The government finally implemented sustained yield
in response to the emerging implications of forest liquidation (that is, when
the limits to the forest frontier were reached). At this time, the adoption of
sustained yield facilitated a secondary purpose of maintaining the structural relationships of the postwar boom during a time of plant closures and

Figure 3.1

Roundwood harvest in BC, 1965-95

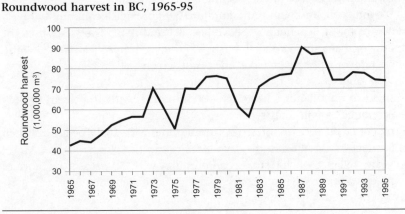

Source: Statistics Canada in Marchak et al. 1999.

rapid change (Barnes and Hayter 1992), serving again to reinforce the development pattern of specialization.

Under the combined influence of sustained yield and the tenure system, the socio-economic landscape of the province in the postwar era changed dramatically. The economic relationship and cultural affiliation between forestry and BC communities was well on its way to becoming firmly entrenched. The connection between timber dependency, local economic specialization in the forest industry, and community stability was complete. To better understand how these development patterns influence community stability in the present day, the following section describes the extent of forest dependency in the province and presents the controversy associated with the concept of community stability, an idea that is largely responsible for justifying high levels of forest dependency.

Forest Dependency
Efforts to define and quantify levels of community dependency and stability draw from a variety of fields with little theoretical backing (Machlis and Force 1990). Adding to the complexity of measuring community dependency is the fact that forest communities themselves differ as widely as the methods used to understand them. The condition of any given community is due to a variety of factors linked to culture, historical background, industry mix, resource endowments, infrastructure, levels of community interaction, and a host of other influences (Williamson and Annamraju 1996). Because of this, identifying important components of community stability is clearly a challenge. We present two illustrations of forest dependency below. They provide an overview of the methods for determining forest dependency in Canada and BC.

First, a regional perspective on forest dependency, using income as the unit of measurement, assesses the economic impact of the forest sector across the various regions of British Columbia (see Table 3.2).

Second, Williamson and Annamraju (1996) provide a community breakdown of forest dependency (see Tables 3.3 and 3.4).[3] The study uses the following benchmarks to establish whether communities have a slight, moderate, or heavy reliance on the forest sector:

- slight or no reliance on forestry – communities with 10 percent of their economic base in forestry
- moderate reliance on forestry – communities with 10-49 percent of their economic base in forestry
- heavy reliance on forestry – communities with 50 percent or more of their economic base in forestry

Table 3.2

Income dependencies on forestry (after-tax incomes, 1991 and 1996 average)

Jurisdiction	1991 (%)	1996 (%)
Vancouver Island/Coast	18	21
Mainland/Southwest (excluding GVRD)	13	13
Thompson Okanagan	15	16
Kootenay	14	16
Cariboo	32	37
North Coast	24	29
Nechako	25	32
Northeast	17	23

Note: Forestry includes logging, pulp and paper, sawmills, other wood products manufacturing, related transportation, construction, etc.
Source: Horne 1999.

Using the Williamson and Annamraju study (1996) as a benchmark with which to assess the degree of timber dependency in British Columbia reveals that the province is one of the most dependent upon forestry in the country. Fully 69.1 percent of the BC population is deemed to live in communities with either a moderate or heavy reliance on forestry, with 14.4 percent of the population and eighty-nine communities experiencing a heavy dependency.[4] In addition, as the Horne study (1999) indicates, forest dependency in the province increased during the years leading up to the Forest Communities project, 1991-96.

As noted earlier, the institutional foundation linking community stability with timber dependency can be found in the historical development of forest policy. This link continues to provide the framework for forestry in the province, although under the pressure of the softwood lumber dispute with the United States, the connection between timber dependency and community stability may face significant changes (see the next section). In the past, governments framed social considerations of community wellbeing exclusively in narrow economic terms: if the forest sector was strong, the community economy would be strong. As we shall see in the next section, however, such economic interpretations require updating and a greater appreciation for the real structure of local and regional economies.

Community Stability
Community stability represents a concept and an objective behind much of the forest policy that emerged in the postwar period. Community stability is a manifestation of a number of overlapping conditions. Accurate mea-

Table 3.3

Degree of reliance of rural communities on the forest products sector in Canada, 1991

Jurisdiction	Total population	Reliance on forestry					
		None or slight	Moderate		Heavy		
		% of population	% of population	No. of communities	% of population	No. of communities	
British Columbia	3,282,061	30.9	54.7	180	14.4	89	
Alberta	2,545,553	93.0	6.3	50	0.7	3	
Saskatchewan	988,928	92.2	7.2	39	0.6	6	
Manitoba	1,091,942	95.5	3.5	21	1.0	5	
Ontario	10,084,885	92.2	6.6	177	1.2	55	
Quebec	6,895,963	74.5	22.7	565	2.8	127	
New Brunswick	723,900	45.2	45.4	128	9.4	40	
Nova Scotia	899,942	74.2	22.8	31	3.0	7	
Newfoundland	568,474	77.1	22.1	85	0.8	35	
Canada	27,296,852	78.4	18.2	1,294	3.4	337	

Source: Adapted from Williamson and Annamraju 1996.

Table 3.4

Distribution of communities heavily reliant on the forest products sector, by size of community, 1991

Province	Number of communities by population size			Total
	<1,000	1,000-4,999	>4,999	
British Columbia	26	33	30	89
Alberta	–	1	2	3
Saskatchewan	4	2	–	6
Manitoba	2	2	1	5
Ontario	22	25	8	55
Quebec	78	43	6	127
New Brunswick	8	31	–	40
Nova Scotia	–	6	1	–
Newfoundland	4	1	–	5
Total	144	144	48	336

Source: Adapted from Williamson and Annamraju 1996.

sures of stability have proven to be an elusive goal. As Marchak (1983) notes, there was persistent confusion between economic and social stability. The traditional method for measuring community stability has been to use economic indicators such as income and employment. If income and employment levels are high, then the community is deemed to be stable. While supporting the notion of the economic base of forestry as the main driver of community stability, proponents of this view argue that it offers a more tangible means with which to assess and compare communities: "Community Stability came to mean anything that increased employment and income in the local area. Higher yields of timber were always better than lower. Community stability became a code word and justification for boosting the cut on public lands ... The timber industry was encouraged to build mills in areas that had never had a commercial timber industry, while communities were encouraged to become dependent on the timber industry" (Power 1996a, 135).

The economic measure of community stability in BC has traditionally been tied to the notion of timber dependency. Trees are harvested, people are employed, income enters the local economy, and stability is achieved, providing that the flow of timber and the number of jobs in the forest sector remain stable, or increase to achieve greater local wealth and stability. As stated earlier, this is known as the economic-base approach to local development.

The economic base of a community is that portion of a regional economy (including income, employment, or earnings) that is generated by export demand (Williamson and Annamraju 1996). The export of goods provides an economic injection into a community that in turn induces local spending and the foundation for a local economy. In the case of forest-dependent communities in BC, the economic-base theory dictates that by exporting timber, communities receive the benefits of employment, income, population growth, increases in local expenditures, and a boost to the local tax base (Power 1996b). This formula guided the dual objectives of industrial and community development policy in BC.

While the economic-base approach is capable of producing significant wealth and community prosperity in the short term, it also programs an inherent weakness into the foundations of local economies in four fundamental ways. First, the focus on exports leaves communities vulnerable to fluctuations in external markets. External dependencies detract from stability achieved through local dependency (Cox and Mair 1988). Second, the economic-base approach ignores an essential indicator of economic stability, the *multiplier*. The economic multiplier refers to the degree of integration and diversity in a local economy. If an economy is specialized (for example, timber-dependent), money that is injected into a local economy "leaks" out through external purchases that are not made to nonexistent local businesses. In this case, the multiplier will be small. On the other hand, if a local economy is more diverse and self-sufficient, money that is injected into the community will circulate within the community, increasing employment and income (Douglas 1994). Third, the economic-base approach fails to account for local transactions based upon the informal economy, which can play a significant role in meeting the subsistence needs of people, particularly in smaller, more socially networked communities. Finally, the economic-base approach does not account for the economic contribution of retaining the natural assets of a community or region, to support, for example, the expansion of local tourism. Arguably, the economic-base approach undervalues the future contribution of natural capital, much like the measurement of the gross national product (GNP). The economic-base approach offers no comparative cost-benefit analysis of the base activity.

A narrow economic development focus on the economic base will also neglect other economic values, such as the amenities of a region that may be in jeopardy due to the increasing demands of the base activity. In BC, reliance on the economic-base approach has left communities throughout the province struggling to survive or to redefine themselves in the transition from an economy of natural resource abundance to one of scarcity. The poor condition of the markets and the impact of international trade agreements are currently amplifying unstable local conditions.

It is important to note that determining the backward, forward, and final demand linkage of base activity depends upon three variables: (1) the sustainability of the base for resource extraction, (2) the extent of local processing, and (3) the multiplier effect. If these features are met by the base activity, the positive contribution to the local economy will be significant. If they are not being met, the community will gain little in the short term and have poor prospects for prosperity or even survival in the long term.

In response to the shortcomings of a purely economic understanding of community and community health, researchers have more recently turned their attention to social factors. Those promoting social factors in the determination of stability argue that the use of economic indicators tied only to timber extraction are too limiting to access the number and complexity of variables contributing to the health and stability of a local economy and its people. We must complement the economic-base approach to understanding local economies with such factors as core population, the degree of leakage from the local economy, the network of social services, citizen participation, and commitment to place. All of these factors contribute to a more holistic view of a local economy and community.

In the case of BC, the social view of stability is strengthened by the changing relationships of the forestry sector to local places. Timber extraction in a local area no longer means that the benefits of the harvesting activities will accrue principally to local residents. Thus, volume harvested is not necessarily indicative of community well-being. For example, in the Mid Coast Timber Supply Area (TSA), a Ministry of Forests study found that out of a total labour force of 1,370 people in the forest sector for the region in 1992, only 144 jobs (10 percent) went to residents within the area (G.E. Bridges and Associates 1994). The vast majority of forestry employees are flown to the Mid Coast from other communities across BC, most notably Vancouver Island and the Lower Mainland, areas that are lacking in available timber supplies. Thus, forestry may be the dominant industry in a region, in terms of employment generated locally, but it will not necessarily have direct linkages to the local economy and therefore contribute to community stability.

Other authors note that the static nature of stability implied by employment and income variables does not adequately account for change at the community level. This is a particularly important factor in resource communities plagued by cyclical variations and constant restructuring (Kaufman and Kaufman 1990). Researchers using social interpretations of community stability point out that an oversimplified view of community stability may in fact enhance instability in the pursuit of a narrowly focused goal, blinding decision makers to the realities of community economies (Lee et al. 1990).

Attempts to reduce the complexity of using social indicators for determining community stability are not devoid of simplifying assumptions, however. The difficulty in measuring social phenomena and drawing useful comparisons between communities for the purposes of constructing appropriate policy acts as a barrier to embracing social measures of community stability. Kaufman and Kaufman summarize the challenge of using social criteria for determining community stability (1990, 32): "Community stability ... is a broad social objective. It is impossible to know all the principal answers, even for one small community. No blueprint is possible. Furthermore, in a democracy it should be the task of the people in the local community to determine finally their goals and procedures."

The complexity and frustration surrounding the measurement of community stability is perhaps responsible for the US Forest Service decision to define community stability as "the rate of change with which people can cope without exceeding their capacity to deal with it." Other studies have adopted this method where it is the perception of local residents that ultimately determines community stability in an environment best defined as a dynamic equilibrium (Machlis and Force 1990).

In British Columbia, although the current economic downturn in the provincial economy is causing a re-evaluation of the economic dependencies and condition of the province, traditional economic interpretations of stability persist. The concepts of sustainable forestry and sustainable communities have managed to influence the debate and raise awareness surrounding broader issues of community stability, but narrow growth-oriented interpretations continue to dominate.

The development patterns and policy instruments of the BC government and the forest sector have tended to define and implement community stability in economic terms of timber dependency. Harvest volumes and employment by large firms with access to the forest land base were the primary instruments of development. Timber extraction became the dominant economic value of the forest and specialization in the forest sector was the principal outcome of local development strategies. The close relationships between communities and large corporations controlling the land base reinforced economic interpretations of timber dependency and community stability (Marchak 1983).

The historic pursuit of community stability in BC through timber dependency and corporate control have had far-reaching implications for forest-based communities and the provincial economy as a whole. As we will see in the following chapter, these forces and trends continue to influence the parameters of community economies today.

Conclusion

Staples theory provides us with a foundation for understanding the narrow parameters of the growth-oriented approach to economic development that dominates policy in Canada and British Columbia. It also provides a window through which researchers may study other social and political phenomena. For our purposes, and the purposes of better understanding the dimensions and challenges of local development, we see that local development has not been a specific strategy unto itself but rather a by-product of a top-down model, if it appeared at all. Certainly, people in communities, as a natural occurrence of community, innovation, and survival, practised local development. Particularly with regard to the forest sector, however, policies that favoured a large-scale, commodity-based industry, resulting in a nondiversified approach to development, settlement, and industrial advancement, stifled early entrepreneurial spirit and the potential for diversified local development patterns.

Chapter 4 demonstrates that BC has largely realized the original goals set out for the industrial forestry model and regional growth. This strategy fuelled the GDP, created numerous communities dependent upon the forest sector, and provided the revenues necessary to build the province's public infrastructure. The simplicity and exclusivity of this approach has not been without consequence, however. The second component of our conceptual framework, *transition,* enables us to explore the concepts and consequences of dependency as it applies to the forest sector in British Columbia and its forest-dependent communities.

4
Transition in BC's Forest Economy: The Implications for Local Development

The purpose of this chapter is to describe the concept and consequences of staples development from a local development perspective as it applies to the forest sector and forest communities in BC. The focus on forestry has obvious connections to the forest-dependent conditions of the Forest Communities project. While the immediate focus is on forestry, the changes taking place in the forest sector reflect broader social and economic changes occurring throughout the province and in other economic sectors.

This chapter introduces the second dimension of our conceptual framework, *transition*. As we saw in Chapter 3, staples development created a foundation for top-down, specialized development in British Columbia. Because of the province's abundance of natural resources, this approach has created tremendous wealth and economic growth. It has also exacted large costs in terms of community dependency, environmental degradation, and lost economic opportunities. The approach to forestry and other resource sector development in the province is being redefined and in fact is constantly in motion. We argue here that locally based development has a significant contribution to make in terms of identifying opportunities to create a more diversified economy in BC.

To structure the discussion, we will introduce three themes. We will begin with a brief overview of the current dimensions of the forest sector and its contributions to the provincial economy. The size of the industry is proof of the success of past policies designed to create a large, forest-dependent economy in the province. Next, we will discuss the consequences of this specialized approach to economic development from a local development perspective. We will present the negative impacts of business cycle instability and corporate restructuring in the forest industry relative to the health of local economies. Finally, we will discuss important forces driving a reconsideration of the forest sector and community and regional development in the province. These forces illustrate the increasing complexity of the economic landscape, providing a more thorough understanding of other enabling and constraining forces that influence local development strategies and actors.

The Modern Forest Sector

Forestry is a significant economic force in British Columbia. In light of the discussion of staples development in Chapter 3, it is not surprising that the forest industry continues to be British Columbia's largest industrial employer, and largest source of exports (52 percent of total provincial exports in 1999, totalling $15 billion). Through the harvest of 76.9 million cubic metres of wood in 1999, the logging and forest products sector provided 100,900 direct jobs, accounting for 5.3 percent of the total employment in the province (BC Stats 2000). The contribution of the industry to the provincial GDP during the midpoint of the project in 1999 was roughly $5.6 billion (1992 dollars), or 6.1 percent of the total.

The average weekly wage paid in the forest industry in 1999 was $899, which exceeds all other weekly wage averages by industry in the province with the exception of utilities. Overall, labour is the largest beneficiary of industry returns, receiving 67 percent of total returns, while Crown and enterprise received 6 percent and 27 percent, respectively, from the overall wealth generated by the forest industry between 1982 and 1993 (Schwindt and Heaps 1996). In the rural areas of BC, this wealth provides a high income for employees who, under comparative circumstances based upon education and rural opportunity, would receive lower wages and have fewer opportunities to contribute to the community economy.

Federal, provincial, and municipal governments received $4.2 billion dollars in 1999 through stumpage royalties and various taxes from the forest industry (Price Waterhouse 1999). These funds contribute to the government coffers, which then sustain public expenditures such as social services and education in the province, both major factors of community stability. The forest industry recently used these figures to criticize the size of payments going to government. The industry complained that in the past ten years, the industry had contributed $36 billion to government and $1.5 billion to shareholders, thereby creating conditions where the industry was unable to meet an appropriate threshold for return on capital employed (Nutt 2000).[1] Others argue, however, that the industry is in fact both heavily subsidized and paying lower than market rates for harvested timber (Gale et al. 1999).

The size and economic contribution of the forest industry to BC makes the health of the industry a critical factor in providing economic opportunities for communities throughout the province. This snapshot view of the industry does not reveal the full economic picture, however. While no comprehensive government or industry accounts exist to track the relative costs of the industry, a recent report published by the Sierra Club of BC uses an ecological economics approach to provide a more comprehensive account of the industry. The Sierra Club report attempts to measure the benefits *and* costs to society as a consequence of the productive activity of the forest sector. While still largely experimental, the report provides an interesting contrast to the standard reporting process used by the industry (Gale et al. 1999).

The Sierra Club report lists a wide range of economic, social, and ecological factors associated with industrial forestry. The report notes that subsidies to industrial forest operations range from a low of $1.6 billion, to a mid-range of $2.93 billion, to a high of $4.23 billion. The report concludes that the methodology used by the firm that produces an annual review of the forest sector in BC, PricewaterhouseCoopers, overestimates the benefits generated by the forest industry and fails to account for the social and environmental costs associated with logging, lumber, and pulp and paper production. Second, the PricewaterhouseCoopers methodology discriminates, according to the report, against ecosystem-based forestry by recording potential declines in employment, government revenues, and corporate profits while not capturing the positive contributions of a decline in subsidies and other social and environmental costs.

It is clear that the forest sector is a significant contributor to the provincial economy. This significance is magnified in rural areas. Given the sharp contrast between the reports provided by PricewaterhouseCoopers and the Sierra Club, however, we are left with questions concerning the costs and benefits of the forest sector to the province and its communities.

The following section evaluates critical dimensions of the impacts of the forest industry on communities throughout the province. We introduce a local development perspective to the role of the forest sector in BC. A local development analysis of the forest sector will move us a step closer to understanding the specific context for local development in forest-dependent communities in British Columbia.

A Local Development Perspective

Despite the significance of the economic contribution of forestry to the provincial economy (and to the individual economies of the project communities), inquiry into community economic development (CED) demands a longer time frame of analysis and a more integrated perspective with attention given to a variety of local economic variables. Recent turbulence in the forest sector exposes many of the cyclical and structural characteristics of the industry, which, when viewed from the perspective of community economic health, illustrate the need for a more diverse approach to community and regional development.

The following section will begin with a discussion of the instability associated with business cycles and structural changes in the forest industry. Second, we will discuss some of the environmental impacts associated with an industrial approach to forestry, with reference to conservation and the long-term viability of the forest economy. We will link the more theoretical discussion of the staples economy in Chapter 3 specifically to the practicalities of the forest sector in British Columbia. We will also illustrate the interrelationships between staples development (forestry in this case) and community and regional development.

Economic Impacts

Business Cycle Instability

A ten-year analysis of the forest industry between 1988 and 1997 reveals that the industry experienced two complete cycles of boom and bust (see Figure 4.1). Murray and Bartoszewski (1998) extend the time frame of cyclical analysis back to 1975, recording an additional boom-and-bust cycle: 1979 and 1982, respectively. The reasons for these fluctuations are linked, in part, to the industry's specialization in commodity markets. Fluctuations in international demand, due to factors such as the downturn in the Asian economy, product substitution, and lower-cost production in other forest producing regions of the world, all affect the demand for, and price of, forest commodity products from British Columbia. International competition places a ceiling on commodity prices in regions. Even when there are conditions of local scarcity, all regions continue to be price takers, not price makers, often further exacerbating conditions of resource depletion due to

Figure 4.1

BC forest sector profit/loss, 1988-97

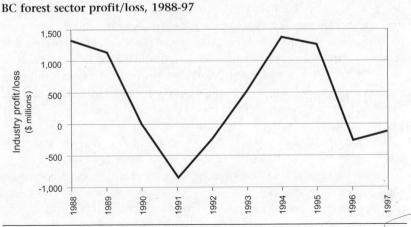

Source: Adapted from Price Waterhouse 1999.

industrial efforts to boost production and efficiency in order to remain competitive and profitable (Clapp 1998).

Boom-and-bust cycles in the forest sector greatly impact the overall health of the provincial economy. At the local level, cyclical instability in the forest industry both directly and indirectly influences the health of local economies in three fundamental ways. First, the most direct impacts are linked to fluctuations in employment, income, and the overall centralization of business operations during market downturns. These changes can have devastating effects on a community economy with a heavy reliance on the forest sector, resulting in permanent job losses in hinterland areas. Estimates are that over 10,000 BC forest workers, or about 10 percent of the industry's employees, were laid off for varying amounts of time during a six-month period between 1997 and 1998, coinciding with the start of the Forest Communities project (Beatty and Hamilton 1998). As the slump continued to the end of 1998, mills closed throughout the province and analysts predicted no clear end to the troubles in the industry. Over eleven mills closed indefinitely in 1998, adding to a sense of urgency and uncertainty in the project communities (Wilson 1999).

End of the road for pulp-mill town in British Columbia: Gold River. The heaviest blow yet to province's forest industry leaves residents struggling to envisage a future. *Globe and Mail,* 26 October 1998, A3

Bail out foundering communities, BC minister suggests to big banks. *Vancouver Sun,* 12 December 1998, E1

A second impact on local economies relates to levels of investor confidence. Internal or external investor confidence in a community dependent upon the boom-and-bust cycles of the forest industry may be shaken to the point that investments are not made to support or diversify the community economy. The lack of investment and diversity in a local economy exacerbates the instability already facing the community due to specialization in the forest industry itself. As a result of lower investment levels, there are fewer economic opportunities to support the local economy and to provide employment.

The mobility of capital places at-risk communities at a severe disadvantage when seeking to attract the type of capital necessary for economic diversification. Capital is fainthearted. The effects of investor confidence are amplified in the context of rural BC, as the remoteness of many communities dependent upon forestry adds another barrier to attaining economic and community stability through a more diversified economy. The coastal region is at a particular disadvantage because of remoteness, difficult terrain, and overall poor accessibility.

Finally, the boom-and-bust cycles of the forest industry create dependency at the local level, inhibiting proactive planning for economic diversification (Randall and Ironside 1996; Picot and Heath 1992). Local expectations that another boom will follow the immediate hardships of a downturn lead communities down a path of declining possibilities. Long-term restructuring in the industry means that fewer jobs return following each bust cycle, and economic opportunities linked to a healthy forest land base become less viable as environmental protection may be reduced in order to achieve short-term social and economic objectives.

Despite the significant contribution made by forestry to the rural economies of British Columbia, the inconsistency, or rather the consistency of industry fluctuations, leads to local instability. Industry responses to each bust period, coupled with increasing levels of global competition, necessitate wide-scale restructuring, increasing the pressure on governments and communities to incur greater social, economic, and ecological costs for fewer direct benefits from the industry.

Community instability linked to fluctuations in the marketplace serves as a motivating force for reconsidering the role of industrial forestry in community economies. Such analysis also calls for a closer examination of the costs and benefits associated with forest dependency and market specialization. The province requires a long-term, balanced transition strategy to address the negative impacts of industrial forestry, to capture the positive features of industrial forestry, and to consider a new approach to fostering CED. The alternative to this balanced transition approach is a cyclical process of incrementally progressive community and ecologically based regulation during boom periods and corporate lobbying and regulatory erosion during bust periods. Clearly, a seesaw approach to forest policy fails to serve the long-term interests of community stability and corporate sustainability in the province. The current reforms taking place under the threat of the softwood lumber dispute represent perhaps a sea change in forest policy, but at the time of writing there has been no definitive resolution to the crisis.

Concentration, Consolidation, and Market Dependency in the BC Forest Industry

The legacy of the two Sloan Commissions and subsequent policy changes provided large corporations with dominant control over the forest land base. The government purposely replaced historical patterns of diversity in the forest industry with increasing levels of corporate concentration (Hayter 2000). For example, in 1999 ten companies controlled 59 percent of BC's total allowable annual cut (AAC) of timber (Table 4.1).

Table 4.1

Allowable annual cut (AAC) in BC, 1998-99

Company	Total AAC (m³)	% of BC harvest
Canfor Corp.	8,305,438	11.8
Weyerhaeuser Canada Ltd.	7,252,374	10.3
Slocan Forest Products Ltd.	6,209,038	8.8
West Fraser Timber Co. Ltd.	4,204,134	6.0
Doman Industries Ltd.	4,080,471	5.8
International Forest Products Ltd.	3,554,877	5.0
Skeena Cellulose Inc.	2,337,550	3.3
Riverside Forest Products Ltd.	2,306,776	3.3
Weldwood of Canada Ltd.	2,111,909	3.0
TimberWest Forest Corp.	1,492,596	2.1
Total	41,855, 163	59%

Source: Canadian Forest Service 2001.

One of the most fundamental influences of corporate control on community economies is linked to the transition of the industry towards capital-intensive means of production. Besides fostering the cyclical conditions noted earlier, intense capitalization has also facilitated declining employment prospects despite increasing harvest volumes. For example, in 1961 the BC forest sector produced two jobs per 1,000 cubic metres of wood. By 1991, the number of jobs per 1,000 cubic metres of wood had declined to 0.88 despite a 57 percent increase in the volume of wood harvested (M'Gonigle and Parfitt 1994).

The dynamics of the industrial forest industry are justified under the logic of competitive markets. Using parameters of market competitiveness, the BC forest industry is essentially faced with a choice between increasing efficiency, and therefore capital intensity, or accepting the risk of becoming uncompetitive. Due to global competition, the entire industry is jeopardized if it becomes uncompetitive. Industrial innovation and change are common and often socially and ecologically beneficial; however, the forest industry in BC produces substantially fewer jobs per unit of wood than the rest of Canada and other Organisation for Economic Co-operation and Development (OECD) countries (see Table 4.2). Lower employment levels in BC are due in part to the highly mechanized state of the industry, both in harvesting and processing (that is, capital-intensive, not labour-intensive, and high volume, low value), and also to the comparatively small value-added industry in BC.

Low values extracted from wood place pressures on the forest industry and the government to maintain high harvest rates and low costs of production. Decreases in volume and tenure reallocation to accommodate the protection of the environment, to provide for community forest tenures, or

Table 4.2

Comparison of selected economic and social benefits of timber production, 1995

Location	Log supply (million m³)	Shipment value ($ million)	Unit value ($/m³)	Value added ($ million)	Unit value added ($/m³)	Direct forest industry employment (jobs)	Direct jobs (jobs/1,000 m³)
British Columbia	76	25,127	332	8,978	119	76,403	1.01
Rest of Canada	114	46,241	405	21,974	193	18,0884	1.59
Canada total	190	71,368	376	30,952	163	257,287	1.36
United States	524	382,460	731	166,724	318	1,369,400	2.62
New Zealand	17	10,979	640	4,246	247	30,495	1.78
Sweden	59	29,159	494	10,501	178	120,000	2.03

Note: All monetary amounts are in Canadian dollars.
Source: Ray Travers media briefing, The David Suzuki Foundation, 18 November 1998.

to protect other economic interests such as tourism and fisheries generate intense resistance from industry due to low profit margins. The industry must maintain the status quo of low-cost, high-volume production (Schwindt and Heaps 1996).

Capital intensification also leads to the agglomeration of the forest industry into larger centres. Centralization occurs primarily in response to the higher transfer costs in remote locations and to the ability of technology to increase the mobility of capital resources (Berck et al. 1992). The mobility of capital creates a tension with the rootedness of place, as many of BC's more remote forest-dependent communities lose valuable processing jobs and their ability to attract or retain investment due to instability.

The centralization of forestry processing operations in response to downturns in the forest industry has particularly negative consequences for smaller communities. Losses of key harvesting and manufacturing jobs occur when operations move to larger centres. For example, the fact that almost half of the forest industry's contribution to the provincial GDP is generated by industrial activities in the Greater Vancouver area illustrates centralizing trends (Hamilton 1998). Companies transport wood from rural regions to the Lower Mainland for processing and shipping.

The Environment
The environmental impacts of the forest industry have been a source of much contention and conflict in British Columbia. The purpose of this section is to outline a critical outcome of the management of the forest resource: overcut. Overcutting and the environmental impacts associated with it are major contributors to the current instability in the forest industry. In the past, downturns were a regular market occurrence from which the industry and communities would recover. Recent evidence shows that many of the current problems facing the industry are being compounded by limits to the resource base itself. Given that many forest product markets remain strong and that other forest-based economies are performing well, internal factors (BC forest policies and practices) are attracting increasing attention from policy makers: "In spite of an elaborate partnership between the government and industry and the expenditure of several billion dollars of public money, BC still has a woefully inadequate forest-management capability ... We have not learned how to become stewards of our forests, and to manage them as well as others do in parts of Europe, the United States, and elsewhere" (Drushka 1999).

Management of the Forest Resource
The dependency of the BC forest sector on commodity markets has had a negative impact on the ability of communities to achieve economic diversification. In order to facilitate commodity-based production, policy makers

have perpetually set harvest levels above government-determined, sustainable levels, resulting in an overcut. Overcutting occurs when the volume of timber harvested from a Timber Supply Area (TSA) exceeds the area's ability to regenerate. Overcutting negatively impacts the future viability of the forest industry and places added pressure on BC communities when excessive harvest volumes can no longer be sustained. Excessive cutting also reduces economic opportunities for other sectors of the economy that depend upon the forest resource.

The economics of discounting represents a fundamental force driving the mismanagement of the forest resource. In essence, discounting is based on the fact that forest ecosystems reproduce themselves more slowly than capital (Clapp 1998; Hammond 1991). Forest corporations receive a higher rate of financial return by clearcutting a forest and investing the money earned from the activity in other areas than by harvesting at slower, more sustainable levels. Discounting also absorbs or hides the cost of damages inflicted through poor harvesting, or the possible benefits derived through other, more sustainable uses of the forest ecosystem (the basis of the Sierra Club argument noted earlier). When we harvest forests solely on the principle of discounting, ignoring even a basic cost-benefit analysis that compares different harvesting techniques or forest uses, long-term community stability is threatened.

The record of overcutting in the industry, facilitated by the use of clearcut logging, has severely depleted the most easily accessible timber. Overcutting is causing a limit in supply, which is contributing to the current downturn in the industry. A former Forest Alliance of BC director describes the overcut situation: "In their search for new timber, forest companies are being forced to log in the hard-to-reach 'guts and feathers' areas of BC's coastal forests" (Hamilton 1998). Limits to the remaining timber supply also affect the cost of logging in BC, as the harvesting of less accessible wood at higher elevations or on a steeper slope increases the costs of extraction and the risks of environmental degradation.

For people living in a forest-dependent community, there is a significant difference between a downturn in the industry caused by demand (market instability) and one caused by supply (lack of timber). Downturns in demand are cyclical and the impacts on community stability can be anticipated and addressed using shorter-term measures and long-term development strategies. The depletion of the resource base itself implies a longer-term process of economic restructuring and ecological restoration, or, depending on the degree to which a local economy is timber-dependent, may spell the end of a community itself. If the integrity of the local ecosystem has been compromised by harvesting activities, the economic impacts on a community may be severe (Power 1996a).

The record of overcutting in BC violates the fundamental principles of sustained yield in terms of ensuring long-term community stability. Long-run sustained yield (LRSY) has now been replaced with the concept of "long-term harvest level" (LTHL). LTHL is a more constrained version of LRSY, as "LTHL recognizes that maximum sustained yield will not be achieved in

Table 4.3

Extent of overcutting in British Columbia, by Timber Supply Area (TSA), 1996

Timber Supply Area	Annual allowable cut (m³)	Long-term harvest level (m³)	Overcut (%)
Nass	1,150,000	410,000	180
Revelstoke	230,000	98,000	135
Bulkley	895,000	424,000	111
North Coast	600,000	300,000	100
Queen Charlotte	475,000	248,000	92
Mid Coast	1,000,000	550,000	82
Lillooet	643,500	362,600	77
Golden	540,000	309,000	75
Kispiox	1,092,611	630,000	73
Robson Valley	602,377	350,572	72
Invermere	591,500	360,000	64
Merritt	1,454,250	925,000	57
Williams lake	3,807,000	2,469,000	54
Kingcome	1,399,000	936,000	49
Arrow	619,000	422,000	47
Kootenay	700,000	490,000	43
Kamloops	2,679,180	1,958,000	37
Arrowsmith	400,000	296,000	35
Cranbrook	850,000	633,000	34
Fraser	1,555,000	1,180,000	32
Strathcona	1,420,000	1,088,250	30
Okanagan	2,615,000	2,022,000	29
Boundary	700,000	560,000	25
Morrice	1,985,815	1,614,000	23
Dawson	1,733,033	1,452,000	19
Quesnel	2,340,000	1,995,500	17
Kalum	464,000	400,000	16
Sunshine Coast	1,140,000	986,000	16
Soo	506,000	442,000	14
100 Mile House	1,362,000	1,202,000	13
Mackenzie	2,997,363	2,810,000	7
Lakes	1,500,000	1,441,000	4
Fort Nelson	1,500,000	1,500,000	0
Prince George	9,363,661	9,630,000	–3
Fort St. John	2,015,000	2,475,000	–19
Cassiar	400,000	867,000	–54
Total TSAs	53,325,290	43,836,522	22

Source: Resource Tenures and Engineering Branch, Ministry of Forests, 1996, in BC Wild 1998.

practice due to operational and environmental constraints which delay the timing of logging and prevent the realization of the full timber yield from each stand" (BC Wild 1998). A study measuring the rate of overcutting in the province by Timber Supply Area reveals that the current rate of cutting exceeds the LTHL by 22 percent, or roughly 9.5 million cubic metres of wood (see Table 4.3). Previous years have exceeded this level of overcut. The degree of overcut is also exacerbated by insufficient restocking of harvested lands. In 1997, 22 percent (787,000 hectares) of harvested Crown land in BC was understocked, although the record of replacement and regeneration is improving (Canadian Forest Service 2001).

The foregoing TSA review is particularly insightful as it highlights the need for further reductions in volume, under existing regulation, which are necessary to establish a government-defined sustainable forest industry in the province. This means that the current rates of employment in the industry will remain linked to an artificially high rate of cutting unless the industry can develop further value-added processing. Employment reductions in the industry will be necessary in the coming decades if current patterns and practices are maintained.

TIMBER SUPPLY REVIEWS

Mid Coast Timber Supply

The Timber Supply Reviews for the Mid Coast and Lillooet Timber Supply Areas (TSAs) illustrate the extent of the overcut in BC and the potential job impacts of returning to sustainable harvest levels. For the Mid Coast, by moving from an AAC in 1992 of 1 million cubic metres to a long-term harvest level (LTHL) of 680,300 cubic metres (a level still in excess of the latest LTHL set in 1996 of 550,000 cubic metres), it is estimated that 313 direct local and non-local TSA jobs will be lost over the next 50 to 100 years.

Lillooet Timber Supply

In Lillooet, reductions from an AAC in 1993 of 636,000 cubic metres to a LTHL of 363,000 cubic metres over a period of 120 years would result in the reduction of 207 person-years of direct jobs in the TSA.

Uncertainty

It should be noted that the predictability of such long-term harvest level estimates is tenuous at best. Changing ecological conditions, declining returns due to ecological degradation from past harvesting methods, or different forest practices may reduce or increase the volume of timber available. (Clapp 1998)

The legacy of the policy of sustained yield and the systematic overcutting of BC forests culminate in what is known as the "falldown effect." Falldown is predicated on the fact that once old-growth forests have been liquidated, second-growth forests, being cut in 70- to 120-year cycles, will not be able to replicate the biomass volumes provided by old-growth forests. Cut levels must then fall to account for the decreased volume of timber that can be sustained from the second-growth forest alone. Past forest practices, which have degraded soils and limited replanting, also contribute to the decline in the potential volume of second growth.

There are numerous reasons for allowing the levels of overcut to continue over time, but two factors are of particular importance. First, as stated earlier, high levels of corporate concentration facilitated the development of a capital-intensive and commodity-dependent forest industry in the province. The industry therefore relies upon high volumes of timber to offset high capital costs and to remain competitive in the marketplace. Second, governments allow higher cut levels in return for the jobs, revenues, and investments being offered by forest companies. For example, previous policy required forest companies to maintain specific harvest levels regardless of price.

BC forest communities and the provincial economy as a whole are now confronting the economic realities of reaching ecological limits (Hutton 1994). Government and industry leaders of the past made forest policy decisions with social and economic considerations in mind. These actors succeeded in generating significant growth throughout the province. Current leaders are faced with a much more complex decision-making environment. They must now add ecological considerations and community viability factors to the social and economic mix in order to weigh the full costs and benefits associated with various uses of the forest resource.

The forest industry in British Columbia fundamentally shaped the development of the province. A cornerstone of the economy, the industry provides employment, is a foundation for community development, and contributes significant resources to government coffers. It is also clear that the industry will remain an important sector in the provincial economy in the future, particularly for rural regions. Chapters 2 and 3 illustrate, however, that the growth mentality that drove industrial expansion and development in the province has not been without cost. The province's First Nations peoples, who were isolated and excluded from any productive role in the resource economy, felt immediate impacts. More recently, many communities throughout the province are facing instability and decline.

Until very recently, the mainstream policy faction in BC has considered as heretical debates about the forest industry that highlight the negative consequences of industrial forestry or question the significance of the industry relative to other approaches to development (Cashore et al. 2001). In summary, through the foregoing discussion, we have attempted to contribute two ideas to an expanding dialogue concerning the link between the forest industry and local economies. First, given the legacy of staples development in BC, there is clearly space in the province within which to explore development alternatives. Second, availing of this space will require fundamental changes in the entrenched attitudes of governments, industry, and communities. A strong community perspective must be added to the complex relationship between forest management and economic development. The following section identifies a variety of additional forces of change, which are challenging us to adopt new approaches, policies, and attitudes towards economic development in BC.

Forces of Change

A more challenging development context is emerging in BC. This section describes a variety of forces contributing to change, including: environmentalism, First Nations activism, economic diversification, government policy, globalization, and community proactivity. A review of these forces provides a more comprehensive understanding of some of the development prospects and challenges facing the province.

Environmentalism

Hayter (2000) notes that the emergence of forest-based environmentalism in BC is linked to three phenomena. First, in the 1970s, "falldown" was acknowledged, resulting in serious questions being raised about the stewardship of the land base. Second, the economic recession of the early 1980s highlighted the vulnerability of the forest industry, the lack of economic diversity in the province, and the extent to which forestry was a negative influence on alternative forms of economic development. Finally, in the late 1980s and early 1990s, a general awareness of the importance of biodiversity increased throughout the world, leading to a more mainstream realization of the ecological significance of BC forests:

- Canada holds 10% of the world's forests
- Canada houses 25% of the earth's remaining frontier forest (large, relatively undisturbed forest areas with sufficient area to maintain all of their native biodiversity)
- Coastal BC is home to 20% of the world's remaining temperate rainforest (World Resources Institute 2001)

As a result of these forces and a general global awareness of the importance of the environment, a powerful environmental movement emerged in BC. The movement is composed of a diverse range of organizations, each seeking to draw attention to a wide variety of environmental issues. From a forestry perspective, local or regional groups, which spring up in response to local environmental hot spots, have worked in concert (and occasionally in opposition) with a select group of province-wide and transnational organizations, such as Greenpeace and the Sierra Club of BC.

The tactics of environmental groups have varied and increased in sophistication over time. The approach that defined the movement and that continues to drive numerous environmental campaigns throughout the province is lobbying for environmental protection through the creation of parks. More recently, environmentalists have varied an exclusive park protection approach with a focus on larger-scale conservation, recognizing that the battle to create islands of preservation amid a sea of environmental damage is not meeting broader biodiversity objectives (Sanjan and Soulé 1997). Conservation implies a push to change forestry practices altogether and to secure a balance between appropriate industrial forest use, land-base protection, and community resource access.

Despite the diversity and compromise of the conservation objective, the fundamental goal of environmentalists remains the protection of the environment. During a time of transition, where status quo forces remain significant, if not dominant, calls for environmental protection create varying degrees of discord among environmental groups and the communities situated within and dependent upon the forest resource for a number of reasons.

First, the extent of existing environmental problems combined with the pace of logging activity fosters a sense of urgency in environmentalist campaigns that may be expressed and perceived as authoritarian from a community perspective. It is common for communities and First Nations to resent the fact that environmental groups have not adequately observed protocols of consultation and local involvement. The urgency to protect ecosystems may cause environmentalists to develop strategies that supersede or run contrary to local decision-making processes (Hayter 2000).

Second, despite the size and sophistication of select environmental groups, they remain poorly resourced compared with the industrial sectors that they confront. Given limited resources, environmentalists are forced to concentrate on the selective use of specific campaign skills. Leaders in the movement have been moulded by, and are necessarily skilled in, conflict-based tactics, including blockades, media wars, and market campaigns. Groups often lack the resources and skills necessary to become more directly involved in issues of local economic transition, necessary once environmentalists have realized preliminary conservation objectives. In addition, moving from a conflict-based to a consensus-based approach requires a transition in skill sets. From a local perspective, the willingness of local actors to work with environmentalists to achieve newly defined local development objectives is not a given. Resentment about the authoritarian style of campaigns, and the problem of accepting change in the first place, quite independent of how or who motivated it, may constrain working relationships between communities and environmental groups.

Finally, environmental groups in BC have been routinely criticized for lacking a vision of development in the province (M'Gonigle 1997; Drushka 1999). Thinking has generally stopped short of asking the question "what then?" As stated earlier, to some extent this is understandable given limited resources and the scale of the problems. As environmental issues and concepts such as sustainable development become more mainstream, however, environmental groups must ask new questions and develop skills and resources to forge adequate answers. In other words, the environmental movement has a role to play not only in identifying problems but also in proposing solutions.

The most promising approach being put forward by the environmental sector for balancing ecological values with economic activity is ecosystem-based management (EBM). EBM offers an approach to managing the land base that incorporates direct principles to protect human well-being. The use of EBM challenges environmental organizations to enhance the sophistication of their economic and community-based strategies while also challenging governments and corporations to improve their environmental performance. EBM is defined as "an adaptive approach to managing human activities that seeks to ensure the coexistence of healthy, fully functioning ecosystems and human communities ... The intent is to maintain those spatial and temporal characteristics of ecosystems such that component species and ecological processes can be sustained, and human wellbeing supported and improved" (Cardinal et al. 2003).

The environmental movement in BC has strong local roots, including the formation of Greenpeace itself. Over the years, campaigns have been effective in raising public awareness about the environment and the importance of BC forests on a global scale. Observers criticizing the movement generally focus on the bluntness and simplicity of campaign strategies and the extent to which they ignore or under-represent local values. However, the sector is constantly changing and adapting to new economic, ecological, and social realities and impulses, such as through the promotion of independent forest certification. Overall, the sector has played a pivotal role in creating the space necessary to consider and adopt alternative forms of development. The challenge now is the extent to which environmental groups will contribute to human well-being within new conservation-based land-use arrangements.

First Nations
Recent changes in the legal and political landscape have resulted in significant advances in the struggle for recognition of Aboriginal rights and title,

particularly with regard to claims to lands and natural resources. The landmark *Delgamuukw* decision provides perhaps the strongest evidence of this trend, along with the ongoing negotiation of land claims under the BC treaty process.[2] Other legal cases, such as the 1990 *Sparrow* decision,[3] have also ruled that the Canadian Constitution preserves Aboriginal rights to resources such as fisheries, wildlife, forests, and water.

Just before the start of the Forest Communities project in 1997, the courts delivered the *Delgamuukw* decision, which legally recognizes the existence of Aboriginal title in BC. As stated earlier, however, between 1870 and 1991 it was the de facto policy of the BC government to formally deny land title to First Nations. This tactic, combined with other early twentieth-century policies designed to further curtail Aboriginal people's rights, led to the use of two pivotal strategies by First Nations in BC to reassert their rights: blockades and litigation (Tennant 1989).

First, Aboriginal blockades emerged in BC during the mid-1970s and peaked in the summer of 1990, when researchers documented thirty blockades, involving twenty different Native groups throughout the province. The blockades symbolized "a Native rejection of generations of systemic racism, territorial dispossession, and economic marginalization ... To be able to assert some claim to, and control over, space (albeit temporary) through a blockade both relies upon, and further sustains, First Nation claims to unabrogated sovereignty over specific territory" (Blomley 1996, 8-9). Second, the Nisga'a First Nation initiated litigation in 1967 with the Supreme Court of BC asserting that their Aboriginal title had never been extinguished. A trial judge initially ruled that if title had ever existed, a series of colonial statutes that enabled the Crown to grant land to settlers had extinguished any current claims. The BC Court of Appeal later upheld the decision, forcing the Nisga'a to the Supreme Court of Canada in 1971. The final ruling in 1973 was a technical defeat for the Nisga'a, but ultimately a moral victory, as three of six judges ruled that title did exist prior to contact, that title had not been extinguished, and that the Nisga'a could assert legitimate title rights in the present day.

Inspired by the moral victory of the Nisga'a and disturbed by the ever-increasing encroachment on their lands and resources, the Gitksan and Wet'suwet'en filed a suit in 1987 asserting their jurisdiction over 58,000 square kilometres of territory in central BC, including control of fishing, forestry, and water rights. The suit also asserted their right to self-government within this territory. In the opening statements, Hereditary Chief Delgam Uukw stated: "The evidence will show that the Gitksan and Wet'suwet'en are and have always been properly counted amongst the civilized nations of the world; that their ownership of their territory and their authority over it has always existed ... The challenge for this court is to hear this evidence, in all its complexity, in all its elaboration, as the articulation of a way of looking at the world which pre-dates the Canadian Constitution by many thousands of years" (Monet and Wilson 1992, 24).

Other cases followed. In 1990, the *Sparrow* decision ruled that the Aboriginal right to fish is preserved in the Canadian Constitution. Other Nations have since applied the decision to other resources, including wildlife, forests, and water.

The Gitksan and Wet'suwet'en lost their case in 1991 and also a subsequent appeal. The appeal decision was a significant victory, however, because the judge ruled that governments had not extinguished Aboriginal rights. In response, the BC government joined with Canada and the leadership of many BC First Nations to create the BC Treaty Commission to address outstanding treaty issues. According to the government, a concern for social justice and the need for investment certainty related to the land base provided the necessary incentive to confront title issues (British Columbia 1995). Currently, 53 BC First Nations are participating in the treaty process, representing 122 Indian Act Bands (114 in BC and 8 in the Yukon) (British Columbia Treaty Commission 2003).

After over a decade, the Supreme Court of Canada ruled in favour of the Gitksan and Wet'suwet'en people in December 1997, stating that, in the absence of treaties, Aboriginal title continues to exist in Canada. All interests continue to wrestle with the implications of this decision, representing yet another factor of considerable uncertainty regarding investment in the land base. However, the *Delgamuukw* decision has caused a significant shift in the negotiating powers available to First Nations. There has been an increase in consultations with First Nations communities regarding economic activities taking place within their traditional territories and an empowering effect on First Nations communities regarding their prospects for economic development.

From a local development perspective, title represents a foundation for justice, healing, and economic development. Title offers First Nations peoples the opportunity to overcome a legacy of economic marginalization to play active and proactive roles in the development and restoration of their communities and surrounding communities. At a broader level, the reclamation of and/or compensation for Aboriginal lands creates new development conflicts and opportunities at regional and local levels. The project research shows that inter-community competition for resources is evident, as are new regional initiatives to pool development resources. The resolution of title issues is a significant force that will continue to shape prospects for local development in the province for years to come.

Economic Diversification
Some of the biggest changes taking place in the BC economy are in the service sector. The reputation of service sector employment has changed a

great deal from the "burger-flipping" stereotypes of the past: "There is nothing insubstantial or unproductive about services. They are what energize the productive side of our economy. They are also what we increasingly want from the economy to make our lives more satisfying. It is goods production that ultimately threatens us and our communities: a constantly increasing flow of raw materials from the natural landscape and a constantly increased flow of material waste back into the landscape" (Power 1996a, 62). BC Stats reports that three out of every four jobs in the province are in service industries (as opposed to one in ten for forestry), which includes a diverse employment spectrum:

- public administration
- finance, insurance, real estate
- transportation, storage, communications
- business services
- education
- accommodation and food
- personal services
- health and social
- wholesale and retail

Total employment in the service sector reached 1,478,900 in 1999. In terms of provincial GDP, 74.6 percent originated in the service sector, compared with 25.4 percent in goods production. Although the service sector encompasses a wide selection of industries and occupations, it is the largest contributor to the provincial economy.

Tourism and high technology are service-related industries that are experiencing considerable growth and increased policy attention. Tourism and high tech are now the second and third single largest industries in the province behind forestry. Tourism contributed $5 billion to the provincial economy in 2001, employing 7 percent of the workforce (BC Stats 2003a). The high-technology sector in BC has been one of the province's fastest-growing industries. The industry contributed $3.3 billion to the BC economy and employed approximately 45,550 people in 2001 (BC Stats 2003b). While larger centres will undoubtedly be the major beneficiaries of the growth in the high-technology industry and the knowledge-based economy more generally, the possibility of telecommuting and the quality of life offered in BC's rural areas may create opportunities for high technology to contribute to existing resource-dependent communities.

A number of researchers, however, question the value of tourism and information-based diversification efforts in resource-dependent communities. Mitchell (1995) notes the difficulties associated with economic diversification into sectors such as tourism. Problems associated with tourism include lower wages, seasonal employment, and a cultural clash or transition as communities struggle to integrate the tourism economy with the economic expectations and values fostered through resource-based histories.

Coffey (1996) states that optimistic views of the potential for the service sector to enhance the economic development of Canada's peripheral regions are largely unjustified. He notes that ten large metropolitan areas contain approximately 70 percent of all Canadian FIRE (finance, insurance, real estate) employment.

As presented in the community profiles, Coffey's findings are supported by the fact that hinterland communities in BC remain heavily dependent upon the public sector and forestry. A recent survey of sixty-three rural local economies in the province reveals the following breakdown of economic dependencies (BC Stats 1999a):

- public sector   24%
- forestry   21%
- construction   21%
- transfers   16%
- other non-employment income   10%
- tourism   7%
- other   6%
- mining   4%
- agriculture   3%
- fishing   2%

Finally, growth in the small business sector indicates a change in the make-up of the provincial economy. In 2000 there were approximately 343,300 small businesses in the province, accounting for 98 percent of all businesses in BC.[4] Small businesses employed 893,300 people in 2000, representing 58 percent of all private sector jobs in the province. The steady growth of small business employment in the province is an important factor to consider from the perspective of community diversity. Small businesses accounted for 31 percent of the BC payroll in 2000. While wage levels are higher in large firms, small businesses are closing the wage gap (BC Stats 2001d).

Government Policy

We have discussed the influence of government policy in shaping the forest sector and patterns of economic development in the province during the immediate postwar period. The policy actors during this period (and arguably at present) consisted of a close-knit triad of government, industry, and labour. This triad represents the collective agenda of the Fordist period. More recently, however, given the enhanced profile and significance of groups such as environmentalists and First Nations, the network of policy actors has become more complex and diverse. These new voices are calling for different approaches to policy making and for new policies to reflect the increasingly complex demands for resources in the province.

In BC, the 1990s represented an intense period of policy making in the forest sector. In the five years leading up to the start of the Forest Communities project, the provincial government implemented policy reforms in an attempt to accommodate the mushrooming of different values and interests attached to the forest resource. The policies and the policy process of this period are significant to local economies for a number of reasons. First, the provincial government used the policies to integrate the principles of sustainable development into the structure and practices of the forest sector. Sustainable development represents an important variable for the continued existence, viability, and diversification of rural communities throughout the province. As we saw in Chapter 3, failure to implement a sustainable approach to resource use results in declining community and industry economic performance and a decrease in the value of the resource itself.

Second, economic diversification in the province is very much dependent upon an approach to forestry that sees timber as one of many values of the forests. The section on economic diversification above illustrates that tourism, the service economy, and the ecological values of the forests are dependent upon a more holistic interpretation of the forest resource.

Third, the policies enacted and pursued by the New Democratic Party (NDP) government in BC during the 1990s represented the most environmentally oriented range of reforms ever undertaken in the BC forest industry (M'Gonigle 1997). The success or failure of these efforts provides an indicator of the ability of governments to initiate and implement structural reform in forestry – and a microcosm of policy development more generally. The development literature is replete with references to the critical role that governments must play to facilitate and enable local development efforts (Friedmann 1992). From a local development perspective, where power over and access to resources must be redistributed to create the necessary conditions for greater degrees of self-determination at local and regional levels, government involvement in the redistribution process is crucial. It is important to note, however, that while the NDP government could be given high marks for its environmental and conservation agenda, it did relatively little to directly assist communities bearing the brunt of restructuring.

The following section provides a brief overview and assessment of selected policies pursued in the forest sector during the 1990s – the policy environment during the Forest Communities project. As Table 4.4 illustrates, many of the principles of sustainable forest management that governments and nongovernmental agencies promote at national and international levels are present in the BC agenda, including conservation, enhanced and more diversified participation, and better information and monitoring. Despite their promise in principle, in reality the policies failed to live up to their stated objectives or significantly alter the structural conditions of the industry. Moreover, the current Liberal government is enacting significant regulatory streamlining, which will further erode the impact and intent of recent policy changes.

First, in terms of conservation, the Forest Practices Code (FPC) has been repeatedly weakened since its inception in 1995. In fact, the government did not implement important sections of the code designed to make forest operations more sustainable (Hume 1999a). Economic goals in the face of a downturn in the forest industry prevented the government from fully implementing the code and, in fact, prompted regulatory streamlining. In addition, the government stated that the impact of the FPC on the annual allowable cut (AAC) would not exceed 6 percent. As Palmer (2001) notes, efforts within the NDP to move towards a results-based code (greater corporate flexibility and less monitoring) resulted in industry not following the code. This represents an important lesson for the current provincial Liberal government in its desire to further streamline the code through results-based management.

Second, the NDP government determined preservation goals based upon its stated target of protecting 12 percent of the provincial land base. Inasmuch as the Protected Areas Strategy (in Table 4.4) is to be applauded, real preservation goals are uncertain due to questions surrounding the validity of the strategy. The province promoted the strategy as a ceiling on protected areas. Meanwhile, biologists continue to question the validity of the science behind the selection of the 12 percent goal (Sanjan and Soulé 1997). Questions remain concerning the size, representative balance, and connectivity of the selected protected areas. In essence, you cannot have too much biodiversity, whereas you can have too much development. The two are asymmetrical.

Third, the NDP's economic diversification efforts were mixed at best. On the one hand, researchers have praised the mandate of the NDP's centrepiece of diversification and restoration, Forest Renewal BC (FRBC). Government succeeded in getting the forest industry to agree to cost increases in order to finance economic diversification and environmental initiatives. One the other hand, the Crown corporation experienced severe implementation problems and the provincial Liberal government terminated the agency upon entering office: "Might the people of British Columbia have been better served by using those resources to foster a transition to an economy based less on industrial forestry, a hazardous, ecologically disruptive commodity sector perpetually buffeted by the unpredictable swings of fickle global markets? Even asking the question is equivalent to heresy in the province,

Table 4.4

BC forest policy in the 1990s

Principle	Policy response
Conservation	• The *Forest Practices Code* (FPC), 1995, is an evolving document with sweeping powers aimed at influencing all aspects of forestry and forest land management. Regulations are incorporated into five-year Forest Development Plans (FDP) that identify cutblocks, timing, and silviculture and harvesting techniques. Penalties are issued for noncompliance. • The *Timber Supply Review*, 1992, is charged with producing timber supply analyses that reflect current integrated resource management, including developing policy, methods, and models for timber supply analysis. The review was initiated in response to the recognition that prior to 1992, there was no regular, comprehensive process to determine the annual allowable cut (AAC) in BC. • The *Clayoquot Scientific Panel*, 1993, was charged with developing world-class forestry standards suitable to the unique ecological conditions and values in the Clayoquot Sound and based on traditional Aboriginal knowledge of resource management as well as the best available scientific knowledge.
Preservation	• The *Protected Areas Strategy* (PAS), 1993, established the objective of increasing the amount of protected areas in the province to 12 percent of the land base by the year 2000. Areas are intended to cover a diversity of representative ecosystems and significant cultural and recreational features throughout the province. Within the areas, lands and waters may not be sold, and mining, logging, hydro, and oil and gas activities are prohibited (British Columbia 1999a).
Diversification	• *Forest Renewal BC* (FRBC), 1994, was an investment agency charged with supporting a full range of forest renewal activities in every region of the province. FRBC was created through the Forest Renewal Act. • The *Jobs and Timber Accord*, 1997, was intended to be an agreement between the government and the forest industry to increase employment in the forest sector, increase the harvest yield, and build value-added capacity in the province.

▶

◀ *Table 4.4*

Principle	Policy response
Decentralization	• The *Community Forest Pilot Program*, 1998, was created to establish a number of short-term pilot agreements that would provide an opportunity to test new community forest legislation, experiment with a range of administrative models and forest management regimes for community forestry, provide long-term opportunities for achieving a range of community objectives, and meet government economic and stewardship objectives (British Columbia 1999b).
	• *Land and Resources Management Plans* (LRMPs) constitute the subregional integrated resource planning process for British Columbia. LRMP considers all resource values and requires public participation, interagency coordination, and consensus-based land and resource management decisions. LRMPs provide direction for more detailed resource planning by government agencies and the private sector, and provide a context for local government planning.

Source: Adapted from Markey et al. 2000.

and that fact is testimony to the enduring legacy of a provincial economy dominated by the forest industry" (Cashore et al. 2001, 231).

In addition, calls to do more with less in the development of value-added and diversification strategies are lacking. The Jobs and Timber Accord, a major forest sector announcement, failed due to a lack of industry participation from the very beginning (Palmer 1999). The end result is that BC continues to lag behind other regions in Canada in fostering value-added enterprises (BC Stats 2000).

Fourth, the NDP's goal of decentralization was given a promising start through the introduction of the Community Forest Licence pilot project. However, the government awarded only seven community licences, representing an insignificant amount of the total AAC (0.1 percent). In addition, the community licences suffer from having to meet regulations designed for industrial-style forest operation. Prospects for tenure reform and the allocation of more timberlands for community licences may open up through the changes introduced to resolve the softwood lumber crisis.

The NDP's most promising policy of decentralization is the Land and Resource Management Planning (LRMP) process. The province designed LRMP processes to reflect interest diversity at the regional level by having a diverse range of stakeholders sit at the planning table. Overall, researchers praise the LRMP program for the fact that it has exceeded all previous attempts to enhance participation in the land-use planning process.

Here again, however, researchers question the structural significance of the LRMP process. As Cashore et al. (2001) indicate, the process designated contentious land use areas as "Special Management Zones" (SMZs). Table participants determine land-use designation and forest practices within SMZs at a later date in order to not impede the ability of the planning table to reach consensus. The process directed that forest practices within SMZs would be more ecologically sensitive. As of early 2000, there were 275 SMZs throughout the province, representing 21 percent of the area covered by LRMP plans. Early indications reveal that it is business as usual in the SMZs (Cashore et al. 2001). It would appear that in some cases the LRMPs were able to achieve regional consensus by simply avoiding the more contentious issues. In addition, the long time line of LRMP table resolution and the fact that many Aboriginal interests are not participating in the program represent considerable forces of uncertainty for the future of the plans.

Perhaps the best that can be said of such a sweeping attempt at forest policy reform is that the NDP government achieved incremental change (Cashore et al. 2001). The significance of the changes will depend upon their longevity, particularly under the provincial Liberal government and the challenges posed by the current softwood lumber dispute. Overall, we are left with the impression of regulatory flux and rollback.

Despite these broadly based policy changes, a combination of internal and external forces continues to erode the performance of the BC forest sector. Recent figures documenting the woes of the industry illustrate the need for change:

- Twenty-seven mills have closed permanently, and 13,000 forest workers have lost their jobs in BC since 1997.
- Forest revenues have fallen by over $600 million since 1997.
- From 1996 to 2000, the BC forest industry's average return on capital employed was 3.3 percent – less than half the 7.1 percent earned in the rest of Canada during the same period.

The BC Liberal government is seeking to adopt a more market-based approach to regulation and forest management in an attempt to reverse the fortunes of the forest sector. The Liberals proposed a twelve-point plan for a "New Era of Sustainable Forestry" before taking office (Hoberg 2002):

- Establish a working forest land base, to provide greater stability for working families and to enhance long-term forestry management and planning
- Streamline the Forest Practices Code to establish a workable, results-based code, with tough penalties for noncompliance

- Apply 1 percent of all direct forest revenues, not including "super stump-age," to global marketing of BC's forest practices and products
- Create a market-based stumpage system that reflects global market realities and local harvesting costs
- Either fix or scrap Forest Renewal BC, starting by removing the political appointees on the board
- Invest in research to promote forest stewardship
- Cut the forestry regulatory burden by one-third within three years, without compromising environmental standards
- Protect private property rights in treaty negotiations
- Work to expedite interim measures agreements with First Nations, to provide greater certainty during treaty talks
- Increase the allowable annual cut over time through scientific forest management, proper planning, and incentives to promote enhanced silviculture
- Implement market-based pricing to reflect local harvesting costs
- Scrap the silviculture hiring hall policy that discriminates against silviculture workers

The Liberals have taken some steps to implement their forest policy agenda, including eliminating FRBC, introducing a $32 million Forest Innovation Account for research and marketing, establishing a one-time $75 million BC Forestry Revitalization Trust to assist workers and contractors with transition in the industry, and introducing a "results-based" forest practices code (Forest Range and Practices Act), although the environmental standards envisioned by this legislation have yet to be clearly outlined. Perhaps the most significant change introduced by the Liberals was to cut 35 percent from the Ministry of Forests budget (equal amounts were also cut from the Ministries of Sustainable Resource Management and Water, Land and Air Protection). These cuts transfer responsibilities and costs associated with forest management from government to licensees, including strategic planning, timber supply analysis, and public consultation.

Overall, however, the Liberals have made relatively little progress on their forest policy agenda. The softwood lumber dispute continues to present an insurmountable barrier to internally directed policy reform. At the time of writing, the US and Canada have failed to reach an agreement to settle the dispute, but the inevitable policy changes associated with an agreement will have a profound impact on the shape of the forest industry in BC. We can gain some insights into the future regulatory environment of the industry and its community implications from some of the proposals being advanced by the provincial government to deflect US charges of subsidy in the industry. Some of the following reforms are already represented in the original Liberal forest policy package (Hoberg 2002; Hamilton 2003):

- Increase minimum stumpage rates (so that timber will not be sold at less than the Ministry of Forests administrative costs, thereby removing charges of subsidy)
- Award new timber rights on a competitive basis (to the highest bidder)
- Allow TFLs and Forest Licences (FLs) to be subdivided
- Reduce restrictions on tenure transfers
- Eliminate "cut control" (for example, ±5 percent of AAC)
- Eliminate utilization requirements (companies can sell timber within BC instead of processing it themselves)
- Eliminate appurtenancy provisions that tie harvesting rights to requirements to process the timber in company-owned mills (BC's 600 mills can obtain BC timber no matter where it was logged)
- Eliminate mill closure penalties

Another significant barrier to the full implementation of the Liberals' forestry reforms is the slow pace of the First Nations treaty process. Following the relationship-souring experience of a controversial provincial referendum on the principles for treaty negotiation, however, the Liberals have adopted a more conciliatory approach through their BC Heartlands Strategy. The Heartlands strategy includes a variety of measures to enhance the economic development of non-metropolitan regions, including a claim to engage in new partnerships with First Nations through economic development support, revenue sharing, co-management, and facilitation of partnerships with resource companies (British Columbia 2003). Regardless, the success the Liberal forest policy reforms hinges on the resolution of the softwood lumber dispute and the extent to which the eventual reforms meet the interests of industry, labour, First Nations, environmentalists, and the general public – no small task.

Returning to our local development lens, the role of government is obviously important and capable of initiating reform, but external constraints and internal attitudes also inhibit attempts to create structural change. One possible conclusion is that peripheral actors in the policy process will inevitably turn to other venues and strategies to create change. For example, environmentalists designed their market campaigns to force change in the industry by jeopardizing forest markets through publicizing abroad stories of unsustainable logging practices and environmental degradation. Similarly, communities may turn to their own development strategies to initiate and implement change. Increasingly, communities are not waiting for government intervention and are working to implement their own agreements and economic development plans.

Community Proactivity
Communities across Canada have long played an important role in creating

and maintaining their own vitality (Bryant and Joseph 2001). Despite the overbearing presence of the staples economy, local action and cooperation during times of decline or throughout the normal course of everyday life represent an under-recognized aspect of the Canadian economic landscape. However, given the recognized limitations of a staples economy, the rapid pace of social and economic change, the declining power or will of governments, and the global reach of the marketplace, local action must be elevated to a more prominent, sophisticated, and organized role in the development process.

In British Columbia, as elsewhere, it is clear that the profile of local development has increased. Increasing community proactivity on matters of economic development is evident on numerous fronts:

- Communities throughout the province have implemented their own economic development strategic plans.
- Dozens of communities submitted applications for a community forest licence during the initial proposal stage of the Community Forest Licence pilot project, indicating a broad base of support for local resource management.
- National networks such as the Canadian Community Economic Development Network (Canadian CED-Net) and local development organizations are dedicated to raising the profile and capacity of local development activity.

Despite growing recognition of the benefits of locally based development, there are significant capacity barriers at the local level. Local weaknesses are usually identified with more market-based interpretations of development processes, but viewing weaknesses from the historically and contextually informed perspective of staples theory does reveal certain insights. In general, it is evident that there is a lack of capacity at the local level for articulating and implementing local economic objectives. This lack of, or variable, capacity has far-reaching implications for the design and implementation of policies aimed at supporting local development efforts and for more general considerations of the perpetuation or exacerbation of uneven development across the province.

In order for local development to become more influential, researchers and governments must pay serious attention to building the capacity and awareness of local development practitioners and leaders. Local development actors and networks are already assuming a sophisticated approach to development; they are no longer content to wait for direction or action from above. In many respects, this approach is congruent with the wishes of governments, which are seeking to reduce the degree of responsibility they have for community and regional development. As a result, there may be many fruitful opportunities for collaboration, capacity building, and decentralization in the future, driven and enabled by an empowered and well-organized local development sector.

Conclusion: From Community Stability to Community Resiliency

In Chapters 3 and 4, we have provided an overview of the contextual details facing the forest sector and, more generally, forest-dependent communities. We have included such detail in order to introduce a local development perspective to a review of the economic development process and the transition taking place in the province over the past fifty years. It is clear from our review of development in BC that a top-down, resource-dependent approach to development was successful in providing an economic foundation for the province, but that longer-term limitations and costs have accompanied this success. There are things, in retrospect, that we can do differently and better.

The attitudes and beliefs that forged a narrow path to development in BC were based upon a relatively one-dimensional approach to creating growth in the economy. The forces of change listed above reveal that the emerging economic landscape in BC is far from simple and that a more complex development environment has emerged in the province. We have begun to question previous assumptions. The legacy of staples development in combination with these forces of change inform us that there is space in the province to consider alternative forms of economic development more suited to dealing with complexity at local scales.

In Chapter 5, we will present the final component of our conceptual framework: community resilience through community economic development (CED). We will provide a review of the principles and origins of CED and outline the components of a CED framework for analyzing the activities of the project communities and understanding the dynamics of CED more generally.

5
Community Economic Development

This chapter outlines the third and final component of our conceptual framework, community resilience, as fostered through community economic development (CED). In Chapters 3 and 4, we prepared the historical, contextual, and conceptual groundwork illustrating that traditional approaches to development in British Columbia have left an uncertain and complicated development legacy for rural and small-town communities throughout the province. Community-based strategies will play an increasingly important role in fostering the organizational flexibility and community resilience necessary to respond to new economic opportunities and governance demands.

The overall purpose of this chapter is to answer a deceptively simple question: what is CED? Building upon the basic definition provided in Chapter 1, three components form the basis of an integrated answer. The first section will outline five principles that represent an ideal form of locally based development using a CED approach. Second, a discussion of market failure, past regional development approaches, and traditional forms of local economic development (LED) will link the origins of CED to actual development experience. CED represents an ideal form of localized development, but the principles that guide CED action are hard-won from the lessons researchers and practitioners have learned from past development experiences. Third, we will propose a CED framework to enhance our overall understanding of CED practice and to provide some organizational and conceptual structure for an evaluation of the project communities in later chapters. Finally, we will identify a series of challenges facing CED. These challenges represent strategic points for continuing research and capacity building within the CED sector.

The CED Ideal
CED is a practical undertaking. It is concerned with improving, in a

quantitative and qualitative manner, the social, economic, and environmental conditions of communities. Despite the practical orientation of CED, it is also an approach to development that is held to a higher and more contingent set of standards than mainstream economic development. The literature commonly represents such standards as a series of principles that are intended to guide CED practice, ultimately contributing to the successful implementation of CED initiatives (Roseland 1998).

The existence of a set of principles attached to CED serves to elevate the approach to an ideal form of locally based development. It is the pursuit of these principles within CED practice, however, rather than the attainment of a certain standard within each principle, that serves as the ultimate objective. We must recognize the contingency and comparative value inherent in any evaluation of the principles within an actual case, as well as possible conflicts between them; however, we present CED as an ideal based on these principles in order to stimulate continuous improvement within and between CED practice and theory.

The principles of CED stand in stark contrast to the theories and methods of more traditional forms of economic development. The following section provides a brief description of core CED principles: that development be community-based, participatory, sustainable, asset-based, and self-reliant. A discussion and summary of the main shortcomings of traditional approaches, as represented by market failure, and state and community responses to market failure in the form of regional development and local economic development (LED), follows.

CED Principles

CED begins with the understanding that communities have a latent capacity to contribute directly to the development of the local economy (Lloyd 1996). The most obvious starting point for a discussion of CED principles is the principal orientation towards a *community-based* approach to development. In CED, the community, and all of its contextual specificity, provides the foundation for projects and development-based relationships. Within CED, communities are not universal recipients of top-down decisions and externally based technocratic advice, but rather the starting point for a more contextually grounded discussion of appropriate development opportunities and specific needs or barriers (Galaway and Hudson 1994).

Second, CED must include the direct and meaningful *participation* of the local community (Roseland 1998; Douglas 1994). Meaningful community participation calls for active citizen involvement in a development process that brings together a diversity of community interests and sectors. The central credo of CED is to develop the competency of community members to deal with local problems and opportunities (Douglas 1994). Real participation is an essential ingredient to building community competency.

Participation within CED projects is generally divided into three categories that seek to integrate community members into an overall process of
collaboration (Bryant and Preston 1989):

- The local community plays an active role in articulating its own goals
and objectives.
- The local community is actively involved in the choice and implementation of development strategies.
- Local resources are a significant component of the initiative.

The ideal of participation within these three categories applies to both
the scale and the scope of community involvement. In terms of scale, Midgley
(1986) provides a simple framework for evaluating community involvement
as either authentic participation or pseudo-participation. Other researchers
propose more sophisticated scales for evaluating participation, such as
Arnstein's well-known ladder of participation (1969), which presents an eight-
stage evaluative framework for assessing participation.

The scope of community involvement is also critical when assessing the
"authenticity" of participation. CED is particularly concerned with the
meaningful participation of groups (differentiated by gender, ethnicity,
or socio-economic status) that are traditionally excluded from decision-
making processes (Lloyd 1996). The active involvement of a diversity of
actors and interests serves as an indicator of the success of the participatory
ideal within CED.

Third, CED seeks to implement *sustainable* development. The Brundtland
Commission and its final report, *Our Common Future* (1987, 8) defines sustainable development as "development which meets the needs of the present
generation, without compromising the ability of future generations to meet
their own needs." The report warns that we may no longer consider the
environment and economy in isolation from one another or as contradic-
tory objectives. The environment sustains our economies, and if the health
of the environment is threatened, so is the health of our economic system
and, by extension, the social health of communities (Pierce 1992). The integration of the environment/economy relationship is evident in British
Columbia's forest, fishing, and mineral sectors, where depletion of resource
stocks results in plant closures and job losses (Drushka et al. 1993). These
symptoms are typical of "mature, advanced" staple economies that overex-
ploit resources and are then left with a painful period of adjustment (Davis
and Hutton 1992). Ultimately, ecosystems support human life and economic
activity.

Although researchers have defined the concept of sustainable development in many ways since the publication of the Brundtland report, the
original description serves as a common conceptual benchmark. The

Brundtland report attempts to show how economic, environmental, and social development can be compatible. Sustainable development has three fundamental variables. First, it recognizes that there are limits to economic growth in specific contexts. Technological change may enhance and alter our relationship with specific resources, but for nonrenewable resources we must consider limits. Second, sustainable development stresses qualitative development rather than the more narrow pursuit of strictly quantitative economic growth. Qualitative considerations add a third dimension to the environment and economy relationship: social development. Qualitative development implies the enhancement of social, cultural, and spiritual qualities of human life as part of the economic process. Finally, sustainable development recognizes the importance of local issues and actions, which together determine our global situation – the essence of "think globally, act locally." This provides the most obvious link between sustainable development and CED: that sustainable development requires sustainable communities (Roseland 1998; Nozick 1992). The concept of sustainable communities serves as a core goal attached to the definition of CED used by the CED Centre. Other interpretations of a sustainable approach to CED use the term "sustainable community development," but we seek to make the sustainability component of CED inherent within the concept.

Fourth, CED is an *asset-based* approach to development. "Community assets" is a term that is receiving increasing attention in the development field (Kretzman and McKnight 1993). The central idea behind asset-based development is that local development must be based upon the strengths and resources of communities, rather than their deficiencies. Kretzman and McKnight (1993) use the term "community assets" to refer to individual skills, local organizations, and local institutions.

Asset-based development inverts the traditional needs assessment approach to community development, whereby experts assess critical weaknesses within a community and design programs and policies to treat community decline. Asset-based development does not ignore community weaknesses, but it is not fixated on them as a foundation for policy and project design. Asset development may ultimately address community deficiencies, but the starting point for community renewal and development must be with locally based community strengths. These strengths are described in the following chapters as forms of "community capital."

Finally, *self-reliance* is a common CED principle discussed in the literature due to the underlying goal of CED to seize some measure of control over the local economy (Boothroyd and Davis 1991). There are two broad interpretations of community self-reliance in relation to CED. First, the origins of a locally focused approach to building self-reliance may be found in E.F. Schumacher's *Small Is Beautiful* (1973) and in later incarnations of the idea, such as bioregionalism (Sale 1985). The basis for a locally focused approach to development is to build community self-reliance by disengaging from unequal and destructive economic relationships with external economic interests (Friedmann 1988). A strict interpretation of local self-reliance dictates that we should seek to meet local needs through local production, address economic leakage, and manage local resources locally and sustainably.

A more moderate view of self-reliance recognizes the interdependence of communities at regional, national, and increasingly global scales. The focus of an interdependent approach to self-reliance is reduction of the influences of external decision-making and economic dependencies, diversification of the local economy to avoid the pitfalls of product or sectoral specialization, and the building of better, more locally advantageous external relationships (Friedmann 1988; Blakely 1994). We will explore the different interpretations of self-reliance below in terms of different CED strategic orientations.

These five core principles of CED represent an idealized methodological approach to local development. As stated earlier, the principles are not intended to serve as narrow benchmarks for development but rather as goals in the process and implementation of CED initiatives. The principles must be more than rhetoric used as "spin" to justify the actions of elites, community organizations, or government agencies in the pursuit of narrow self-interest. Although the CED principles represent an ideal, they are attainable in practice. The origins of the principles exist ultimately in the practice of development itself. If we compare alternative development techniques with mainstream approaches, and seek to learn from the local disenchantment and economic failures associated with past development efforts, we may understand the principles of CED in more practical terms.

Market Failure and the Development Response

This section presents market failure, regional development, and local economic development (LED) in the spirit of the counterfactual – that we may gain a greater understanding of CED by describing what it is not. The discussion is contextually grounded in the experience of developed, industrialized countries from a theoretical perspective and more narrowly based in Canada through a discussion of regional development.

Attention to market failure and to traditional forms of regional and local development inform our understanding of CED, given their overall contribution to the emergence of CED as a more rigorous and formal mode of development, particularly in a rural, resource-dependent context. The origins of CED in Canada and other Western countries are directly related to three factors: (1) market failures and their impacts on peripheral and urban core communities; (2) the frustrations and failures associated with postwar regional and local economic development practices designed to mitigate market failure; and (3) the negative implications of restructuring given the government program and sectoral dependencies fostered by mainstream approaches to development.

Neoclassical Theory and Market Failure

> By invoking their favourite phrase, *ceteris paribus* (all other things being equal), neo-classical economists often throw away most of the useful variables for understanding development in one society and retardation in another. (Laxer 1989, 36)

As the quotation by Laxer illustrates, neoclassical economics is extremely selective in interpreting the costs and benefits of development. A common critique of neoclassical economic theory is that disciplinary abstraction distances it from reality (Daly and Cobb 1994). The range of problems in society that are not formally recognized by neoclassical economics exist in part because of the narrow functional simplicity of the theory. These problems may also be identified as forms of market failure.

Neoclassical theory at the microeconomic level is based upon a simplified understanding of the economy where people are viewed as rational utility-maximizing consumers and businesses are viewed as rational profit-maximizing producers. The economic system is said to exist in a state of perfect competition, where neither consumers nor producers are directly capable of manipulating price. The prices of goods, services, and labour are determined by the point at which the demand of consumers equals the supply of producers, leading to a state of equilibrium in the economy. If prices are high, supply will increase but demand will decrease. Likewise, if prices are lower, demand will increase and supply will be reduced, eventually causing shortage (Howlett and Netherton 1999).

Neoclassical theory also envisions a balance at the macroeconomic level. Firms provide money to the public in the form of wages, profit, interest, and rent. In turn, the public spends this money consuming goods and services, thus transferring funds back to the firms. Money not spent on direct consumption exists as savings, which are then free to be invested in productive activities – generating growth in the economy through the creation of new economic enterprises (Ross and Usher 1987).

The simplicity and exactness of this model is designed to reduce or eliminate the need for intervention in the economy. A number of problems (or market failures) exist in the operation of the market economy, however. Market failures produce negative consequences for society and provide the rationale for local and extra-local intervention designed to reduce negative impacts and to recognize otherwise excluded local economies and (conventionally speaking) non-economic factors.

Economists use the term "market failure" to describe situations in which the regular functioning of the market performs a disutility to select individuals, the environment, or society as a whole (Howlett and Netherton 1999). The existence of market failure stands in marked contrast to the notion that the market is best left alone as the determinant of social, economic, and environmental decision making. For example, neoliberal thinkers posit that interference from governments in regulating the marketplace creates inefficiencies and unnecessary political interference in the economy (Brohman 1995). While factors such as self-serving political interference and certain forms of taxation may reduce the efficiency of the market, the existence of market failures and other inequities in the unfettered market creates a role for government regulation. Governments provide a critical function in the operation of the market by helping to determine the boundaries and rules for market activities. Indeed, as Homer-Dixon (2000) argues, the increasing complexity of our lives demands innovative social and institutional responses. Researchers cite market failures as examples where the abstract purity of necolassical theory clashes with reality, resulting in social and/or environmental costs (Aglietta 1979). Four forms of market failure are particularly relevant to a discussion of CED, which both acknowledges and attempts to address these flaws: externalities, the space economy, lack of markets, and self-interest.

Externalities and Full-Cost Accounting
Ross and Usher (1987) define externalities as costs to society, resulting from poor (or selective) accounting. When the price of certain products does not reflect the full cost of producing those products, negative externalities exist. For example, industrial forest practices, by virtue of their scale and methods, may generate a variety of externalities that forest companies are not held to account for by government regulation or standard accounting practices. Timber production may cause damage to fish habitat, cause sediment to taint water supplies, increase the risks of flooding, reduce tourism values, or compromise the spiritual integrity of the forest for indigenous cultures (Hammond 1991). If externality costs are not accounted for by the corporation, their existence does not impede the actions of individuals and companies mandated to pursue more narrow economic gains. Externalities become costs to society or to the environment.

The Space Economy
The existence of the "space economy" imposes very real transaction costs on smaller and remote communities (Bryant 1994). The relative costs associated with transportation, infrastructure, access to labour markets, and

other locational dynamics in the hinterland environment mean that rural businesses may face competitive barriers compared with centrally located enterprises (i.e., information failure).

In addition, Cox and Mair (1988) highlight the market failure associated with the free flow of labour and capital as expressed by the concept of equilibrium. Their analysis of the various forms of firm and individual local dependency introduces a level of complexity to the interpretation of local and regional economies absent from neoclassical thinking. For example, as discussed further in succeeding chapters, people are unsurprisingly attached to place and family. Various forms of local dependency also impede the mobility of firms, such as access to labour, infrastructure costs, prior investments in facilities, proximity to resources, and a corporate commitment to place.

Lack of Markets

A third form of market failure is the concept of incomplete markets. Markets simply do not exist for many of the goods and services that perform valuable and necessary functions in our society (Ross and Usher 1987). The drive for efficiency and the use of narrow economic indicators to portray societal health place selective pressures on the determination of value (Roseland 1998; Henderson 1994). A common outcome of this form of market failure is the inability of many smaller or socially oriented enterprises or services to raise sufficient amounts of capital to either start or sustain their activities, creating a need for subsidy.

Also, more commonly, markets do not exist for pure public goods such as air and biodiversity. Our inability to attach market mechanisms to these functions leads to abuses and ignorance of the services and inherent importance of public goods. The field of ecological economics has made some progress towards addressing this lack of understanding.

Self-Interest

Finally, a central tenet of neoclassical theory, which we may interpret as a form of market failure, is self-interest. As stated earlier, a fundamental premise of neoclassical theory is that the economy consists of a large number of small producers and consumers, each pursuing their own self-interest, without the power to influence the overall operation of the market. As such, the market recognizes only the propensity of individuals to act in order to optimize their own self-interest (Daly and Cobb 1994; Aglietta 1979). The only way to satisfy self-interest, in neoclassical thinking, is through the consumption of goods and services. Social dynamics are not formally recognized as part of the economic process (Aglietta 1979). This view fundamentally influences the argument that the best way to contribute to society is through the narrow pursuit of individual satisfaction. The grounding of neoclassical economics in the concept of individualism leads Schumacher (1973) to state that "the market is the institutionalization of individualism and non-responsibility." Individualism is a propelling factor in the socio-economic polarization of society and between societies (Savoie 2000). Recent research documenting the importance of social capital is unrecognized within a more narrow, neoclassical interpretation of economic development (Woolcock 2001). Yet, as humans, people do act in ways that benefit others and consider their self-interest in non-economic terms. The influence of social capital on CED and development more generally is discussed further in the following chapter.

WHAT CONVENTIONAL ECONOMICS DOES RIGHT

Despite the problems of market failure, the market economy does a variety of things extremely well.

Participation
The market system facilitates millions of transactions between producers and consumers (Ross and Usher 1987). Despite the structural and personal limitations on the choices that define participation, from both producers and consumers, the extent of participation is enormous. Local and national boundaries and control are transcended, offering a wide variety of choice.

Efficiency
The market distributes resources and provides a diversity of products and services in an efficient manner not possible through central planning (Daly and Cobb 1994). Despite the problems that this zeal for efficiency creates, under fair conditions the quest for profit that serves as the motivating force behind efficiency is a powerful force. As Daly and Cobb state, the key to combining the positive effects of efficiency and diversity lies with the power of governments to establish clear rules for market engagement (1994, 14):

> The role of government is to set fair conditions within which the market can operate. It is also responsible for setting the overall (scale) size of the market. The market is not the end of society and is not the right instrument through which the ends of society should be set. We favour private ownership of the means of production. We favour the widest possible participation in that ownership, including worker ownership of factories, against its concentration in a few hands.

Potential to Deal with Rules

The market shows vast innovative qualities once governments have established the rules governing production. A recent example of this is the progress that car manufacturers are achieving in the production of energy-efficient automobiles despite decades of stalling. Another example concerns the potential of tools such as full-cost accounting to force companies to internalize their externalities. Schumacher (1973) illustrates the impact of cost-benefit analysis, highlighting a broad spectrum of market-based strategies for sustainable development – again, possible only when they are imposed on the system.

Source of Information

Pierce (1990) notes that markets are imperfect but they nevertheless do provide important sources of information through price. The relative scarcity of resources serves as one example. Clapp (1999) reiterates this positive function of the market, but cautions that such information must be recognized for its narrow interpretation of the economy and society.

In summary, the narrow economic imperative of the mainstream economy creates a myriad of problems when applied to the messy and interconnected realities of the lived world (Dale 2001; Daly and Cobb 1994). We face problems concerning environmental conservation, marginalization of people and places, access to capital, and the maintenance of social cohesion in society due to the individualizing and polarizing tendencies of the mainstream economy.

Formal recognition of market failures leads to a variety of state interventions designed to correct or to mitigate the negative impacts of an unfettered market on society. From a local and regional development perspective, governments act to enhance the competitiveness of peripheral regions and to ease the restructuring shocks associated with the market economy through regional development programs (Neil and Tykkylainen 1998).

Regional Development in Canada

Before the 1950s, Canada lacked a formal program for addressing the structural problems associated with rural and hinterland economies (Fairbairn 1998). During the 1950s, however, the federal government began to adopt explicit regional development policies (Savoie 1992). As Reed (1990) states, staples theory proved influential to the adoption of regional development strategies as official government policy. Staples theory provided governments with the theoretical justification for intervention in the economy in order to reduce regional disparities. In the optimistic market interpretation of staples theory, government intervention in creating the infrastructure and assigning the regulatory mandate for resource development set the stage for a modern, diversified economy. There was, however, no real plan to facilitate or to improve development prospects once senior governments had established a staples economy (Reed 1990). As a result, governments and communities lack a more comprehensive, holistic understanding of development, and Canada has lacked a consistent regional development strategy throughout the postwar period.

Regional disparities and attention to uneven development in the postwar period, along with a period of relative national prosperity, were key motivating forces in directing governments to become more directly involved in promoting regional development. The original focus on regional disparities greatly influenced the policies and programs launched by successive governments to address underdevelopment. Governments tended to visualize communities and regions in terms of what they were lacking (needs or weaknesses) and measured comparative prosperity and regional health using limited economic indicators (Savoie 1992). In effect, a focus on poverty reduction, not on comprehensive development or on the structural conditions of underdevelopment, shaped government thinking and policy making (Fairbairn 1998). By addressing economic deficiencies through regional development programs, governments envisioned that regions would be propelled along a linear path to prosperity. In this interpretation of development, the region is simply a spatial unit, very much conducive to an empty-vessel approach to development: pour financial resources into an area to produce development opportunities. This approach is supported by *growth pole theory*.

The growth pole theory of development complements a deficiency-based development perspective. Introduced by François Perroux in the 1950s, the growth pole concept includes both sectoral and spatial dimensions of growth. Sectorally, policy makers can divide industry into two subsectors: leading "propellant" industries and those derived from propellant industries, known as "impelled" industrial sectors (Martinussen 1997). From a regional development perspective, proponents of the growth pole approach believed that a few dynamic sectors or geographical clusters of industries could form the foundation of a spatially balanced and economically diversified regional and national economy. Growth pole theory states that a growth pole, centred around a dynamic leading sector, is capable of achieving rapid growth in the regional setting through spillover and multiplier effects throughout the surrounding economy.

Hirschman (1958) elaborates upon the growth pole concept, verifying the positive impacts of spread effects and arguing that the concentration of capital inherent in the growth pole is justified based upon the "trickle-down" effect. Trickle-down is based upon the idea that a concentration of capital will eventually lead to higher levels of overall investment and prosperity, thereby providing opportunities for employment and economic diversification.

Five reasons help to explain the government appreciation for the growth pole concept during the middle parts of the last century. First, the theory suited a large bureaucratic approach to government and policy development that stressed central control and uniformity across the country (MacNeil 1997). Second, implementing the growth pole approach relies heavily upon the direction of development experts. Professional expertise and scientific approaches to development complement an overall technocratic approach to planning. Third, achieving service and economic parity across the country was an underlying goal for all development strategies at the time (Savoie 1992). Regardless of whether a person lived in Toronto or rural Newfoundland, governments used the same narrow economic indicators to measure standard of living and the overall health of the local economy. Grand theories facilitated the universalization of development objectives. Fourth, providing financial resources and policy support to a limited number of communities designated as growth centres was more efficient and less resource-intensive than attempting to address the economic circumstances of all communities. Finally, the trickle-down assumptions inherent in the growth pole theory promised enhanced development for all, without necessarily challenging existing power relations or the more systemic and complex features of underdevelopment.

Savoie (1992) indicates that the growth pole theory is a confused concept that was poorly implemented as policy through the concept of growth centres. Despite the lack of adequate evaluation attached to the implementation of the growth pole approach, however, certain features of the theory show remarkable persistence in regional development policy. During the early 1980s, for example, development officials emphasized the comparative advantage of Canadian resource industries as a foundation for regional development planning, providing a sectoral rather than territorial approach to development, but based upon similar principles. Government intervention and support was designed around a series of megaprojects (Weaver and Gunton 1982). Governments designed megaprojects to act as propellants in the economy, with the surplus generated from the activities to be used for purposes of industrial restructuring. However, the economic recession in 1982 and the collapse of international commodity prices made the megaproject approach largely irrelevant (Howlett and Netherton 1999). In summary:

> Megaprojects had the advantages of attracting and focusing public attention. Their scale seemed to match the scale of the economic problems perceived by Canadians. The number of jobs they promised was respectable in comparison to high levels of unemployment. They were also regional in

nature, and spoke to regional interests and regional grievances. The one significant downside was that they required immense investments or guarantees at a time when governments were plunging head over heels into debt. (Fairbairn 1998, 29)

A number of researchers consider the approach to regional development adopted in Canada between the 1950s and mid-1980s to be flawed (e.g., Savoie 1992, 1997). The ineffectual experience with regional development is not a uniquely Canadian experience, however. The failure of regional development policy has been instrumental in drawing attention to locally based alternatives throughout Western industrialized countries (Neil and Tykkylainen 1998).

Five points illustrate the main shortcomings of the variety of regional development programs launched in Canada. First, different levels of government did a poor job of coordinating their regional development policies and policy objectives (Savoie 1992; Brodie 1990). The desire to generate political capital – gain votes – through development programs, a common criticism of Keynesian-inspired development policy, often led to poor intergovernmental coordination at best and political feuding at worst.

Second, as noted earlier, government use of regional development policies was driven by a reliance on weak theories that were overly abstract and poorly interpreted. Government interpretations of the growth pole theory fundamentally misunderstood or ignored what we now consider to be basic features of successful development programs. For example, in early programs, there were limited opportunities for public participation, which is symptomatic of an overall failure to adequately support the development of human capital (MacNeil 1997; Fairbairn 1998; Savoie 1997). A propensity to focus solely on infrastructure without adequate attention to human development and capacity (e.g., entrepreneurialism) limited development effectiveness and ignored the broader benefits of economic diversification. This selective and narrow approach to regional development is consistent with an approach that sought a separation of the social from the economic, which, as Coffey and Polese indicate, is due in part to the political realities of the development process (1985, 89):

In strictly political terms, it is far easier for decision-makers to deal with problems of infrastructure and capital rather than become involved with policies designed to alter a population's behaviour and perceptions, especially since such policies are at the same time less visible, less immediate, and less predictable; this probably accounts for the capital bias of most existing policies. The element that may be seen as the principal virtue of a local development approach, its focus on the local population, may also be its greatest source of weakness.

Third, the theoretical underpinnings of development policies infused programs with a sense of quasi-environmental determinism. Policy attached common political, social, and cultural characteristics to often very diverse communities and regions simply because they were located in the same geographic location or shared certain socio-economic similarities (Savoie 1992). Regional development policies ignored differences in the economic and social attributes of communities and regions that we now know are very significant to the development process.

Fourth, as stated earlier, a deficiency-based approach defined the traditional approach to regional development in Canada. Governments designed and developed programs to address "needs." For the most part, policies treated regional deficiencies in a symptomatic manner, failing to address underlying conditions and causes of underdevelopment or to capitalize on unique community strengths (Savoie 1992; Brodie 1990). In effect, Canadian regional development policy lacked an appreciation for historical specificity and recognition of the long-term implications of the development process (both in creating underdevelopment and in achieving development).

In addition, critics of Canadian regional development argue that the deficiency perspective that guided rural regional development programs helped to foster perceptions of rural backwardness (Fairbairn 1998). Perceptions of backwardness may have exacerbated problems associated with migration and impeded proactive local responses. The idea of rural backwardness also lends greater credibility to and fosters a reliance on technocratic, top-down planning. Local participation and the use of local knowledge are devalued. The perpetuation of rural backwardness may also have helped to create forms of learned helplessness in certain jurisdictions and to inhibit the various factors of CED success introduced in the next chapter (MacNeil and Williams 1995).

Finally, the existence of varying degrees of dependency among communities and regions is associated with the interventionist activity of the state. Regions become accustomed to the efforts of the state to address underdevelopment. Intervention through various program cycles to address periodic or sustained economic decline creates expectations for future interventionist activity (Martin and Sunley 1998). As a result, Keynesian-inspired regional development programs did help to underwrite regional economies in a variety of ways: through support for manufacturing regions, resource management policy, and industrial location programs. These programs stimulated growth in particular regions, although few were self-sustaining. In addition, a major contribution to the growth of regional economies during this period was the expansion of public sector employment that provides full-time, high-wage employment (Fairbairn 1998; Martin and Sunley 1998). This again may stagnate proactive independent or complementary local development responses to economic decline.

The tradition of government intervention through regional development programs stands in stark contrast to the extent of deregulation and budgetary restrictions that have dominated government agendas since the 1980s. As a result of past dependencies and the shift in government direction, communities and regions are generally ill-prepared to deal with change. Despite the more recent attention to neoliberal-inspired government retractions from the rural environment, Fairbairn argues that the withdrawal of government programs began almost immediately after the first forays into regional development (1998, 33):

> Overall, the history of the period can be seen as the saga of the federal government's entry and its substantial retreat from regional development in Canada. The entry might be seen as a result of a particular perception of decline and backwardness in the 1950s, as well as the populist mobilization of regional and rural grievances by Diefenbaker and others. The retreat, this paper argues, began almost immediately, and proceeded in several stages. No sooner were rural and regional development grievances articulated, than they were reconceptualized in terms of modernization-oriented regional-planning theories. Before the end of the 1960s, planners had taken control of the issue away from rural people, and the shift was underway from rural development to industrial development. In the 1970s their efforts fell afoul of the conflict-ridden federal-provincial relations of that era, so that in the end provincial planners had to be allowed into the game. In the 1980s all of this was swept away by a perception of economic crisis and of globalization, by megaproject theories, and by business-development programmes at federal, large-regional, provincial, and local levels.

Given the shortcomings of past development programs, researchers have yet to determine how shifts in government policy will affect the development aspirations of communities and regions. What is certain, however, is that a universal frustration with past development approaches has created space for alternative means of addressing matters of uneven development and economic restructuring:

> What we are suggesting essentially is to remove, as much as possible, the responsibility for planning and implementing regional development measures from the hands of bureaucracies, particularly those in central governments. The past thirty years have taught us that large bureaucracies are not well suited for formulating and operating regional programs – they do not have the necessary freedom to move quickly, to be flexible, to be creative and to look down to the community level. (Higgins and Savoie 1995, 403)

Specifically, the failure of regional development strategies in Canada and in other industrialized nations is a contributing factor to the rising interest in community-based economic development. Local government and community frustration with the inability of the central state to balance growth among regions, maintain standards of living, manage resources, maintain access to services, and manage the impacts of a changing economy fuel interest in CED (Boothroyd and Davis 1991). We also find evidence that the federal government has learned from past regional development experiences, as is evident in the development approaches of Western Diversification (WD) and the Atlantic Canada Opportunities Agency (ACOA), both launched in the late 1980s. These agencies promote a more locally oriented and facilitative model of government intervention and, despite some criticisms, are generally lauded by researchers and practitioners. The Canadian Rural Secretariat has also promoted and adapted a policy framework since the mid-1990s that is supportive of human capital development and territorial approaches to development.

Before expanding on the concept of CED as an alternative approach to development, it is important that we review an approach to local development that features industrial attraction and a top-down approach to planning. Local economic development (LED) is a common term used to represent these local strategies that are driven by a more narrow economic imperative.

Local Economic Development: The Local Growth Imperative

Local economic development (LED) is differentiated from CED in the literature by its narrow economic and externally oriented approach to creating economic growth (Lloyd 1996; Gill and Reed 1997; Douglas 1994). At the core of LED lies the basic premise that growth is driven by the decisions of the market, as represented by individual entrepreneurs.

Traditional LED strategies rely upon the provision of land, infrastructure, and favourable tax incentives to entice business location. In LED, the community becomes the product, seeking to attract the "buyer" (i.e., the corporation). As a result, the community is "packaged" according to the interests of external entrepreneurs and investors (Blakely 1994). Given the business attraction focus of LED, success is relatively easily measured (employment, income, businesses attracted to the area, and changes to the tax base of the community), although causality is not necessarily a direct outcome of LED efforts.

A number of weaknesses associated with the LED approach are influential in informing the practices of CED. First, the tax incentives associated with business attraction often undercut the overall advantages accruing to the community. Communities may overestimate the potential returns of business attraction and, as a result, overcommit local resources to provide costly and unnecessary infrastructure (Power 1996b). In the end, budgetary pressures resulting from infrastructure improvements may increase local tax rates (i.e., citizens directly subsidizing new businesses) or force communities to cut program delivery, all without any real guarantees of a return on their investment.

Second, there is a range of problems associated with the fact that LED strategies may have very tenuous connections with the community itself. The external focus of LED means that it does not necessarily seek to capitalize on local human capital (Newby 1999). A lack of community participation, in terms of designing strategies, allocating community resources, and assessing results, means that LED is often associated with an elitist or selective approach to growth. In addition, business attraction may succeed in bringing new employment to the community, but if there are weak connections to the existing employment base of a community, there is no guarantee that the new jobs will help to address *local* unemployment. New jobs may be imported into the community, but if the purpose of the strategy is to improve the unemployment rate of the community, little progress may be made.

Third, the narrow economic imperative underlying LED fails to adequately capitalize on the social, cultural, and ecological dimensions of a community or region (Douglas 1994). A more comprehensive understanding of the community economy recognizes the interconnectedness of different community attributes. Researchers and practitioners are increasingly recognizing the social, cultural, and environmental assets of communities and regions for their tangible economic value. Fostering a multifaceted approach to development may yield added value to internally and externally derived approaches to building the local economy.

Finally, a local development approach driven by marketing and industrial attraction does little to reduce dependency on external decision makers and the vagaries of market forces. When considering the low rate of success attributed to business attraction, and its potential "beggar-thy-neighbour" impact on inter-community relations (for example, undercutting neighbouring community incentives), the external focus of LED loses credibility further (Power 1996b; Lipietz 1994, 2001).

We list these limitations of LED to provide points of contrast with CED and to highlight lessons of development that must now be incorporated into a CED approach. That said, the knowledge and expertise of LED concerning matters of local entrepreneurship, adapting a locally appropriate approach to business attraction, and concern for local infrastructure and competitiveness represent strengths that are lacking in CED (Douglas 1994).

The literature reflects the potential overlap between CED and LED, by often failing to differentiate between the two approaches and terms (Bryant and Preston 1989; Reed and Gill 1997). On the one hand, there is increasing mainstream recognition that the principles and practices of CED offer substantive economic advantages. On the other hand, recognition of the limitations in management and entrepreneurial capacity within traditional CED circles leads to an increasing acceptance of the need to integrate more tangible business skills and thinking into the CED approach. The space between CED and LED on the continuum of development is narrowing. Incorporating the strengths and addressing the limitations of each approach leads to an integration of CED and LED as an appropriate framework for addressing community-based development (Reed and Gill 1997).

Summary of Origins

The foregoing discussion illustrates the extent to which a more integrated and participatory approach to development is lacking in traditional development methods designed to confront regional disparities and to promote economic growth. Researchers and practitioners have ignored critical components of the development process by relying on abstract theories and narrow economic measures of success.

Regional science, which dominated the economic development literature in the immediate postwar period, was of little help in identifying problems and proposing possible solutions (Savoie 2000). The dependency of regional science on abstraction and technical methodologies made the literature largely inaccessible to both policy makers and development practitioners. Practitioners of regional science accumulated a general recognition of existing problems, but the gap between experience and inquiry meant that there was no widely recognized base of knowledge from which to design solutions and amass iterative disciplinary knowledge. Nor was there a collected body of information relevant and accessible to individuals and community organizations attempting to put local development into practice.

The modern crisis in development in a Canadian rural context peaked with the recession of the early 1980s. The recession painfully illustrated the persistence of regional disparities and the intense vulnerability and dependency of select regions (Boothroyd and Davis 1991; Dykeman 1990). The recession also focused the attention of community leaders, researchers, and governments on the latent potential of communities to participate more directly in the project of development. The forced awareness of the potential contribution of local development during the early 1980s in Canada coincided with broader challenges to traditional economic development theory. For example, the work of Stohr and Taylor (1981) and others granted greater mainstream legitimacy to the concept of bottom-up development, while governments began to search for partnerships in service delivery under the cost-cutting pressures of high debt loads. Thus, dire practical circumstances in combination with the increased academic and policy attention being directed towards bottom-up development provided the early foundation for CED to unfold as a more rigorous discipline and legitimate form of development in rural areas.

A BRIEF HISTORY OF CED ACROSS CANADA

Although CED has only recently been gaining the attention of researchers, policy makers and practitioners in Canada, there is a long history of CED efforts across the country. Various groups have applied CED-type activities in many different ways, through many types of initiatives and strategies, ranging from training and education to business development to arts and cultural activities.

Cooperatives and local, self-help initiatives have been common in Atlantic Canada since the early 1900s, a function perhaps of the need to work together to survive under adverse conditions. These cooperatives provide the roots of the CED approach in Canada.

In Quebec, rural development initiatives have been underway since the early 1970s, and Montreal serves as a focal point for urban CED activity dating back to the 1960s, with initiatives born out of the Roman Catholic Church. In the 1990s, the city of Montreal supported CED by investing millions of dollars in Community Development Corporations (CDCs) in disadvantaged urban areas.

In Ontario, CED initiatives thrived in the early 1990s under the provincial policy of the Bob Rae government to promote and encourage CED. Support for the CED approach diminished following the election of Mike Harris in 1995, however.

As in Quebec, CED in Manitoba got underway in rural and northern areas in the 1960s and 1970s with the Rural Economic Development Agreement of 1967-77. This agreement dealt with issues such as resource management, human resources, and infrastructure, and shaped programs according to the priorities of community-based boards.

In Saskatchewan, agricultural cooperatives and Aboriginal development initiatives have thrived for years. The Kitsaki Development Corporation in Lac La Ronge is considered one of the most successful Aboriginal-owned CDCs in the country.

BC has tended to focus on resource-related endeavours, such as fish coops and salmon enhancement. However, Vancouver is home to the nation's largest credit union, VanCity, with outstanding community and environmental programs as well as alternative lending options. A variety of urban-based initiatives serve areas such as the Downtown Eastside. In addition,

CED continues to play an important role in BC First Nations communities as they work towards self-determination.

In many ways, however, Canada lags behind the United States, where community reinvestment, community development financial institutions, and peer lending began in the inner cities in the 1960s and 1970s in the War on Poverty, spawning similar movements in Canada (Blakely 1994). More recently, Canada has adapted US-based leadership training programs in rural development in the 1980s and conservation-based development in the 1990s under the leadership of organizations such as Ecotrust Canada.

The limited extent and variable quality of CED literature for both urban and rural areas inhibits the advancement of CED as a means for conceptualizing and promoting local development. Whereas the regional science literature is too abstract to be of practical use, CED literature is generally considered to be too practical to be of any abstract (or generalized) use – abstraction and generalization being necessary ingredients for theoretical modelling and policy development.

Savoie (2000) further criticizes much of the early literature in CED for its "missionary zeal." While this may be so, the purpose of the early literature was promotional rather than analytical. In order to advance the concepts and practices of CED, however, greater rigour is necessary in CED practice and research. In particular, students of CED need to balance the need for flexibility and diversity in project and program development with the need for accountability (Savoie 2000; Filion 1998). Accountability is vital to ensure government support for CED, and also to enable practitioners and researchers to learn from the best practices and failures in a consistent yet adaptive fashion.

In summary, the following factors represent limitations in the policy relevance and practical advancement of CED: the practical and multidisciplinary nature of CED; the inconsistencies and failure of past regional development policies, which tarnish potentially productive intervention on the part of governments; and the failure of traditional locally based economic strategies, which may be confused with CED. In addition, the contingency associated with CED impedes the cumulative progression of knowledge, while simple models and general explanations offer little directly substantive utility to the diversity of community conditions (Murdoch and Marsden 1995; Neil and Tykkylainen 1998). In order for CED to be adopted at a larger scale, it must continue to reflect local context, but it must also contain elements of generalizability and even predictability. These two conditions are necessary to scale up the impact of CED in policy and practice.

Despite the organic emergence of CED into mainstream discussions of development, three factors contribute to the advancement of CED theory and practice. First, a growing CED-oriented literature does exist, which has helped to chart a more coherent and systematic progression of CED knowledge (e.g., Economic Council of Canada 1990; Douglas 1994; Galaway and Hudson 1994; Pierce and Dale 1999). Second, there is a wide variety and increasing number of CED-related programs within Canadian universities, which will add much-needed research capacity (Markey and Roseland 2001). Third, practitioner-based CED networks exist at provincial and national levels. These networks disseminate knowledge and will build local practitioner capacity for CED (Canadian CED Network 2001).

In effect, a reverse process defines the emergence of CED as a legitimate and influential development approach. Traditionally, using regional development as a guide, the main source of policy development and program implementation is academic and policy literature, leading ultimately to case evaluation. In CED, the practical work of communities and the deficiencies associated with past development efforts provide the starting point for CED-inspired policy development and systematic research. The challenge is to construct an effective literature from this inverse approach to disciplinary emergence.

In order to create some internal coherence to inquiry into CED, we propose a framework to assist with the presentation of project community experiences. The foregoing discussion presents CED as an ideal, represented by select principles that should be attached to the intentions and actions of both policy and practice. We have outlined the shortcomings of traditional regional and local economic development in order to trace some of the conceptual and practical roots of CED. The framework that follows completes our discussion of CED by defining critical components of CED practice.

CED Framework
The following framework serves to contain the relative contingency of CED for analytical purposes. The model identifies different aspects of CED, while recognizing the limitations of capturing the true diversity and creativity of CED practice within a single mould. We have selected the following framework components for project analysis and reflection: (1) the CED process, (2) strategic orientations, and (3) community capacity. Accordingly, following an introduction of the components below, the next three chapters discuss these themes in greater detail from a project perspective.

The CED framework provides direct linkages to the development of greater community resilience. When confronting the forces of restructuring, communities need to be well organized, have access to quality information, understand options for action, and find ways to reinforce the learning process associated with independent action. The CED framework addresses each of these themes.

The CED Process

CED is a process of direct local intervention into the community economy. Rather than leaving communities to the vagaries of market forces (and market failures), CED offers a bottom-up approach to addressing local opportunities and challenges. The effectiveness of CED is ultimately determined by the planning and implementation capacity of the community – the organizational structures, local actors, and relationships that drive the process.

Community Organizing and Planning

The community organizing and planning component of CED addresses a key gap in past regional development policy, namely, overlooking the fact that communities directly contribute to the process of economic renewal and innovation. Individuals and organizations within the community may proactively launch the planning process, or governments may instigate programs seeking to promote community participation.

CED recognizes that the health of the local economy is dependent upon more than the individual aspirations of entrepreneurs (MacNeil and Williams 1995). However, CED may facilitate entrepreneurial activity through accountability to a community planning process. Community planning processes represent one area where research and practitioner accounts have successfully and systematically contributed to the theory and practice of CED.

Early inquiries into CED sought to design and explain a series of developmental stages through which a community would attain development objectives. For example, Coffey and Polese (1984) describe a staged model of local development by linking local entrepreneurialism with the development of a broader regional economy. The stages included:

- the emergence of local entrepreneurship
- the "take-off" of local enterprise
- the expansion of these enterprises beyond the local region
- the achievement of a regional economic structure that is based upon local initiatives and locally created comparative advantages

Other researchers stress the dynamics of community-based planning processes that help to shape local economies. For example, Bryant and Preston (1989) adapt the principles and process of strategic planning to local development. Strategic planning offers a number of advantages to CED. First, strategic planning is easily recognized in the mainstream planning movement, which grants a greater degree of legitimacy to local efforts. Second,

Figure 5.1

The strategic planning process

Source: Adapted from Douglas 1994; Lewis and Green 1992.

strategic planning assists with the organization and systematization of CED practice. A systematic approach to CED facilitates the spread of community planning processes across communities and enhances policy relevance and recognition. Third, the organizational structure of strategic planning improves the effectiveness of CED practice by simplifying the complexity of the development process and linking investments of time and resources with community strengths, potential, and capabilities (see Figure 5.1).

As Bendavid-Val (1991) indicates, the function of a planning model is to provide a frame of reference in order to deal with the complexities of reality. In practice, CED planning and implementation will rarely follow the precise sequence of steps outlined in any model. It is likely, however, that participants will observe a variation of core strategic planning stages at different times in the development process. Feedback loops to earlier steps may occur, for example, as groups identify new information needs or ideas during planning or implementation.

The successful integration and modification of the strategic planning model (through an adherence to CED principles) serves to promote and, from a conceptual perspective at least, standardize the CED process. Strategic planning provides CED with an internal focus to assess, organize, and mobilize local resources, while at the same time recognizing that the community is not an isolated entity. As Bryant states (1999, 81): "Strategic planning implies an effort that takes account of the dynamic environment, with all its uncertainties, and that attempts to position the community in question in this dynamic, open, and competitive environment." Strategic planning provides a vehicle with which to represent various community interests and integrate, more generally, the principles of CED into practice: "The difference between strategic planning and development planning is primarily one of scope. Development planning is defined as the application and broadening of strategic planning principles to include promotion of individual and community well being" (Lamontagne 1994, 210).

Researchers commonly link community organizational development, the capacity of key local actors, and the fostering of relationships between these actors as well as outside sources of support with the successful implementation of a CED planning process (Economic Council of Canada 1990; Bryant 1999). Community-based economic development organizations, local actors, and CED networks represent, therefore, particular areas of research and development within CED.

Organizations, Actors, and Networks

Creating an organization that can develop and sustain a consistent yet flexible community strategy facilitates the long-term commitment necessary to engage in CED planning (Blakely 1994). Community-based economic development organizations (CEDOs) are formal social structures that enable people to work together in the pursuit of common goals. CEDOs may be strictly third-sector organizations, implying independence from usually municipal or regional government, or they may be the product of governments choosing to create an organization specifically mandated to address economic development issues (Pell 1994). There is an enormous range in the form and functions of CEDOs. Several thousand CEDOs exist in all regions across Canada (Pell 1994).

In terms of what CEDOs do, Bryant (1995b) groups a diverse range of functions into four categories. First, CEDOs serve an *integrating* role in the community. CEDOs act as hubs within the community for facilitating inter-community and external relationships. They may also help to represent different and often excluded or marginalized interests within the community in local planning processes. Second, CEDOs generate and disseminate *information* needed for local planning and decision making. Third, CEDOs are often responsible for *community planning*. Finally, CEDOs are responsible for *action,* such as organizing meetings, producing research reports, or undertaking specific development projects.

CEDOs assume a variety of organizational forms. For the tasks of CED specifically, however, the community development corporation (CDC) has become a common organizational structure to house and facilitate CED

efforts at the community level. CDCs are umbrella organizations that operate or provide support for new small enterprises and nonprofit community-
service projects within a specific geographic area (Pell 1994).

Communities all over the world have adapted CDCs to serve a wide variety of purposes since their incarnation in the US during the 1960s war on
poverty (Blakely 1994). Specifically, there are generally two CDC models:
the *assistance* model and the *equity* model (Consilium 1997). The assistance
model describes CDCs with a mandate to provide grants, loans, technical
assistance, information, and training to support community and business
development. The goal of the assistance model is to ensure organizational
survival in order to maintain its support functions.

The CDC equity model assumes a more active and direct role in establishing or investing in businesses that are owned, wholly or in part, by a development corporation. The goal of the equity model is to build an equity base
and to develop business assets in order to redirect profits towards community projects and job creation.

The equity model responds more directly to the local effects of market
failure concerning the provision of social services. As a result, CDCs may
offer "patient capital," which supports community-based development
projects at a low rate of return, provided that the project or business advances the social, economic, cultural, or environmental well-being of people
in the community.

Researchers and practitioners are increasingly recognizing CEDOs for their
contribution to local development (Douglas 1994; Canadian CED Network
2001). CEDOs face significant barriers, however, including a lack of access
to capital, a lack of information, limited amounts of management capacity
at the local level, and a lack of appropriate training opportunities and resources (Douglas 1994). Successful CED is strongly associated with having a
local organization with a clear mandate and sufficient resources to engage
development issues within the community.

Equally important are the skills and commitment of people working directly or indirectly with the CEDO, and CEDO capacity is directly related to
the capacity of these individuals. Community capacity is ultimately dependent upon individual capacity: "In short, it is not unreasonable to suggest
that regional growth and development depends as much, if not more, upon
the composition of the population as upon locational, structural, and resource characteristics" (Coffey and Polese 1985, 87).

Increasingly, the development literature is recognizing the contribution
of human resources (termed "local agency") to the development process.
According to MacNeil (1997), a lack of attention to human capital was a
critical weakness of past regional development policy. In the recent context
of economic restructuring, researchers recognize the role of local agency in
the transformation of local conditions as a critical force behind processes of

uneven development (Bryant 1995a). Such recognition was slow to infil-trate development policy, however, despite some early observations that development "starts with people and their education, organization, and discipline ... without these three, all resources remain latent, untapped, potential" (Schumacher 1973, 138). The gap in recognizing local agency in a development context is surprising given the pivotal role accorded to lead-ership in the business case study literature.

Researchers have translated attention to local agency into theoretical terms through a discussion of local actors. For example, local actor theory con-cerns itself with conceptualizations of the role and effectiveness of local actors. Local actor theory views communities as consisting of networks of relations. The theory adds to our understanding of local development by attempting to discover and represent how individual actors, at local and extra-local scales, influence processes of development (Murdoch and Marsden 1995; Bryant et al. 2000).

Bryant et al. (2000) define actor effectiveness within the context of (1) their own inherent characteristics and (2) their ability to mobilize and gather internal and external resources from the networks to which they belong. By concentrating on the importance of networks, these researchers introduce a third critical component of the CED process: social dynamics, as defined by the relationships between the various organizations and ac-tors engaged (or who should be engaged) in the development process. These personal and organizational relationships form networks of resources, con-sisting of connections that support and drive the process of CED planning and implementation.

The effectiveness of local actors in meeting their stated objectives repre-sents a critical connection between local actor theory and the practicalities of CED. Naturally, a focus on local actors introduces perhaps the largest single variable of contingency into the CED process, because all people are different. However, attention to human capital development and to under-standing which methods are appropriate for supporting and training new CED actors represents an area in need of further research (Filion 1998). Ac-cordingly, we discuss our project experiences and reflections concerning community capacity building in Chapter 8.

In summary, despite internal contingencies, the basic structure of the CED planning process introduces a significant level of consistency and predict-ability to the theory and practice of CED. The process provides a common framework for comparison and enables researchers to begin speculating as to appropriate expectations and time lines within the practice of CED. As such, the framework also provides the necessary criteria for effective policy development related to local development.

As Filion (1988) illustrates, however, there is often a significant gap be-tween CED-inspired planning and implementation. The visions and consensus achieved at the planning table are often challenged by the realities of dynamic local and extra-local factors. As a result, a frequent tendency at the community planning table is to revert to conventional development strategies. CED must effectively implement and then sustain its process and strategies. An important contributor to achieving CED success is the degree of clarity attached to the pursuit of CED strategies themselves. The following section of our CED framework outlines different orientations of CED initiatives.

Strategic Orientations

The second component of the CED framework addresses the importance of action. Specifically, this section will clarify areas of confusion concerning the variety of contexts in which CED may be applied and the specific internal and/or external orientations of CED strategies. Orientations refer to the initiatives, decisions, and actions that determine the pattern of development at the community level (Bryant 1999). Strategic orientations reflect the values and interests of community members driving the CED process and the specific needs/assets of the community.

Within accounts documenting CED activity, there is often either a contextual rigidity (an implication that CED can be applied only under certain conditions) or simply a lack of information describing the conditions under which a community is implementing CED. Similarly, researchers and practitioners often uniformly promote CED projects, despite the potentially very different values and actions associated with different strategic orientations. Understanding the possible orientations of CED will lead to a more strategic implementation of different CED approaches – in other words, finding a better fit between the needs of a community and a menu of different CED approaches. The following pages will provide a simple framework for presenting different strategic orientations for CED. First, we will present a distinction between CED in marginalized areas compared with more mainstream applications. Second, we will distinguish between strategies that are directed at the internal dynamics of the community economy (localist) and strategies that seek to foster stronger or more appropriate economic relations with external economies and partners (linking).

Marginalization and the Mainstream

First, a critical question for practitioners and policy makers is, "When and where is it appropriate to pursue CED?" More specifically, "Is CED for marginalized communities only, or is CED relevant in more mainstream situations?" Many authors make a clear connection between CED and marginalized communities. For example: "Communities will turn to community economic development measures to assist them in dealing with an economic crisis. More to the point, they have little choice. In most cases, therefore, community economic development measures will be designed for and by communities confronting difficult economic circumstances" (Savoie 2000, 117). Savoie also indicates that well-performing communities do not necessarily have the sense of urgency necessary to initiate CED. Similarly, Lloyd draws a link between marginalized communities and the appeal of CED (1996, 19): "While CED can, of course, be applied to all places and to all communities, it is most appropriate to those deprived areas of industrial and urbanised regions where geography itself adds a magnifying effect to the conditions of social exclusion." Lloyd is writing in the context of CED in European Union regional development policy, which identifies CED as a strategy for reducing uneven development and for directing development programs towards least-favoured regions.

Both Savoie and Lloyd make connections between marginalized communities and their willingness (or simply lack of alternatives) to adopt CED. In the absence of mainstream economic attention, marginalized communities must capitalize on the economic opportunities offered by a more endogenous approach to development. Clearly this represents an appropriate environment in which to apply CED.

From our perspective, however, to limit the application of CED to already marginalized conditions is overly restrictive. First, in contrast to Savoie's statement concerning CED and economic crisis, CED is not necessarily an appropriate strategy for communities facing a sudden decline in the local economy. CED should be a strategy that is put in place in *anticipation* of economic restructuring. When faced with a crisis, communities require an immediate response mechanism to deal with short-term job displacement and the social impacts associated with economic uncertainty. CED often delivers results in the medium to long term. Second, CED is a strategy that is ideally pursued under conditions of relative economic stability. If a community is stable and not facing imminent crisis, it will have more internal resources to allocate towards an effective CED process, including a stronger local economy (implying that there may be capital available for reinvestment) and the situational flexibility necessary to implement longer-term strategies.

In effect, there is a continuum of circumstances within which practitioners may appropriately apply CED. The critical variables that determine one's place on the continuum are the capacity of the community to engage in CED and its existing and potential economic circumstances. If CED is viewed solely as a strategy for the economically marginalized, there is a risk that CED itself will be marginalized within a two-tier society – in which communities are either included in or excluded from the dominant capital, labour, and commodity markets (MacNeil and Williams 1995).

In an environment of exclusion, CED is a strategy for building an internal economy or cushioning the inevitable effects of the restructuring process.

However, CED is also capable of being more than a coping strategy. Many authors look to CED as a means to form linkages with the mainstream economy, capitalizing on the economic opportunities and advantages offered by a community-based and more sustainable approach to development. Localist and linking strategies offer a second complementary way to conceptualize these different strategic orientations of CED.

Localist and Linking Strategies

It is indeed all too easy to retreat into an anti-system view of quasi-regional protectionism in order to promote local development in a particular region. But a local development model, one relevant to western nations, must reconcile regional development objectives with the imperatives of economic integration: the free movement of people, goods, information, and capital. From an integrational perspective, it is perhaps preferable to think in terms of "balanced" local development rather than to adopt a narrow and exclusive interpretation of the concept. (Coffey and Polese 1984, 10)

Coffey and Polese refer to a second point of confusion concerning the applicability of CED: is the purpose of CED to promote a locally focused, self-reliant community economy, or may CED also be used to forge better links with the mainstream economy? Such a distinction may be clarified through an interpretation of CED strategies as being either "localist" or "linking."

Localist strategies are concerned with building stronger localized economies through community ownership. Under this approach, communities seek to meet local needs through local production (i.e., the more uncompromising version of community self-reliance discussed earlier). Localist strategies represent a core application of CED to support local economies, particularly (although not exclusively) in marginalized communities, where positive integration with the market is less likely, if it exists at all. On the other hand, practitioners may also choose to design linking strategies to address issues of marginalization, innovation, and decline by seeking to close the gap between communities and mainstream economic forces.

Within the current context of economic transition, linking CED strategies are relevant given the dynamics of post-Fordism and sustainable development. Economic change and new technologies make it increasingly easier for communities to establish their own linkages with the broader provincial, national, and global economies, and also to be more vulnerable to global competition. Community resilience in this sense refers to increasing the entrepreneurial capacity of residents and community leaders to respond to economic opportunities. The trick, of course, is to establish appropriate linkages with the broader, external economy, so as not to simply recreate conditions of dependency or to indirectly decrease the net value to the community economy (for example, through environmental externalities or a fundamental clash with local values, thereby creating excessive community conflict).

Filion (1998) identifies a variety of economic opportunities associated with the transition from Fordism to post-Fordism:

- prospects for new small/medium-sized firms
- devolution of job creation by government
- growing currency of self-help
- reduction in government social programs
- high unemployment
- cohorts of economically marginalized people

There is obviously the potential that each of these conditions will create an equal or greater amount of social and economic turmoil. A community's capacity to organize itself and to react proactively to new opportunities (i.e., to adopt an effective CED process) will determine whether post-Fordism represents a negative force or an opportunity to add value to the local economy.

Coffey and Polese (1984) and Dykeman (1990) highlight the entrepreneurial focus of local development that is of particular relevance in the post-Fordist climate described above. The demand for niche products creates opportunities for local innovation and product development. From an internal perspective, the decline of the conditions of stability associated with Fordist structures (government and corporate dependency) creates a need for communities to become economically proactive, thereby facilitating economic and social development.

Second, the relative mainstream status of sustainable development places increasing demands on the capacity of local communities to directly participate in matters of economic development (Pierce and Dale 1999). As a result, locally oriented strategies represent important sources of innovation in advancing a more sustainable economy (Roseland 1998). As Gibbs (1996) argues, sustainable development has received only limited attention from work on economic restructuring. CED, with its emphasis on sustainable forms of development, represents an appropriate forum within which to explore local dimensions of sustainability and their impacts on the broader economy.

Clearly, there will be some strategic overlap between localist and linking approaches to CED. For example, community-based training programs may differ in their objectives, but not necessarily in method. The main contribution of the localist-linking differentiation of CED strategies is consideration of a diversity of strategies in seeking to strengthen the local economy: "CED can, therefore, be defined as an approach which comprises a continuum of actions across a range of possibilities ... CED represents, in effect, a menu from which choices are made according to local needs and the set of local capacities for action at a particular time" (Lloyd 1996, 21). In addition, if CED is truly a bottom-up process, then the decision as to which CED approach to take lies at the community level. Having a clear idea of the different contextual and strategic orientations of CED will add to the effectiveness of CED research, policy, and practice.

Increasingly, researchers and practitioners are promoting a *balanced* approach to CED (House and McGrath 2004). This means that communities must pursue strategies to both strengthen the internal dynamics of their local economies and explore appropriate economic linkages with external interests and markets (Coffey and Polese 1984; Bryant and Preston 1989; Newby 1999; Pierce 1999). It is possible for localist strategies to complement linking efforts and vice versa. In addition, prosperous communities will undoubtedly contain marginalized sectors, requiring the use of a more balanced and mutually supportive CED process containing a variety of targeted strategic responses.

If a community has been bypassed and has been economically marginalized by changes in the economy, then the decision to pursue a more self-reliant approach to CED is easily decided upon – pursue greater economic self-reliance or wither away. In a more dynamic community context, however, analyzing trade relationships and levels of reinvestment may be very difficult. Significant research and planning are required to understand how the community itself may benefit from a more self-reliant economy, particularly if this approach challenges existing economic relationships. Understanding the potential downsides of a more isolated economy is necessary, including the possibility of lower living standards. This is one area where there is a significant gap in the CED literature and a source of rich research opportunities. Nevertheless, integrating a self-reliance component into a CED planning process may be beneficial and work in harmony with other strategies. A report from Atlantic Canada illustrates the importance of adopting a balanced and contextually appropriate approach to development:

> The Commission has rejected both a romanticized yearning for the past and an unrealistic expectation of becoming a heavily industrialized society ... While the Commission has advocated that big industries be developed here to the extent that makes sound economic sense, our research has shown that big industry alone will not provide jobs in the numbers we need. This is why we have stressed instead a balanced approach to economic development. This approach encourages medium and small-scale enterprises, and takes advantage of modern forms of communication and technology, in

order to build upon the latent strengths of all parts of our society, including our small outports, our resource towns and our regional service centres. (Commission on Employment and Unemployment in Newfoundland 1986, 446)

Community Capacity

There are numerous locally detrimental impacts associated with past economic development practices, as illustrated in Chapter 3. Research has shown that the local capacity to undertake sustained development efforts is lacking in many communities, particularly in smaller rural communities (Walzer 1991; Reed and Paulson 1990; Halseth 1998; Hayter 2000). Efforts to reverse community decline and seek an economic development approach that is more tolerant of contextual diversity and more supportive of local control require significant levels of community capacity.

A focus on community capacity provides a direct contrast with the needs-based approach of past regional development policy. Clarke et al. (2000), for example, note that rural development policies and strategies rarely contain provisions for the training and support of local actors. Despite the relative ease in understanding the conceptual difference between needs and capacity, the utility of a capacity-based approach to development lacks the same operational clarity as addressing community needs. Needs are relatively easy to identify, to target with programs, and to monitor. Capacity is a much more elusive concept. A needs-based approach targets weaknesses and generally seeks to address them through the delivery of externally based capital and expertise. A capacity-based approach to development seeks to develop, from within, the abilities of individuals and communities to address their own problems and to capitalize on their own assets. As such, capacity building is a necessary ingredient of CED.

Across various literatures, the term "capacity" is generally employed in a respectful and proactive manner with a view towards building community or individual skills, resources, and processes for community or individual self-reliance in the long term. This section describes a variety of definitions in the literature used to define CED capacity. Each definition is accompanied by a set of criteria designed to assist in the measurement/assessment of capacity in communities. These capacity assessment criteria help to operationalize the concept of capacity for development and policy purposes.

Reimer (1999), as part of the Canadian Rural Restructuring Foundation, describes community capacity from a systems perspective as the ability to identify issues, be reflexive, realize objectives, and self-organize. High capacity is implied when a community shows strength and agility within market relations, bureaucratic relations, associative relations, and kinship relations.

The Aspen Institute defines community capacity as "the combined influence of a community's commitment, resources and skills that can be deployed to build on community strengths and address community problems and opportunities" (1996, 1). The Aspen Institute provides eight outcomes that serve as indicators of community capacity (1996, 11):

- expanding diverse, inclusive citizen participation
- expanding leadership base
- strengthened individual skills
- widely shared understanding and vision
- strategic community agenda
- consistent, tangible progress towards goals
- more effective community organizations and institutions
- better resource utilization by the community

Human Resources Development Canada (HRDC) adopts a suitably vague approach to defining community capacity: "Capacity is simply the ways and means needed to do what has to be done. It is much broader than simply skills, people, and plans. It includes commitment, resources and all that is brought to bear on a process to make it successful" (Frank and Smith 1999). HRDC describes ten outcomes/criteria of capacity building:

- stronger community relationships: healthier people, caring families and safer, welcoming communities
- an increased number of community-based opportunities identified
- the enhanced ability of community members to share their ideas on a course of action
- increased competency in setting and realizing common goals
- expanded intuition in sensing what to do, when to do it, and when to quit
- an enhanced respect for limited resources, including people, so that shortages, duplication, or waste are minimized
- an increased awareness of the importance of protecting, advocating for, and improving the conditions for vulnerable people, distinct cultures, floundering economies, and environments
- skilled leadership
- an increased interest among young people to become future leaders
- an increased ability to handle disappointment, threats, and hazards to community pride and well-being

Lewis (1994) offers an operational perspective to community capacity by outlining four integrated dimensions of CED practice (and therefore areas in which to concentrate capacity-building efforts):

- *growth/equity* – stresses the building of equity or wealth-generating assets in a community through direct ownership of businesses and industries that will be accountable to community goals, goals that focus on generating profits for reinvestment, developing management capacity and influence, and the creation of jobs.
- *loan/technical assistance* – focuses on debt financing and the provision of loans and loan guaranties to small and medium-sized entrepreneurs and community businesses. This is an important aspect of CED since credit to small-scale producers and self-employed individuals is often very difficult to access. This difficulty is exacerbated in marginalized areas or areas experiencing economic instability.
- *employment development* – places the emphasis on human resource training, job readiness, skills training, job placement, self-employment training, and matching needs of employers with training for employment. Having a skilled employment pool is essential in planning for CED. In communities where most people have depended on the forest industry for their livelihood, there is typically a lack of education and low skill level related to other forms of employment and business. The forest communities of BC are in transition, moving towards a more diversified economy. It is essential, therefore, to provide support and infrastructure to retrain and upgrade educational levels as a way to build community capacity for more diversified development.
- *planning and advisory services* – provide planning and research assistance to communities doing CED. Examples within the Aboriginal community are tribal councils that provide services to their constituent communities. In other cases, a community organization, agency of government, educational institution, or a specifically set up community economic development organization (e.g., community development corporation) may take on this role. The type of activities undertaken may include marketing assistance, strategic planning, feasibility studies, product research, import-substitution studies, community profiling and mapping, coordination of services, public information, and public promotion.

Each of the models described here makes an important contribution to advancing our understanding of community capacity. We will review different features of the capacity component of the Forest Communities project in Chapters 7 and 9.

Challenges Facing CED
With the conceptual framework now in place for analyzing CED in the project communities, this section outlines a variety of documented challenges facing CED. A number of researchers have identified various barriers

associated with using a CED approach. We identified these challenges before proceeding with the project in the hope of avoiding them in the field and contributing to a better understanding of their eventual resolution.

First, CED researchers recognize *evaluation* as a particular challenge. For example, Coffey and Polese (1985) discuss the problems of how to measure and communicate the return to society on investments in human capital. The current measurements of the economic system lack the longevity and subtlety to tap into such changes. Others discuss the difficulties of measuring the "soft benefits" of social capital. As Ross and Usher state (1987, 110), "the absence of measurement inevitably leads to an under-evaluation of the activity, as well as the people who perform it." Thus, CED practitioners and researchers face particular challenges in communicating the direct and indirect outcomes of their actions.

Second, CED is challenged by the fact that community *capacity* exists in a catch-22 relationship with the capital necessary to successfully launch CED activities. You need community capacity to raise capital and implement projects – and you need capital to raise community capacity. Areas of capacity lacking in CED projects include entrepreneurialism, planning, organizational development, and basic managerial skills (Blakely 1994; Douglas 1994).

Third, linked to the second point, limited financial *capital* for community-based projects remains a central barrier to implementing and, more important, sustaining community-based initiatives. The lack of funds necessary to initiate significant projects and then to sustain them through their start-up phase is a consistent barrier cited in the literature and was echoed by each of the communities engaged in the Forest Communities project. Heightened factors of risk in hinterland communities present barriers to secure and adequate financing and funding.

Two main barriers block access to capital in unstable forest-dependent and other marginalized communities. First, bank policies require collateral on loans to minimize loan risk. People who are low-income, who do not own houses or cars that they can use as collateral, are deemed high-risk and do not qualify for traditional bank loans. This challenge is pronounced in First Nations communities, where, under the Indian Act, reserve land is "owned" by the Crown and set aside for the collective use and benefit of a First Nations band (Indian and Northern Affairs Canada 2003). While the band council may allot land parcels for individual use, the land cannot be used by that individual as collateral. Second, in order to cover administration costs associated with each loan and make a profit on it as well, banks tend to specialize in large loan portfolios ($100,000-$250,000) to large companies, thereby denying microbusinesses and small entrepreneurs access to credit (Bellan 1995). In order to fill this gap left by banks, governments, credit unions, and nongovernmental organizations (NGOs) have established a variety of community loan funds and loan guarantee funds to provide investment capital to capital-starved communities and small loans to low-income individuals who want to start businesses.

Fourth, the *role of government* represents yet another dilemma for CED, depending upon the type and degree of government intervention. From a negative perspective, too much reliance on government funding and technical support may simply transfer or perpetuate conditions of community dependency. This may be seen as an attempt by government to control community organization and action, monitor activities, or integrate areas of the informal economy into the formal system. Less cynically, but no less destructive for CED initiatives, overreliance on government support can lead to a lack of consistency in training and development activities. Changes in government and changes in government programs occur on a much shorter time line than is necessary for a sustained approach to CED.

Fifth, CED activities are intensely *political*. CED practitioners are often unaware of the potential for certain initiatives to create conflict at the community level; there is a feeling that local initiatives are inherently good and therefore beyond controversy. Challenging traditional approaches to growth, seeking greater participation in decision making, and creating new forms of employment and economic action are all intensely political activities. Divisions may exist between the status quo and new economic interests, or within the CED community as to which approaches are most effective. Adding to the political poignancy of CED is the role of funding, or the competition among CED-type groups for access to the same sources of support. Greater political awareness and analysis is required for CED to play a more influential role in the local economy and in broader policy processes (Roseland 1998).

Finally, the *small and medium scale* of CED activities, when viewed in isolation, appears insignificant and unable to replace traditional jobs and sources of capital. Smaller local initiatives may be unable to replace jobs based upon unsustainable practices (for both economic and ecological reasons). There is, however, potential for smaller initiatives to reconstruct and to diversify the basic foundation of local economies over time. In order for this to occur, CED must capture the imaginations of local leaders, entrepreneurs, and government agents. CED researchers and networks must do a better job of explaining the cumulative and gradual changes that CED is capable of contributing to the local economy – and cumulatively to provincial and national economic diversification.

Conclusion

The history of development in Canada illustrates that governments have designed policies to serve the economic interests of provinces and the nation as a whole. Given the wealth of Canada's natural resources, this macro, growth-oriented approach has served the interests of a diversity of rural communities, with the clear exception of First Nations. More recently, the complexity of the global economy, the collapse and volatility of traditional resources and resource industries, and the subsequent decline of many hinterland communities are challenging many of our previous assumptions concerning economic development. The simple yet persistent development formulas of the past are under increasing scrutiny from a variety of perspectives.

From a local perspective, a new approach to development is needed that is capable of building upon and adapting to the diversity of cultures, capacities, and specific economic circumstances found across rural Canada. A new balance between national, provincial, and local interests needs to be negotiated. However, new approaches face the added challenge of pursuing economic development within a more complex framework of community sustainability and conflicting boundaries of jurisdiction and competing values. Rural communities are entering a new phase in their development, moving from being sites of resource extraction to testing the boundaries of their resilience and permanence – they are experiencing a tenuous second growth.

CED has the potential to play, over time, a significant role in overcoming the deficiencies of conventional approaches to development and mapping a more sustainable approach to economic renewal. However, serious challenges exist in terms of practice and theorization: "I maintain that the CED movement is in a log jam, the result of the sharp dissonance between the wave of interest it presently generates and the insufficient availability, within the current context, of economic and political resources to assure its success" (Filion 1998, 1102).

Part of the reason for this "log jam" is the lack of theory and consistency in reporting CED activities. CED is a practical endeavour, directed by the individual actions of people and organizations at the community level. The practical nature of CED is a source of great appeal and strength for CED, in policy and practice. People respond to problems and gather the capacity and resources necessary to do the job. No one is necessarily instructing people to do CED, and the vast majority of practitioners are not being well paid for their renewal efforts. The lack of systematic research and theorization in CED is a weakness, however. The political realities, which govern the decision-making process for community and regional development, rely on the certainty that models provide. At the political level, the lack of theory in CED reduces its influence. Theory helps to convince leaders that a CED approach is tested and reliable: "The lack of systematic, well-documented evidence is not surprising given the absence of a clear consensual definition and the conceptual immaturity this absence reflects. More rigorous theoretical descriptions of CED will be required before systematic data gathering efforts can progress beyond individual case descriptions" (Galaway and Hudson 1994, 96).

As stated in Chapter 1, it is the purpose of this book to contribute to the systematic documentation of CED and to present a conceptual framework that is contextually and theoretically informed. Chapters 3, 4, and 5 have outlined our framework for understanding CED against the backdrop of general theories of development and the specific contextual circumstances that define the resource-based, hinterland economies of British Columbia. The following chapters apply this framework to our work with four forest-dependent communities.

Chapter 6 explores different dimensions of vibrant communities and successful local initiatives. We hope to learn from development examples of the past to identify key characteristics of CED success. The chapter presents a "success factor" framework that communities may use to reflect upon their own capabilities and opportunities.

6
Success Factors in Community Economic Development

Successful community economic development (CED) can help address the impacts of changing socio-economic, political, and ecological conditions within forest-dependent communities by bringing more money and employment into a community, increasing community control over planning and resources, and creating resilience to external changes. But are all communities capable of achieving success in CED? Are some communities more suited to certain kinds of CED endeavours than others? And how do we recognize success in CED as it occurs?

This chapter attempts to respond to each of these questions by presenting a framework for understanding the complex and dynamic concept of community in terms of success factors in CED. Success in CED depends on community capacity – the presence of various forms of community capital and the ability to mobilize this capital for development purposes. We have identified common conditions associated with successful communities through an extensive literature review, and distilled these conditions of success into indicators of community capital. We have organized community capital in four categories: human, social, economic, and ecological. By adding indicators to each of these categories of community capital, we have formed a success factor framework. This framework provides a tool for data collection and analysis (steps 2 and 3 of the CED process presented in Chapter 7), as well as for planning and ongoing monitoring/evaluation (steps 4 and 6).

This chapter begins by providing a review of the importance of community capacity and ongoing research efforts to determine how capacity might be measured, followed by a discussion of each success factor (capital) category and its origins in the literature. The final section reviews the contribution of the success factor framework to understanding and implementing CED, including monitoring changes in community capacity. A variety of suggestions for future directions in research and CED framework development are also outlined.

This chapter focuses on the internal capacity of communities. Many external factors, ranging from government policies to international market shifts, as discussed in the opening chapters, also affect local CED efforts. Both internal and external factors must be considered when developing feasible CED strategies. The success factors framework provided here, however, encourages communities to begin the CED process by looking inward at how their capabilities and the conditions of their community either facilitate or serve as a barrier to the implementation and sustainability of successful CED initiatives.

The framework is intended to help clarify the complexity of understanding and working with various community dynamics. We have designed the framework to be used by communities as part of a larger CED planning process, providing examples of appropriate indicators for assessing current conditions and tracking the impact of CED efforts. The framework is also a useful tool for external researchers. Conducting a community assessment based upon the success factors aided our own comprehensive understanding of the communities.

In order for the framework to be most effective, it must be combined with community research, reflection, and a process that draws upon the participation and knowledge of local residents. Ultimately communities must choose for themselves what constitutes success in a continuous cycle of development, identifying and pursuing goals and objectives that will enhance capacities and dimensions of well-being considered to be of the highest priority by community members. It is hoped that the following framework will assist in this process.

Searching for the Ingredients of Success

Communities and the circumstances they face are unique and diverse. As a result, definitions of what constitutes success in CED are also diverse. The definition and pursuit of success will vary greatly at the local level, reflecting the different values, cultures, and resources found within communities. The development of a "one size fits all" recipe for CED success is therefore neither appropriate nor realistic.

However, the identification of favourable conditions for success in CED, based upon lessons from development-oriented literature and the past experiences of other communities, can provide four useful services in expanding the understanding and use of CED. First, identifying success factors will provide communities with information and ideas that they can use to assess their own strengths and weaknesses. A better understanding of conditions in the community will help identify which CED strategies are most appropriate for meeting community goals and objectives, or even whether or not CED is a suitable response. Second, reflecting upon the ingredients of success noted by researchers and theorists may stimulate new ideas for local development. Third, identifying common conditions for success will aid policy makers in constructing a positive, enabling environment for CED by identifying more universal characteristics of, and strategies for success in, CED and the contributions policy can make to enhance and support these activities. Finally, the development of a framework of commonly cited conditions for success or failure in CED will help build a body of knowledge and stronger theoretical foundations in a field often criticized for theoretical weakness and lack of a systematic framework for inquiry into the development process (Filion 1998; Hayter 2000).

Research on Community Indicators: Measuring Community Capacity
Recently there has been a dramatic rise in interest in the concept of assessing and building community development capacity (Aspen Institute 1996; Kusel 1996; Chaskin et al. 2001; Colussi and Rowcliffe 1999). Two factors are fundamentally responsible for the rising interest in capacity building: (1) a concern for the decline of communities under conditions of severe restructuring, and (2) a broader trend of increasing political and institutional attention to the social, economic, and ecological benefits associated with local control.

From a local perspective, there is increasing disenchantment with the strategies that governments and corporations use to sustain the social, economic, and ecological health of regions and communities. Devotion to a sectorally based, externally driven, growth-centred approach to development has contributed to economic instability and proven detrimental to the long-term aspirations of communities regarding economic diversification. As outlined in previous chapters, in BC forest communities, staples dependency has had a range of negative or "capital-reducing" impacts on the various dimensions of community capacity. Efforts to reverse the decline and seek an economic approach more tolerant of diversity and more supportive of local control and contextual difference will therefore require enhancement of the capacity of communities to pursue their own potential. This in turn requires an understanding of the strengths and weaknesses within a community and methods for monitoring how capacity changes over time.

We define capacity as the ability to identify, enhance, and mobilize the human potential, economic opportunities, social relationships, and ecological resources found in a community for the purpose of improved community resilience. This definition links the concept of community capacity with a framework for community monitoring that consists of four categories: human, economic, social, and ecological. We describe these categories as types of community capital.

CED practitioners have been recently drawn to the term "capital," previously reserved for describing financial assets. Rees explains this economic metaphor in ecological terms (1991, in Roseland 1999, 193): "Human kind must learn to live on the 'interest' generated by remaining stocks of living 'natural capital.' Any human activity ... cannot be sustained indefinitely if it not only consumes annual production, but also cuts into capital stocks." Ecological, social, and individual/human assets also warrant attention, accounting, and responsible management. Attention to each form of community capital reveals and categorizes different dimensions of community, recognizing the value – in monetary and non-monetary terms – of all forms of community assets to the development process.

We explored these four categories of community capacity independently for the purposes of identification and analysis, but the integration of human, economic, social, and ecological forms of community capital is essential for good CED planning. Externally driven economic development has tended to segregate these interconnected elements of community, with the aim of maximizing the economic benefits of short-term growth within specific sectors. The challenge of achieving long-term community sustainability and resilience demands that all areas of capacity be nurtured over time and applied to the pursuit of appropriate community goals and objectives. Thus, success in CED can be defined as the degree to which local initiatives improve the quality *and* integration of the various types of community capital and the ways that CED planners employ these capital reserves to improve community well-being. Before we can effectively mobilize community capital assets, however, we must be able to identify and measure them.

The identification of success factors in CED is part of a growing body of research to devise effective monitoring and evaluation indicators for sustainable community development (see Table 6.1). While we are starting to see some signs of convergence between different community indicator programs, three factors help explain why there will always be some variety between different approaches. First, communities and regions are different, and localized monitoring systems reflect this variety. Communities vary in terms of their values, access to data, and development goals, all of which will affect a monitoring system.

Second, specifically related to sustainable development, the inclusion of people and the study of human well-being in ecosystem-related studies is in its infancy (Kusel 1996). As researchers conduct more indicator research, comparisons between different monitoring frameworks will yield insights into which systems are most effective in different environments. This research is important because a failure to define and monitor sustainability, through establishing benchmarks and subsequently tracking trends, will ultimately relegate the concept of sustainability to "buzzword" status (Beckley and Burkosky 1997).

Table 6.1

Examples of community capacity/sustainability assessment and monitoring systems

System	Researchers	Capacity/sustainability categories	Framework components
Sustainable Community Initiative (SCI)	University of Victoria	Ethics, conservation, competition, cooperation	Auditing questions, indicators and sectoral categories for each category of community relationships
Willipa Indicators for a Sustainable Community	Willipa Bay Alliance	Environment (water, land use, species viability), economy (productivity, opportunity, diversity, equity), community (life-long learning, health, citizenship, stewardship)	Indicators within each of the 11 categories with information on baseline data and trends
Indicators of Sustainable Community	Sustainable Seattle	40 economic, environmental, and social indicators	40 indicators, presented bi-annually in a "report card"
Quality of Life Reporting System	Federation of Canadian Municipalities	8 sets of indicators: population resources, quality of employment, quality of housing, community affordability, stress, health, safety, and participation. Quality of environment and social infrastructure under development.	4-7 quantitative measures in each of the 8 categories
Elements/ Circle of Development	First Nations Development Institute	2 main axes make up the circle – control of assets-kinship, and spirituality-personal efficacy, all within ecology	2 axes, 4 quadrants, with 16 elements, goals, and indicators for each
Sierra Nevada Wealth Index	Sierra Business Council	Social/human capital, natural capital, and financial capital	42 indicators measuring each of the three categories

▶

◄ *Table 6.1*

System	Researchers	Capacity/sustainability categories	Framework components
Community Vulnerability Checklist	Canadian Association of Single-Industry Towns	Vulnerability of industrial base, vulnerability of local economy, development environment	35 indicators measuring each category
Measuring Community Capacity Building	Aspen Institute	Inclusive citizen participation, expanding leadership, strengthened individual skills, widely shared understanding/ vision, strategic community agenda, progress towards goals, more effective organizations and institutions, better use of community resources	Indicators or measures corresponding to each of the 8 categories or "outcomes"

Sources: Walter 1996; Schoonmaker and von Hagen 1995; Sustainable Seattle 1998; Federation of Canadian Municipalities 1999; Canadian Association of Single-Industry Towns 1989; Aspen Institute 1996; Sierra Business Council 1996; Salway Black 1994.

Third, indicator approaches vary according to what is being measured. Researchers and community planners have focused on methods for measuring the state of community sustainability or well-being. Additional forms of community monitoring seek to provide insight into the future state of the community, rather than focusing on the present situation. Still other indicators measure the effectiveness of community capacity building efforts.

The variety of community monitoring systems again illustrates the importance of diversity. Each community or organization entering into a monitoring process will be striving to reach different objectives and communicate with different audiences. It is possible, though, through ongoing comparative research, to share ideas, compare methods, and adopt standards of continuous improvement within each system.

CED Success Factors: A Conceptual Framework

The following success factor framework contributes to the community monitoring literature by concentrating on aspects of community capital deemed to be of significance to a community's capacity to engage in CED. The link between the success factor framework and the principles of CED has influenced our design and choice of indicators in three ways. First, we wanted to identify indicators that were easily accessible, informative but not overly complex, and comparable with other communities. The comparative point is important due to the realities of community diversity and the relative nature of the concept of success. For example, a 12 percent unemployment rate may be considered high for some communities or an employment windfall for others.

Second, we use both quantitative and qualitative indicators. Combining local knowledge with aggregate statistical data yields a more informative and accurate picture of community capacity. CED demands that development be conducted *by* and *for* the community, so the capacity assessment process needs to be participatory, a central tenet of CED (Roseland 1998). The inclusion of local knowledge is imperative and often cannot be measured in a quantitative form.

Finally, comparing different types of data is also a capacity-building exercise. For example, local perceptions may challenge or be informed by different indicators. In this manner, community assessments help raise awareness about a community and how different sources of information can influence the development process and shape the community's image for both residents and external observers.

The following success factor framework illustrates and briefly describes the conceptual origins of each of the twenty-four success factors selected by the Forest Communities research team (see Table 6.2). We have identified success factors within each of the four categories of community capital along with indicators, measures, and data sources for each factor (presented in the Appendix). The Forest Communities project provided a valuable opportunity to test the application of this framework. We will provide examples throughout this chapter, and in the chapters that follow, of how project findings shed further light on the importance of each of these factors.

Human Capital

The heart of a community, and of a community process or project, is its people. Without individuals who possess certain knowledge, skills, values, and sense of commitment, CED will not happen and organizations and communities will not exist to facilitate the process. Human resource strengths and requirements therefore represent a logical starting point in the evaluation of community capacity.

We have identified in the literature six forms of human capital of particular value to CED: skills, education and training, leadership, civic engagement, entrepreneurial spirit/attitude, and labour force readiness. We will describe each factor in greater detail below. Measures and data sources for determining the presence or absence of these factors in a community are outlined in Appendix Table A1.

Table 6.2

CED success factors: Indicators of community capacity

Type of capital	Success factors
Human	Skills Education and training Leadership Civic engagement Entrepreneurial spirit Labour force readiness
Economic	Economic health Diversity Adaptability Health of local businesses Sustainability Informal economic activity Local control Access to capital Location/infrastructure Service amenities
Social	Sense of community Community-based organizations Community participation, planning, and cooperation
Ecological	Ecosystem health Natural resources Commercial and subsistence harvesting Ecological amenities Stewardship

Skills

In general, a skilled labour force is a critical community asset. The range of skills within a community that are important for success in CED varies according to the venture or strategy being considered. The suitability of a proposed venture to a community's existing human resources is an important consideration at the project selection and feasibility analysis stage of the CED planning process. Once the project has been selected, planners can design CED initiatives to best take advantage of the human resources available and to build human resource capacity (increase human capital). In some cases, the presence of unique or exceptional community skills will lead to a project idea.

For a CED initiative to have a real impact on improving the capacity of a community, it must be designed with existing skill levels in mind. If the demands of a strategy exceed existing human capacity, the project will require external skills in the short to medium term. To develop the capacity of the community, efforts should be made to foster the internal skills of community members and workers over time. For example, both the Nuxalk and Upper St'at'imc communities recognized the skills of their community members in the areas of arts and culture as significant human resource strengths. As we will see in Chapter 8, arts and cultural skills and community assets were important sources of CED inspiration and projects.

Specific skill requirements are project-dependent. However, valuable foundational skills in a CED process include: marketing and communications abilities; managerial, business development, and fundraising skills; professional, trades, and other technical skills (e.g., lawyers, accountants, engineers, construction workers, scientists, and engineers); and creative and artistic talents. Researchers have also identified computer skills to be important in rural development projects (Halseth and Arnold 1997). In addition, CED planners must consider local skills associated with the informal economy.

A variety of techniques are available to identify the range of skills present in a community. For example, planners can use community skill inventories or asset-mapping exercises (Kretzmann and McKnight 1993) to gather information on a community's skill base. It is also important for a CED process to value a variety of skills held by community members. An inclusive process will help build local participation and create unforeseen project linkages and partnerships.

Education

High unemployment and welfare rates, susceptibility to wild employment variations, and low education levels – these are the products of a resource extraction society. (100 Mile House participant)

Education is a critical success factor at many levels of the community development process. Education contributes to creating a productive labour force, effective leadership, and informed citizens. Evidence of a commitment to learning and continuing education within a community indicates a willingness to adopt new information, ideas, and perspectives. Continuing education contributes to the ability of individuals and communities to adapt to changing circumstances. Education increases earning potential (Courant et al. 1997), can prepare individuals with the skills and knowledge to take advantage of future economic opportunities, or reintroduces people to their past and forgotten ways of making their communities viable. Finally, organizations themselves are more successful if they are committed to a process of ongoing organizational learning (Argyris and Schön 1978). This process of self-reflection and learning is dependent on the willingness and ability of individuals within community organizations to engage in the learning process.

The availability of training programs, education, and learning opportuni-ties (including adult education, conventional educational institutions, and informal/peer learning settings), therefore, is an important factor in sus-taining and building CED capacity. Referring to the "brain-drain problem," Crihfield (1991) cautions, however, that increased education spending does not necessarily result in greater community stability. Educated residents may leave the community or region for work or education and not return, particularly if local jobs are not available or wage rates are not competitive. Strategies aimed at human resource retention and matching training and education with current and future local labour market needs are required to maximize benefits from the human capital available within a community's labour force and from initiatives aimed at human resource development. As one Bella Coola resident says, "What is the point of being trained for non-existent jobs?"

Leadership

Leadership is a critical and challenging human resource requirement, and the subject of much discussion among CED practitioners and authors (Com-mission on Employment and Unemployment in Newfoundland 1986; Flora and Flora 1991). Most CED success stories come about because of the hard work of a small group of dedicated people. CED requires volunteers who are willing to play a leadership role, and/or funding to hire a professional CED facilitator, as in the story of the Nuxalk presented in Chapter 7.

Rural communities may face particular leadership challenges due to a smaller population base from which to draw leadership potential and a smaller core of professional staff and consultants (Hustedde 1991). How-ever, rural communities often overcome these shortcomings with a larger overall volunteer commitment from local residents. Bollman (1992) points out that despite economic strain and a smaller population base to draw from, in Canada's small, rural towns a higher percentage of people volun-teer their time than in urban areas.

The challenge of finding appropriate CED leaders is complicated by the range of skills that are required by CED processes. These skills are rarely found in one individual. In fact, while some authors suggest that success is dependent on the presence of a "sparkplug" or "champion" (a single key individual), others argue that leadership is frequently a collective endeav-our (e.g., Flora and Flora 1991; Miller et al. 1990). Wismer and Pell (1981) identify two often conflicting skill sets required in CED leaders – the initia-tor (someone with a vision) and the manager (someone able to implement the vision). Finding an initiator and a manager, either in one person or in a team that works well together, is a difficult but critical task. The many skills required of a CED leader are outlined in Table 6.3. We compiled the table

Table 6.3

CED leadership indicators

Leadership theme	Indicators
Leadership identification/ recruitment	Diversity of leadership (e.g., gender, culture, age) Inclusion of retirees, youth, and new residents Forums for public participation Support for volunteerism Delegation Mentoring programs Active recruitment strategies
Qualities of leadership	Tolerance for diversity Interest-based dialogue Networking between community associations, formation of internal and external alliances Process transparency Accountability Community vision, long-range plans Willingness to take risks, openness to change Facilitation skills Acceptance by the community (respected, trusted) Awareness of and responsiveness to community needs Ability to innovate and motivate Strong coordination, management, and organizational skills Cross-cultural sensitivity

based upon our literature review. Chapter 7 continues our discussion of CED leadership within the parameters of the project.

Although the quality or appropriateness of local leadership is a difficult thing to define and evaluate (Hustedde 1991), communities undertaking CED initiatives must attempt to identify their current and potential leaders and assess their skills and characteristics. In addition, specific individuals or organizations may be very effective, but given the demands being placed on community capacity, leadership may be spread too thin. In situations where few people or organizations are responding to multiple tasks, monitoring the health of community leaders is important and developing recruitment or mentoring processes can be very effective.

Leadership stress and burnout can take its toll on impassioned and committed individuals. CED organizations and leaders must take proactive steps to avoid the burnout of key volunteers and staff, a problem identified by three of four project communities. In many First Nations communities in British Columbia, for example, individual leaders are overburdened with community affairs, policy debates with senior governments, treaty negotiations, and other responsibilities.

One strategy for avoiding burnout and mentoring future leaders is to establish recruitment and succession plans and to continue seeking ways to support volunteers and staff in their efforts. Leadership training has become a key component of community and organizational development. Savoie (2000) further suggests leaves of absence and the provision of staff backup.

Civic Engagement

For CED to be successful, residents must be well informed and active in their communities. Rural areas tend to rely heavily on volunteer efforts and community spirit for development (Reed and Paulson 1990), particularly during the initial stages of a CED project. Once a project has successfully secured financing, organizations may reduce the demand for volunteers by creating salaried positions. However, before the CED process is able to secure paid positions (and even then projects may continue to require volunteer support), the availability of surplus time for households and individuals is important. "Surplus time" refers to the ability of residents to engage in development activities over and above the demands of subsistence livelihood. This has a significant impact on the levels of citizen involvement within CED (Friedmann 1992).

Communities must also assess the health and well-being of their population and consider implications for the ability of local residents to be actively involved in their communities. In marginalized communities, individuals cut off from mainstream society may suffer from low self-esteem and low confidence in their ability to change the circumstances of their lives and their community. In these circumstances, civic engagement and leadership may be hard to achieve. CED processes must strive to empower participants by applying principles such as inclusiveness, understanding, and respect for differences and cultural sensitivity:

> There is a long history of top-down development work and community division in Bella Coola. A number of projects initiated in Bella Coola have failed. This was said to be because of the lasting effects of the trauma caused by residential schools and conditions of dependency. These effects include a loss of self-esteem and a lack of a sense of responsibility. Strategies for gradually overcoming health and social problems in the community have been outlined in the Nuxalk Nation's Healing Plan, which promotes an attitude shift towards positive thinking, motivation and self-reliance. (Nuxalk Selection Survey)

Entrepreneurial Spirit

CED requires the creativity and opportunistic spirit of entrepreneurialism, a mix of both skill and attitude. A community rich in entrepreneurial spirit is more likely to be rich in development ideas and full of people willing to work towards putting them into practice. This fosters adaptation and community resilience.

Entrepreneurialism in CED generally applies to small and medium-sized enterprises (SMEs). Small business has become an increasingly important contributor to our provincial and national economies, accounting for 98 percent of all businesses and more than 40 percent of all jobs in the province (Dufour et al. 1998). Small business development is particularly important for community economies that are experiencing significant transition or restructuring. Small businesses offer the opportunity to diversify both within and outside of traditional economic sectors.

Both private businesses and community enterprises require entrepreneurial spirit. Furthermore, both traditional and social/nonprofit enterprises require entrepreneurial spirit. These initiatives all require risk management, innovation, and operational management skills to ensure their viability. Entrepreneurship is both an individual and a collective endeavour. Providing the foundation for entrepreneurial development demands a proactive approach composed of building individual skills, creating the necessary regulatory and infrastructural environment, and clearly articulating a CED vision from which to assess the feasibility and desirability of different enterprise options.

Flora and Flora (1991) cite a variety of characteristics that are common to entrepreneurial communities. These attributes may help to facilitate individual and community enterprise development:

- acceptance of controversy
- a school system that emphasizes scholarly endeavours
- surplus wealth in the community
- a propensity to invest locally
- a willingness to raise and invest taxes in infrastructure
- an ability to see themselves as part of a regional community, to work with adjacent communities and with senior levels of government
- flexible, dispersed community leadership

Community-based services that support entrepreneurial development, such as community loan funds, technical assistance, business libraries, and mentoring programs, are also important.

As seen in our discussion of staples theory, the shift for rural communities from resource dependency to a more entrepreneurial economy is often

difficult. Economic dependency on resource extraction may foster a community culture that discourages innovation and change. Psychological dependency in workers and local leaders on the business cycles of the industry,
for example, may create an environment of economic "addiction," as bust
cycles are endured with the expectation of a boom cycle to follow (Freudenburg 1992). The dynamics of the welfare state may also inhibit entrepreneurial spirit. Social assistance may postpone or reduce the local initiative
necessary to engage in entrepreneurial endeavours. These externally driven
inhibitors of entrepreneurial spirit highlight the necessity of having a complementary or enabling environment based upon both internal and external
forces, attitudes, and policies. The market does not create entrepreneurs.

Labour Force

Finally, the existence of a healthy and available labour force helps facilitate
development projects, particularly job-creation initiatives. Some sources (e.g.,
Economic Council of Canada 1990) suggest that greater success can be
achieved with a labour force that has a substantial number of workers between the ages of twenty-five and forty-four. Out-migration of younger residents who are about to enter or have recently entered the labour force is
seen as one of the negative consequences of unemployment and a barrier to
future development efforts. Groups of all ages and physical capacity are
capable of implementing successful CED initiatives. CED planners must seek
to include youth under the age of twenty-five and seniors in their planning
process and project efforts.

Social Capital

"Social capacity" refers to the collective characteristics of the individuals
within a community and the quality of their social interactions, as well as
the groups of community members that have organized themselves around
a common goal or set of shared values (for example, community organizations; see Table A2). An increasingly common way to describe the role of
social organization in development activities is to refer to a community's
"social capital." Social capital comprises the formal and informal features of
social organization within a community, such as networks, trust, and norms
of behaviour that facilitate collective action. Social capital forms the bonds
of community by turning the "I" of individualism into the "we" of community (Putnam 1995; Wilson 1997; Roseland 1998). Contrary to the indi-
vidualist assumptions of the market, social capital reflects the propensity of
individuals to address mutual needs and pursue common interests, influenced by a sense of common good, belonging, and custom (Wilson 1997).

Researchers now recognize that social capital, long relegated to the fringes
of consideration for economic development, plays important functions in
the productivity and viability of business and CED ventures (Mitchell et al.

2001). Marshall et al. (2001) further suggest that income and social inequality, leading to declines in social capital and social cohesion, are connected to human health outcomes. Unfortunately, we are recognizing the significance of social capital during a time of intense social and economic polarization associated with the impacts of resource scarcity, competition, restructuring, and globalization, which may diminish opportunities for social capital development in certain locales (Longo 1998).

The success factors listed below are building blocks of social capital at the community level. The principles and practice of CED draw heavily on the bonds of social capital. Collective planning and action, based upon local knowledge and directed towards locally appropriate development needs and opportunities, require a foundation of social capital. CED also exists in a symbiotic relationship with social capital, as CED activities will contribute to the formation and strengthening of existing or new social capital relationships.

Sense of Community

A sense of community is a collective awareness of what makes a community unique. It is a sense and celebration of shared history, experiences, belonging, and identity (Stacey and Needham 1993). Flora and Flora (1991) refer to it as "community solidarity." A strong collective sense of community contributes to resident commitment to place, which in turn enhances community resilience. A sense of community identity is directly relevant to CED activities such as tourism, museums, and other cultural initiatives, and helps to sustain all forms of collective endeavour. A sense of community can also contribute to a desire to look after one another and seek ways to address issues of poverty and income disparity, often through the informal economy. Studies have shown that communities with one dominant culture or religion have a greater capacity for planning and implementing community solutions, but that common concern for community survival can be a sufficient common bond for community consciousness (Savoie 2000).

One of the stumbling blocks that CED must overcome is the possible negative connotation attached to the word "community." A sense of community may be fostered in such a way that particular interests or groups are narrowly defined as constituting the community, to the exclusion of others. Attention to the principles of CED, such broad-based participation, and equity, will help guide a community-building process towards more empowering and enabling definitions of community.

Community-Based Organizations

The basic form of community organization for empowering individuals and mobilizing their capacities is the association. Associations provide a middle ground between the state and individuals that enables citizen-based synergy to contribute to the construction of a civil society. Associations can amplify the gifts, talents, and skills of individual community members, connecting them more intimately with specific issues and the political process at community and extra-community levels (McKnight 1995).

Community-based economic development organizations (CEDOs), one particular type of association, offer a number of advantages to the development process by virtue of their organizational structure and location within the communities in which they operate. First, CEDOs are generally small organizations. Their small size fosters organizational flexibility and responsiveness, thereby enabling them to respond quickly to opportunities and crises. Second, CEDOs are responsive to and knowledgeable of particular local issues and cultures. Local knowledge may enhance the appropriateness of the development response. Third, their location within the community and their association with community residents may foster a sense of community ownership over projects and programs. Such ownership may not be associated with projects that are imposed by or managed from the top down, thereby impeding their successful integration into the communities.

Community Development Corporations (CDCs), discussed in Chapter 5 and through the Salmon Arm example in Chapter 7, are one form of CED organization. The presence of a range of CED-related organizations – CDCs, community kitchens, health centres, community loan funds, and so on – is an indication of experience and CED capacity within a community. The existence of organizations that are concerned with social, economic, and environmental matters is a good indication that a community takes each of these issues into consideration, as are public debates within each of these realms (Bryant 1999).

Organizational development in CED is important for four main reasons: recognition, ownership, credibility, and accountability. First, an organization gives a development idea or cause greater recognition in the community. Increased levels of community awareness and support can be fostered through the organization. Second, an organization helps to facilitate collective ownership over a project or planning process. Housing a CED activity in an organization rather than keeping it an individual or ad hoc project can create greater levels of commitment and synergy in planning and implementation. Third, the formal structure of a group through a constitution, board of directors, and/or legal registration will lend credibility to an organization and it purpose, which is often important for mobilizing financial resources. Finally, organizational structure helps to build accountability into the CED process. Organizations help to facilitate collective responsibility through their management structure and other legal requirements. Responsibility within organizations builds the credibility of individual and collective action within a community, addressing the accountability gap referred to in Chapter 5. Despite these advantages, in some communities and groups or for some issues, an informal (versus incorporated) association or network may be more appropriate, particularly in the early stages of a project or process or in communities suspicious of bureaucracy and formal systems of this nature.

Participation, Planning, and Cooperation

In addition to having experience with the formation of CED-related organizations, communities may have other forms of CED experience, such as planning and consultation processes, that provide them with background and learning that will help them with future CED endeavours. As discussed in Chapter 5, effective planning processes are key to successful CED organizations and their initiatives. The presence of an ongoing community planning process and/or CED strategy is an indication of a commitment to and experience with strategic planning. The lack of a formal CED plan may mean that efforts are not organized or coordinated, or that there is little activity taking place. Communities may also choose, however, not to put a formal plan into effect.

While proper planning and process design are important, Edwards (1994, 15) points out that without some tangible results and immediate rewards, the required momentum for pursuing a desired direction may be lost. Edwards, chair of a local round table organization in Central Canada, believes that "the right mix of rousing old-fashioned, sleeves-up community work and what some would consider unproductive high-brow visioning" is required.

An important contributor to the success of most CED organizations and efforts is the ability to overcome conflicts. Conflict can both enhance and limit community participation in CED. To approach conflict positively, participants must recognize that communities are not composed of homogeneous, harmonious individuals and groups. Open conflicts can be a healthy part of community life. Conflicts may allow otherwise unresolved and unspoken tensions to surface and be resolved rather than fester and persist. Unless conflict is explicitly acknowledged and discussed, the "partnership" model introduced below may stigmatize conflict as a purely negative force and therefore feed into the homogenizing forces and market bias of society (Poncelet 2001). Chapter 7 provides examples of how conflict has influenced CED, both positively and negatively, in the case communities.

In order to make conflict a constructive force in CED, four conditions must be considered. First, the nature of the conflict must be understood. Conflicts may be based on difficulties with communication, information, or process/organizational structure. Other forms of conflict include those that are based on relationships, interests, or values (Markey and Vodden 2003). It is difficult, if not impossible, to resolve conflicts that are not understood by the proponents. Second, the CED process must be transparent. Transparency enables the broader community to follow the CED process, including discussions over conflict. Transparency builds trust and provides opportunities for challenging assumptions and plans, which may lead to more informed and balanced decisions. Third, the planning process must create real opportunities for participation by community members and organizations. Communities must consider different forms of participation to encourage the full range of interests that may be affected by CED decisions to come forward with their ideas and opinions. Finally, a community must have strong leadership. It takes strength and courage to invite into a process those with whom we disagree, in the belief that a better, more lasting outcome may be the result. It should also be noted that there are both good and bad times for engaging full-scale community participation through open public meetings, particularly when planners expect heated debate. Open meetings must be skillfully facilitated and well prepared in order to encourage participation and to vent disagreements in a civil and constructive manner. Processes may require more subtle forms of communication, participation, and conflict resolution under certain circumstances.

Building and maintaining partnerships and communication links (or networks) among community members, associations, local and external firms, government agencies, and other communities is yet another ingredient in CED success (Bryant 1999). Recent literature points to the importance of networks in local development, suggesting that communities may be differentiated in their development success by virtue of their local, regional, national, and international connections. By building strong local and external alliances, CEDOs can create what Birner and Wittmer (2001) term "political capital," increasing their ability to access resources (including funding and information) and influence change. Research on rural development within the European Union further emphasizes the role of both local governance and internal and external networks among actors in economic performance outcomes (Bryden and Hart 2003; Terluin and Post 2003).

Partnerships with governments and other outside agencies are critical in most initiatives (MacNeil 1994), but the significance of local alliances should not be overlooked. New partnerships within a community can broaden an initiative's base of public support, provide access to a wider range of local resources, and/or result in more efficient use of resources through sharing and collaboration (Vodden 1997). Lack of communication and coordination between local groups is a major barrier to CED success (Savoie 2000).

In many cases, cooperation among communities in a shared geographic region is also an important contributor to CED success (Young and Charland 1992). For example, we will illustrate the importance of cooperation between neighbouring Aboriginal and municipal communities in the case communities (see Chapter 7). Competition between communities for benefits such as business location, tourism dollars, economic development, and infrastructure funding may represent a significant barrier to local and regional development efforts. Community-to-community information sharing and partnerships can help increase the reach and influence of CED. Provincial and national CED networks formed in the late 1990s, such as the Coastal Community Network in BC and the Canadian CED Network, have helped to facilitate this process. In this regard, one workshop participant argued the following: "Rural communities must work cooperatively, set their own agenda, share information, and learn lessons from each other, particularly successful examples – what works" (Workshop Four Report).

MacNeil (1994) identifies trust and time as important factors in successful CED partnerships. Fallows (1989) expands on the notion of trust as a key factor in a community's ability to foster collaborative efforts, suggesting that the "radius of trust" in an area be used as an indicator of this ability. The area within which people are considered "one's own kind" and where the boundary of "outsider" is drawn defines the radius of trust. In some communities the radius of trust does not even reach beyond the community's own borders, while in others it may encompass an entire geographic region (Flora and Flora 1991).

Partnerships bring new resources, influence, and ideas to a project, but they are challenging and have both costs and benefits. They are positive in terms of accessing or sharing resources, avoiding potential conflicts, and building participation. If they are pursued from a position of weakness, however, they may ultimately be harmful to the objectives of the CED process. Kretzman and McKnight (1993) warn that seeking partnerships from a position of weakness or disorganization may be detrimental to the capacity of community-based organizations and their members. The development of partnerships should proceed only under mutually beneficial conditions. Issues of power imbalances between partnering organizations must be addressed. For example, the issue of forming an equitable partnership was raised by the Nuxalk in the early stages of the project:

> We readily admit that the challenge in achieving this [CED] currently outstrips community capacity. We need to build partnerships with those who have the expertise generally to help communities diagnose their needs and act upon this assessment ... We need to transfer expertise from outside consultants to community members. We wish to participate in the project to gain awareness, information, skills and control over the future ... We need to know how to partner and on what terms. We need partners who do not act on self-interest but on shared goals and visions. (Bella Coola Selection Survey)

Finally, participation of a wide range of community members in planning and implementing a CED initiative is also reflective of a community's social capital. Participatory development has many benefits, including access to new and creative ideas and a proactive approach to handling potential conflicts between community interests. Broad-based public participation and support requires a personal sense of citizenship along with appropriate leadership with experience in and a commitment to public participation. Reliance on a local elite or reluctance on the part of those elite to share power is a common leadership pitfall. Bryant (1995a) warns that the control of bottom-up processes by local elites may be equally or more oppressive than top-down governing. He argues, in fact, that local agency is now a driving force in uneven development, and that the relative power of local actors in the development process must be considered along with the tendency of powerful actors to steer the process in a manner that protects their interests.

Partnerships between community organizations can facilitate more widespread involvement and support, connecting their individual members. Ensuring that public input is given serious consideration and working to either minimize or subsidize expenses can also help address participation barriers. Finally, all process participants must be willing to genuinely listen to one another and engage in meaningful dialogue. In the following chapters, we will discuss the methods employed in the project and in the project communities to engage community participation.

Economic Capital

Understanding the economic capacity of a community from a CED perspective requires a holistic and historically sensitive interpretation of the local economy. CED seeks to address the impacts of staples development and other forms of traditional economic development by reducing dependency on external forces such as commodity markets; expanding the economic multiplier through increased local control and economic diversity; recognizing the contributions of the informal economy; and understanding and comparing the costs and benefits of various economic opportunities over the long term (see Table A3). Analysis of the following success factors will help create a clearer, more holistic picture of a local economy and a community's capacity to improve it from a CED perspective.

Economic Health

A healthy local economy is more conducive to promoting CED. While CED is often used in response to economic uncertainty or weakness, the long-term nature of the capacity-building process limits the effectiveness of CED as a crisis response tool. Building on the arguments of Chapter 5, there are advantages to implementing CED when economic conditions are relatively stable. First, a healthy economy is more attractive to investment. The paradox of economic instability is that you need investment to build the local economy. If conditions of instability exist, when development is most urgently needed, investors will be reluctant to place capital in the community. Local capital is also more readily available when there is no immediate threat of an economic downturn. Further, a healthy local economy can create an environment that is more conducive to planning, particularly the kind of inclusive planning that is essential to the success of CED. That said, the social and human aspects of capacity building through CED might certainly be beneficial in creating a more positive environment for confronting instability in the short term. We define economic health below using the variables of diversity, adaptability, the health of local businesses, and sustainability.

Diversity
Long-term economic stability for a community, much like stability in the natural environment, is dependent upon diversity. Economic diversity means that communities are able to weather downturns in any one sector of the economy by relying on economic contributions made in other areas. Reliance on one or only a few sources of employment and income ignores the complexity of local and global economies now defined by constant and fast-paced change. Diversity in a local economy provides communities with much-needed flexibility and security, which are necessary in order to maintain a positive climate for internal and external investment and the commitment of the local population to a community. Unfortunately, as described in Chapter 3, a lack of diversity is a characteristic of staples economies, and thus of many rural BC communities.

The presence or lack of economic diversification may influence a community's willingness to engage in CED planning. Dependency often leads to fears that other economic efforts may threaten the status quo and undermine a dominant employer. Those who continue to benefit from past production models and relationships may be slow to adopt change or may simply resist it.

New sectors such as tourism and locally dependent small business are likely to be supportive of a more diversified approach to development. A commitment to economic diversification demands a commitment to the sharing of power and resources found within and around a community. Those in positions of leadership must seek to understand the costs, benefits, and potential of a community economy and each of its individual sectors. Communities will continue to encounter economic fluctuations linked to such factors as market volatility and technological change. Economic diversification will not guarantee economic prosperity, but it will contribute to long-term community resilience and the potential for viable CED initiatives that will help maximize the health and potential of a community.

Local Control

Closely linked to the factor of economic diversity is local control. Local control over a diverse economy represents a prime condition for economic stability and minimal dependency. Local control over the economy may also help create a more positive enabling environment for CED initiatives. Externally based employers may openly discourage CED efforts and economic diversification in an attempt to maintain their control of the local labour force, economy, and resources.

Local companies are more likely to wait out hard times than threaten to leave the community. Owners that have greater ties to the community and therefore a greater stake in community well-being encounter a broader range of social and economic pressures in their business decision making, summarized as greater accountability to and responsibility for the community (Gill and Reed 1997; Halseth 1998). However, the size of local businesses may also affect local stability. Larger, externally controlled companies may be better able to weather systemic fluctuations in the performance of the broader economy (we saw this rationale used for the transfer of forestry harvesting rights from smaller to larger corporate entities). Offsetting concerns regarding market durability within a CED context creates opportunities to link smaller community-based companies through joint marketing, collaborative project bids, and cooperative structures more generally. There are many mechanisms for scaling up the economic weight and reach of community-based enterprises.

Sustainability

The goal of CED is long-term community resilience. Resilience is jeopardized if the economic base of a community does not adhere to the principles of sustainability. The get-rich-quick approach of the postwar North American economy must be tempered by a new understanding of economic sustainability and quality of life. Harvesting local resources in an ecologically destructive manner, beyond the natural carrying capacity of the environment, or engaging in production that is ecologically destructive due to pollution, ultimately detracts from the future economic and social viability of communities. Understanding how various economic activities affect the environment and are integrated, directly or indirectly, with other economic activities is an important step for CED and a fundamental requirement of sustainability.

Informal Economy

An element of the local economy that is often overlooked is the so-called informal economy. Unpaid personal, voluntary, and household activity makes up the informal economy. Like the formal, monetary economy, the informal economy is a source of wealth and well-being in a community. Informal economic activities can also support the formal economy and buffer its vagaries. Ommer and Sinclair (1996, 7) describe this situation in Newfoundland as an "accordion-like pattern whereby informal economic activities could substitute for the formal, when the economy was in crisis" and add that Newfoundland's "mercantile economies relied upon the flexibility of the community and its seasonal exploitation of a range of resources to support an otherwise too expensive labour force." Informal economic activities such as barter, gift giving, and harvesting of wild food products are thought to be more common in rural than in urban areas.

For example, in Bella Coola, and among the Nuxalk in particular, the local economy relies heavily on non-market activities – such as lumber for construction, fuel, carving for artistic and ceremonial purposes, medicines, and foodstuff. Similarly, members of the Upper St'at'imc communities identified high levels of informal economic activity as one of their strongest forms of economic capacity, along with their young and growing populations. Salmon Arm residents also noted the informal economy among their community's economic assets (particularly a strong rate of local volunteerism).

The provision of services such as elder and child care by friends and family has not only an economic value (such as the market rate of a service provider) but also social and cultural significance. The informal economy can strengthen ties of kinship and friendship and provide a role for community members (such as the chronically unemployed) who may not otherwise feel they are contributing. Informal economic transactions can also have environmental benefits, such as helping to manage economic demand by reducing the need for paid products and services.

Community volunteer work is an important aspect of the formal and informal economy. Approximately one in seven Canadian jobs, employing 1.8 million people, is generated by the voluntary sector. One reason for the sector's continuing growth is cutbacks in government funding and the increasing delegation of services to nonprofit organizations, largely supported by volunteerism and community goodwill (Quarter 1992).

Access to Capital

Inadequate access to capital is among the most frequently cited barriers to the success of CED initiatives. These initiatives often do not meet the requirements of mainstream capital sources, in part because economic returns are not the sole objective and may therefore be lower than those from alternative investments. Further, those involved may be considered a credit risk (such as low-income and unemployed citizens).

Public funding is also limited, particularly in an era of fiscal restraint and deficit reduction. Further, the tax base of economically depressed communities perhaps most in need of CED is often depleted. Local governments have little funds to invest in the CED process. Competition for limited funds among community organizations and reliance on government dollars are often outcomes of this situation:

> We're all after the same dollar ... We need to look beyond government funding. (Workshop Four Report)

> Our community has tried to diversify with little or no funds from provincial or federal governments, but our municipal government is strapped. (South Cariboo resident)

In response to these challenges, CED practitioners have devised a range of alternative forms of financing. These include micro-enterprise lending and borrowing circles, community loan funds, government loan guarantees to ensure security for loan fund investors, credit unions, community banks, and business development centres/Community Futures programs (Smith 1999). By obtaining funds from such sources, it is often possible to acquire additional capital from conventional sources (Jackson and Pierce 1990).

Other CED financing mechanisms include share purchases, joint ventures, venture capital, socially and environmentally responsible investment, and other equity arrangements, such as worker ownership (Meeker-Lowry 1988; Dauncey 1988; Van Gils 2000). Forgivable grants can also be obtained from foundations and corporate donors. Churches, rotary clubs, and labour funds have also been known to contribute. Despite this range of options, obtaining project financing remains a significant CED challenge, particularly in communities where few of these mechanisms exist.

Location and Infrastructure
Location is an important factor to consider when assessing and designing realistic and locally appropriate CED strategies. Location, in terms of distance from markets, may influence the viability of export-oriented business ventures and reliance on local demand. Proximity to other communities and retail/business centres can provide market opportunities but may also be detrimental to the local retail sector in rural communities due to competition for limited local spending dollars (Harden 1960; Johansen and Fuguitt 1973).

While location has traditionally been an important factor in economic development success, John and colleagues (1989) found that location had little to do with changes in employment in US farm states throughout the early 1980s. The exception to this consisted of cases where proximity permitted commuters to bring dollars into the community by working outside. Communications technology has revolutionized rural access to outside markets. Successes in rural CED have been achieved in areas such as Internet marketing of rural products and services and the establishment of call centres. Urban growth in technology-based development continues to outdo that of rural areas, however, exacerbating the rural/urban divide (Polese and Shearmur 2002). Educational levels and access to communications infrastructure are among the challenges.

Remoteness affects not only market access but also the costs of production. Millerd and Nichol (1994) cite inadequate infrastructure (such as sewage and water systems, power, waste disposal) to support industrial development, high inventory costs, long waits for supply orders, delayed product delivery times, and higher transportation costs as disadvantages for BC manufacturers operating in remote locations. Infrastructure such as plants, public facilities, water and sanitation, transportation, and communications infrastructure represents a community's material or physical capital (Roseland 1999). It is important for a community to carefully assess its capacity to attract and develop business investment and consider what types of businesses the community can realistically support. There is a danger of communities overburdening themselves with heavy debt loads to finance infrastructure projects that fail to attract or foster the anticipated development, thereby representing a drain on the local economy.

Amenities

Amenities refer to local nontransportable goods or services that contribute to the pleasant characteristics of a place and satisfy both psychological and physical needs (Power 1996a; Coppack 1988). Cultural and service-based amenities contribute to the local economy in three ways. First, the presence of amenity services decreases the amount of leakage in a local economy and may attract regional or tourist expenditures. Second, cultural and service amenities add to the attractiveness of a community, helping to foster a greater commitment to place. Third, amenities make communities desirable places to invest in, or locate to, for outside interests: "Amenities exert an influence on the location, structure, and rate of economic growth. One of the ways this influence occurs is through the so-called people-first-then-jobs mechanism, in which households move to (or stay in) an area – triggering the development of businesses seeking to take advantage of the household's labour supply and consumptive demand" (Courant et al. 1997, 63).

Another strength of an amenity-rich economy is a strong connection with varying demographic interests. For example, communities across BC are beginning to recognize the growing economic value and clout of retirees, who are drawn to amenity-rich areas. Retirees with adequate resources are in a position to seek out areas that offer a unique combination of climate, beauty, and culture. Flora and Flora (1991) caution, however, that recruiting elderly residents may result in an expansion of low-paying service employment and resistance to tax increases for social services that may help attract and retain younger families. Younger families tend to look for a quality educational system and recreational facilities/amenities. Arts and culture are also significant components of the overall amenities found in communities and regions.

Ecological amenities will be discussed below.

Ecological Capital

Ecological health and diversity are critical indicators of community capacity and stability. Economic connections to ecological health include the viability of natural resource stocks harvested for commercial or subsistence purposes, as well as ecological amenities that attract residents and visitors. There are also non-anthropocentric values associated with ecological health that CED must consider, such as biodiversity and basic ecological functioning. Finally, a sense of stewardship, or respect for and responsible use of the natural environment, among local residents helps to protect and enhance various ecological capital values (see Table A4).

CED adheres to environmental sustainability through two fundamental principles. First, local control increases the likelihood that local resources and the environment will be treated with respect for values beyond short-term economic gain. While providing no guarantee of sustainability, local rootedness adds additional personal and interpersonal dimensions to economic decision making. These connections may then broaden what might have been a more narrow economic rationale, thereby creating the space to consider longer-term questions of sustainability. Second, the legacy of E.F. Schumacher is interwoven into the theory and practice of CED through the phrase "small is beautiful." When economic opportunities that are smaller in scale are pursued, the degree of ecological impact tends to be reduced. It is often easier to correct practices to suit sustainable environmental management objectives (practice adaptive management) when development occurs at a more moderate scale. The counter-argument that a certain scale of economic activity is necessary in order to afford pollution abatement technology and other environmental management efforts also deserves consideration, however. Regional cooperation and other coalition arrangements can help facilitate larger-scale environmentally sustainable production processes.

As the world faces increasing scarcity of intact ecosystems and healthy, productive, livable environments, opportunities and the need for CED will increase. The need to manage resources sustainably and at a scale that is conducive to sustainability yet economically viable will open numerous opportunities for CED in the future. The following success factors outline five broad areas of ecological capital: a general assessment of ecological health; status of natural resource stocks and sustainable productivist harvesting of forest, fish, and agricultural resources; post-productivist use of ecological resources defined by amenity values; and acts of environmental stewardship and responsibility practised by community organizations and governments.

Ecosystem Health

While we may tend to think of assets that can be directly used to support CED activities when assessing a community's CED capacity, the category of ecological capacity is an excellent example of the whole being greater than the sum of its parts. Communities depend on healthy natural environments for their long-term health and survival. Long-term community stability relies on a livable environment that provides ecological services such as continuing supplies of clean air and water. A degraded environment will offer limited economic opportunities and foster little commitment to place among local residents. Further, the availability of harvestable natural resources and ecological amenities relies ultimately on the overall health of the ecosystems of which these individual components are a part. The impacts of natural resource extraction on ecosystem health must also be taken into account. In Lillooet, for example, community members voiced concerns about the impacts of logging practices on ecosystem functions such as water levels, wildlife, and slope stability (creating avalanche danger).

CED and Natural Resources

Many communities, particularly in rural areas, derive a significant portion of their employment and income (in cash and goods) from the extraction of natural resources. Sustaining such an economy in the long term depends upon the availability and sustainable use of healthy resource stocks or "natural capital": "Natural capital refers to any stock of natural assets that yields a flow of valuable goods and services into the future ... The forest or fish stock is natural capital and sustainable harvest is 'natural income'" (Roseland 1998, 5). An assessment of a community's capacity for CED based on natural resource extraction must consider both the current availability and productivity of harvestable natural resources and the sustainability of resource management and extraction practices (an indication of future resource availability). Once again, staples dependency has taken its toll on natural capital, in the form of both resource exhaustion and attitudes of resourcism, introduced in Chapter 3.

Incorporating sustainable natural resource extraction into CED activities involves a variety of prerequisites. First, local control must exert influence in the process of resource management (Vodden 1999; Gunter 2000). This can be accomplished in a variety of ways, ranging from outright community control to co-management arrangements (see Chapter 8).

Second, a variety of local interests must be involved in management decisions. Broadening management participation in the community can have numerous advantages, including increased capacity and understanding within the community concerning natural resource management and the quality of the surrounding environment, proactive identification of potential conflicts associated with resource extraction, and awareness of a range of benefits and uses of the environment. Broadening the use of natural resources will contribute to diversification and community building. For example:

> Communities recognize the value of participation in resolving existing and potential resource conflicts. The prospect of an Upper St'at'imc Nation forestry joint venture has proven complicated and caused some concern in the community. The Nation generally is seeking to lower the AAC in the TSA, and to implement ecosystem-based forest management. Other potential partners would like to uphold the current AAC to maintain local jobs. To date, there has been little community participation in the planning of this initiative. Representatives recognize the time has come now for the LTC to engage the public in meaningful discussions regarding this bold move and to address concerns that the joint venture might compromise values of the Upper St'at'imc Nation – and if so, how to mediate different interests. (Workshop Four Report)

Third, CED-directed resource management must consider both economic and non-economic values associated with land and water. For example, forestry activities must consider the impact of extraction on fish habitat and tourism, biodiversity, and culturally or spiritually significant areas and uses (Schwindt and Heaps 1996).

Fourth, the interest, not capital, of renewable resources must be the deciding factor when setting harvesting rates. Harvesting beyond this level will either reduce the potential economic benefits or increase the restoration costs of resource-related economic activities for future generations. Living off the interest, or "natural income," of the earth also motivates the development of value-added activities, that is, making the most of the resources that are harvested: "Natural resources have been exploited for over 100 years here. The cream has been skimmed, now the principal is being taken" (100 Mile House Capacity Survey).

Ecological Amenities

Ecologically-based amenity values include such factors as visual aesthetics, recreational opportunities, and the overall quality of life that stems from a healthy natural environment surrounding and within a community. Ecological integrity carries intrinsic value linked to such factors as biodiversity. However, as noted by Gale and colleagues (1999), these values are difficult to quantify and compare with the economic contributions of resource use and extraction. As a result, decision makers have found it easier to dismiss ecological or intrinsic values associated with the environment. That said, researchers are increasingly recognizing the economic value of such amenities, offering protection for ecologically based values while providing planners and developers with tangible economic rationales for the preservation or sustainable use of natural resources (Rasker and Alexander 1997). As discussed earlier, the economic benefits of amenities include the attraction of new residents, businesses, and tourism dollars (Coopers and Lybrand 1996).

Ecologically based amenities are also significant because of their connection to trends in the economy. Continued increases in the service sector, high technology, tourism, and retirement incomes represent economic interests that may compete, directly or indirectly, with traditional resource extraction interests. Amenities have the potential to attract these interests and thus contribute significantly to economic health and diversity. Communities must now weigh the costs and benefits of land-use decisions much more carefully in a world moving towards scarcity of intact ecological areas and in an economy no longer dominated by specialization in resource extraction.

Stewardship

The manner in which residents treat their environment is an indication of a community's commitment to long-term stability. If ecological degradation defines how a community and its businesses interact with the environment, then efforts devoted to CED strategies aimed at long-term community stability are likely to be unsuccessful. That said, CED can be used to foster environmental awareness and responsibility, or a sense of "stewardship," among residents, businesses, and local leaders. The now-popular term "stewardship" embodies the concept of a reciprocal relationship between human communities and the natural environment, where humans act not as manipulators of the land but as dependents and caretakers simultaneously, who share a common responsibility for leaving the environment in a healthy condition for future generations and other species.

In this vein, watershed and stream stewardship groups in BC, for example, have taken responsibility for monitoring pollution, cleaning up habitat damage due to past logging practices, monitoring and enhancing fish populations, and other activities. The benefits of their activities include not only ecological restoration and protection but, in the shorter term, community building, public education, skills development, job creation, improved information for resource management, and an increased sense of pride and hope for the future (Vodden and Gunter 1999). Stewardship activities can range from political action (such as lobbying for protection) to habitat restoration or activities that reduce the environmental impact of day-to-day life (such as energy conservation and waste reduction).

Conclusion: Future Directions

CED is complex and can be difficult to measure. The conditions for success presented above are daunting, particularly for communities with little prior CED experience. Further, even if these conditions are met, success cannot be guaranteed. External factors such as shifts in international markets, government policy, environmental conditions, or demographics (among countless others) influence community futures (Hussmann 1993). It is doubtful that any community has all of the conditions for success outlined above. However, many of the conditions can be created through CED strategies designed specifically to build capacity – to enhance a community's ability to launch and maintain successful CED initiatives. In fact, the process of planning and implementing any CED initiative is itself a capacity-building effort.

The absence of a number of the conditions listed above, therefore, should not be viewed necessarily as a recipe for failure. When assessing community capacity, answering two questions helps to assess the importance of missing conditions:

- How critical are these conditions to the success of CED in the community or to the specific CED initiative being considered?
- Is it likely that the community can create or acquire those conditions that are absent (or weak) but considered important?

Consequently, such a checklist of "ideal conditions" also serves as an assessment of training and development needs and can help communities decide which CED strategies to pursue.

Critical to the usefulness of the success factor framework is ongoing monitoring and consistent checking against the values and priorities of the community. CED is a long-term process requiring a long-term commitment. A key aspect of measuring success in CED is being able to determine whether or not CED efforts are having any impact on the four areas of community capital over time. Monitoring changes in these indicators will help foster accountability within the CED process, build credibility, ensure that success is recognized and rewarded, and draw attention to lessons learned.

This chapter and the appendix are intended to serve as a tool to be used in practice and as a basis for further discussion and research. We compiled the list of success factors based on previous works and our project experience. These indicators of success must be further tested and refined. The findings of the Forest Communities project indicate the need for more work on matters such as weighing the relative importance of each factor and finding ways of better incorporating cultural elements of community capacity and local and traditional knowledge into the assessment process. We must also wrestle with the issue of complexity. The framework, with twenty-four factors and over 140 possible indicators (see Appendix), is complex and may be overly time-consuming to implement for some communities, depending on the availability of indicators and previous planning experience. It is also important to modify the key elements of the framework to suit each community's needs and circumstances. Simplifying the process of community assessment and monitoring remains a challenge for CED researchers and practitioners.

Communities, CED practitioners, and researchers alike need to continue to reflect on appropriate indicators of community capacity for CED; the degree to which these factors of success may vary from one situation to another; how agreed-upon indicators can best be measured, evaluated, and presented; and, finally, how capacity assessment results can be applied in the selection of appropriate strategies for community renewal and resilience. The application of the success factor framework in the project resulted in an opportunity for reflection on existing initiatives and the identification of new initiatives compatible with the strengths and values of the community. Chapter 7 highlights a variety of CED strategies undertaken by the communities in an effort to diversify their local economies and enhance community capital.

7
The Community Economic Development Process

Community economic development (CED) is a process that offers new ways to conceptualize and plan economic development to target specific local needs and assets. The development benefits derived from a sense of place and a local commitment to the survival and prosperity of a community offer a counterbalance to the challenges associated with attempting to implement a more sustainable approach to development, often in economically depressed areas. It is through an effective planning and development process that CED practitioners may harness and nurture the positive forces of community for the purposes of economic development.

As mentioned earlier, a common criticism of CED is that it is too unruly. The purpose of this chapter is to illustrate that through the implementation of a specific local planning process, it is possible to view CED as a more predictable and orderly – less unruly, albeit still diverse – development response. In addition, it is through an adherence to a planning process that CED may expand its influence throughout the local economy. By integrating the principles of CED into a development process (including meaningful participation, equity, and sustainable development), CED moves beyond being a random and isolated form of job creation to being part of a broader process to create revitalized and viable local economies.

This chapter outlines the basic features of the CED planning process used in the Forest Communities project. We will discuss the central components of the CED planning process, including organizational structure, strategic planning, and capacity assessment. In each section, we will provide community examples to animate the theoretical presentation of CED in Chapter 5. Following the presentation of the CED process, we will provide an analysis of our experiences related to three themes: *preparing* for the CED process, *managing* the CED process, and *sustaining* the CED process.

The CED Process

In Chapter 5, we outlined the basic features of the strategic planning process. For the purposes of the Forest Communities project, an adaptation of this classic strategic planning model provided a suitable framework with which to guide the process, selectively explore components of complex community conditions, integrate local knowledge, and facilitate community and researcher learning. Following a review of different strategic planning methods, we designed a simple six-step model to facilitate the research and development process. Community-based workshops served to apply and adapt the model to the different community environments.

It is important to note that the development process at the community level is far more dynamic than our linear model suggests. Numerous ideas for development initiatives lie dormant in every community and the opportunity to exploit them may simply be a serendipitous event, such as responding to a new government program or policy or the timely commitment of an energized local actor. Communities may begin midway through the process and return later to earlier steps. As a collaborative team, however, we moved relatively methodically through the planning process in an attempt to instill a stronger institutionalized CED presence in each community, not simply a one-time, short-term funding-dependent event.

THE CED PROCESS MODEL

1. Process Initiation
The focus of this first step is to set clear objectives and to build community awareness and participation. Community organizing techniques and the formation of a CED working group, committee or development organization may help to initiate and guide the planning process. Important questions during step 1 include:

- Why launch a CED process? What is the problem or opportunity to be addressed?
- Who should be involved in the CED process?
- Who will manage the CED process?

2. Community Data Collection
The data collection phase is critical to the CED process to ensure that decisions are being made using quality information. Gathering community-based information and using it as a foundation for planning may raise a

new awareness of community economic potential. The CED process may also draw upon information not previously considered in development planning. Important questions during step 2 include:

- What information do we need?
- What information is available?
- How can we use local knowledge?
- How should we collect the information we require?

3. Data Analysis

We include a specific data analysis phase given the importance of using community-based information correctly. Sharing and understanding community-based information and applying it to a development context is necessary for the identification of appropriate strategy options. This information is later vital for step 4. Important questions during step 3 include:

- What does our research tell us?
- How can we share this information with the community?

4. CED Planning

If CED planning is initiated at this point in the planning process it is more likely that decisions will be made from an informed position. Community visioning, asset and need assessments, and project identification will benefit from the informed position fostered by the previous steps. It is necessary at this point to review a broad variety of CED strategies, which may not be common knowledge among planning participants. Important questions during step 4 include:

- What are our community assets?
- What are our community needs?
- What do we want for our community: vision and goals?
- What is the range of strategy options available to us?
- Given what we know about our community, which strategies are best suited to our situation?

5. Implementation

The steps up to this point will foster a degree of confidence among planning participants that they are making informed decisions. The next steps require action. It is important at this point in the process to select strategies that will not overwhelm the capacity of the community, and if necessary, to select smaller projects or engage in partnerships to build experience for future initiatives. Important questions during step 5 include:

- What is the capacity of the community to implement various projects?
- What resources are required to implement projects?
- Do partnership options exist that would enhance the likelihood of project success?
- What is our plan to implement the strategies and projects – what steps will be taken, where, by whom, and when?

6. Monitor, Reflect, and Revise

Having an evaluation plan in place will increase the confidence of planning participants. Monitoring the community and the strategies implemented will enable the community to adapt to changing circumstances, identify barriers to successful implementation as they are occurring, and assess whether or not local efforts are making a difference to the well-being of the community. Important questions during step 6 include:

- How will we know if our process has been successful?
- How can we measure and communicate our success?
- How can we improve and sustain the CED process?

A number of projects involving different community members and initiated independently of our work were in progress throughout the duration of the Forest Communities project. Our intent was to introduce the six-step model as a planning example and as a capacity-building exercise for the communities. Communities could then apply the knowledge and tools fostered by the project to both current and future development efforts taking place in the community. In addition, people who were involved in other planning processes were generally able to integrate their activities with the larger community process, thereby creating important planning networks at the local level.

Organizational Structure

The first act of a CED process is to provide some form of organizational structure within which to house local efforts. Chapter 6 presented different models of community-based economic development organizations (CEDOs), but less formal committee or network relationships may suffice under certain conditions. In some cases, as illustrated by Salmon Arm and the Nuxalk, a single coordinator position represents a starting point. It is particularly important to pay attention to the principle of participation at this stage in the process. Understanding the social dynamics of a community is essential in order to appropriately represent various community interests. It is not necessary for every CED initiative to represent all community interests, but a broader planning process should account for and include a diverse representation of community sectors. Quality leadership of the CED process is critical at this early stage. The following case examples illustrate how the project communities dealt with the issues of organization in order to facilitate the CED process.

The Salmon Arm Economic Development Corporation

The Salmon Arm Economic Development Corporation (SAEDC) serves as a hub for the local development process in Salmon Arm. The activities of a single organization are obviously not representative of every local development effort or nuance taking place in a large community. However, the degree to which the SAEDC is closely networked with other community-based organizations and with local and senior levels of government makes possible a reasonably comprehensive view of the local development process in Salmon Arm.

The start of a community-based local development process in Salmon Arm is largely credited to the mayor who first came to office in the 1996 municipal election, in which the community economy was a key issue. Items raised in campaign debates included concern about the stagnation of the community economy, increased economic competition from surrounding communities, and the extent to which locals and external investors perceived Salmon Arm to be "anti-development" and therefore experiencing economic decline.

Upon being elected, the mayor and council moved quickly to initiate a local development agenda. A number of factors contributed to the ultimate selection and creation of a Salmon Arm economic development agency. First, local officials recognized that, at the time, local governments had no legislated mandate to conduct economic development. Local governments are not completely without direct and persuasive power, however. As one local government official in Salmon Arm states: "In local government, we know what the problems are but we don't necessarily have the resources."

Local officials recognized that local governments could play a variety of facilitative roles in the promotion of local development. First, local governments can direct funding to a development agency, thereby providing some certainty to the local development process and allowing for additional financial leveraging. Second, the mayor and council can encourage individuals to become involved in their community, thereby promoting participation and directing human capital towards the local development process. Third, local governments can set a positive tone for development, creating an atmosphere of confidence, which may help motivate participation and encourage local investment.

A second contributing factor leading to a more community-based development approach was the perception that Salmon Arm was not receiving adequate development services from the Columbia-Shuswap Regional District (CSRD). Salmon Arm was the largest contributor to the regional district prior to the election, and interviewees expressed a common feeling that the community was receiving little in the way of direct benefits from the various regional initiatives.

Third, the CSRD and surrounding regions contain a number of communities with established, successful local development agencies. Revelstoke and Kamloops each have what are largely regarded as highly effective local development corporations. Each of these organizations provided important advice to Salmon Arm during the start-up of the SAEDC.

Finally, the hiring of an economic development coordinator advanced the community-based development approach in Salmon Arm. The coordinator was semi-retired and had a strong business background. The early approach adopted by the coordinator mirrored a corporate approach to planning and development, as illustrated by an early promotional document entitled *Salmon Arm Inc.*, which depicted the mayor as the chief executive officer of Salmon Arm and the councillors as members of the board. The purpose of the document was to instill a sense of responsibility in the local council concerning matters of economic development.

The business tone being adopted to further local development activities created some controversy in the community. An aggressive corporatist approach exacerbated an inherent pro-development/anti-development rift in the community. However, an extensive process of community research and participation eventually tempered the parameters of a narrow business model.

An initial community survey conducted by the development coordinator revealed some of the concerns present in the community, which provided the motivation necessary to forge a community-based approach to development:

Salmon Arm is at a critical point of its economic development. Former lack of economic direction, objectives and strategies combined with recent Government cutbacks, both Provincial and Federal, have left Salmon Arm in a very tenuous position.

With a heavy reliance on existing core industries (forestry, tourism, retirement) and the subsequent downsizing, redistribution of, and new Government controls affecting these core industries there is now an urgent, critical need for development of a decisive and shared industrial economic direction and appropriate initiative for Salmon Arm.

Proactive economic planning and initiatives will determine the long-term future prosperity of Salmon Arm. (SAEDC 1997)

A summary of key challenges facing Salmon Arm reveals some of the concerns raised within the community concerning its development future (SAEDC 1997):

- forest dependency
- government regulations
- world markets and increased competition
- erosion of "community fabric" due to government cuts
- poor quality of recreation facilities
- becoming a satellite community to other centres: Kamloops, Kelowna, Vernon
- lack of educational opportunities
- youth out-migration
- declining health care resources
- government cutbacks for service delivery
- lack of local representation in either level of government

The combination of consultations with other communities, local research into the state of Salmon Arm itself, and the dynamics of the individuals involved in promoting economic development in the community each contributed to the decision to establish the Salmon Arm Economic Development Corporation as a means of taking greater control over the local economy. The following section describes the form and functions of the organization, and reviews the strategic planning process adopted by the SAEDC to facilitate CED in the community.

The SAEDC was incorporated in 1997. It is a nonprofit entity administered by a board of directors and a community advisory board (Figure 7.1).

Mission
The SAEDC lists nine mission statements that guide its role in the community (SAEDC 2001):

1   to develop strategic initiatives to foster CED and employment opportunities in and about the District of Salmon Arm
2   to provide information and assistance to individuals and businesses wishing to relocate to or invest in Salmon Arm, including referrals to appropriate community organizations and government agencies
3   to seek input from individuals and groups interested in CED issues and to sponsor meetings and events to encourage public discussion of those issues
4   to sponsor local employment initiatives in conjunction with municipal and regional planning authorities

Figure 7.1

Salmon Arm Economic Development Corporation (SAEDC) organizational chart

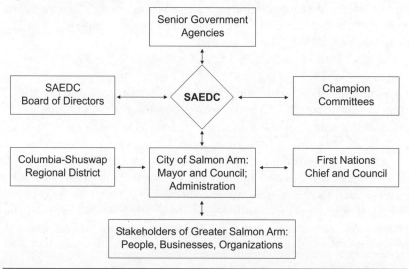

5   to attend meetings, trade shows, and other events to represent the interests of Salmon Arm and to promote Salmon Arm as a desirable location in which to live and do business
6   to provide assistance to projects and activities initiated by volunteer and not-for-profit community organizations, and to provide information on community projects and events of interest to Salmon Arm residents
7   to secure the confidence of the residents of Salmon Arm that it will, to the extent possible, represent the interests of all members of the community in matters relating to economic development
8   to be supportive of economic development initiatives that are being proposed by First Nations groups outside the District of Salmon Arm when possible
9   to be cognizant of issues relating to development and the potential impact on the environment

Structure

The structure of the SAEDC consists of an economic development officer (EDO), three part-time staff members, a board of directors, and a series of project-based volunteers associated with the advisory council. The structure of the organization is important for clarifying roles and responsibilities, and for providing the SAEDC with the resources necessary to play an active and far-reaching role in the community: "We started with a very sound organizational basis. Three things were of particular importance: first, the municipal government was kept at arm's length (i.e., they could be board members, but not voting members). Second, we tried to make the board as representative of the community as possible. And third, board positions were given a fixed term of service – this has been a real strength of the organization" (Salmon Arm resident).

The EDO position is the most critical role in the organization. As mentioned above, the first EDO brought significant business experience to the organization, which proved highly effective during the start-up and initial strategic planning stages. The Economic Development Association of BC awarded the EDO honourable mention for Economic Developer of the Year in 2000, and bestowed the top award the following year, providing external recognition of the early success of the organization.

We worked with the EDO and the community working group to design a strategic plan for the community and to implement specific action plans. The EDO evinced a very positive attitude in communications with the broader community, seeking to raise the confidence of the community concerning its ability to initiate change:

> "It's all about attitude: we can and we will," says EDO. (*Salmon Arm Observer,* 26 May 1999)

> EDO: Communities today are becoming more aware that if they are to continue to prosper, maintain and enhance their lifestyle, economic and environmental well being, they must initiate and generate their own solutions to the challenges facing them. Community based economic development will allow Salmon Arm to be proactive in planning and establishing its own vitality and future prosperity, creating an environment that will in the end see new businesses, industry, culture, and residences here. (*Shuswap Sun,* 12 February 1998)

Residents recount, however, how many in the community were concerned with the pace of implementation and the extent to which the organization modelled a business approach to development. One local councillor questioned the representativeness of the SAEDC and asked critical questions pertaining to the approach being adopted by the organization, mainly:

- What is our philosophy of "economic development"?
- Are we looking for outside business to come here?
- Are we concentrating on maintaining and strengthening our existing business?
- Are we a combination of both approaches?
- What other approaches are there?

The EDO did eventually adapt the tone and structure of the organization to fit a more community-based development approach. Interviewees give credit to the SAEDC for improving the networking and working relationships between various community organizations concerned with development issues.

Second, the SAEDC board serves important visioning, fundraising, and representative functions. Through revolving board participation, the SAEDC is able to include various interests in the community, including seniors, the business community, socially oriented organizations, the arts community, the unemployed, and so on. Given the range of activities adopted by the SAEDC, staff and board members realize that the board must play an active role in the organization. Without active board involvement, the burden on the EDO would be too great.

Third, volunteers in the community play critical roles in the planning and implementation functions of the SAEDC. A local advisory council consisting of a wide cross-section of organizational representatives and interests in the community also form subcommittees to explore various aspects of development in the community. For example, community volunteers, called "champions," participated in a variety of committees when designing the initial strategic plan for the community. Committee topics included:

- entrance signage
- Web page design
- storefront economic development
- infrastructure and industrial park
- district bylaw review
- new business development
- existing business support and development
- media relations
- tourism
- funding
- education

Interviewees consider volunteerism a significant asset in Salmon Arm. There is a large volunteer base in the community, as exemplified by the extent of advisory committee functions. The influx of new residents to the community is also cited as a good source of community volunteers with good skills and a willingness to become involved in community issues.

Finally, community residents cite the relationship between the SAEDC and the local government as a key reason for the SAEDC's organizational success. The municipal council has played a critical role in providing support for the organization; moreover, it has been willing to let go of the process to allow the organization to establish its own legitimacy and direction in the community:

> The corporation exists at arm's length from the local government. There are times when you are in sync with local government and times when you are not – you need the distance to maintain the integrity of the organization. (Local resident)

> The local government is often more politically driven than community driven. You need to be able to look at community issues more objectively. (Local resident)

COMMUNITY VOICE: BOB MCKAY, FORMER EXECUTIVE DIRECTOR, SAEDC

Community-based Development in Salmon Arm: Looking Back on the Process

What I wish to share with you in this short piece is the idea that community-based economic development, if done correctly, will have significant influence and impact on the prosperity and well-being of any community.

The approach we have taken in Salmon Arm is somewhat "grassroots" – meaning starting from fundamentals and advancing from there. It is an approach that is, in many cases, ignored or downplayed by municipal or local governments, provincial, state, or federal governments, and even citizens of communities when they are attempting to engage in establishing economic policies or economic initiatives.

A definition of community-based economic development is: "A process whereby citizens can actively engage in planning, assisting, and investing in the development of a more locally controlled economy, one that is aimed at meeting the needs of local people, particularly those who have been most marginalized by the economic system such as welfare recipients, youth, the unemployed, and minorities." In other words, it's a process whereby communities can initiate and generate their own solutions to their common economic problems and thereby build long-term capacity and foster the integration of economic, social, and environmental objectives. Community economic development entails having the right attitude, drive, and willingness to become involved, and willingness to try something new. These qualities are important not only in a business context but also in a community economic development perspective if you are going to succeed. And from my perspective, change and success cannot be realized unless all stakeholders – you, me, neighbours, agencies, etc. – share a common sense of understanding and a proactive positive attitude. Attitude is everything.

Having said all this, let me take you back a few years ago to 1997, on a journey when we started to create change in Salmon Arm from a *can't* attitude to a *can do* proactive attitude. The focus was: how do we enrich our community to be prosperous and healthy?

My simple belief is that if you have a healthy economy, which stimulates and creates healthy and prosperous businesses, you will probably have healthy families, and a healthy community. I would also emphasize that by embarking on a journey or a process, you must realize that you do not change the complexities of human behaviours or issues in your community or understandings of the issues overnight.

To give you an idea of some of the serious problems we were facing in 1997, they included:

- There were leadership and administrative issues.
- Our sole dependency on forestry was at risk.
- Tourism was at risk.
- Our retail sector was struggling.
- Additional facilities and programs for retirement were needed.
- Health care erosion was one of the largest concerns to growth.
- Our local college enrollment was dropping.
- Government cutbacks and downloading (without funding) was a reality.

To compound this, we had a series of dysfunctional activities – protectionism, power struggles, organizational and agency relationship problems (chamber of commerce, DIA [Downtown Improvement Association], tourism, Regional EDC) – and problems in civic administration, which was perceived by many as being bureaucratic, nonresponsive, difficult to approach, and development-unfriendly.

So, as you can imagine, this was affecting attitudes and perceptions across all sectors of our community and economy, reflecting directly on perceived or real "individual successes," "business successes," and "lifestyle successes." The community by many people's standards was somewhat unhealthy from an economic, socio-economic, and environmental perspective.

It was realized that changes had to occur. We had to change and change quickly not only for the short-term and long-term prosperity and health of our community and its citizens and culture but also for our overall social and economic well-being.

We needed a plan. We needed results – not more studies and research programs to accompany the others that had piled up on shelves, gathering dust. We also recognized very quickly that we needed community participation and buy-in, and we required all community citizens and agencies to work together to develop and implement change. In business terms, if you do not have every sector and employee of your business pulling towards a common goal or vision, you probably will not succeed or be as successful as you could otherwise be. In effect, this meant changing mindsets and attitudes through leadership.

Now, ironically, the citizens of Salmon Arm (whom I refer to as the ultimate stakeholders of the community) recognized many of our difficulties, as they were feeling the direct impacts of our community's situation. They voted in a totally new council and mayor and sent a strong message that said: we want changes – we are not happy with the direction in which we are headed. The timing and situation was right to be proactive and forward-thinking, and to begin a process of addressing the community's discontent. We had a new council and they needed direction and help as well.

At this point, I became more involved and took the community through a series of community exercises known in business as directional planning (not strategic or operational but directional), where you identify your willed future, you blatantly assess your existing realities, you then determine what the issues really are, and finally you try to determine the initiatives you must now undertake to achieve your willed future. We also recognized the inherent strength within our community through its citizens, businesses, and organizations. I certainly did not have all the answers, nor did anyone else. We determined early in the journey (process) that we needed community participation, knowledge, wisdom, and so on, and we needed to harness that energy. We also determined that we needed leaders (or what we eventually called "community champions"). Who is a champion? Someone who has a passion, desire, drive, tenacity, respect, and leadership for something and is willing to make things happen through the leadership of others.

It was recognized that we needed some form of structure at arm's length from political or vested-interest organizations to truly represent the social, economic, and environmental interests of the community from youth to seniors. Through a series of evaluations and discussions across Canada and with learned experts in the field of economic development, we formed the Salmon Arm Economic Development Corporation in November 1997. I was hired to form the organization and formulate an action plan.

We established a board of directors from key sectors of our community's pillars (professional, education, seniors, youth, retail, industry, district, arts and culture, etc.), formed a twenty-one member advisory committee made up of all community agencies, movers and shakers, youth, seniors, chambers, regional, and so on, and got underway. From the output of the directional planning exercise we went through earlier, we determined our action plan and approach to the undertaking ahead of us. We also determined that we needed partners and money. We needed someone to share the vision, and invest in the risk. We drafted a detailed business proposal and letter to the federal government (Human Resources Development Canada [HRDC]) detailing our goals, aspirations, and benefits in employment if we were successful, and sold the concept as a three-year journey in community-based economic development.

We adopted and encouraged the practice that community-based economic development is a process or a journey whereby communities can initiate and generate their own solutions to their common problems and foster the integration of economic, social, and environmental objectives. In simple terms, we suggested driving towards becoming more self-reliant.

From this we established our mandate as a corporation, which is to:

- support and provide services to existing businesses and to assist local business expansion and retention
- attract new businesses and industry development to our community
- engage in advocacy
- engage in strategic planning

Through a series of public forums we developed the Salmon Arm Economic Development Strategy and set our priorities as to what we could achieve given the money and resources available.

We also formed strategic partnerships with Simon Fraser University, HRDC (for community projects), the District of Salmon Arm, and the Adams Lake First Nation, and cooperative partnerships with other communities (namely, Sicamous), with whom we shared everything we were doing, and community agencies such as the chamber [of commerce], DIA, Community Futures, and so on. We wanted everyone to feel part of the process and part of the solution and part of the successes – breaking down barriers, obtaining focus, changing attitudes – celebrating successes no matter how small or large.

We set up a financing plan and arrangement whereby HRDC would finance 100 percent of the corporation in year one, two-thirds in year two, and one-third in year three, with the district contributing the remaining in each with a new budget and set of goals and achievable outcomes.

We also set out to demonstrate immediate tangible results that stakeholders (citizens and businesses of our community) could see and benefit from. We therefore put a number of public/private partnerships together on community projects that put people to work, produced community benefit, and were environmentally and socially friendly. The partners were nonprofit organizations that could provide materials; HRDC, which could supply training and labour; and the district, which could supply machinery, materials, and civic projects that were beyond their current mandate to accomplish.

What this approach did was to provide immediate community benefit while the EDC and others were working on other long-term, more complex issues. We also set up a series of "Champion Task Forces" driven by individuals who had an interest and passion to accomplish certain tasks. These champions put teams of community citizens together to solve or highlight issues and then resolve them. For example:

- The former mayor and a team he established did a detailed evaluation and generated recommendations to council on needed bylaw changes to make our community more business/development-friendly.
- There is a champion and team looking at our entrance signage.
- There are several committees: Website, Industrial Park, New Business Development, and Tourism.

We accounted for about a thousand individuals in our community who were now involved one way or another. As a result, attitudes were changing, and then the successes started to surface. For example:

- New industries started to move into Salmon Arm.
- New businesses started to appear (Wendy's, Boston Pizza, new Chrysler dealership, three new hotels, major manufacturer, etc.).
- Upgrades to storefronts and malls were initiated (community pride).
- Major business expansions began taking place in manufacturing, retail, and service industries.
- New initiatives were started (tourism, partnering, Adams Lake Indian Band Developments, etc.).
- Twin-sheet multiplex development was initiated.
- A new RCMP building was constructed.
- New infrastructure initiatives were started.
- The Business Enhancement and Retention (BEaR) program and Shuswap Construction Industry Program (SCIP) were started.

Successes building on successes – momentum beginning – creativity happening! It all sounds so easy, but it is a tremendous amount of work, with lots of frustration at times, wondering how to do or tackle something, but we persevered.

If you're going to be successful, you must involve the community as a whole, recognize and deal with the economic, social, and environmental issues and aspirations (the makeup of any community), and provide leadership, encouragement, and willingness to understand and listen. You must keep an open mind and be willing to entertain new ideas and business/growth options and opportunities.

I do not believe in top down but rather bottom up. For some elected officials, this is difficult to do. Many feel they are giving up power, control, authority, and so on. They're not! What is being done is enabling your community to become involved and mould its future with full buy-in by the people of the community who will ultimately make it happen. If you can create a sense of buy-in, community pride, volunteerism, and positive reinforced attitudes, anything is possible.

The Nuxalk CED Coordinator

The Nuxalk Nation was a challenging community to work with, given the combined influences of distance separating the university from the community and the degree of inter- and intra-community fragmentation and conflict in the region at the time of the project. These factors hindered the establishment of the participatory research process and limited the effectiveness of CED planning. In reality, we quickly realized that the community was at a pre-planning stage and needed to address issues of community conflict resolution and healing, which we will discuss in greater detail in Chapter 8.

Progress towards the implementation of a CED process did occur in June 1999, however, when the band leadership hired a CED coordinator as a focal point for local development efforts. Commentators from within the community attribute the creation of this position largely to the expanded awareness of CED resulting from the Forest Communities project. For example, one participant writes: "Before SFU came along, the Nuxalk Nation tried to fill its need for a coordinator with financial officers, like accountants. They saw the challenge of development mainly as getting almost any kind of business to set up and hire Nuxalk people. After the exposure to CED through the Forest Communities project, a broader concept of CED developed and this set the stage for hiring a CED specialist rather than an accountant."

The purpose behind the creation of a CED position within the Nuxalk Nation was to provide a sustained presence for CED in the community. The coordinator was to provide an impetus for further training, the creation of a strategic plan for pursuing various development opportunities, and the creation of a "capacity group" to serve as a core of trained individuals to facilitate development activities.

A variety of entrepreneurial projects did surface during the tenure of the coordinator, and there was a renewed emphasis on development on the part of the band council and the community, who were very eager to "get something going." The efforts of the CED coordinator also helped to facilitate dialogue and cooperation with other non-Aboriginal organizations and neighbouring communities (see Chapter 8). Although the capacity group built up around the coordinator position did not receive additional funding, continued technical assistance, a dedication to reflection on how to move forward, and a change in leadership have led to a continued emphasis on CED planning.

Despite these ultimate breakthroughs, however, the difficulties associated with the CED planning process and the variable level of support granted to the CED coordinator raise interesting questions about the clash between the theory of a participatory CED process and the reality of complex community dynamics. In the following community voice section, Norman Dale, a former Administrator for the Oweekeno-Kitasoo-Nuxalk Tribal Council, reflects on some of the barriers to implementing CED in Aboriginal communities and how the model of CED may clash with cultural circumstances and practices.

COMMUNITY VOICE: NORMAN DALE, FORMER OWEEKENO-KITASOO-NUXALK TRIBAL COUNCIL ADMINISTRATOR

The Undiscussable in Native Community Economic Development

Introduction

> People can differ on verifiable, measurable facts. They can also differ about pragmatic, or realistic non-confirmable ones ... But the most difficult of all are those concealed, painful experiences, which some people cannot relate, and others try to devalue. (Bar-On 1999, 288)

I am writing here about what is not discussed. I mean this in two ways. One is that this essay brings up unusual, some might say eccentric, ways of looking at Native community economic development (CED) and its restraints. But more specifically, the focus here is on the impact of there being much that happens in Native organizations (including CED ones) that is undiscussable. Often members cannot or will not discuss matters that most any sympathetic outsider would say they had better talk about. Bad things appear to happen as a result of undiscussability, bad at least if the economic progress of the community and the success of projects it undertakes are highly valued.

Open discussion, rich in constructive criticism and shared reflections about problems, including internal and personal ones, is a tenet of CED practice. Community gatherings are a taken-for-granted mainstay of planning process. The ubiquity in CED exercises of so-called SWOT analysis (assessing community strengths, weaknesses, opportunities, and threats) attests to the good currency of the idea that community members need to get together and speak openly, not only of their strong points and of the external situation but also of their own failings. But what if this norm is unheeded, perhaps can't be heeded? What if the most contentious and important factors and incidents affecting and reflecting a First Nation's CED experience are inherently undiscussable? And why might that be?

This essay relates a small case, embedded in one First Nation's economic struggle, where the undiscussable was left so. I focus on the dynamics that seem to me to make undiscussability so rampant in the Native economic development experience.

The argument is not advanced as having general validity across all Native communities. I am especially loath to make any such claim, having spent enough time with a limited but diverse set of British Columbia First Nations to understand how easy it is to slip from generalization to cultural stereotyping. The differences between First Nations are usually more interesting than any generalities adduced by a decidedly non-Aboriginal "participant-observer" like me.

Instead, I say what I have to say here as no more or less than one person's incomplete story, based on fragments of direct experience. Readers should use their common sense and inference – as would anyone listening to something that is "just a story." The ideas may resonate with their experiences or, by contrast, astound or even offend. Either way and in between, the result will, hopefully, be more than a moment's reflection on the much larger unfinished narrative about how Native economies develop, or fail to.

The Story of a Recurrent CED "Error"

The Nuxalk are a Nation of approximately 1,400 whose modern core community is Bella Coola on British Columbia's Central Coast. With the falldown in Central Coast forestry and the decline and economic concentration of the BC commercial salmon fishery – the two leading sectors in which Nuxalk had come to participate – the community has reached a point where an estimated 80 percent or more are on social assistance. It would be natural to expect that every resource, including skilled professional help, which might offer a way forward would be openly embraced.

Let me begin my story at the epilogue, in mid-2002, when the Chief and Council were recruiting a new economic development officer (EDO). There has been a vacancy for over a year. The job advertisement and prepared interview questions carry a familiar upbeat tone – the need for a self-starter with, among other sterling attributes, impressive communication skills. These skills, the detailed prospectus elaborates, should include being able to engage in a clear and candid exchange of ideas with political leadership, other staff, the Native community at large, and other actors significant to economic development.

This was the third such competition in just over four years. The EDO hired in 1998 was an accountant of non-Native ancestry who stayed for only about ten months of what was to have been a two-year contract. The job description had been quite similar back in 1998, and yet the EDO almost from the outset had been given a working situation and assignments that seemed starkly different from "as advertised." Despite being a senior professional, the EDO had been assigned a small cubicle lacking in any privacy, just outside the larger and private office of the band's financial clerk. Almost from the start of the position, this EDO had been given an almost daily changing set of priorities, much of which involved correction of old bookkeeping problems. Very little work time was left, or was assigned any priority by Chief and Council, to engage in matters more usually seen as the core activities of community economic development.

Some years before, the band had built an ice plant for fishermen as an economic venture. By 1998 the plant faced serious technological and financial problems. The EDO was told to "make a plan" to correct this. However, the band did not have the files and financial records of the plant. These were in the hands of a financial advisor who had been given control over the enterprise some years before and with whom, by 1998, the then Chief and Council had, at best, strained relations. Despite this, the former advisor kept on making decisions about the plant and retained the relevant records, ones essential to making that plan. The EDO was unable to obtain the information needed to take stock of the situation, and the Chief and Council preferred to ignore rather than confront the former advisor.

As time passed, the EDO grew discouraged with what to him appeared to be predestined ineffectiveness in doing what he had been hired to do. His lack of office privacy concerned him, especially since alone among the senior staff he was never allowed keys to access the building in off-hours. He confided in me that he felt this was "racial," as he was the only non-Native working in the main office. Discussions with the Band Manager and Chief Councillor seemed to never get to the point, although there were frequent vague agreements to "do something" about the former financial advisor who controlled the ice plant. But this did not happen.

Eventually, as the EDO had expected, elected councillors began to complain, although never to the EDO's face, that he was "not doing what he was asked." Relations grew strained and the EDO resigned. The community was informed that the departure was for "health reasons," effectively sealing off any further discussion on why an initially promising professional employee resigned.

A short few weeks later, a competition was held and a search committee was directed to put a high priority on finding a band member as a replacement. Indeed, a Nuxalk was successful and brought on as the new EDO in mid-1999. He was someone who had worked for other BC Nations on economic development as well as on a much earlier Nuxalk-owned enterprise, a fish-smoking facility that had failed after generating wide community enthusiasm. Even as he was hired, some elected councillors were already privately disclosing their misgivings, for now they had a "devil they knew" and, contrary to the old aphorism, found this just as worrying as the "devil" they hadn't! More by innuendo than assertion, the failed fish-smoking business was seen as a portent of problems that had not had time to start.

This new EDO was successful in rapidly obtaining a federal grant aimed at developing enterprises based on off-reserve natural resources (the BC Capacity Initiative). But very soon, unrealistically so and perhaps because he was being "watched closely" in memory of the defunct fish smoker, he came under pressure to produce jobs. Perhaps because of this, he used the federal grant almost entirely for wages to hire a four-person staff of very inexperienced workers. After all, what kind of economic development would it be if, instead, the new EDO had lured away employed people from the Nation's limited talent pool?

The EDO's team spent many months training and setting up a pleasant workspace in a disused former youth centre, one built decades before with funds from an earlier generation of nonrenewable short-term grants. A visitor to the office of the EDO and his team would almost always find them busily "work-shopping" away with flipcharts of flow diagrams and lists of strategic priorities draping the walls. Several successful efforts were made to have nationally known CED practitioners from far and wide come in and do training and seminars. Meanwhile, however, the same scenario was playing out with regard to the still uneconomic band-owned ice plant, the project that had gotten the earlier EDO in trouble with Chief and Council.

As with his predecessor, the second EDO was expected to take over the reins and files of the facility from the former financial advisor, and thereby come up with a forward-looking renewal plan. Again, information was asked of the advisor, but the request was ignored. The EDO, whose dislike for open confrontation was now culturally similar to that of Chief and Council, basically acquiesced to this and turned back to the almost full-time job of watching over his four-person team. On the surface, this failure to do something about the ice plant fulfilled the dire expectation of those who had doubted that this EDO would do anything more effective than with the long-closed fish smoker.

Once again, Chief and Council began to blame the EDO for not accomplishing anything tangible. Despite the deteriorating relationship between the EDO and his political bosses – during which I was often confided in by both – at no time did the EDO and Council sit down and, together, try trace the roots of this persistent problem. After fifteen months, the second EDO was laid off. The official reason given was that economic development grant money had run out.

Twice, then, within two years the fate of two very different EDOs had run quite a similar course, with these common features: not really getting down to substantive CED work; in particular, not being able to come to grips with what Chief and Council deemed a priority economic development file (the "ice plant"); and, in my view, most significantly, no frank communication about "the problem" that might have led to shared diagnosis and problem solving. A Chief and Council who represented and cared deeply about their community failed sequentially to retain two very good people and then obscured why this had twice happened with substitute public explanations ("health problems," no more grant money).

In recounting this tale, I have erred well on the side of discretion but would guess that my description has already resonated, at a general level, with not at all infrequent experiences of those involved in Native (and non-Native) community economic development. My purpose in bringing up these not very remarkable events – ones which brush on sensitive matters such as possible discrimination, political lack of responsibility, allowing personal likes and dislikes to govern what is done and not on the job, etc. – is not to lead us into further discussion of such micro dynamics and dysfunctions. Rather, I wish to call attention to the broader issue of *undiscussability.*

The Undiscussable as an Organizational Barrier
The idea of undiscussability as a serious impediment to organizational effectiveness was developed in the frameworks of Argyris and Schön in a series of widely studied books and articles that go back almost three decades (Argyris 1980; Argyris and Schön 1974, 1978, 1996). The general task they set themselves as researchers and practitioners was to understand and thereby help to change forces that inhibit inquiry into organizational error or failure. As they worked at the levels of individuals, groups, and whole organizations, they examined "theories-in-use," the ways that organizational actors recurrently behave in response to troubling conditions. Argyris and Schön

found a pervasive pattern. Even in ostensibly sophisticated and successful organizations, a veritable dark undergrowth of unspoken issues lurked, painstakingly hidden not only from organizational development (OD) consultants but, more importantly, by members of the organization *from themselves.*

> From the viewpoint of an individual living in such a system, the organizational world is apt to be particularly frustrating and constraining ... A staff member ... is likely to experience a world of ambiguity in which he fears punishment for delays he does not see as his responsibility; fears the consensus-seeking process and fears to avoid it; feels he does not understand the problem; and believes he cannot raise with others the issue of the factors that have put in this situation ... These are situations that meet the conditions Gregory Bateson has laid down for "double binds" ... namely, one is caught in a no win game and the rules of the game are undiscussable. (Argyris and Schön 1978, 118)

Although the analogy to Freudian psychotherapeutic constructs of repression, sublimation, and transference springs to mind, Argyris and Schön were not interested in the psycho-dynamics of undiscussability. For them, the potentially constructive route was to explore with the members of the organization the fine structure of "defensive routines" and well-hidden errors that made significant problems – ones universally understood throughout the organization as root causes of dysfunction – undiscussable. Thereby the undiscussable would no longer be so and, presumably, the organization could learn and do better.

Argyris and Schön's work and that of an ever-growing school working within their paradigm implies a ubiquitous phenomenon day by day of elaborate organizational cover-ups. In bringing up this phenomenon, it is not my intention to be one of those "borrowers" who lifts some fashionable if esoteric management science construct and drops it down into a hitherto unfamiliar context. Given the superfluity of OD fad books and argot, that could be a full-time job. But it is my inference, based on about a decade of working in Native CED, that there are some characteristics particularly common or exaggerated in First Nations' organizational culture that make undiscussability a far more widespread and potent factor than in most other contexts.

Undiscussability in a Culture of Blame

One of my reasons for saying this has to do with what seems to be endemic blaming within Native communities, including their CED apparatuses. I must hurriedly add that this "blame game," commonly linked to the medium of gossip and whisper campaigns, is a ubiquitous human experience and has particularly occupied and concerned organizational analysts (Dubnick 1996). Intricate webs of blaming and scapegoating are seen, not necessarily most often but most clearly in all sorts of smaller and traditional social groups. Yet having worked and lived in both First Nations communities and within other communities and organizations, I feel that it is palpably more prevalent and destructive in the former.

This difference of degree has been explained, sometimes by First Nations people themselves, as an outgrowth of the residential school system. In those repressive, indeed dangerous, places, the argument runs, the best survival strategy was to offload responsibility for any of the myriad offences for which the masters each day sought an object of punishment. Squirming away from responsibility by blaming someone else makes good sense when the consequences are utterly disproportionate to the violation. In general, blame flourishes in an atmosphere of crisis and intimidation. Vann Spruill vividly captures the suspension of thoughtful causal reasoning under duress (1989, 259): "If an adolescent pokes a gun in my ribs on Conti Street in New Orleans, I certainly will blame him. I will not care in the least about his motives, or his unfortunate past. At that moment I will not even care about him as a human being. Only if he were neutralized, no immediate threat, could I afford to be more objective, conceivably even compassionate. Nevertheless, my regression to blaming, provided it was temporary, would have been immediately adaptive."

Another related reason for the ostensible prevalence of blaming in First Nations communities is the self-hatred and inevitable culpability that the dominant white society imposed. Bluntly put, individuals were taught in and out of a residential schools to hate themselves – the Indian was a problem, no, *the* problem. Even in today's seemingly post-colonial context, it remains all too easy to do exactly what one always saw authority figures do, day in and day out: blame Natives for whatever is amiss. Immersed in a dominant society, living under a system that Dyck (1991) aptly calls "coercive tutelage," is it not likely that one comes to emulate the apparently successful masters?

Finally, it has been suggested that blaming and its preferred means of conveyance, "gossip," are inherent in the communication patterns of small, traditional communities everywhere. In fact, these mechanisms work reasonably well when the limited size and distance a negative message must travel makes it quite certain that the alleged wrongdoer will quickly hear of his offence and be able to take corrective action without losing face (as he would if confronted openly by the aggrieved party).

Whatever the reasons, the implications of this high incidence of blaming for undiscussability are direct. From the blamed person's standpoint, it goes: "I expect to be charged, behind my back, for even the smallest of blunders, whether I made them or not. Therefore, keeping individual or collective errors in the shadows of the unspoken makes good sense."

Native Social Discourse versus Discussability

The second and broader reason the undiscussable is likely to be more influential in Native than other communities has to do with norms and taboos around what we of more Anglo culture call candour, frankness, and so on. Here, the theory and practice of popular mainstream interventions, ranging from alternative facilitation guidebooks (e.g., Kaner 1996; Health Canada 1998) to Argyris and Schön's and countless other forms of "dialogue-centred" problem solving (Senge et al. 1994) may not be of clear application and relevance.

In most frameworks for community self-help, a very central normative position is reserved for open, interpersonal discourse. Without highly participative and candid face-to-face discussions, communities cannot grapple with the complexity of understanding their economic world and changing it. In recent years, there has been what could be called the candour revolution. A plethora of loosely related methods of personal, organizational, and social change have come to the fore, most of which share a foundational and seemingly unassailable value – being as clear and open as possible to debate with others about one's "diagnosis" of problems (e.g., Senge et al. 1994). It is argued that we must "get at" the deep underlying sources of personal or organizational difficulty, and in the group setting this means open and frank dialogue, or "collective reality-testing" (Etzioni 1968)

Most versions of community economic development share this ideal, and for good reason – if a community is unable to surface and freely discuss what went wrong on matters small and large in its economic initiatives, the organization will, as Santayana's famed aphorism suggests, be condemned to relive the past and its mistakes.

Well and good, but now embed this imperative within a community where open critical commentary is taboo. There is fairly wide agreement in ethnographies of many traditional societies, and certainly of those along the Pacific Northwest Coast of North America, that discourse does not proceed according to such norms (Hymes 1962; Boelscher 1988). Indeed, direct discussion, especially of potentially contentious matters, is often proscribed.

Commonly this is described as a cultural aversion to confrontation, nothing more complicated than that. I have heard this quite often, especially about the Nation in which I work, that they are just "very nice people" and therefore wish not to offend. But this is an oversimplification that could lead to a misguided "solution" – a facilitator who just keeps trying harder to encourage assertiveness and assure workshop participants that "it's safe here to disagree." Safe perhaps, but is it appropriate?

It turns out that there is quite a bit more than passivity working against the use of direct and candid discussion in many Native cultures. Marianne Boelscher concludes her extensive analysis of discourse among the Haida Nation by saying (1988, 201):

> This style of discourse, action and thought ... thrives on ambiguity, allusion, and elusion, even silence ... Likely because of the traditional values so closely associated with this style, younger Haida grow up with a sense of the allusive quality of social and political discourse, of the importance of implicit negotiation, of silence, of many types of symbolic action or gestures ... It is this intricate and deeply meaningful style of indigenous communication which is so easily misunderstood by White outsiders.

Importantly, Boelscher here is linking very long traditions of what a Native people would and would not find discussable (in the mainstream sense of the word "discussion") to current cross-cultural communication difficulties.

Conclusion

Mix a modern culture of excessive blaming with a communicative style not so much proscribing "frank and open" discussion of contentious issues as just doing discourse differently: the result is a rather formidable barrier to achieving one of the widely touted necessary conditions for successful CED.

Having posed a wicked social problem, one is usually expected to take leave with some sage advice on how to solve it. There is no shortage of practical advice and tools for openness, dialogue, improving organizational dialectic, or collective reality-testing from development experts. The trouble is that these abundant "solutions" almost all presume that a community is willing to embrace foreign communicative ends and means.

This is culturally presumptuous. Non-Native professionals may diagnose First Nations communities as simply deficient in the skills of open and candid discussion, just because *they do not do it our way.* But thereby we replicate the pattern of ethnocentric, negative judgments of indigenous cultures that has gone on since the era of early European contact (Berkhofer 1978). Mainstream Euro-Canadian society took centuries to learn that North America never was *terra nullius,* an empty land, wanting in spirituality, ethics, political organization, rationality, and the knowledge of the world around. We, who so badly want to help First Nations communities along their paths of development, should first spend a lot of time working to grasp however dimly the subtleties of Native interpersonal communicative tradition.

There is no easy solution to offer, fundamentally because what we outsiders may choose to see as "the problem" may be but a reflection of our naiveté, a failure to understand that things may be undiscussable because some peoples want it that way. To paraphrase the metaphor Boelscher drew from Haida ethnography for her book title, the *curtain* within and between Native communicators is not there by accident. Who can insist that it be lifted?

I do not want to leave an impression of being personally content that CED errors just pile up, merely shrugging off that that is the "Native way." But the open dialogue and frank constructive criticism I might prefer and may even still deem essential for CED may just have to wait. It may have to wait for Native community healing, now so avidly and widely sought. In the long run, this may reduce blaming behaviour and replace it with more penetrating causal analysis, shifting the response to error from a search for the guilty to a reflection on what can be learned.

But we should also recognize the possibility that openness and candour are not the only modes of socially constructive discourse supportive of CED. In the future and in a way I have not the ken to imagine, First Nation communities may adapt time-honoured modes of discourse, indirect and allusive as these are, to re-establish their once thriving economies.

The Strategic Plan

Once a community has designed the organizational structure to facilitate CED, the next step is to engage in a structured strategic planning process. To illustrate different approaches to strategic planning within CED, we present project findings associated with the Salmon Arm Economic Development Corporation (SAEDC) and the Lillooet Tribal Council (LTC). Both organizations dedicated significant time and resources to their strategic planning efforts, believing that the plan would serve as a solid foundation for future development activities.

Salmon Arm Strategic Plan

Regional and local economies are more volatile and vulnerable to increasing levels of economic dislocation ... It is therefore vital that communities such as Salmon Arm understand and develop strategies and initiatives to address the changing economy we are faced with and live in.

A strong local economy makes several important contributions to a community such as Salmon Arm including employment, opportunities for investment, and a tax base to support community infrastructure, services, and social programs. The provincial government is cutting back on the support of many programs, services, and opportunities, while downloading more responsibilities onto the District. Salmon Arm can influence its economic prospects and prosperity through an effective approach of CED initiatives. (SAEDC 2001, 12)

The strategic plan drafted by the SAEDC marks the first time the community had conducted a long-range, integrated economic development plan *for* and *by* itself. Earlier planning processes in Salmon Arm relied upon outside consultants or the planning functions of the regional district. The SAEDC followed a standard strategic planning process, consisting of the following steps:

- *background research* – assessment of community challenges and opportunities conducted by the EDO and community "champions" associated with the advisory council
- *community participation* – survey, community forum, advisory council
- *vision* – compiled based upon a survey of past community planning related documents
- *goals* – establishment of broad goals to guide the activities of the SAEDC
- *objectives/strategies* – identification of nineteen potential strategies, each with specific actions and a suggested workplan (see below)
- *implementation* – priorities determined as part of the yearly workplan for the SAEDC

The strategies listed in the strategic plan provide an interesting illustration of the type of economic development activities the SAEDC believes it can either directly or indirectly contribute to, and the plentiful economic development opportunities available in Salmon Arm:

1 Establish Salmon Arm as a safe, modern community welcoming sustainable business
2 Continue to build a strong light, medium industrial, and high-technology sector
3 Maintain and support Salmon Arm's forestry sector and value-added forest-related industries
4 Strengthen Salmon Arm's role as a major centre of education and take maximum advantage of the economic opportunities presented by educational institutions
5 Continue to improve and diversify Salmon Arm's commercial retail and service-based sectors
6 Create a supportive environment for new entrepreneurs, home-based businesses, small businesses, and local economic initiatives
7 Promote the economic development potential of culture and arts in Salmon Arm

8 Expand the tourism sector by improving Salmon Arm's ability not only to enhance and host new forms of tourism but also to attract four-season destination visitors

9 Maintain and support Salmon Arm's agricultural sector

10 Develop and expand Salmon Arm's sports, recreation, and open-space resources as opportunities for economic development

11 Develop and enhance Salmon Arm's community infrastructure and services

12 Continue to expand Salmon Arm's role as a hub city community for business, institutions (health care, education, etc.), and government (CSRD, Provincial Access Centre, Community Futures, etc.)

13 Identify and tap the economic opportunities associated with Salmon Arm's multiculturalism and Native character

14 Establish Salmon Arm as a major hub community centre for the film and video industry within the Columbia-Shuswap Regional District and regional strategic plan

15 Promote the economic opportunities associated with housing and services for youth and seniors and the retired sector of the community

16 Develop and maintain a high level of community involvement and access to the economic/social development process, thereby building long-term community capacity and buy-in

17 Advocacy: Develop and present a strong positive image and identity for Salmon Arm to aid ongoing efforts to promote and market Salmon Arm – attracting the kinds and qualities of development desirable to Salmon Arm's future

18 First Nations: Identify and develop the economic opportunities associated with Salmon Arm's First Nations communities

19 Provide an environmentally friendly community, protecting the natural environment and increasing awareness of environmental issues

It is important to note that the plan recognizes that undertaking all nineteen initiatives would be "somewhat dangerous," noting that there is a risk that "none of the strategic initiatives would be accomplished well." As a result, the plan stresses the importance of inter-group cooperation and coordination in order to divide and integrate the various strategic initiatives adopted by the various CEDOs in the community.

Community members note that the strategic plan makes three particular contributions to the community. First, it increases the confidence of the community; according to a Salmon Arm resident, "The strategic plan gave us a sense of confidence in the local economy, regardless of the overall economic climate." Second, the confidence associated with the plan is due in part to the sense of direction it provides. As noted above, the list of nineteen strategies outlines a variety of possible directions. Third, the planning process and the final document provide important educational and networking services to the community. A Salmon Arm resident stated: "Conducting the plan and then revising it again in 2001 gets people involved and raises the level of awareness in the community about the organization and about CED in general. The planning process also brought organizations together to discuss priorities."

Interviewees associated with the planning process provided three additional pieces of advice concerning the strategic planning process. First, the fact that community members and organizations (and not an external consultant) designed the process and constructed the plan built a sense of ownership over the results. SAEDC staff also note that if a community hires consultants to do the planning and submit a report, no real local knowledge is gained. Second, the plan itself stresses that it is a "living document." The plan will be revised according to changing internal and external conditions; nonetheless, the existence of the plan provides a long-term sense of accountability and a benchmark for updating development activities and priorities. Finally, despite the size and significance of the strategic plan, interviewees stressed the need to balance planning with action: "You have to do things too. You can't plan things to death."

Lillooet Tribal Council: Heritage Strategic Plan

For the Lillooet Tribal Council (LTC), CED centres on a strong commitment to community revitalization through health, capacity building, and the cultural and economic opportunities and practices associated with their territories. Within the LTC, there is a strong connection between economic development and heritage revival. This connection served as a starting point for defining the social, economic, and environmental values that would guide the development process. The Upper St'at'imc hold a broad understanding of the term "heritage," which encompasses values associated with culture, Aboriginal rights, governance, ways of life, land, and natural resources. Heritage development and its linkages with both education and economic opportunity clearly represent a critical strategy for First Nations in BC to pursue in their journey towards greater levels of social and economic capacity and well-being.

COMMUNITY VOICE: LARRY CASPER, LILLOOET TRIBAL COUNCIL NATURAL RESOURCES COORDINATOR

Building a Heritage Strategic Plan

It's interesting to note that while CED has the most in common with the Native community's holistic approach to the environment, prior to European contact Native nations did not have the same concept of development as is common today. As there was no concept of development, there was also no concept of underdevelopment. In contemporary society, however, where the effects of colonization have profoundly impacted Native communities, CED may still be viewed as the best option for First Nations' economic independence. The following excerpt is from our Heritage Strategic Plan, which we see as a vital way to build a successful long-term strategy for rebuilding community health and gaining greater levels of economic independence.

Lillooet Tribal Council Heritage Strategic Plan
The CED process of the Upper St'at'imc Nation is closely associated with the development of a heritage strategy.[1] The Lillooet Tribal Council (LTC) formed a Heritage Committee, which served as the working group for the Forest Communities project. The group identified five purposes:

1 Visioning: The group will develop a vision for St'at'imc land management that respects cultural traditions, respects nature, outlines St'at'imc stewardship, and serves St'at'imc communities.
2 Education: The Heritage Committee will assist efforts in language revival, the exercise and practice of Aboriginal rights, and traditional use.
3 Technical support: The Committee will document history and traditional use, conduct mapping and resource inventories, and develop monitoring standards.
4 Policy development: The Committee will draft resource policies for governance, issue permits, and collect rents and royalties.
5 Political: The Committee will integrate technical, leadership, and community members, and build alliances with other First Nations communities.

Specific tasks undertaken by the Heritage Committee during the project included:

- the development of a multi-Band community profile
- community meetings (visioning, land use, and forestry operations)
- meetings with outside "experts" on issues such as title rights and treaty, community economic development organizations, forestry operations and resource management, and community planning
- a mediated conflict resolution exercise to resolve differences with the Lillooet Forest District and the local logging corporation
- participation in a certified Archaeology Training program

The Forest Communities project provided research, technical assistance, and personnel support to the Heritage and Resources Committee. The committee embraced the CED process as a way to move through a community planning process. The LTC and members of the Heritage and Resources Committee initiated a long-term process to build an integrated and holistic approach to development for their communities.

The Heritage Strategic Plan lists five broad goals. There is overlap between areas, reflecting the holistic worldview of the Upper St'at'imc people. The creation of categories is for clarity and not intended to separate issues or actions. The five goals of the plan include:[2]

1 Health of the Land: Return the land to a healthy state for the benefit of future generations.
2 Health and Natural Resources: To preserve and protect St'at'imc culture and heritage as a way of life.
3 Culture and Heritage: To preserve and protect St'at'imc culture and heritage as a way of life.
4 Community Economic Development: To have St'at'imc people equally represented in all facets of resource management, harvesting, and processing in the territory.
5 Community Education: To have St'at'imc involvement/ownership in formal and informal education processes that promote St'at'imc values and/or identity.

Specific strategies for CED outlined in the Heritage Strategic Plan include:

• Create joint ventures and co-management agreements with forest licensees
• Create a tribal economic development corporation or business entity
• Establish community-based silviculture and harvesting companies
• Establish road-building companies
• Increase St'at'imc involvement in the processing of wood harvested in the territory
• Establish an ecosystem-based plan that adheres to the principles of sustainable development

Plans are also in place for a St'at'imc Cultural Centre, for which we are now raising funds.

Generating CED Information: Community Capacity Assessment

In Chapter 5, we reviewed the importance of community capacity to the CED process. Ultimately, CED initiatives are locally driven, requiring skills and resources at the local level to make things happen. The capacity assessment process provides practical meaning to the term "community capacity." In other arenas of decision making, an obvious and critical factor (yet an often assumed variable in the CED planning process) is information. Quality local information represents a significant gap in many CED processes. Basic statistical data are relatively easily available but are quickly obsolete, often at an inappropriate scale, or lacking qualification by local knowledge. Traditional sources of information also generally fail to capture a more holistic impression of the community and region, that is, conveying or supporting the integrated dimensions of CED. There is perhaps no greater indicator of the fact that CED represents a relatively new and unproven approach to development than the lack of quality, supportive information available to community leaders. In addition, if the information is available, it is often not being used by local development practitioners or widely available to the broader community.

Once the community has determined the organizational elements of the CED process, therefore, the next critical step is to generate local information for use in the planning process. The challenge is to gather relevant information (you don't want to waste time and resources with an unfocused search). Ultimately, the objective of the information-gathering process is to match an understanding of community capacity with appropriate development initiatives. We used the term "capacity assessment" for the process used to generate local information for the project.

The Capacity Assessment Process

The capacity assessment process conducted in the project consisted of a series of steps:

1 We conducted a review of the development literature to identify best practices or conditions of success associated with local development projects and initiatives.
2 Using the literature review, we constructed a framework of indicators with which to assess various dimensions of the project communities. We separated indicators into economic, social, environmental, and human development categories, corresponding with the objectives and integrative principles of CED and key forms of community capital (as described in Chapter 6).
3 We produced a community profile for each community to use in gathering and presenting quantitative and descriptive information.
4 We gathered local qualitative knowledge using focus groups and a survey. We drew upon the success factor framework to guide the selection of questions.
5 We compiled the profile and survey information into a community assessment matrix to facilitate an easier presentation of community information (see example below).

6   Finally, we used the matrix as baseline information with which to identify local opportunities and challenges. We reviewed the information in community-based workshops and discussed how various CED initiatives could contribute to the community in light of assessment results and local values/aspirations. We produced and distributed working papers on various CED initiatives prior to the community workshops to expand local knowledge of different CED strategies and possibilities.

On a more practical level, we used a variety of community-based research methods to generate the information for the capacity assessment process. Both quantitative and qualitative techniques can yield useful data. Combining both types of data sources ensures that local insights and knowledge are balanced with aggregate statistics. The following research methods illustrate a variety of techniques that researchers or practitioners may use to effectively collect data when assessing community capacity.

Research Methods

Community Profile – Aggregate Quantitative and Descriptive Information
The community profile is a logical starting point for the capacity assessment process. Combining quantitative statistical data with descriptive data about the community, the profile will provide a rough indication of the current condition of and issues within the community. The types of aggregate statistical data presented in a profile may include information on labour force, income, educational levels, population, and so on. The advantage of statistical data is that they are usually easily attainable from Statistics Canada or a provincial statistics department. Statistical information also provides developers with the opportunity to compare the profiled community with other communities, and to analyze trends over time. Both applications provide an even more accurate picture of decline, stasis, or improvement in community conditions. It is important to note, however, that smaller communities may not benefit as much as larger communities from statistical data, as the sample size of the statistics may be too large to capture local variation.

Descriptive data about the community may include information about local infrastructure, services, natural amenities, government, and other details that provide an on-the-ground picture of the community. Practitioners or researchers may gather this information through community interviews, documents, and community observation (see below).

The information we collected for the community profiles in the project is shown in Table 7.1.

Table 7.1

Community profile components

Category	Components
Quantitative (Trend analysis, 1986-96: local, regional, provincial)	*Economic* Employment Income Income source Labour force by sector *Social* Education Population Demographics Migration Health Ethnicity Crime rates *Biophysical* Biogeoclimatic zone Air quality Water quality Wildlife and fisheries populations Harvest rates
Community descriptive (Community-specific)	Local history Health services Governing structure Recreational and cultural facilities/programs Infrastructure Community associations Land-use designations Ecological amenities Stewardship programs

Community Survey

Surveys can be an important tool for measuring the perceptions of community residents. Researchers may tailor surveys to ask specific questions relating to tangible development issues or to general thoughts on the future direction of a community. Surveys serve the added function of involving a broad cross-section of members in the community, and therefore help inform people about community issues and planning processes. A survey may also help identify residents with development ideas, resources, or an interest in more involved participation. Reporting to the community with results keeps the momentum of the process going and creates positive conditions for future community involvement by establishing the credibility and sincerity of the development process. A word of caution, however: designing quality surveys – that get the information you want ... and are completed by local residents – can be challenging. Consult survey research tools or seek assistance from local colleges or universities for survey design.

Advisory Committee

Advisory or steering committees are important for any community development process. Having a core group of volunteers and/or staff with specific areas of interest and knowledge about the community will create synergy for community development and help ensure that the process leads to action. An advisory committee can provide ongoing input and assist with the process of gathering and interpreting research data related to the capacity assessment process. The advisory committee will also be responsible for moving the CED process from data collection and analysis to initiative selection and implementation. Individual members of the committee may also champion different aspects of the capacity assessment process, thereby distributing the workload among staff and volunteers.

Key Informant Interviews

Key informant interviews can be an efficient way of assessing community capacity. By targeting specific people who are knowledgeable about the community, researchers can gather detailed and thoughtful insights in a relatively short time period. It is important to identify a range of people who will be able to reflect upon the community from different perspectives. Individuals in formal governing positions, local business people, and community-based organization leaders all represent ideal potential key informants. It is also important to recognize the limitations of identifying select community voices.

Methods Summary

The capacity assessment methods we list above do not provide a comprehensive overview of all possible research methods,[3] but they offer a sampling of different techniques that communities may adapt to suit their specific needs and development interests. Each of these methods has a variety of strengths and weaknesses. In order to refine the method selection process, the following section outlines five criteria for selecting the most appropriate methods for collecting community-based information.

Criteria for Selecting Research Methods

We have condensed the selection criteria for assessing different research

Table 7.2

Criteria for selecting capacity assessment methods

Assessment method	Criteria			
	Resident involvement	Leadership involvement	Time requirements	Cost
Profile	Low	Moderate	Moderate	Low
Survey	High	Moderate	Moderate	Moderate
Focus group	Moderate	Moderate	Moderate	Moderate
Advisory committee	Low	High	Moderate	Low
Key informants	Low	High	Low	Low
Community interviewing	Moderate	Low-Moderate	High	High
Asset mapping	High	Moderate	High	High

methods into a single integrated chart (see Table 7.2). Ideally, an assessment method would involve both the general residents and community leadership, and would require only a modest investment of time and money. As such, criteria for selecting a set of data collection methods for conducting capacity assessments include the following: resident involvement, community leadership involvement, time, and cost.

Clearly there is no one best method for collecting community capacity information. In fact, communities and researchers should balance the strengths and weaknesses of different data collection options by employing more than one method. Besides improving outcomes by combining methods, the weaknesses of the individual methods reported here can be overcome through adaptation and adjustment. For example, partnerships can be created with educational institutions to decrease the cost of profile research and interviewing.

CED researchers may wish to weigh the criteria of the various capacity assessment methods against the resources of their organizations. Perhaps time and cost are not significant factors and resident involvement is considered a priority. In this case, asset mapping or extensive community interviewing would be a preferred approach.

Capacity Assessment Matrix

Inputting local information into a capacity assessment matrix provides an easy way to identify areas of community strengths (community assets) and weaknesses. We used the matrix shown in Table 7.3 to increase the breadth and depth of information being considered in the planning process, thereby attempting to avoid reactive or uninformed decisions leading to inappropriate development initiatives. Ultimately, our intention was to have each community select specific features of the matrix to be used as a foundation

Table 7.3

Sample capacity assessment matrix

Indicators (success factors)	Measurement	Data source/ notes	Profile results	Survey results	Regional/ provincial comparison
Economic health					
Employment	Unemployment level				
Labour force participation	% of participation				
Labour force by sector	Distribution of labour force				
Income	Income average and median				
Others					

for a community monitoring system. We prepared tables for each of the four forms of community capital: economic, ecological, human, and social.

Applying the Capacity Assessment Results

The communities were already considering numerous initiatives before the start of the Forest Communities project. The collaborative research team used the capacity assessment tables to identify new initiatives and to reflect upon existing projects. In addition, a working paper inventory of potential CED projects helped to stimulate ideas for local development among the working groups (Smith 1999). One of the key steps in the CED planning process is increasing awareness of CED options – many strategies are simply not common knowledge to community members.

The community assessment process provided insight into the challenges and opportunities facing each of the four communities. Specific questions asked by the research team during the planning workshops addressed the links between the matrix information, the planning process, and the selection of CED strategies. For example:

- How would a specific CED initiative capitalize on the strengths exhibited by the community?
- How would a CED initiative address community weaknesses?
- Which CED strategies does the community have the capacity to undertake?
- If the community currently does not have the capacity to build an initiative, how could it be developed or acquired?

These questions link steps 3, 4, and 5 in the CED planning model presented in the sidebar above (p. 171-73), moving the process from research to action in an informed, methodical fashion.

The assessment process identified opportunities and challenges in each of the communities and for each area of community capacity. For example, the Nuxalk Nation identified weaknesses in human resource capacity, particularly business-planning skills. The working group determined that business training would be required before the Nuxalk could pursue economic opportunities in a more self-reliant manner. In Lillooet, the working group identified the need for an organization mandated to own and operate community business enterprises. It is ultimately up to each community to select its own indicators and review the capacity assessment information from the perspective of its own values. Communities may weigh some variables differently than others and choose only a select number of indicators with which to review the condition of the community. In fact, the process of selecting indicators and matching initiatives can be a revealing one that communities should not ignore.

The capacity assessment process was an exploratory exercise designed to increase awareness of the condition of the communities and their ability to initiate a variety of CED strategies. The capacity assessment matrix succeeded in facilitating a discussion linking capacity with CED planning, and ultimately in facilitating the implementation of CED strategies and projects. In some cases, working groups made direct project development decisions based upon assessment findings. In other cases, the matrix served to reassure the communities that they were moving in the right direction, or that they simply needed to make slight adjustments by expanding the local development process to include other interests in their community.

Summary of the Capacity Assessment Process

We identified five overall benefits associated with the capacity assessment process. First, development decisions that are based upon a clear assessment of a community's capacity will have a greater likelihood of success and therefore make a greater contribution to the desired future of the community. Communities and development organizations that pursue projects and funding in a less informed and more reactive manner will face greater barriers to success. Without a capacity assessment process, initiatives may not represent an appropriate fit with the community: financially, ecologically, or in terms of human resources. If a community is unable to generate viable development initiatives, external forces will play a larger role in determining the future of the community, thereby creating or perpetuating conditions of dependency.

A second benefit of the community capacity assessment process is that it can help the community avoid development pitfalls associated with the step from dependency and specialization towards the uncertainty and complexity of a more diverse local economy. There are numerous approaches to generating growth and development. Communities must be careful to avoid short-term strategies that may merely repeat cycles of dependency. The list of development "fix" options is long, including: (1) get-rich-quick strategies that may overburden communities with unmanageable debt; (2) strategies that inadequately represent local values; (3) strategies that sacrifice longer-term ecological health (i.e., development that impoverishes rather than enriches [Daly and Cobb 1994]); and (4) strategies that cater to corporate boosterism in an attempt to achieve short-term political objectives and immediately reverse perceptions of a poor investment climate.

When communities develop investments that are based upon quality information, they reduce the risk of becoming overburdened with false hopes or poor investment decisions based upon development fads. Empowered by the knowledge of their human, social, economic, and ecological resources, communities are able to pursue locally appropriate development options that mobilize and build upon local strengths. The ability to create stability through diversity may involve aspects of a community that communities have not previously considered to be of any economic value. Attention to the four areas of community capacity will highlight a variety of development options, and an awareness of these options will contribute to the overall search for community diversity and resilience. Community capacity assessment is vital if communities are to identify locally appropriate and diverse development strategies. The assessment process provides a new lens with which to view community and economic opportunities.

As communities increase their capacity to conduct their own affairs, the negative consequences of core/periphery relationships that define many rural communities will decline. Figure 7.2 illustrates the value of the capacity assessment process in terms of increased self-reliance and decreased external dependency.

Figure 7.2

The community capacity assessment process

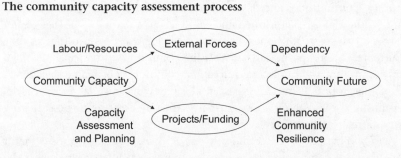

Third, capacity assessment creates a database of information about communities, which then have the option of turning the database into a community monitoring system. Community monitoring is linked with the CED process in step 6. Communities can use the capacity information to measure the viability and appropriateness of initiatives proposed in the planning stage of the CED process (step 4), and to measure the impact of development decisions and the process of community change, both internally or externally generated, over time (step 6). With a prolonged commitment to community monitoring, longitudinal analysis of various capacity trends will help foster proactive development in the community. Viewed over time, trends in education, the quality of the environment, or resource sustainability, for example, will become apparent to community decision makers, encouraging them to act in a proactive manner.

Fourth, the capacity assessment process causes local decision makers to think differently about the local economy. The different dimensions of the capacity assessment framework facilitate development of an integrated perspective of the community. People are clearly able to draw connections between social, economic, environmental, and cultural features of the community. In addition, simply documenting different features of the community fosters a sense of ownership over the local community and economy that were previously considered to be someone else's responsibility.

Finally, the process of capacity assessment is in itself a capacity-building exercise. The information generated may provide new insights or perspectives for community leaders and CED practitioners, and can be communicated to the community at large. Sharing information not only increases local education and awareness but also generates increased participation and support for development activities.

Evaluation of the CED Process

We divide our observations of the CED process followed in the Forest Communities project into three categories: preparing for the CED process, managing the CED process, and sustaining the CED process. In this section, we reflect on how we implemented the process in each community, and identify lessons learned in relation to the CED framework presented in earlier chapters. We hope that this reflection will help reduce uncertainty about CED planning and build capacity for CED planning more generally. The section will also serve as a guide for community leaders seeking to implement or re-energize a CED process.

Preparing for the CED Process

There are a variety of factors that a planning team must consider before initiating a planning process. The team must select a planning model, identify relevant stakeholders, gather the resources to sustain the process, and consider the overall capacity of the community to engage in a CED process. Important steps in the pre-planning stage include assessing community readiness, assessing the underlying motivation for engaging in a planning process, and considering or conceptualizing the process in terms of asset-based CED.

Community Readiness

A community's degree of readiness to engage in a CED process is crucial to achieving CED success. Things to consider include the level of internal conflict present in the community, the willingness of community members to participate in the planning process, the level of community-wide awareness of the need for planning, the availability of information, and the overall level of political support for CED planning at local and senior government levels. Further, the planning team should be aware of the community's past experiences with local development. Assessing readiness will help communities choose the appropriate scale of projects and determine what preliminary work may be necessary to prepare a solid foundation for planning and project implementation.

Motivation for Initiating CED

All four communities stated that their interest in participating in the research project stemmed from a concern for future generations in their communities and from the immediate need to create employment opportunities – a balance between long-term and short-term thinking. Regardless of variations in the capacity and conditions in the communities, the communities viewed the CED process as a way to create economic opportunity. The selection and capacity assessment surveys also note that the timing of the project coincided with a particular crisis in employment and economic instability. In many ways, the downturn in the forest industry that coincided with the timing of the project and the ongoing economic struggles of the First Nations communities created opportunities to view the local economy from a different perspective. As a resident from the South Cariboo noted, "We've lost our sense of complacency towards the forest industry." Likewise, a member of the Upper St'at'imc community said, "We are moving from survival to living," recognizing both the challenges and opportunities now facing First Nations communities.

A lack of satisfaction regarding previous development approaches lowered many of the political and ideological barriers to exploring alternative forms of development. The communities were, at least initially, approaching CED more from a position of need. This is a typical response to the boom-bust patterns of resource dependency. Ironically, community conditions are rarely questioned during the boom: a time when a community has more resources at its disposal to address development issues (Freudenburg

1992). As noted earlier, bust periods create the motivation for change, an opportunity taken by the four project communities.

Assessing the motivation of the community for engaging in a CED process prepares the community and the planning agents for the process itself. The willingness of the community to participate, the level of interest being expressed by community members, and the willingness of the community to allocate resources to the process all reflect the motivating circumstances that support the local decision to pursue CED.

Conceptualization: Asset-Based Development

> As a result of the project, I think we realize the assets we have and how we can use them to grow and succeed. Personally I think we have a greater sense of community. (South Cariboo resident)

Initially, the research team promoted the concept of asset mapping as a starting point from which the communities could assess and mobilize existing community capacity for the purposes of CED. Asset mapping is a technique that produces a visual representation and inventory of the resources, talents, and strengths in a community (Kretzman and McKnight 1993).

In the end, we did not formally implement an asset-mapping process in the communities. Members of the planning workshops decided that the exercise would be overly resource- and time-intensive. However, the idea of community assets did prove to be very powerful in the *conceptualization* of economic opportunities. The term "assets" remained with the project throughout the CED process and became commonly used in the language of working group members in their planning efforts.

At the technical level of strategic planning, identifying and building upon a community's strengths (assets) is the logical starting point for any action. As a concept of value and ownership, *community* assets fundamentally redefine a community's relationship to its human, economic, natural, and physical resources. For example, from a land-use perspective, if a community comes to realize that its natural surroundings are an asset for tourism or amenity-based development, the community automatically gains an interest in how that land will be used by others. The value that the community attaches to the land and the value government or industry attaches to the land may vary. These differing values create the need for more inclusive planning and for the empowerment of the community to have more influence or control over the decisions affecting their well-being.

The concept of community assets fundamentally shifts the emphasis of community and larger-scale development. At the community level, the idea of local assets internalizes development thinking and moves people from a booster approach to economic development towards an internally oriented approach. From a provincial perspective, the infrastructure and resources previously conceptualized as part of province building must now contend with the pressures of community ownership and local demands for re-investment and resource control.

Managing the CED Process

Effective management of the CED process is a difficult task. The line between process and action is a fine one. In addition, the variety of interests and the range of skills that coalesce within a planning process require a multitude of management capacities in order to maintain an appropriate balance (i.e., not acting too quickly yet still managing to move towards implementation). Important process observations from the project relate to the following: skills, governance models, resources and mandates, and conflict.

Process Skills

The effectiveness of the six-step process and the degree of participation it is able to generate depends largely upon the process skills present at the community level. The CED process requires the following skills: facilitation, communication, decision making, consensus building, financial management, and conflict resolution. In our experience, the presence of these skills varied widely both between and within the communities. Clearly, it is unrealistic to expect all of these skills to exist at a high level in any single individual. It is the responsibility of the community to determine which skills are lacking and identify strategies for addressing gaps – from within the community or from external expertise if necessary.

The process skills of community members also determine the speed and certainty with which a community can move through the series of process steps. It is critical to find the correct balance between process and action. Our experience shows that using the same process and time line in four different communities meant that we were ahead of schedule in some and behind in others in terms of the continuity of the six-step process. This variability did not detract from the educational and reflective value associated with the process, but there were delays or limitations in our ability to adapt to the realities of the community development process on the ground.

Governance

"Governance" in CED refers to the way in which communities manage the CED process. The research team witnessed two approaches to governance in the Forest Communities project: *directed* and *facilitated* CED. Both models depend upon the style of leadership underlying the CED process and the resources available to the community. *Directed* CED governance relies upon a central organization (such as a development corporation or a municipal or band council) to take a leadership role in coordinating and directing the

CED process. The process may involve a broad range of other community and government organizations, but a central body serves as the conduit for process and planning. This directed model requires that funding be available for a CED organization (CEDO), over and above other community organizational groupings.

The second model of governance, *facilitated* CED, maintains a more organic organizational structure in the community. In the facilitated model, various groups conduct their own projects independent of a broader, more inclusive planning process. The leadership within the community may assist community groups in achieving their goals (for example, by providing resources or networking opportunities), but the responsibility for specific development projects remains with individual organizations.

In the project, the Nuxalk Nation and Salmon Arm followed a directed CED governance model (Table 7.4). Salmon Arm developed the Salmon Arm Economic Development Corporation (SAEDC) to serve as a central CED organization in the community, with other community organizations joining the process through steering committee representation. In contrast, the Nuxalk Nation relied upon the band council to direct its development operations. Because the Department of Indian Affairs concentrates resources and authority within the band council system, the facilitated model is more difficult to implement in Aboriginal communities. The tribal council system, however, does serve a more facilitative role, as demonstrated by the Lillooet Tribal Council, where different communities pursued independent development activities but were also able to enter into cooperative ventures. Communities may also create development corporations to serve a central economic development role. Other organizations may, and undoubtedly will, implement separate projects, but there is a clear emphasis on coordinating and integrating local activities.

The South Cariboo used a facilitative approach to CED. While the mayor of 100 Mile House created an economic development committee, CED projects within the community continued to be housed quite independently within specific community groups. Groups worked with the district to obtain funding and other resources necessary to conduct projects, network

Table 7.4

CED governance models followed in the Forest Communities project

Governance model	Community
Directed CED	Salmon Arm
	Nuxalk Nation
Facilitated CED	South Cariboo
	Lillooet Tribal Council

with others, and raise awareness in the community about their efforts, but the community did not develop a cohesive and comprehensive plan.

The effectiveness of different models of governance depends upon attention to appropriate intra-community protocol. Clear and open communications between groups, which define organizational or individual responsibilities, are necessary to ensure that groups work together in an effective manner, independently or as a central group. Without clear protocols between groups, communication barriers, lack of trust, and outright conflict may impede local development efforts.

Mandate and Resources

Closely associated with the concept of governance, "mandate" refers to the degree of authority granted to or attained by a CEDO or CED planning process. The extent and effectiveness of community participation are heavily dependent upon the importance the community attaches to the CED process and the resources allocated to do the job.

The communities in the project that had a specific development organization to serve and lead the CED process were ultimately more effective at moving through the planning process and implementing projects. CEDOs offer an effective way to house and manage both process and action at the community level. CEDOs also provide an arm's-length forum from government: as a Salmon Arm resident said, "When development is the responsibility of local government, it is politically driven, not community-driven." CEDOs, however, require human and financial resources to ensure their success, particularly in the medium to long term, thus necessitating a role for local government.

Individual capacity is obviously important to CED. Volunteers play a critical role in CED, but providing direct financial support for individuals to direct the CED process elevates the status and recognition of CED as a meaningful strategy for strengthening local economic capacity. In order to scale up the effectiveness of CED, paid positions enable a more sustained local development effort and help prevent volunteer burnout, the latter of which may jeopardize long-term projects. In project communities where CED was an unpaid responsibility, or an add-on to an existing job description, the community made less direct progress. Conversely, communities that created paid CED positions dramatically enhanced the effectiveness and variety of CED tasks, including communications, grant-proposal writing, project coordination, and implementation.

Managing Conflict

As discussed in Chapter 6, conflict can be both a negative and positive force in CED. The research team witnessed positive conflicts at the community level driven by a development-versus-conservation debate. This dualism proved to be a positive force because of the degree to which the debate enables communities to avoid stagnation and decline on the one hand, and overdevelopment and thoughtless growth on the other. Provided there are effective resources for resolving development conflicts, open debate and disagreement can lead to a more lasting and successful CED plan.

Inter-community negotiations between First Nation communities and their municipal neighbours was another example where conflict was a positive force in the project. In Salmon Arm, initial conflicts ultimately facilitated a more constructive relationship between the municipality and the surrounding Aboriginal communities concerning service provision and joint projects for economic development.

The research team also witnessed a variety of destructive conflicts throughout the course of the project. Examples of negative conflicts included Aboriginal and non-Aboriginal community struggles over tourism, Aboriginal/industry disagreements regarding land-use decisions, and personal conflicts within communities that impeded development progress and consumed valuable local resources. In each case, a lack of transparency, mistrust, and a long history of poor communication seriously impeded the economic prospects for the communities and regions.

Overall, the project had the opportunity to view and experience conflict in a variety of forms common to everyday community life and politics. Positive conflicts helped the CED process achieve the innovative qualities and openness necessary to move from positions of competition to cooperation. Negative conflicts stalled the development process and resulted in a circular process of draining repetition and drifting initiatives. Projects and processes aimed at facilitating discussion of positive conflicts and moving negative conflicts into more positive forms of resolution and debate were valuable outcomes of the project and of community efforts.

Sustaining the CED Process

Sustaining the CED process is necessary for the simple reason that CED is a long-term approach to development. Conditions both within and outside the community that affect the local economy are constantly changing. This is the essence of the new economy and an important variable in the process of economic transition. Communities must be prepared to revisit their CED plans and maintain a constant advisory role, either through a CEDO or a less formal advisory committee.

Communities should devise strategies for sustaining the development process at the *beginning* of any CED process. This includes considering such factors as fundraising capacity, access to capital, entrepreneurial opportunities, levels of volunteerism, burnout avoidance, mentoring, and determination of appropriate decision-making procedures. Based upon the project, keys to sustaining the CED process include the following: effective leadership, balancing process with action, effective project evaluation, and the presence of government.

Leadership

Leadership was a critical factor in the Forest Communities project. Workshop participants listed the following characteristics of an effective leader, many of which reflect the characteristics identified in the literature review given in Table 6.3 (see p. 149):

- an effective facilitator
- innovative
- encouraging
- motivating
- entrepreneurial
- well known
- trusted
- knowledgeable
- willing to let go of the process (share control and responsibility)
- willing to forgive
- problem solver
- good listener and communicator
- promotes a positive attitude
- role model
- respectful and compassionate
- focused
- team player
- deals effectively with feedback, learns from mistakes
- good time manager
- ability to handle stress

Further examination of the role of leadership in CED reveals a rich source for future research. In addition, leadership training in a CED context would greatly enhance the prospects for CED across the province. We discuss the CED training efforts associated with this project in Chapter 8.

The Project-Based Approach: Balancing Process with Action

As mentioned earlier, the communities were immediately interested in moving to action. A critical challenge facing communities is how to balance the need for a quality process with the desire to create change. This tension was succinctly stated by a resident of Salmon Arm as "the need to find a balance between certainty and action in the pursuit of CED." The university research team was interested in taking a step back from action in order to pursue better planning, while the communities focused right from the beginning on identifying and implementing various CED strategies. The result of this tension was mutual learning and a deeper appreciation for the process/action dichotomy in CED.

In some circumstances, community members did not match the expressed urgency for action with real implementation. Often communities were hesitant to make the leap into action. Some participants suggested that because of previous economic development failures, community leaders were understandably fearful of being associated with local development projects. It is much safer to identify opportunities than to pursue them.

In an attempt to resolve the tension between process and action, the research illustrates the advantages associated with a project-based approach to CED. This means that you must balance planning with action. There are two main benefits associated with an early focus on implementation. First, doing something generates community interest and enthusiasm. As one Salmon Arm resident put it, "Focus on projects right away to generate interest and build momentum, then modify things as you move along." This strategy helps ensure that CED meets the criterion of meaningfulness to the individuals who are directly involved and to the broader community. Second, a focus on implementing achievable projects offers demonstration value to both the community and its internal and external supporters. Funding agencies in particular are interested in tangible evidence proving that their support is having a direct impact. Economically, the impact of a project on a community will depend upon the scale and time line of the activity.

Conversely, there are three advantages associated with quality process. First, patience for process will help a community avoid a reactive response, or the "quick fix," for what are undoubtedly complex problems. Quick fixes may have a variety of negative repercussions at the community level, including wasted resources, exacerbation of dependency, ecological degradation, and spoiling of community interest in further development activities. Second, good process will help communities avoid the common mistake of overlooking community capacity to manage and sustain initiatives (Blakely 1994). Finally, a quality local planning process helps build participation. If the process is transparent, wide participation helps to expose and negotiate between different interests, explore different ideas, and build a broader base of support for community-based projects.

From a research perspective, the development of better community research and decision-making tools will help bring about an effective balance between process and action. The capacity assessment framework provided the research team and the communities with a good starting point. Further modifications to the framework and more experience at the community level will result in circumstances where communities realize the advantages of both *efficient* process and *appropriate* action.

Project Evaluation

Project evaluation is critical to sustaining the CED process. Without effective evaluation, it is unlikely that a CEDO will be able to effectively justify its existence in tangible terms. Community development organization are generally uneasy about the selection of specific targets, which may simply become targets for failure given the complexity of mixed causality of the local development process. However, evaluation that includes an organization's staff, membership/constituents, and volunteers can become an effective tool for defining and confirming/redefining the purpose of the organization, improving its capacity, and illustrating its impact to funders and to the broader community. We will explore evaluation in the Forest Communities project further in Chapter 8.

The Role of Government

The project identified a variety of roles for government in the CED process. Governments can play a positive role in terms of funding CED processes, making policy adjustments to accommodate community needs, facilitating networking, and providing new information to community decision makers. However, governments and communities must avoid the risks associated with depending too much on government assistance. The inconsistency of government funding programs means that CED processes that rely solely or primarily on government funding risk failure if (and usually when) governments decide to discontinue program support.

Researchers often present CED as an appropriate strategy for achieving political decentralization. However, we see from a consideration of what makes for an effective CED process that the role of government may not necessarily be reduced quantitatively, but rather changed qualitatively. Effective community-based participation, decision making, monitoring, and management may not necessarily reduce the need for government resources, at least in the short to medium term. As the capacity of the community increases, however, negotiations may take place between local development organizations and government, or between different levels of government, to redefine jurisdiction and responsibility. A facilitative role for government introduces problems associated with variability in government management (in terms of protecting the broader public interest) and in community capacity for self-governance. Nevertheless, local diversity must be allowed to express itself in more decentralized, innovative ways to stimulate economic development. Through CED, we may mediate new standards and boundaries for top-down and bottom-up development.

Conclusion

The CED planning process is a critical step for understanding and reconceptualizing communities and local economies. If we are to conduct a successful CED process and persist through to the design and implementation of appropriate CED strategies, it is necessary to understand what to look for: what are the key dimensions of a community that will enable it to prosper? More specifically, what would a healthy CED-based economy look like? The answers to these questions enable us to create a comparative benchmark for community assessment and to focus precious CED resources where they will have the greatest impact on the economy and on the society of the community.

Generating quality community information and implementing efficient CED processes are critical steps in fostering more flexible and adaptive communities. Through CED, communities gain an awareness of different assets and resources and how to deploy them more efficiently. The CED process ideally brings together a diverse group of people and organizations to share resources and, hopefully, to foster a sense of synergy in working towards common goals. Perhaps most important, the CED process provides communities with a system for managing the complex economic development process. If the process becomes an ongoing practice in the community, community members will also learn from past experiences and apply these lessons to future efforts, leading to a more responsive and sophisticated local response (and again enhancing community resilience).

In the following chapter, we move from process to action. Chapter 8 describes a variety of development strategies that resulted from the CED process in each community.

8
Community Economic Development Strategies

In this chapter, we outline various strategies undertaken by the communities in the Forest Communities project to enhance their economic capacity. A description of the strategies serves two purposes in relation to the project, this book, and the promotion of community economic development (CED) generally. First, the most powerful educational tool we used in the project was the ability to provide community working groups with examples of what was possible, namely, examples of CED activities from other jurisdictions. This reduced the learning curve for project development and implementation and allowed internal reflection on how various initiatives may apply in their own communities. Concrete examples also reduced the level of anxiety felt by community members, assuring them that they were not alone in their struggles and that a different approach to economic development was possible. We hope that sharing the experiences of these four communities will in turn help others who are seeking solutions to their own economic challenges.

Second, there is a need for systematic case studies in CED that can be used for educational purposes. Case study components are a common educational technique used in other fields, such as business education. Through case studies, students and practitioners have an opportunity to learn from the success or failure of real-life examples, enhancing both the relevance and absorption of the material.

This chapter introduces a broad range of strategies employed by the project communities, including (1) business development and support; (2) arts, culture, and heritage development; (3) community resource management and land-use planning; (4) tourism development; and (5) network building and community relationships. We will describe each of these strategies with supporting community-based information. The range of strategies being pursued demonstrates a commitment to building diverse, healthy economies. We must note, however, that the strategies and stories presented here represent only a small selection of local initiatives.

The chapter concludes with a review of some of the lessons and observations drawn from the project communities as they implemented their CED plans. The communities illustrate a strong commitment to adopting a more self-reliant and proactive approach to developing their local economies.

CED Strategies

CED is a combination of principles, process, and action. Strategies represent a key link between planning and action – or, in community terms, "where the rubber hits the road." Strategies should be selected that are appropriate to a community's aspirations and abilities. Every community has particular strengths (assets), needs, and concerns that will determine which strategies are best suited to their circumstances. For resource-based communities, control over and sustainable use of natural resources are likely to be key areas of concern. Community strengths may lie in the skills and knowledge of local workers, the uniqueness of local cultural products, or particular natural amenities (Smith 1999). As outlined in Chapter 7, the process of capacity assessment can help to identify which strategies are a good fit for communities.

Within each strategy, a number of specific initiatives can be undertaken. For example, as part of an overall strategy to encourage new business development, communities may choose to create a business incubator facility or to provide business support and mentor services. Numerous strategies for economic renewal and enhancement of community well-being have been employed by communities and identified in the literature on CED. The list of strategies provided is not comprehensive but does illustrate a variety of CED initiatives that are possible:

1 plug the leaks (outflow of resources)
2 initiate and encourage new enterprises (business and social entrepreneurship)
3 support and improve existing enterprises; business retention
4 develop human resources
5 encourage work-sharing arrangements
6 strengthen the informal economy
7 recruit compatible businesses from outside the community
8 increase local ownership of businesses and resources
9 develop required physical infrastructure
10 improve environmental management of local organizations, institutions, and firms
11 increase community involvement in natural resource management
12 restore the local environment
13 undertake other quality-of-life improvements (e.g., health, social, recreational amenities)
14 celebrate local identity and culture

15 create sectoral development strategies (e.g., tourism, high tech)
16 develop local mechanisms for financing CED (Vodden 1999)

The five strategy themes highlighted below illustrate that it is necessary to match the development strategy with the socio-economic conditions, values, and capacity found at the community level. Elements of the CED process may be generalized, but the end product of that process should be infused with local information and knowledge to find viable and contextually appropriate projects.

Business Development and Support
Business development and support initiatives help generate or retain local dollars and increase employment. Business development and retention strategies work to promote, protect, and enhance local business ventures. Examples of business development and support initiatives include worker cooperatives, micro-enterprise programs, enterprise facilitation, technical assistance and support services, business incubators, alternative financing mechanisms (e.g., peer lending, community loan funds), value-added and import replacement initiatives, conservation-based development, joint ventures, and nonprofit and community enterprises (Smith 1999).

Increasing levels of support for existing businesses can be accomplished through a variety of initiatives. Communities should consider strategies such as buy-local programs and local purchasing policies, improved marketing, financial restructuring, research and business development assistance, money-saving energy and waste reduction initiatives, and business retention programs such as early warning signals analysis and import substitution (matching local suppliers with local purchasers). Business networks – groups of businesses (often small or medium-sized) that come together to collectively share information and support each other through their business purchases, connections, and joint ventures – may also prove effective at improving the local business climate.

When assessing the benefits of potential new enterprises, it is important for communities to consider whether they will meet community development objectives and fit with the overall vision of their area. Communities should work to establish their own criteria (a useful learning process in itself), but the following criteria are examples that will help with the decision-making process for establishing or reviewing new businesses or attracting external enterprise (Blakely 1989):

• local employment potential
• destination of corporate profits (net gains to the community)
• expected length of operation and overall viability
• impact on community culture

- environmental implications
- expected wage ranges
- working conditions
- potential to use local goods and services as inputs
- sales to local markets
- attraction of new investment or ancillary employers
- competition with local firms

Business development aspects of the Lillooet CED strategy included resource-related joint ventures and community and individually owned enterprises. Increasingly, Aboriginal communities across the province are looking to entrepreneurship as a strategy for economic revitalization. In fact, although small business growth is a widespread phenomenon, the number of Aboriginal entrepreneurs in Canada is increasing even more rapidly than that of non-Aboriginals (Vodden et al. 2001).

For Salmon Arm, business development and support was a central component of the Salmon Arm Strategic Plan. We provide examples from the retail and construction sectors, along with the community's Business Expansion and Retention (BEaR) program, below.

Salmon Arm Business Development

Business development was a primary objective in the Salmon Arm Strategic Plan. Originally, the Salmon Arm Economic Development Corporation (SAEDC) adopted a mainly externally oriented approach to business development, seeking to attract industry to Salmon Arm. The SAEDC printed brochures, produced a marketing video about the community, and bought a mobile trailer advertising unit and drove it around western Canada and the US to promote the community. The SAEDC also streamlined a process for dealing with outside expressions of interest from business owners, mobilizing a quick-response team and process that included meetings with the mayor, a tour of the community, and a full presentation about the community by SAEDC staff. While we strongly recommend having a process in place to deal with outside interest in the community, the economic development officer (EDO) quickly realized that promoting the community to random external parties was a time-consuming, resource-intensive, and not particularly effective strategy. As a result (and due to some prodding by the local business community, which felt that the SAEDC was not allocating sufficient resources to local needs), the SAEDC adopted a variety of proactive internal business development strategies. According to a revised version of the community strategic plan (SAEDC 2001):

Salmon Arm is in the midst of a number of new retail, commercial and service sector developments that will enhance its position as a regional commercial/retail centre. To support, improve and diversify these sectors the Salmon Arm Strategic Plan includes a commercial/retail strategy that includes:

- maintaining and increasing the quality of its commercial and highway commercial corridor, and beginning to plan how and where the highway commercial corridor should expand to in the future (the Trans-Canada Highway being its main street)
- revitalization and downtown beautification planning and programs
- development of Salmon Arm's waterfront and providing access to the Shuswap Lake across the mainline CN tracks of the transcontinental railway
- development of a mentoring program on "taking care of and supporting existing businesses"
- foster working relationships between business groups to support and present a unified image of our commercial community, yet promote uniqueness
- conduct an import substitution study to identify business opportunities for local residents and improve the self-reliance of the Salmon Arm local economy
- explore opportunities associated with the potential of stopping the "Rocky Mountaineer" train in our community (carries 65,000 travellers through our community per annum)

The following three initiatives are examples of the type of actions implemented by the SAEDC to support the *local* economy.

Construction Industry Program

Local knowledge and community profiling confirmed that significant economic opportunities associated with the construction industry existed in the community due to the predicted high growth rates throughout the Salmon Arm area. Research also indicated that nonlocal contractors were completing a majority of the larger projects in the Salmon Arm region. The local construction industry in the Shuswap was missing out on opportunities to bid on local projects.

To address this gap, a local champion presented a proposal to initiate a local construction industry network. With research assistance from Simon Fraser University[1] and financial support from Human Resources Development Canada (HRDC) to fund initial coordination and research expenses, the SAEDC served as an incubator to create a not-for-profit association that was eventually called the Shuswap Construction Industry Program (SCIP). SCIP's mission statement is "Shuswap Construction Industry Professionals working together to create opportunity, to ensure maximum use of local businesses and individuals on construction projects in the Shuswap."

SCIP quickly assembled over 200 member businesses across the Shuswap region. The organization implemented a number of services for the local construction industry:

- A local "plan room" showcases blueprints for construction projects in the Shuswap to facilitate individual or coordinated bids from SCIP members.
- A labour pool registry provides access to qualified workers in the region.
- A membership directory is produced and widely distributed each year to market local products and services.
- A construction industry coordinator now manages SCIP operations.
- A community awards program now recognizes projects that use local contractors (measured at 50, 60, and 70 percent).

Beyond the benefits to the local construction industry, SCIP has expanded its network to serve other community objectives. SCIP has partnered with the local college to provide educational opportunities for businesses to upgrade their knowledge and abilities to compete in the construction industry on a competitive basis. SCIP also makes direct investments into the capacity of the community by supplying four Shuswap high schools with scholarships to promote entry of students into the trades. (For more information, see: <http://www.scip.bc.ca/about.html>.)

The BEaR Program

As mentioned earlier, the SAEDC quickly realized the value of the local business community. Once this strategic shift in thinking occurred, it became evident that the quality of information about the local business community was poor, particularly from a development perspective (i.e., in terms of how to exploit new opportunities and provide assistance to avoid business loss).

To facilitate local business expansion and retention, including in the commercial/retail and construction sectors, the SAEDC launched the Business Expansion and Retention (BEaR) program. BEaR is a community-driven initiative that aids communities in understanding the issues and opportunities facing existing local businesses. It identifies, supports, sponsors, and/ or assists in the implementation of activities that can be undertaken to help businesses survive and thrive. The intent of the program is to address local economic issues, bolster what exists, and help maintain these activities in the future. The SAEDC sought to achieve the following objectives through BEaR:

- demonstrate a community commitment to existing local business
- take action to resolve business concerns
- strengthen coordination and collaboration among local business and community development and service providers

- provide the business community with a greater level of awareness about the groups and programs available to assist business, and improve the competitiveness of local firms

The SAEDC hired a private marketing firm to conduct the research. The firm conducted 250 interviews, collecting information on business tenure, locations, facilities, customers, revenues, competition, challenges, and community. Of the 250 businesses, 188 identified areas of assistance or concern, primarily in marketing and the use of the Internet. In response to the project findings, the SAEDC has launched a variety of secondary business-oriented initiatives (Salmon Arm Economic Development Corporation 2000):

- a business mentor who now works with businesses to provide information and assistance (with financing, marketing, exploration of export opportunities, and human resources)
- promotion of website development seminars
- initiation of a marketing/training team
- facilitation of local educational and service provider organizations in addressing identified business needs
- provision of information on the "Secret Shopper Program" and similar customer service programs
- initiation of relationship building and linkages between professionals and business services, identifying opportunities for them to support the business community
- promotion of the Business and Community Employer Network Technology System (BCENTS) with local business as a marketing tool
- referral of businesses to the tourism coordinator to explore product promotion opportunities
- establishment of a resource library at the SAEDC office

Economic Leakage: Salmon Arm Buy Local

The final business strategy we will present concerns stopping the flow of money out of the community (otherwise referred to as "leakage"). Economic leakage refers to community income that is spent outside of the local economy. For example, each time a resident makes a shopping trip to a different town or larger centre, the amount spent represents dollars and income lost to the home community. There are two basic forms of leakage: immediate and secondary. Immediate leakage occurs when, as in the foregoing example, members of a community travel to another centre and use their locally generated incomes to make nonlocal purchases. Secondary leakages occur when a resident makes a purchase in the community but buys a product that was purchased or manufactured outside the community (thus most of the profit leaves the community). The sidebar "A Story of Local Spending" illustrates the concept of economic leakage.

A STORY OF LOCAL SPENDING

Imagine a community called Localtown. In Localtown, people and organizations tend to spend most of their incomes on local items, such as groceries, repair work, child care, clothing, and so on (approximately 80 percent of their incomes are spent locally). For example, as a resident of Localtown, let's say you win $10 from a local lottery. To celebrate, you decide to spend $8 dollars at the local florist (80 percent of $10). The florist, closing her shop for the day, decides to get a haircut at the salon next to her shop for $6.40 (that's 80 percent of $8). The hairstylist, after a long day's work, realizes that he is hungry and goes to a local restaurant, where he spends $5.12 (80 percent of $6.40) on a sandwich. Figure 8.1 illustrates this flow of money in Localtown.

In this small example, we see that from an original amount of $10, the local community's economy gains a total of $29.52 (and that is just from the first three rounds of local spending). If you had decided to spend your $8 on a catalogue purchase and only $2 on local purchases, the impact on the local economy would be significantly less. The potential income for the florist, the hairstylist, and the local restaurant would have leaked from the community, making these local businesses less viable and reducing the diversity and stability of the local economy – and perhaps ultimately the population of the community itself.

Figure 8.1

Local money flows in Localtown

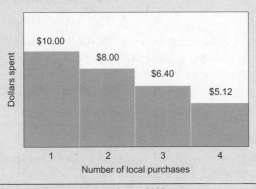

Source: Adapted from New Economics Foundation 2002.

Economic leakages are important because money that is spent outside the community represents a loss to the local economy, in this case to the economy of Salmon Arm. The SAEDC and the Salmon Arm Chamber of Commerce were concerned that local residents were not supporting local businesses and did not understand the connection between local spending and community well-being, thereby lessening the vibrancy and diversity of the downtown core. To learn more about this potential problem and to identify possible solutions, we worked with both organizations to conduct research on the consumer spending habits of Salmon Arm residents. We designed a survey to assess immediate leakages by measuring personal spending habits, categories of goods and services bought nonlocally, and total dollars spent outside the Salmon Arm economy.

From the results of the survey, it was estimated that over 10 million shopping dollars leak out of the community every year: "Only a healthy local economy will keep the circle of community going strong in Salmon Arm. That was the message given to 98 business people attending last week's Shop Local forum at the McGuire Lake Inn. The Chamber of Commerce sponsored the evening dinner meeting to address the issue of $10 million in shopping dollars, which are spent outside the community every year" ("Businesses told shopping locally critical to healthy economy," *Salmon Arm Observer,* 17 November 1999).

Specific problem areas (or opportunities for local businesses to address) in Salmon Arm included:

- few men's clothing stores
- lack of children's clothing selection
- poor selection of mid-range dining establishments
- poor selection of music and books
- problems with parking downtown
- need to improve customer service in some stores

In response to the survey, the chamber of commerce and the SAEDC implemented a variety of actions. The chamber sponsored customer service workshops. Representatives of local businesses made a formal presentation to the local council regarding problems with downtown parking. A coalition of organizations launched a *Buy It Right ... in the Shuswap* campaign, which included store advertisements, a local media campaign, and incentives to purchase goods and services locally.

The purpose of the buy-local program is not to isolate the community from the outside world. Every person buys goods and services nonlocally as items may be less expensive, of a better quality, or simply available elsewhere when we travel. However, local spending and the integrity of the local economy play critical, and often overlooked, roles in preserving the diversity and stability of the local economy. If consumers support the local economy, those dollars will go back into the community and support many intangible aspects of community that are beyond the scope of, but rely on, economic well-being. The buy-local program identifies business opportunities, facilitates a better relationship between local consumers and local businesses, and reminds the entire community of the importance of supporting the local economy.

Arts, Culture, and Heritage Development

"Every community and every society has a unique personality or identity, shaped by its physical surroundings, traditions, values, forms of expression, and past experiences" (Stacey and Needham 1993). A sense of community identity, expressed through arts, culture, and shared community history, can enhance quality of life for local residents. As a community amenity, a strong local identity can serve as a selling feature, attracting residents, business people, and visitors who understand and appreciate a community's unique features, traditions, and way of life. Celebrating community identity and culture can also help build a spirit of cooperation and involvement (community mobilization) and a sense of belonging that provides security, stability, and strength, helping communities cope with change (Stacey and Needham 1993).

CED should be an expression of community history and culture. The discovery and revival of community culture is itself a CED strategy (Nozick 1992). Nozick (1992) distinguishes culture as a sense of identity and common purpose (community spirit). The Union of BC Municipalities (1997) adds that terms such as "culture," "arts," and "cultural development" mean different things to different people, ranging from multiculturalism to heritage preservation and street mural projects. Regardless of how we define culture, the arts and culture sector makes significant contributions to the social and economic development of BC communities. Statistics Canada estimates that this sector generated $3.3 billion in revenues and employed over 157,000 British Columbians in 1996 (Union of BC Municipalities 1997).

South Cariboo Arts and Culture Centre

The residents of the South Cariboo and 100 Mile House were drawn to a strategy that built upon the natural and cultural amenities found in their area. Amenities represent a wealth of relatively untapped potential for CED in British Columbia. In the South Cariboo, the working group discussed options and pursued strategies related to outdoor activities, local recreation, heritage, and the arts. Each of these areas makes communities more attractive places in which to live, visit, and invest. Following the completion of a Community Forest Pilot proposal (discussed below), we redirected efforts towards the enhancement of tourism and amenity values in the region. A local arts committee drafted a proposal for an Arts and Culture Centre. A community workshop sponsored by the project provided the committee with an opportunity to work with the local administration to design the project. Ongoing negotiations between the arts committee and the town administration eventually resulted in a decision to renovate an existing unused facility in the area to create an arts centre:

> The Arts and Culture Centre will be the home of literary, visual and performing arts in our community. Here, textile artists will meet and work alongside writers, painters, dancers, potters, singers and musicians. It will be a dynamic centre of teaching, learning and creating. The Centre will also be the home-base for groups like the Arts Council, the Cariboo Artists Guild, and the 100 Mile Festival of the Arts. We feel it is important to recognize and honour the Lions Club's contribution. (Arts and Culture Centre brochure)

In addition to bringing together citizens and community-based organizations, the Arts and Culture Centre space is used for a variety of activities and programs. Space uses include: a workspace, meeting place, office space for groups, teaching space for courses and workshops, a site for talks and lectures, a rehearsal area for the performing arts, and a small performance centre. In addition, groups deliver a variety of community programs in the facility, including: day camps for children and youth, a Summer School for the Arts, workshops and lessons, shows and sales, volunteer programs, and work experience. Local residents recognize that this relatively simple arrangement contributes to the process of community building and offers added value for the entire region by capturing benefits from the growing tourism market. The Arts and Culture Centre opened in June 2000, and serves a vital cultural, economic, and social function in the community and surrounding region. The initiative provides a strong example of mobilizing underutilized resources within the community and adding value to individual initiatives through networking and collaboration between different community interests.

Community Resource Management and Land-Use Planning

Community-based natural resource management (CRM) is an important and increasingly accepted CED strategy whereby communities gain management rights, responsibilities, and increased local benefits from local or regional resources. CRM strategies include resource sectors such as forestry, fisheries, wildlife, water, and minerals, as well as more comprehensive land and resource planning initiatives that account for all of the various uses and values associated with the land base and natural environment surrounding a community or region. Examples of CRM initiatives include community watershed management, community forests, fisheries co-management agreements, alternative harvesting techniques, community-shared agriculture, habitat restoration, ecosystem-based planning, and community resource boards and committees.

In British Columbia, decision-making agencies and corporate headquarters are typically geographically removed from rural communities. Decisions are frequently made without a clear sense of the ramifications for resource-dependent communities (Burda et al. 1997). "Basically the post-contact status quo is intact. The Nuxalk are neither recognized as nor able to act as the stewards of their forest homeland as they did for countless centuries. Oddly enough, they are treated as newcomers, sometimes even intruders in an industry based on their own resources!" (Selection Survey).

For both ecological and economic reasons, however, communities and regions are now less willing to accept outside decisions (Gallaugher et al. 1996). At the same time, senior governments are seeking ways to share the costs of management with resource users and to calm the political volatility associated with resource conflict (Nixon 1993). As a result, public involvement has increased in virtually all aspects of community and regional planning, including resource and land use.

Community involvement in resource management can have practical benefits for both resource managers and resource communities. The involvement of local communities and other stakeholders in resource planning and decision making can lead to:

- better and more informed decisions (provides a forum for advice and input)
- increased stakeholder commitment to implementation and enforcement (sense of shared responsibility)
- resolution of differing points of view early in a resource decision-making process, resulting in reduced conflict and uncertainty over resource use in the future (anticipatory versus reactionary)
- increased public awareness and understanding (Gale 1996)

Local decision making also tends to be more flexible and efficient, thus lending itself to adaptive management.

For communities, CRM is a strategy that can be used to expand their role in the management of local resources, thereby redressing the imbalance in hierarchical decision making. CRM can empower and build capacity among local citizens and organizations and result in more locally appropriate resource decisions. Case studies demonstrate that community members are likely to bring objectives such as sustainable employment and quality of life to the decision-making table, along with the more traditional resource management goals of economic viability for the resource industry. CRM systems tend to be based on cooperation instead of competition and focus on the collective sharing of a resource (Jacobs 1989). Accordingly, CRM may embrace key principles of CED.

Examples from elsewhere in Canada and around the world demonstrate that CRM has also been successful in encouraging resource conservation as communities develop local systems for preventing overexploitation. Guided by traditional resource-use wisdom and ecological knowledge, CRM encourages communities to harvest their natural capital at sustainable levels because of their long-term commitment to their home place and for longer-term economic viability. Research suggests that the more complete the resource rights given to communities and organizations, the more willing a group will be to take on responsibility for their management decisions (Schlager and Ostrom 1993). A commitment to stewardship arises not only from local rights to manage and benefit from resources but also from the duty felt by community members to each other and to future generations.

Local ownership and/or control do not ensure resource stewardship, but local ownership and the localization of the decision-making process do make it more likely (Gibbs and Bromley 1989). The ability of communities to take on management responsibilities is dependent on factors such as community capacity and a sound stewardship ethic. As a safeguard, management responsibilities in CRM are often shared with other levels of government. The functions of community and stakeholder groups in CRM can range from being informed and offering comment regarding proposed policies or programs, to sharing real decision-making authority with a management agency, to having the sole authority and responsibility to make decisions and to implement and enforce them. In effect, there is a continuum of community involvement in the process of CRM. Cooperative management lies at one end of this continuum of arrangements, co-management in the middle, and community management at the other end (see Figure 8.2) (Vodden 1999; Pinkerton 1989).

Co-management of natural resources may be defined as "the sharing of power and responsibility between government and local resource users." Aboriginal people view co-management as joint decision making that reflects government-to-government relationships. Co-management involves

Figure 8.2

Continuum of community involvement in resource management

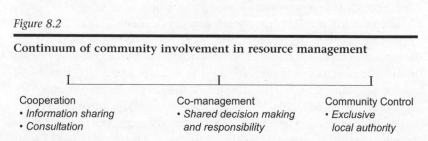

Source: Adapted from Pinkerton 1989.

the integration of local and state management systems (M'Gonigle and Curran 1997). Community forestry is one example of co-management that is particularly relevant to forest-dependent communities. Given that three of four project communities explored community forestry as a potential CED strategy, we allocated significant research attention to the issue.

Developing Sustainable Community Forestry in British Columbia

There is increasing interest in exploring the viability of community forestry as a potential solution to the problems facing forest management and forest-dependent communities in BC.[2] As evidence of this trend, in 1998, over eighty communities responded to a call for proposals from the provincial government to apply for a community forest licence.

Despite this recent surge in local interest, the idea of community forestry is not new. In fact, foresters around the world have practised community-based forest management for decades. The Royal Commission on the Forest Resources of BC first introduced the concept to BC in 1940 by recommending that municipalities manage local forests. This recommendation led to the creation of the Mission Municipal Forest (Burda 1999).

It was not until the 1970s and 1980s, however, that the concept of community forestry began to have broader appeal. Rising public awareness of the need to protect forest ecosystems from the negative impacts of industrial logging practices were partly responsible for the increasing attention. Water and soil quality, fish and wildlife habitat, and wilderness preservation all became prominent issues of public (and therefore political) concern. While environmentalists focused their energies on preservation, a growing number of people who worked with communities in the forest sector were becoming equally concerned with the responsible management of the "working forest" (Pinkerton 1993, 34).

Since the 1980s, the provincial government has sanctioned several community forests in BC. We have also witnessed the development of a variety of conceptual models that promote community forestry and, in general, more ecologically sensitive, holistic approaches to natural resource management (see Pinkerton 1993; Tester 1992; Maki et al. 1993; M'Gonigle 1996; Haley 1997; Burda et al. 1997). Definitions of community forestry are as numerous and diverse as the communities trying to implement it. At its core, however, community forestry emphasizes local control of the benefits from local forest resources, timber and non-timber. These benefits are not only monetary but are derived from the many values associated with forests, including ecological, aesthetic, cultural, recreational, spiritual, and medicinal values. The intent of community forestry is to allow these values, and the diverse interests of local citizens representing them, to be reflected in decisions about forest use (Burda et al. 1997; Betts and Coon 1996).

There are three overarching goals of community forestry: fostering community economic development, promoting sustainable forestry, and enhancing community participation in management decisions. There is a growing realization that in order for social and economic objectives to be met, we must restore and maintain healthy ecosystems (Kootenay Conference on Forest Alternatives 1999; Marchak et al. 1999). As a result, a number of communities in BC are considering an ecosystem-based approach to community forestry. This involves planning that first determines the ecological limits of the land base and then, given these limits, looks at how to harvest resources while maintaining a fully functioning ecosystem (Denman Island Community Forest Cooperative 1998).

The implementation of ecosystem-based forest management is in its infancy in BC. This type of management faces many hurdles, including the low-value commodity export orientation of the mainstream forest industry. In order for ecosystem-based management to be economically viable, community forest organizations must capture a higher price for their resources. Value-added manufacturing and ecological certification represent two such strategies for getting a higher return from local resources. The need for innovative manufacturing and marketing initiatives, developed in parallel with community forest operations, presents additional challenges to small communities that want to protect local ecosystems and provide meaningful, long-term employment.

There is no question that community forestry is a very challenging CED strategy, requiring a high level of commitment and expertise. Tables 8.1 and 8.2 provide lists of key conditions that contribute to the success of

Table 8.1

Conditions necessary for the development of sustainable community forestry in BC

Themes	Conditions
Community	• Strong local desire to assert management rights. Indicators of this include a will within the community to become more self-reliant, as well as evidence of entrepreneurial spirit.
	• A dynamic leader or "spark plug" and/or a core group of committed individuals who are motivated and, together, have the necessary skills, knowledge, and community acceptance to make a community forest happen.
	• Community enthusiasm for forestry in general and for community forestry in particular. Accompanying this should be mechanisms to transform this enthusiasm into commitment over the long term.

▶

◄ *Table 8.1*

Themes	Conditions
Community Forest Organization	• Appropriate Community Forest Organization (CFO) structure that serves to enable effective, accountable, and adaptable management of the community forest in a manner that reflects the values of the community being served. This should include a mechanism for conflict resolution. • Access to financial capital. • Ability to conduct sound business planning. • Participation of a broad spectrum of interests with sufficient overlap of perspective to find common ground. To facilitate this participation, there must be an established process for ensuring fair and equitable representation of all local interests. • Ability of the members of the CFO to learn how to work together to build social capital within the organization. • Ability to build and maintain partnerships and collaborative relationships both within and outside the community. This includes relationships with the Ministry of Forests, neighbouring licensees, and local contractors. This should be coupled with a good understanding of how new partnerships will affect the autonomy of the CFO. • Commitment to long-term planning.
Tenure	• Political will on the part of the BC government to enable sustainable community forestry. • Meaningful tenure with sufficient duration, security, and devolution of management rights on either a formal or informal basis, to encourage community involvement and achieve community-defined objectives. This tenure should include: an area-based, long-term licence with sufficient annual allowable cut (AAC)/geographic area to be financially viable; the right to participate in decisions regarding harvest levels and timing of harvest; a stumpage appraisal system that takes into account the sensitive nature of the community forest land base; and positive incentives for stewardship and the use of a low discount rate. • A large enough area with an adequate stock of merchantable timber in a balanced age-class distribution to sustain the community forest over the long term. However, the area should be small enough that users can develop accurate knowledge of external boundaries and internal micro-environments. • Community forest land base that either encompasses or is directly adjacent to the managing community.

Source: Adapted from Gunter 2000.

Table 8.2

Conditions beneficial to the development of sustainable community forestry in BC

Themes	Conditions
Community	• Strong identification of members of the community with local forest ecosystems. This connection is facilitated when people depend on the forest for their livelihood or other variables that are of importance to them (such as drinking water, viewscapes, and recreational opportunities). • A strong sense of community evidenced by a high level of civic engagement. Sense of community is closely linked to a strong place orientation. Also, community spirit and civic engagement are good indicators of the level of social capital. When residents participate actively in their community, cooperative, trusting relationships grow, and leadership capacity is built. • Willingness of the community to be pragmatically opportunistic. The ability of community leaders to think strategically about resource management issues is very important in the struggle to gain greater decision-making authority over local resources. • The existence of local forest knowledge as well as available local technical knowledge and skills. There should also be a commitment to education and training with a focus on local capacity building where knowledge and skills are lacking. • Available human resources. • Ability to think broadly of community forestry as one aspect of community development.
Community Forest Organization	• Reliable, up-to-date information about the state of the forest. • Reliable, up-to-date information about the availability of natural resources for commercial purposes. • Prior organizational experience. Although not necessary, it does facilitate the development of a new organization. • Agreement on expectations and objectives for a community forest. To some extent, this depends on having a common understanding of the forest, and for sustainable community forestry, a shared understanding of the connection between forest health and community health. • Focus on the multiple uses and benefits to be derived from the community forest. • Ability and commitment to maximize the value to the community of wood and forest products harvested. • Ability to demonstrate the benefits of the community forest to the community. • Capacity to connect to higher-value markets in a timely fashion. • Revenue autonomy.

Source: Adapted from Gunter 2000.

community forests. The lists are intended to serve as a checklist for community forest planners and operators in evaluating their (potential) operations. The information is drawn from an extensive literature review and primary research into community forests in BC.

We consider the conditions in Table 8.2 to be secondary to those in Table 8.1, but still extremely beneficial to the development of sustainable community forestry.

Until very recently, only a few examples of community forestry existed in BC, including Mission, North Cowichan, Revelstoke, Creston, and Kaslo. In 1998, the provincial government passed legislation that makes tenure change possible (British Columbia 1998b). As part of the legislation, the Forest Statutes Amendment Act allows for the establishment of community forest pilot agreements. The government intended the pilot agreements to "increase the direct participation of communities and First Nations in the management of local forests and to create sustainable jobs" (British Columbia 1998a). According to then Minister of Forests David Zirnhelt, "the legislation is the first step towards giving communities the flexibility to manage local forests for local benefits. Community forest tenure will contribute to the long-term economic stability of communities that rely on BC's forests" (British Columbia 1998b).

The objectives of the pilot program are to test new community forest legislation and its compatibility with existing forest legislation; to test a range of administrative models and forest management regimes; to provide long-term opportunities for achieving a range of community objectives; to meet government environmental stewardship objectives; and to provide general social and economic benefits to BC (British Columbia 1999b). As stated earlier, over eighty communities expressed an interest in the program, and the government accepted ten of twenty-seven full proposals. The term of the pilot agreements is five years with provisions for extension or replacement with a long-term community forest agreement of twenty-five to ninety-nine years if the pilot program is successful. The pilot projects represent a significant step in the direction of community-based resource management, and researchers and foresters from around the province are watching with interest.

The incentive for the provincial government to award community forest agreements may increase in many areas of the province. Until recently, the focus of harvesting in most regions has been on areas that are out of view, that are inexpensive to log, and that do not include consumptive watersheds. The available timber in these areas is diminishing, and forest companies are moving into more contentious and expensive areas. Logging in consumptive watersheds, especially those that are on steep slopes, is extremely controversial. There is also widespread opposition to logging important viewscapes. Community forest organizations may be better equipped to incorporate the concerns of community members into harvesting plans and to gain public support for logging in certain areas. Cautious, adaptive management will be required to be successful in these sensitive areas.

South Cariboo Community Forest Pilot Application

The timing of the Forest Communities project overlapped with the call for proposals from the Ministry of Forests for the Community Forest Pilot program. Based on the economic profile information provided in Chapter 5, it is clear that forestry is the dominant economic activity in the South Cariboo region. As a result, forestry was initially the main focus for CED planning for the project.

The community viewed pursuit of a community forest licence as a cornerstone to building a more diversified economy, managing local resources sustainably, and building economic partnerships with the surrounding business community. It is also clear in the excerpts from the community forest application below that the residents of the South Cariboo feel a strong sense of attachment to and *ownership* over the local forests. The South Cariboo assigned responsibility for developing the proposal to a working group with the objective of developing a "home grown proposal."

The 1999 South Cariboo Community Forest Pilot application states in part:

Introduction

This Community Forest Proposal is submitted by the District Municipality of 100 Mile House as a "home grown" proposal. When we first looked at the request for the proposal we decided not to hire outside consultants but to work with our citizens and local associations to prepare a proposal that reflects our visions, our objectives and our goals for our forest. Technical assistance was given by professional foresters from the 100 Mile House operations of Weldwood Canada and Ainsworth Lumber company. We feel this is truly our Community's proposal.

Our proposed Community Forest will benefit the citizens of The South Cariboo by giving them the opportunity to control the resource that drives our local economy and to protect their forest. The process we will set up will always ensure public involvement in the decisions that will be made about their forest. Local control of our forest resource will provide stability for all citizens in the area.

The Province will have the opportunity to partner in a Community run tenure with high environmental objectives, priorities which promote multiple uses of the forest and will be economically viable. The proposal will also strengthen the existing research project in economic development for forest-based communities we are presently involved in with Simon Fraser University. It will supply a valuable model for the Province to use in considering economic opportunities for other resource-based towns.

Statement of Goals and Guiding Principles
Our objective for the Community Forest Tenure is to set up a process which will allow for the stewardship of the resource under the direction of the residents of our community. The goals of the management plan will be to manage the area on a multiple use basis leading to an ecosystem based management plan as the tenure evolves.

Management Goals
1 Preservation and improvement of the quality of life style enjoyed by the residents. Our Community Forest will allow forestry-based decisions to be made which put equal weight on the social, economic and ecological factors specific to our region.
2 Enhanced forestry practices to ensure long-term availability of raw material for all local users of the resource. Emphasis will be placed on forestry practices which will improve the quality and quantity of timber within the tenure area.
3 Local management of the area and Provincial objectives for wildlife habitat, the ecosystem, aesthetics and the watershed.
4 To reduce dependency on volatile commodity markets for our residents. By implementing a sound multi-use management plan geared to the needs of the local forest users a more stable local economy can be realized.
5 To ensure profits generated stay within the community for the benefit of all citizens in the area. A successful Community Forest should relieve some of the tax burden experienced by the small town serving a large trading area.
6 A multi-use promotion of the Forest within the area for forestry, tourism and agriculture. Our community forest will be managed for all users. Local knowledge and participation throughout the process will ensure it is for the enjoyment of all. (District of 100 Mile House 1999, 14)

Administrative Authority and Structure
The 100 Mile House Development Corporation will manage the Community Forest on a multi-use basis with the primary focus on good environmental stewardship, guaranteed recreational and public use opportunities and the continued enhancement of the forest resource. Management objectives will always address the stability of the local economy while preserving the complete community forest resource for future generations.

The proposed 100 Mile House Development Corporation administrative structure was to include representation from council and administration (three members) and the community (two members) on its board of directors, along with various stakeholder representatives on a management committee with an advisory role.

The CED Centre played a variety of roles in assisting in the development of the Community Forest Pilot application. Researchers provided information and resources to the community about community forestry, including examples of community forestry in other jurisdictions. The research team facilitated a number of planning meetings. Finally, the region sponsored a series of community open house meetings to discuss the application.

Ultimately, the Ministry of Forests did not award the South Cariboo proposal. However, community forestry represents a viable opportunity in the area by virtue of the timber supply and the high local capacity for managing forestry operations. The proposal completed by the residents of the South Cariboo served as a valuable capacity- and community-building exercise. As pressure builds from communities across the province to create more community forest licences, the South Cariboo will be well prepared to take advantage of changes in the management and ownership of provincial forests.

Lillooet Tribal Council Community Land- and Resource-Use Planning
As mentioned in Chapter 7, the Lillooet Tribal Council (LTC) developed its Heritage Strategic Plan with a strong focus on land and resources. The natural resource coordinator compiled the plan in dialogue with Upper St'at'imc leaders, technicians, and community members. The plan serves as the basis for a comprehensive strategic plan that addresses the areas of land and natural resource management within Upper St'at'imc traditional territory.

The plan provides the foundation for land stewardship or heritage management activities, and may be used by LTC leadership and staff as a guide, planning tool, and basis for policy development.

One goal of the plan was to "return the land to a healthy state for the benefit of future generations." The plan outlines a vision for

a continuing and renewed relationship between the St'at'imc people (ucwalmicw) and the land (tmicw) which:

• Respects St'at'imc cultural traditions – using the ways, laws and standards of the people passed down through the generations
• Respects nature – putting the health of the water, the plants, the animals and the land itself before all else
• Is under St'at'imc stewardship – letting our people decide collectively how the land resources of the traditional territory will be managed
• Serves the St'at'imc communities – providing livelihood in old and new ways to all our people.

The plan outlines strategies to achieve this vision, including:

- Establish an organization or structure with the mandate to preserve, manage and renew St'at'imc lands, resources and cultural heritage, i.e., Natural Resource Advisory Board (NRAB) to oversee management of forestry, cultural heritage, fish & wildlife, lands and minerals, water and plants and medicines within the St'at'imc Traditional Territory;
- Develop St'at'imc policy, standards and guidelines regarding heritage management and land and resource use within the traditional territory;
- Develop and implement an eco-system based plan and approach to land and resource management;
- Establish an accessible and secure land and resource use information system that stores, retrieves and manages data for land and resource use planning and/or heritage management;
- Support the training of community members in Aboriginal land stewardship, heritage management and wildlife and fisheries conservation. (Heritage Strategic Plan)

Ultimately, the group would like to conduct a comprehensive land-use process for the bands of the Lillooet Tribal Council. The LTC has held forums and community meetings with industry and developed partnership associations to complete the planning process and implement specific development projects. Projects associated with the plan include a proposed joint venture with a local forestry company, archeology training for forestry crew members, the creation of maps with Upper St'at'imc place names, and a workshop on Aboriginal rights, title, and legal strategies with respect to the environment.

Joint Forestry Initiative: Hala'w

Upper St'at'imc Tribal Chief: We have a long way to go and a period of healing to go through. The St'at'imc communities are committed to finding this new direction, protecting the values that are important to the St'at'imc communities while achieving a level of community stability and economic growth for the Lillooet and St'at'imc communities.

Ainsworth VP: We must work together to find a new direction that balances the environmental, spiritual, community and economic needs of the St'at'imc and Lillooet people. We have a responsibility to the people of this area to find a new balance and a new relationship that is win-win for everyone. (*Lillooet News,* 3 May 2000)

The Hala'w initiative provides an example of a locally based decision to develop a local protocol for economic development bridging Aboriginal and non-Aboriginal communities. The initiative consists of two distinct phases. First, there will be an eighteen-month process of community and cross-cultural workshops, leading to the development of a memorandum of understanding; second, the project is preparing to develop a long-term economic development strategy for the Lillooet Tribal Council and a joint LTC-Ainsworth Lumber Company forest practices code.

The Hala'w initiative is not without controversy and difficulties. Both parties have been engaged in numerous failed attempts at negotiations, and both have a lingering frustration with government. These two issues lend additional uncertainty to the planning process. As a local resident put it: "We are working with the LTC to improve relations. It is a very gradual process of building trust. But you have to ask yourself: is this a role for private enterprise in the province? Should the government simply shuffle this off to private enterprise to solve?"

Despite concerns in both communities, the relationship-building process of the Hala'w initiative appears to be contributing to a more methodical and locally based process of conflict resolution and economic development for the region:

> Ainsworth VP: I have finally let go of the desire to make a business deal with the St'at'imc communities as a means of single-handedly solving all of Ainsworth's problems in Lillooet. Instead, the Hala'w Initiative involves taking a step back to work on the relationship first. Ironically, since I have accepted this slower, more methodical approach, we have made some of the real progress I was looking for in the first place. (Hala'w Group 2000)

Nuxalk Land-Centred Development

As a final example, the Nuxalk will pursue a "land-centred" approach to CED: "The premise of the land-centred approach is that when we have begun to assess and derive value from our lands, we will be best able to sit down and speak with others, including the Government of Canada, about the land question and issue of title" (Selection Survey). The Nuxalk wished to pursue a three-part strategy whereby they would: (1) gain greater access to their resources, (2) build community capacity, and (3) develop market relationships to ensure the financial sustainability of their development efforts. Our project planning with the community covered a variety of initiatives related to a land-centred approach, including plans for a community forest, local processing facilities, and the construction of a community longhouse. These projects also displayed a high level of issue integration, combining land and resource management, training, housing, tourism, and cultural development. Connie Watkinson, Forestry Manager for the Nuxalk Nation Integrated Resource Office, provides an update on their progress:

On January 15, 1999 the Nuxalk Nation submitted an application for a Community Forest License Pilot Project. After nine months of negotiation the Nuxalk were offered a Community Forest License (CFL) by the Ministry of Forests. The offer was made subject to a process of public and stakeholder input to verify local community support and further negotiations between the two parties over an exact agreement and forest management plan for the agreed upon area. One year later a number of community meetings, an open house, along with meetings and conversations with individuals, a newly elected Chief and Council and Ministry of Forests had been held. Concerns raised include consideration of cultural values, impacts on trap lines, insufficient volume (20,000 cu. m. per year), cultural sensitivity and low timber quality of the areas offered and high stumpage rates. Further, Nuxalk members were wary of the relationship to the treaty process and asked the question "Why do we need to have a license when we own the land?" At the same time it was projected 19 jobs would be created and opportunities for practicing environmentally sound forestry practices and value-added were identified.

By November 2002 we had cleared a variety of procedural and community steps: we established a Community Forest License Committee, hired a Forestry Manager, and acquired funding from Indian and Northern Affairs Canada Resource Access Negotiations Fund, and gained support for the CFL from a newly elected Chief and Council – providing that logging practices are sustainable and environmentally friendly (e.g., no clearcutting) and that the final decision to implement the community forest is made by the people. The Nuxalk are seeking funding for additional staff to assist in tasks such as business planning, economic and technical analysis. The planning process has been slow and time consuming yet a great deal of learning has taken place, with plans for integrating further forestry-related training programs for the Nuxalk people. Networking with other CFL holders has also proven to be an important source of information and ideas. (Watkinson 2002)

Tourism Promotion and Development
Despite recent downturns in the tourism industry, projections continue to indicate that growth in the tourism industry is a worldwide phenomenon. International tourist arrivals were 25 million in 1950, 183 million in 1988, and 644 million by 1999 worldwide (Remedios 2001).

Faced with an economic crisis due to dependency on declining forest resources, many rural communities are turning to tourism as a strategy for revitalizing their economies. Tourists travel for a variety reasons, including recreation and the opportunity to experience unique cultures and landscapes. Recreational and cultural tourism and ecotourism are three main strategies for tourism development. A number of Aboriginal communities in BC and across the world have discovered that their heritage and culture are of special interest to outsiders. If tourism operations share and develop community culture in a way that is sensitive to a people's history and traditions, cultural heritage may attract tourists to communities, bringing jobs, revenues, and business opportunities. Other communities have found that their natural environment lends itself to development of recreational projects such as wildlife viewing, ski-hill development, or sport fishing. Still others have chosen to capitalize on the small-town heritage and culture of their rural community.

Moving from an industrial resource-based economy to one based on selling a town's image and amenities requires local people to begin seeing their town differently in order to support a new direction for development. The economic transition requires visioning exercises, public debate, and community participation in the development planning process (Gill and Reed 1997). Further, tourism is not necessarily environmentally or culturally benign (Schaller 1996). Local control and careful planning are necessary to ensure that tourism operators implement responsible developments and deliver sufficient local benefits.

There is a strong link between amenity-based tourism development and the strategy of arts, culture, and heritage development described earlier, as illustrated by the objectives of the South Cariboo Arts and Culture Centre as well as the approach to tourism development adopted by both Salmon Arm and the Nuxalk Nation. The Nuxalk have identified ecotourism as an area of opportunity that must be pursued with careful planning and predetermined guiding principles in light of local cultural and ecological concerns.

Tourism Development in Salmon Arm

Strategy number 8 of Salmon Arm's strategic plan is to "expand the tourism sector by improving Salmon Arm's ability to not only enhance and host new forms of tourism but to attract four season destination visitors," with the goal of providing "services and facilities which are attractive to tourists in order to ensure future development of the town as a regional tourism destination" (Salmon Arm Economic Development Corporation 1999).

Like many other communities, Salmon Arm is seeking to extend its tourism season beyond the busy months of July and August and to encourage visitors to stay for longer than a stop to eat and gas up their vehicles. Local research identified low awareness of attractions and limited access to the waterfront as barriers to tourism development. However, a tourism subcommittee recognized significant potential for organizing and expanding tourism and capitalizing on the existence of high-quality sports and recreation facilities, the waterfront, and a rich, highly talented arts and cultural community.

The objectives of Salmon Arm's tourism development strategy include:

- increasing tourism year-round
- maintaining, enhancing, and marketing attractive year-round programs to increase the base of tourism offerings in Salmon Arm
- developing partnerships with surrounding communities to promote regional tourism
- developing Salmon Arm into a regionally recognized tourist destination
- promoting birdwatching and viewing of the grebes

The Salmon Arm tourism strategy recommends that the community seek to expand the tourism sector by not only concentrating on recreational tourism but also expanding into the following markets: sports, heritage/art and cultural, nature/environmental, and business/educational tourism. To implement this strategy, a working committee has implemented a number of actions. First, the municipality and the SAEDC formally recognized the committee as the Salmon Arm Tourism Committee, charged with responsibility for developing a tourism strategy for Salmon Arm. Second, the committee coordinated its activities with the regional tourism associations in the area to ensure synergy and cohesiveness with a minimal amount of duplication of programs. More recently, the committee conducted a study to identify back-country tourism assets and opportunities to complement the existing town- and lake-based services.

Lillooet Cultural Tourism

The Lillooet Tribal Council has an ongoing plan to create a centre to bring together the language, archeological, artistic, and other cultural resources of the Upper St'at'imc peoples. The St'at'imc Cultural Centre will serve an important economic development function for the entire region in terms of cultural tourism. The LTC and the municipal council in Lillooet collaborated to allocate land to build the cultural centre. The LTC continues its fundraising efforts to build the centre.

The LTC vision is to showcase St'at'imc culture to the wider community and to visitors from around world. The objectives for the centre are to:

- revive and maintain the St'at'imc language and heritage
- bridge the cultural gap within the Lillooet area
- educate the St'at'imc and others on St'at'imc culture and history
- provide career development opportunities
- promote the production, sale, and trade of traditional arts and crafts
- develop First Nations tourism-related activities and businesses

The Upper St'at'imc Language, Culture and Education Society is coordinating the centre project. The activities of the heritage resource coordinator are also contributing valuable cultural and archeological information to the society. Besides the future benefits of the cultural centre to the St'at'imc and the region, the society has made plans for the construction of the centre to be a capacity-building exercise. The design of the building will blend with the surroundings and reflect traditional pit houses used by the St'at'imc in a previous era. The society intends to use local labour and integrate a construction training program during the construction phase of the project.

The tourism sector in the Lillooet area is experiencing consistent growth. Lillooet's proximity to the Resort Municipality of Whistler creates enormous potential. Visitors to the area increased consistently from 1990 to 1998, from approximately 6,000 to over 16,000, drawn mainly by the adventure/ecotourism amenities in the area. The addition of a cultural centre will diversify the overall tourism strategy in the area, besides performing an important cultural service for the Upper St'at'imc people.

Networks and Community Relations

CED is ultimately about people working together to share information, generate ideas, and implement actions. At a time when rural and resource-dependent communities are facing tremendous uncertainty and turmoil, cooperation among different actors and organizations may be a particular challenge. Change and the scarcity of resources often lead to tension, competition, and conflict. Thus, a particular strategic focus of any CED effort must be the dynamics of community relations, facilitated through the community planning process.

Effective community-based planning, which is based upon and recognizes the principles of participation and representation, requires productive intra-community relations. A single harmonious community does not represent a realistic picture of the diversity of even small communities. On the other hand, a community rife with internal personal and organizational conflict may suffocate local development initiatives. Finding ways to constructively resolve differences of opinion and conflicts over organizational jurisdiction is a critical component of the CED process.

Developing a sense of shared purpose requires a bond among community members, often through meaningful interaction. Creating a "community of communities" also requires recognition of "unique cultural expression and cross-cultural sharing" and understanding (Nozick 1992, 196).

Formal and informal partnerships form an inevitable component of the CED process. Community groups can maximize the benefits of partnership development by ensuring that they meet a number of conditions, including (MacNeil 1994):

- well-defined, transparent, agreed-upon organizational goals and objectives
- a documented organizational structure
- shared contributions (facilitated by a degree of economic self-sufficiency or a diversity of funding sources)
- clear and ongoing lines of communication
- clear, transparent decision-making processes
- respect for the needs of each party, and encouragement of solutions acceptable to all

Understanding the legal and regulatory environment for more formal partnerships is also important. For example, an understanding of evolving Aboriginal rights and title in the case of partnerships with First Nations is a critical component of Aboriginal/non-Aboriginal relations and potential partnerships.

In addition, external agencies may also promote or link funding to the development of relationships within a community or between the community and external agencies. The stimulus of an external actor may lead to the formation of local partnerships, which in turn facilitate the implementation of CED projects. External agencies, particularly governments, played a critical role in the development of strategies in each community. For example:

- An alliance between Human Resources Development Canada (HRDC) and the local government in Salmon Arm worked to create the SAEDC.
- The Ministry of Forests Community Forest Pilot program provided the impetus for creation of the multi-partner South Cariboo community forest application.
- The development opportunities for the two First Nations communities are intricately linked with court decisions, the treaty process, and program assistance for training, capacity building, and governance, which require intricate partnership arrangements.

In the case of the SAEDC, its organizational hub role provides a sense of planning continuity and a forum in which to explore differences and balance competing interests. Continuity is a critical ingredient in the formation of constructive and lasting partnership arrangements.

Solving the Community "Flip-Flop"
Community residents stated that Salmon Arm was relatively evenly divided between those who wished to preserve the natural beauty and small-town feel of Salmon Arm and other interests in the community who wanted to promote development and community expansion. In the past, residents

stated that this split was responsible for a "flip-flop," or regular rotation in local government representation between "conservationists" and "developers." This split in the community fundamentally influences the dynamics of local development. In the past, residents stressed the extent to which the split has contributed to conflict and inconsistent planning. More recently, however, the split appears to be having a relatively healthy influence on the local development debate, influencing and restraining the perspectives of both sides, with some exceptions.

Residents note that intra-community relations in Salmon Arm have improved significantly since the introduction of the SAEDC. The SAEDC advisory council, which monitors and assists the activities of the organization, also serves as a think tank for the local council, thereby facilitating information sharing. The advisory council has increased participation and openness between various development agencies in the community.

Local residents also state that the working relationships between the SAEDC and other groups is aided by the transparency of the SAEDC planning process, the inclusiveness of the organization through diverse membership on the board and the advisory council, and the extent to which priorities are clearly communicated and shared with other agencies. In addition to the formal organizational structure of the SAEDC, residents feel that informal networking contributes to maintaining open and effective relationships at personal and organizational levels. It should be noted, however, that the networking function of the SAEDC was not automatic. Tensions and differences were common in the early formative stages of the organization, as all community members and representatives struggled to define the mandate of the development corporation. Over time, however, the community outreach and participation skills of the organization improved and a broader spectrum of local interests was represented both within the organization and in its strategic orientations.

Communities may require other forms of intervention in cases where a clear and recognized conflict at the local level is inhibiting any progress. If a community is "stuck," attempts to initiate planning processes and organizational development will repeatedly fail, making future attempts more difficult. We experienced a more entrenched form of community conflict in Bella Coola, which local leaders were quick to point out during our initial rounds of project planning.

Conflict Resolution in Bella Coola
Our work with the Nuxalk Nation, although initially slow, provided a mutually rewarding learning experience as well as definitive action in the later stages of the project. Community conflict can jeopardize community planning if it remains unchecked or unresolved before a CED process is embarked upon.

A two-part conflict confronted the Nuxalk. One the one hand, there was internal leadership-based conflict within the Nuxalk. On the other hand, there were long-standing issues of conflict and mistrust between the Nuxalk community and the non-Aboriginal residents of the valley. The internal conflict was ultimately more an interpersonal issue that was gradually resolved through both individual efforts and a change in local elections that removed the opposing agents from at least the formal local political process.

All parties recognized that the inter-community conflict between the Nuxalk and the non-Aboriginal residents of the valley was a critical barrier to development for both communities. Because of the isolation of the Bella Coola valley and the gradual resolution of title and treaty issues, the two communities must find ways to work together. In the fall of 1999, Simon Fraser University facilitated a relationship between the community and the US-based Kettering Foundation, which specializes in conflict resolution and cross-cultural relations. The foundation selected Bella Coola as one of five North American communities to which it would provide conflict resolution assistance. The project brought together individuals from the Nuxalk Nation and valley locals to engage in a process of "sustained dialogue."

The process consisted of a series of workshops that brought together citizens and community leaders to openly discuss conflict issues in a controlled environment. Reports from community members indicate that the process was beneficial. Continued efforts on the part of the Nuxalk Nation, the tribal council, the valley population, regional government, and organizations such as Community Futures hold promise for long-term relationships in the valley. The resolution of inter-community conflicts and the building of trust between the two communities will be a long and gradual process, perhaps even generational. However, making conflict resolution a focus for the CED process – linking community relations with development – represents a critical first step.

Lessons and Observations

The range of strategies pursued by each of the communities demonstrates a commitment to economic diversification both within and outside of the forest sector, a key overall strategy for addressing the legacy of dependency on a single resource. In general, an economy with a diversity of businesses and industries will be healthier and more sustainable because the risks associated with economic downturns are spread throughout a variety of sectors. A broad base of economic activity helps cushion the impacts of boom-and-bust periods associated with single sectors, regardless of their overall economic contribution. Just as an ecosystem depends on diversity and species richness to keep it functioning and healthy, so a local economy depends on the variety and diversity of businesses and CED initiatives to keep it vital and dynamic (Nozick 1999).

A commitment to diversification serves as a testament to the abilities of the individuals and organizations that have facilitated the CED process in their communities. The process of transition from an economy dependent on resource extraction to a more diversified, and in some cases "post-productivist," economy is not an easy one. Economic transition requires significant social, attitudinal, and institutional change (Gill and Reed 1997). Clearly the communities of Salmon Arm, Bella Coola and the Nuxalk Nation, the Lillooet Tribal Council, and the South Cariboo are accepting this challenge. The following sections offer our final reflections on the strategic orientations and capacities of the project communities.

Common Barriers and Opportunities

A first interesting observation is drawn from one of our final community workshops. All project communities were represented at the workshop, providing an opportunity for mutual learning and reflection. We asked participants to make presentations on the project activities taking place in their communities. We then conducted brainstorming with the entire group to identify barriers, opportunities, and potential solutions for each community. Six themes emerged from the discussion, representing either a barrier or an opportunity, depending on the degree to which they were present in the community (see Table 8.3).

Given the economic and cultural diversity represented by the communities, we were all surprised by the degree of commonality, despite differences in terms of the severity or impact of each issue. The significance of this finding represents opportunities for future research and for the direct promotion of CED across BC. Experimenting with and broadcasting an array of strategies to address these six themes will have universal appeal to communities across the province. The themes also represent a starting point for evaluating and designing various policy interventions.

The common community experiences help in part to explain similarities in the strategic orientations of the communities. The strategic similarities witnessed in the case communities are reminiscent of Filion's observations (1991) concerning the small range of development options being pursued by municipalities in Ontario. Filion (1991) provides five reasons to explain the limited range of actions: (1) all municipalities face budgetary restrictions that place limits on local action; (2) small and medium-sized municipalities face similar forces and effects of the restructuring process; (3) municipalities are limited by the extent of their legislated authority; for example, they are unable to offer grants or bonuses to stimulate private investment; (4) control over the development process by the business class and town councillors narrowed the ideological spectrum of possibilities; and (5) Filion witnessed a limited understanding of local economic devel-

Table 8.3

CED barriers and opportunities

Barrier/opportunity	Examples from the project communities
Individual capacity	• Limits to volunteerism and burnout • Need to transfer expertise from outside consultants to community members
Access to capital	• Need for funding and long-term financial viability of CED processes, organizations, and initiatives • Competition for limited funds • Cautious spending by public and private sector • Challenge of a small tax base with a large regional population
Community education and awareness	• Need for an attitudinal shift in the community towards more self-reliance • Fear/acceptance of change • Concept of economic leakage
Community organizing	• Community participation • Trust between communities • Communications and coordination between community groups • Collaboration between Native and non-Native communities
Policy and the role of government	• Determining local and regional responsibilities • Offloading from the federal government to provincial and local levels without associated resources, knowledge, and experience • Separating economic development from politics
Resource management	• Concern for environmental health and resource access

opment options among local planning staff and elected leaders (generally limited to town marketing).

Analysis of the project communities adds to Filion's representation of local development in four ways. First, inter-community networking and information sharing leads to a contextual modification of tested economic development options. For example, the formation of the community-based economic development organization (CEDO) in Salmon Arm and similar economic development committees in the other communities were, to some extent, borrowed from the experiences of other towns. This networking may reduce the variability of development options, but it also provides an opportunity to enhance the effectiveness of specific strategies and increase local and extra-local confidence in the pursuit of specific options.

Second, the similar nature of strategies reflects the broader dissemination of information pertaining to community development (through organizational websites, consultants, government handbooks, etc.) and the role of network organizations in distributing information and building capacity. Professional training and examples from other communities contain similar methods and processes for conducting CED activities.

Third, the availability of funding for specific initiatives reduces the variability of development options between communities. This creates an opportunity for institutional learning associated with the implementation of specific strategies; however, the cases show that this was not conducted in any systematic or consistent manner at any level.

Finally, the communities add to Filion's analysis by displaying a more sophisticated and varied understanding of local development. The orientation of the case strategies provides information about the impact of a more balanced approach to local development. The diversity of strategies and the concern for a localist approach to development represents an expansion of the narrow, town-marketing approach to development witnessed by Filion.

For example, in Salmon Arm, the SAEDC started with a booster approach to promoting the community and attracting external enterprise. Over time, however, concerns about the elitism of the process and its external orientation began to modify and expand the function of the SAEDC. An internal (localist) and more diverse (inclusive of marginal) focus began to emerge within the organization. The mandate and orientation of the SAEDC changed through increased attention to existing local businesses, sectoral-relational support for construction and tourism, business coaching and mentorship, buy-local campaigns, job transition projects, and expanded board and steering committee representation.

Similarly, 100 Mile House and the South Cariboo originally pursued a resource management option only. Over time, however, the project included a more diverse representation of community interests and development options, including links to small business development and educational programs. This proved important following the rejection of the community forest plan by the province.

Community Organizing and Planning

It is certainly the case that a host of agents – businesses, labour organizations, place-based workers, economic development practitioners – are only too aware of the need for a deeper comprehension of the political economic processes and scales of governance within which their regional economies are often precariously positioned. (MacLeod 2001, 822)

As we saw in earlier chapters, a large number of external and internal forces exert influence over the local economy. Maintaining a grasp of the multitude of impacts and opportunities is a challenging and time-consuming task. Equally numerous are the locally oriented development options and concerns. As a result of this causal and opportunity dynamism, it became necessary in each community to adopt a development process to provide some structure with which to understand and confront the internal and external dynamics of the community. The community organizing and planning functions of a CEDO (or similar community-based organizational structures) and the initiation of a strategic planning process facilitate the development of structure and order.

CEDO

In all cases, the first step towards adopting a more structured approach to local development was the identification of a local actor who would assume responsibility for leading and coordinating the working group response. The selection of a highly skilled individual marks the first critical step in the local development process. The individual must be capable of sorting through the significant complexity of the development process, which requires a broad range of skills. The identification of qualified candidates poses a challenge to smaller communities, given the lower likelihood of finding an individual with the ideal qualifications. However, CED is larger than a single individual and the formalization of the process requires organizational support in addition to legal recognition.

As seen in Chapter 7, CEDOs are a common organizational structure to help facilitate local development. CEDOs provide an identity to the local development process. They act as a platform for the participation of both the broader public and other organizations. CEDOs also constitute a legitimate entity through which to attract and distribute resources. It is clear to us that the communities with an established and recognized organizational structure were more successful in implementing CED strategies. The establishment of a formal CEDO structure simply represents a more advanced stage in the CED process. Salmon Arm was in a position to fund such an organizational structure by virtue of its size and the funding support from HRDC. The other communities made progress towards the organization of their development response, as the South Cariboo and the Nuxalk created CED coordinator positions and the Lillooet Tribal Council created an internal committee to share CED resources and information among the different bands. The main advantage of the SAEDC is that it was able to serve as an incubator for a broader range of community projects. Economic development was not simply an add-on function to an existing position. In total, the SAEDC posted a 419 percent return on investment to the local district between 1998 and 2000.

Overall, a comparison of the communities reveals a variety of lessons concerning the operation of CEDOs in the rural environment, particularly with respect to characteristics of CEDO success. The following are characteristics of the CEDOs that figure prominently in creating organizational success:

- diverse community representation on the board
- active board participation
- broad community representation
- organizational distance from local council
- local government/band council support
- constructive community group relations (well coordinated and clarified)
- clear mandate and clearly communicated mandate and plans
- high degree of volunteerism (increases capacity and representativeness of the organization)
- ability to leverage funds
- long-term funding commitment
- internal focus as strategic orientation
- exploration of equity options
- economic development officer (EDO) style and phases of leadership

This list represents a daunting task of organizational management and personal skill. Clearly, it will be a challenge for any single individual or organization to find the correct balance of skills, functions, and relationships necessary for a given context. A strategic planning process lessens the need for a single highly skilled individual. The strategic plan delivers operational order to CEDOs, helps build local and extra-local relationships, involves more people, and provides a template for action.

Strategic Planning

Strategic planning is a tool that places local action within the context of a specific geography (Barnes and Hayter 1994) and economy (Douglas 1994). The strategic planning process illustrates that it is critical to understand the broader context of development. However, local action depends upon the ability to isolate selected opportunities to which to allocate scarce local resources. Strategic planning in the project communities helped subdue the complexity of the development process into a manageable framework. Overall, a variety of benefits are associated with the strategic planning process:

- increase in confidence – higher degree of local ownership and awareness of the development process

- networking – organizational participation and identification of a variety of community interests
- community assessment – identification of local needs and opportunities
- tailored expectations – realistic expectations and a feasible workplan
- time – outlining of a long-term vision for the community

Strategic planning was critical for the communities to undertake. Despite early resistance to being "studied to death," the planning process was important for group formation, building a base of participation, understanding how different dimensions of the community interact, and identifying development options that existed "outside the box" of traditional local economic development models.

The Role of the State

From a government perspective, the CED challenge lies in defining an appropriate role that supports community-based efforts without overtaking them, empowers community processes while protecting the broader public interest, and offers financial and resource support without fostering dependency or creating duplication. This represents a challenging balancing act with regard to support for CED.

The lack of any coherent senior or provincial government coordination of resources and the lack of a comprehensive rural economic development plan is both a by-product and a cause of this confusion. Similarly, the limited resources, understanding, and powers of local governments, a situation that may be gradually changing in BC, further complicate the promotion of development from the bottom up. The following sections outline lessons drawn from the project communities regarding a clarification of the roles of local and senior governments concerning CED.

Local Government: Municipal

It is clear from the review of the economic transition process taking place in the project communities that local governments are struggling with a wide range of issues that affect the state of the local economy. Local governments have a mandate from the community, and are accountable to the community, concerning matters of the local economy. However, local governments do not necessarily have the authority, staff resources, or expertise to assume a more direct and proactive role in stimulating CED (responsibility without power).

The communities illustrate that the support of local governments is critical to the start-up and success of a CED strategy. Local governments can provide the necessary authority, legitimacy, and start-up resources to organize a more structured local development response. The involvement of local governments also provides an important connection with the municipal administration, linking the development process with town planning and local expertise. Despite the benefits of involving local governments in CED, the cases illustrate that removing selected features of the economic development function from local governments may hold distinct advantages in terms of expertise, resource generation, and sheltering of the economic development process from the vagaries of the political process.

The arm's-length relationship between the local government in Salmon Arm and the SAEDC worked very well. The direct separation of the CEDO from the municipal council may enable it to weather challenges and conflicts that define the local political process. CED requires a long-term commitment and a plan that may extend beyond specific political mandates. Nonetheless, the removal of the economic development function from the direct accountability of the political process raises additional questions of power and the potential for elitism to dominate the economic development agenda.

The Community Charter, new local government legislation in BC, will grant more freedom and responsibility to local government over matters of economic development (Ministry of Community, Aboriginal and Women's Services 2002). The examples drawn from the project raise interesting questions about the capacity of local government councillors concerning economic development, the role of local politics in economic development, and the risks associated with subjecting long-term development processes to the shorter-term fluctuations of the political process. However, removing economic development control altogether from local governments may foster elitism. This implies a complex relationship between local development and accountability to the local democratic process.

Band Councils
Our experiences with the Nuxalk and the Lillooet Tribal Council illustrate the overwhelming influence of these organizations on the economic development prospects of their communities. In the case of resource management and the resolution of title and treaty issues, such a communal governance approach offers a number of advantages, such as pooling of resources and ensuring equity throughout the community. The Aboriginal system of governance also faces some critical challenges, however.

First, the short time line for the band council election cycle severely curtails the ability of councils to design and implement development opportunities within a single mandate. This is particularly problematic in communities where there are frequent "flip-flops" in council representation. Incoming councils may reverse decisions of previous councils, thereby preventing any form of continuity in development progress.

Second, due to the number of demands now facing council members (resource management, consultations with local industry, treaty negotiations, and local administration), council capacity is a serious concern. From an economic development perspective, limited capacity means that multi-faceted development issues will not be adequately addressed. Stressed capacity leads to a narrower or issue-by-issue approach, when an integrated approach is more productive and culturally appropriate.

Finally, while the tribal council system represents a forum for cooperation and resource sharing, we also witnessed a fracturing of economic development funds. Individual bands are responsible for smaller development budgets and the local bands are often too small to support an economic development position or seriously pursue more complex economic relationships or strategies.

Senior Governments

The communities all relayed various frustrations with senior levels of government concerning economic development. The frustrations are drawn from a long list of reasons, including inconsistent program implementation, rigid program designs, urban policy bias, and offloading of services and functions without necessarily transferring authority or resources. The frustration is balanced, however, by a clear recognition of the need for senior levels of government to manage the restructuring process and maintain basic services. In particular, the communities believe that senior governments have a key role to play in supporting local development efforts. As illustrated by the staples discussion in Chapter 3, communities do not easily discard traditional forms of dependency. The transition is particularly acute in terms of reorienting government/community relations and in determining appropriate scales and degrees of senior government involvement in the local development process.

In order for governments to embrace a more facilitative and flexible approach to CED, however, communities must first address the issue of accountability (Savoie 2000). Senior governments are faced with two distinct levels of accountability. On one level, they are entrusted with protecting the broader public good, which may or may not coincide with the interests and objectives of local communities and regions (Bryant 1999). On a second level, governments must secure the accountability of the local community in order to protect broader budgetary interests, but also to ensure the effectiveness of policies and programs. Systematic senior government support for CED efforts is contingent on the accountability of local processes and practitioners.

Two factors emerged from the project that inform the question of community and government accountability in the CED process: evaluation and funding.

Evaluation

In the CED literature, researchers recognize evaluation (of objectives and outcomes) as a particular challenge. In addition to the problems associated with identifying causality in development due to scale flux, a number of local challenges exist. First, the integrated development approach of CED presents a number of particular challenges to effective evaluation. CED seeks to address multiple objectives. CED considers economic and non-economic factors when measuring the outcomes and externalities of local action (Armstrong et al. 2002). Second, given the participatory nature of CED, multiple target groups are affected by local development activity (MacNeil and Williams 1995). Third, there are long lead and implementation times associated with CED. Capacity development leading up to the implementation of specific activities and the time necessary to achieve self-reliance and spin-off effects complicate targeted and time-specific evaluation efforts. Finally, it is difficult to separate often overlapping (and isolated) policies and program areas related to development.

CED practitioners generally resist evaluation efforts for two main reasons. First, CED practitioners are apprehensive about setting evaluation targets for events that are complex and often well beyond their direct control, such as creating a specific number of new jobs. Targets can too easily become signposts for failure rather than tools for critical reflection. Second, meaningful evaluation can be a resource-intensive process. CED organizations generally operate on small budgets and practitioners may see evaluation as an added distraction from actually engaging in development activities. The lack of specific resources from project grants for evaluation also provides little incentive for an extensive evaluation process. As a result, evaluation of CED efforts is more narrowly associated with the achievement of organizational objectives (i.e., fulfilling the workplan) and return on investment, instead of assessment of broader community impacts.

Based on the activities of the communities and the list of success factors identified in the previous chapter, we are able to identify a number of possible CED evaluation variables (see Table 8.4). In effect, it is possible to use a variety of quantitative and qualitative evaluation variables in CED. Baseline information related to specific and tangible indicators is useful for raising awareness and for improving the quality of information available to local actors for planning. From a purely evaluative perspective, however, baseline analysis for CED is weak (Armstrong et al. 2002). Baseline analysis is incapable of estimating the counterfactual (i.e., what would have happened in the absence of local development efforts?) because of the number of variables affecting the state of the local economy and society. Qualitative variables offer useful information to local and nonlocal actors, but again they must be systematically and repeatedly documented. As a result, there is generally no comprehensive understanding of the direct and indirect value of CED organizations and their activities.

Table 8.4

Possible CED evaluation variables

Evaluation component	Variables
Organizational evaluation	• Representation of community by board/steering committee members • Internal versus external organizational effort (time and resource analysis) • Workplan and specific objectives • Community awareness of CEDO activities • Transparency (decision making and information availability)
Direct development	• Funding and return on investment (ROI) • Inquiries from external interests (businesses and private citizens) • Number of jobs created • Number of people trained • Number and total of loans provided or businesses counselled • Process-related activities (e.g., community meetings)

Indirect development	• Community confidence
	• Community organizational cooperation
	• Businesses created
	• Businesses attracted
	• Building permits
	• Assessed values of properties
	• Visitation rates
	• Taxation levels
	• New business licences
	• Socio-economic statistics:
	  – Employment levels
	  – Health
	  – Education rates
	  – Other socio-economic variables

Armstrong and colleagues (2002, 461) provide a useful framework for organizing qualitative analysis of local development efforts. Evaluation should be structured to answer a set of specific questions pertaining to the following:

1 *Deadweight:* would additional directly created jobs (or other forms of economic activity) have occurred anyway?
2 *Displacement:* are the jobs created at the expense of jobs in competitor firms elsewhere in the area?

3 *Supply chain effects:* do the expanding businesses buy significant amounts of their inputs from other local firms, creating additional benefits in the area?

4 *Multiplier effects:* to what extent do the extra jobs trigger multiplier benefits in the area? (leakage or local spending)

A lack of resources is the most common barrier to comprehensive evaluation. Even at the local district level, it is difficult to compile and update evaluation variables that permit trend analysis. Nevertheless, evaluation is critical to raising internal support for CED efforts, and scaling up the attention paid to local development by governments and other supporters. Given the utility of evaluation to senior governments, it may be appropriate for governments to provide or facilitate technical assistance for evaluation at the community level. In addition, governments may help improve our understanding of CED evaluation and the generation of frameworks for use and adaptation by local practitioners.

Funding

Program funding represents the most critical role played by senior levels of government in support of CED. As noted earlier, funding is a significant source of the community frustration with senior governments, a sentiment that is undoubtedly shared in the opposite direction as well. In addition to general comments of frustration, community members offered their prescriptions for how funding relationships should be structured between communities and governments:

- *Community ownership of projects is essential.* In order to facilitate substantial local ownership, communities should commit real financial resources to project development (i.e., not just in-kind). The best government programs are those that commit matching funding (matched to cash and not things like office space and the like).
- *Governments should fund studies in coordination with a serious, up-front commitment to implementation* (such as partnership development and finance options). Studies are essential for supporting the knowledge base and office infrastructure of CED organizations; however, unless governments are willing to fund the capacity necessary for implementation, most studies fail to spur real project developments. Community members somewhat cynically saw studies as a way for government to show support for CED efforts without committing substantial resources that are capable of having any structural impact.
- *Governments should make provisions in programs for the facilitation of technical support.* Prior assessment of the capacity necessary to implement projects should be matched with community resources and not assumed to exist.

- *CEDOs require stable, long-term funding commitments.* Without long-term organizational stability, people and other organizations are less willing to enter into partnerships with local CED organizations. In addition, the leveraging of additional project financing or funding without long-term organizational security is challenging.
- *Direct organizational support from government funding should be set at a realistic sliding scale.* Time lines and options for core organizational self-reliance are critical to avoiding dependency on inconsistent government support for local development.
- *Funders should provide CEDOs with incentives for performance.* For example, an economic development corporation (EDC) could receive 10 percent of any new tax revenues generated by the commercial sector, provided there was a substantial link between the EDC and such development activity.

A more thoughtful and systematic approach to understanding beneficial funding relationships between communities and governments would help reduce uncertainty about the CED process. There is also a clear connection between funding and evaluation in terms of assessing the effectiveness of CED efforts and the value they contribute to the wider society.

Scale

The degree to which CED will be able to offer a viable alternative for local economies will depend greatly on its scale. This does not imply simply becoming larger in order to compete more effectively in a marketplace biased towards large-scale capital. Rather, scale and the process of *scaling up* CED implies both size and diversity. We see from the Forest Communities project examples of each. In particular, each community scaled up the regional representation of their strategies, as can be seen in Table 8.5.

In each case, the line between the community and the region began to blur when specific initiatives were implemented. The community/regional connection exists because neither people nor economic activity necessarily obey strict jurisdictional lines. However, the mechanisms for addressing community/regional relations appear poor in each project area. Regional districts are the formal arena for addressing regional development issues, but the regional districts in the case areas were often a source of tension and conflict, often spurring the decision at the community level to go it alone. Nevertheless, the project demonstrated a variety of benefits associated with linking local CED processes and strategies with regional cooperation:

- the ability to save resources
- enhanced financial viability
- a stronger political voice
- conflict avoidance or resolution

Table 8.5

Community/regional strategies for scaling up CED adopted in the Forest Communities project

Community – region	Strategy
Salmon Arm – Shuswap Region	The SAEDC facilitated a variety of projects bringing together various communities in the Shuswap region for cooperative planning and implementation, including the tourism strategy and the construction industry networking strategy.
100 Mile House – South Cariboo	The project was initially coordinated through the District of 100 Mile House, but the working group expanded its focus to include the South Cariboo region in its pursuit of the community forest licence.
Lillooet Tribal Council – Upper St'at'imc Nation	The project began with a regional, multi-community focus, given the relationship fostered with the Lillooet Tribal Council. Strategies highlighted common concerns and opportunities, including heritage revival and development and regional land-use planning.
Nuxalk Nation – Bella Coola Valley	The Kettering Foundation conflict resolution process facilitated by the project addressed long-standing issues of contention between the Nuxalk and the regional district authority, representing the non-Native residents of the valley.

- increased economic linkages and business development opportunities
- community building
- access to a larger pool of expertise
- community sharing and learning
- participation
- decrease in competitive relationships (increase in levels of trust)
- dilution of isolated conflicts in the larger regional pool
- mutual aid
- economies of scale

The challenge that accompanies these multiple benefits is being able to maintain the principles of CED as the process becomes more complex. This requires different skills in organizational development, decision making, and, as seen specifically in the project, conflict resolution. Once again, the ability to scale up the reach and effectiveness of CED is dependent upon the capacity of the individuals and organizations in the specific development context. The community/regional linkages identified in the project highlight a significant development gap in the province. The province requires new governance structures and attitudes to forge innovative regional economic development alliances.

Conclusion: A Change in Thinking

The diversity of communities and regions combined with the contextual orientation of CED means that there will be great variety in the outcomes of development processes. The diversity of development opportunities and constraints present in BC, in addition to differences in the capacity of local actors and organizations, leads Barnes and Hayter to conclude that in matters of local development, anything is possible (1994, 307): "In some cases, crushing outside structural forces will weigh against any local initiatives, while in other cases, by dint of perseverance, luck, skill, and opportunity the force of agency will win through. But neither of these cases can be known in advance."

The prospect that anything is possible when it comes to local development does little to help communities or the agencies with a mandate to assist them in achieving their development objectives. As stated earlier, poor conceptualizations of CED arise for a variety of reasons: limited systematic research, weak theorization, lack of capacity, and the small-scale nature of interventions. As a result, our present understandings of CED fall somewhat short in providing the necessary security, conceptual or practical, that communities can implement local development in a systematic and reasonably predictable manner. Researchers, policy makers, and practitioners require an element of predictability if they are to progressively build coherent research agendas, policy frameworks, and best practices.

The CED examples presented here illustrate that there is some element of a systematic local response. Certain processes and forces may lead to specific results regarding the impacts of restructuring, the response of communities to the uncertainties of restructuring, the strategies communities seek to implement, and the role of governments in either hindering or facilitating local development. Such conformity in process and strategy is to some degree, as Filion (1991) noted, due to common constraints. However, conformity in CED is also a by-product of, and testament to, the work of local researchers and practitioners throughout the 1980s and 1990s. Their ability to share lessons learned and to disseminate best practices for CED are clearly influential.

Two main points summarize the general lessons for the implementation of local development strategies. First, the cases illustrate the importance of starting small and building up to larger initiatives as the capacity of the organization and the support of the community increase. Small and early successes help build a reputation for a development organization. Early and, in particular, localist action builds support within the community. This may also lead to increased volunteer resources. In addition, finding an appropriate scale for local initiatives will help prove to both internal and external interests that local development efforts are more than simply another process. Time spent on larger projects, without an equal or even greater amount of time invested in specific local initiatives, may leave development organizations with nothing to show the community but endless hours of meeting time and staff/volunteer burnout.

Second, the communities illustrate the advantages of pursuing a balanced approach to CED, by which we mean both localist and linking initiatives. Unless communities pursue a balanced approach to development, they will be less likely to attain the broad participation and diverse representation necessary to support local development organizations. Both the literature and development practitioners are clearly familiar with the practices and strategies of a booster approach or a specifically linking approach to economic development. They are less familiar, however, with integrating a local and a broader representational perspective into the local development process and thinking differently about the structure of the local economy.

As the Salmon Arm business community discovered, however, the inclusion, if not dominance, of a localist orientation in CED efforts is necessary to maintain organizational support and to launch appropriate and less risky projects. A purely external approach will leave little time to foster cohesive local coalitions. It may also lead to concerns over the elitism of the process. People may also raise objections about the fact that local resources are being used to assist external and as yet unproven interests (i.e., "what about me!?").

Ultimately, the booster approach does little to decrease the dependency of communities on external forces or to meet the needs of existing business and employment interests. What emerges from the analysis of the case communities is a blending of internal and external approaches to CED. Clear lines in the literature between elite boosterism and general community development blur in practice as communities cope with the real complexity of development – in terms of identifying internal and external opportunities and balancing an appropriate representation of community interests.

Throughout the project, we witnessed a change in the approach communities were adopting to confront economic development issues, becoming more confident in the internal capacity of the community to create and sustain economic opportunities. It is the change in thinking that is perhaps the most important and lasting transition that must take place at the community level before CED will truly be an effective approach to economic development. As Donna Barnet, mayor of 100 Mile House during the project, explained in a letter to Sean Markey: "We must show leadership at the community level and continue to move forward no matter how difficult the task may seem."

9
The Community/University Relationship

This chapter describes in greater detail the specific dynamics of working with communities from the university perspective. First, we will discuss participatory research techniques. Our intent is to contribute to the dialogue on participatory research, which is gaining increasing currency within academic circles. This section will conclude with a more generalized discussion of lessons for community-based researchers. Second, we will discuss techniques and insights associated with building local capacity for community economic development (CED). Capacity building was a major strategic focus of the CED Centre within the project. We will identify lessons from our experiences with the hope of generating insights in other individuals and organizations associated with capacity issues through training and education in the rural and small-town environment. This chapter also contains lessons for communities on how they may establish constructive external capacity-building and consulting relationships to aid them in their CED endeavours.

Mediating Research Tensions

Universities are under increasing pressure to demonstrate their relevance to society. Coincidentally, communities are expressing a greater interest in becoming active participants, rather than passive subjects, in research and development activities that take place within their jurisdictions. In theory, participatory research represents one approach for mediating these tensions and ensuring the production of both quality research and constructive community action.

Participatory Research

Participatory researchers face a critical balancing act between maintaining the rigour of the research process and ensuring the relevance of its findings and outcomes. The search for this balance encapsulates the many tensions inherent in the participatory research process as it is undertaken in academic situations: theory/practice, university/community, and researcher/ subject relationships. The participatory research ideal informs us that by placing these conceptual and institutional opposites on an equal footing, the role of research in society surpasses its abstract, distanced traditions to become useful to both the production of knowledge and to the more concrete advancement of society. On the one hand, participatory research generates theoretical insights and rich new information that is contextually significant and detailed. On the other hand, the participatory research ideal suggests that action associated with the research process will be locally appropriate, empowering to those who implement it, and educationally transforming.

The community-directed and driven nature of CED makes the adoption of participatory research techniques almost a necessity in terms of negotiating relationships between universities and communities that are designed to advance our understanding of CED processes. It is hoped that by including this information in this book, our detailed reflections will resonate with other researchers, leading to an improved understanding of the theory and, in particular, the practice of participatory research.

As with any theory, the participatory research ideal sets a high and clear standard for designing and comparing research processes in practice. It is through discussions and critiques of participatory research that researchers may collectively work towards attaining the ideal (namely, quality research and societal relevance) and towards modifying our expectations and practices accordingly. To begin our discussion, we will briefly review some of the conceptual origins of participatory research.

The Origins and Rationale for Participatory Research

The origins of participatory research are found in proactive and reactive responses to traditional research that is founded upon the scientific method. As Chesler (1991) notes, a positivist and deductive approach to research dominates the social science academy. The scientific method demands a number of conditions from researchers engaged in the research process, including the search for general laws, objectivity, neutrality, standardized assessment, and the reduction of reality into its constituent parts (Reason 1994). Above all, the research process itself is to be separated from its application (i.e., action) in any context (Chesler 1991).

Practitioners of participatory research challenge this distanced notion of research, although driven by concerns for the rigour of the research process, on a number of fronts. First, participatory researchers suggest that combining research and action leads to better understanding. The inclusion of action in the research process does not necessarily jeopardize the integrity of research findings and may offer prescient insights on how to enhance the quality and relevance of the information being generated by researchers (Aguinis 1993). Situating research within the dynamism, complexity, and diversity of practical problems presents researchers with opportunities, not obstacles, for understanding (Greenwood et al. 1993). Second, collaborative interaction between researchers and what were traditionally deemed to be "research subjects" creates opportunities for local knowledge to be directly integrated into the research process (Schroeder 1997). The contextual sensitivity of local knowledge may lead to higher-quality and more relevant information and, as a result, better research and action-based decision making. Third, despite the intentional distance of the scientific method, a variety of disciplines and methodological perspectives challenge the presumed objectivity of the traditional researcher (Reason 1994). Finally, advocates of an emancipatory approach to participatory research note the often strong connections between traditional research and researchers and the status quo responsible for perpetuating conditions of oppression (Brown and Tandon 1983). The need to democratize knowledge and to involve people in the research process to create conditions of empowerment or "conscientization" necessitates the direct and collaborative involvement of people in the research process (Schroeder 1997; Freire 1970). Through participatory research, the traditional role of the researcher to generate knowledge is linked in a dialectical relationship with application of that knowledge.

Participatory research techniques emerged in the 1960s and 1970s, but did not receive more serious recognition until the 1980s. A variety of reasons help to explain the gap between the introduction of participatory research techniques and their acceptance within the broader academy. Chambers (1994) notes a common belief that outside "experts" (such as government officials, academics, planners, etc.) have knowledge superior to that of local people. This leads to an overall exclusion of people from research and developmental processes. It has taken time to record and analyze the errors of this approach in the field of development and in other areas of research, and it has taken time to develop widely recognized alternative approaches and expectations. Today researchers increasingly recognize the validity and importance of local knowledge and participation in research and development programs (Grenier 1998).

Action Research and Participatory Action Research

As stated in Chapter 1, the research team selected action research as the specific participatory research model for the project. Chisholm and Elden (1993) observe that a variety of approaches to action research have emerged since its postwar origins. The diversity of action research methods is a source of confusion in the literature, which has undoubtedly affected practice (Brown and Tandon 1983). In an attempt to clarify the meaning of action research, the following section will describe action research (AR) and its more emancipatory research relative, participatory action research (PAR). Following this review, we will discuss specific theory/practice tensions that emerged in our participatory research process.

Action Research

> Action research aims to contribute both to the practical concerns of people in an immediate problematic situation and to the goals of social science by joint collaboration within a mutually acceptable ethical framework. (Rapaport 1970, 499)

Lewin (1946) was the first to explore the direct relationship between action and research in advancing (social) scientific understanding while at the same time contributing, in a more direct manner, to change (Aguinis 1993). The foregoing statement by Rapaport maintains a sense of the original Lewinian intent and highlights critical elements of the context-based nature of AR and the collaborative links between social science researchers and the people facing problematic situations.

The role of the researcher in AR is to stimulate people to change, serving as a catalyst or process enabler. In working with people as co-researchers in the process, AR seeks to "build collaboratively constructed descriptions and interpretations of events that enable groups of people to formulate mutually acceptable solutions to their problems" (Stringer 1996, 143).

Participation in AR is often implied, despite claims by other researchers who state that it is necessary to emphasize the participatory nature of AR.[1] The failure of some researchers to clearly distinguish between AR and other forms of participatory research creates some confusion in the literature. Researchers and practitioners often contrast AR with participatory action research (PAR), a form of participatory research originating in the developing world. Without a clear distinction between AR and PAR, the original intent of PAR may be weakened and co-opted by a status quo application of the participatory approach (Greenwood et al. 1993).

Participatory Action Research

> PAR values the people's knowledge, sharpens their capacity to conduct their own research in their own interests, helps them appropriate knowledge produced by the dominant knowledge industry for their own interests and purposes, allows problems to be explored from their perspective, and, maybe most important, liberates their minds for critical reflection, questioning, and the continuous pursuit of inquiry, thus contributing to the liberation of their minds and the development of freedom and democracy. (Reason 1994, 329)

Participatory action research (PAR) combines the research process with the dual objectives of conceptual and physical liberation. PAR begins with questions of power and powerlessness and seeks to reveal inherent power relationships and to reveal latent or suppressed resources in order to transform situations of oppression.

The conceptual and descriptive differences between AR and PAR represent the root cause of many debates in the literature. For our purposes, the differences between AR and PAR are clearly outlined by Brown and Tandon (1983), who use a political economy perspective to situate and separate the two research approaches.

Researchers use AR when working directly with formal authority. The implementation of the AR process is consensus-based. The AR process envelops the status quo in the research process and generally addresses problems associated with efficiency and improved relations (rather than with structural power relations).

Conversely, researchers use PAR when initiating collaborative research with oppressed groups. Researchers and community partners seek change in the status quo through their actions within the research process (Brown and Tandon 1983). The distribution of power is central to both research approaches, but the situation and practical intentions of the participants determine the nature of the research process. The following section highlights this practical tension in participatory research as it applied to the Forest Communities project.

Participatory Research in Context
Before discussing the specific dynamics of the research process within the project, however, a brief discussion of the university and provincial/community context helps to situate the motivation for, and resistance to, participatory research more generally.

The Role of Participatory Research in Universities
At present, acceptance of the use of participatory research in the university setting is growing for a number of reasons. First, researchers themselves are increasingly adopting a critical approach to research. Academics are seeking not only to understand but also to change and influence communities and societies as a whole. Second, many communities and the subjects of traditional research have become frustrated with the traditional research process. Cries from the community level of "we have been studied to death" are common sentiments researchers are likely to encounter when leaving the protective boundaries of the university library or lab to test their hypotheses. The frustration felt by communities and local organizations towards outside research and researchers leads many to request or demand a greater role in the research process, making the participatory approach a

necessity rather than an option for those engaging in community-based research. Third, funding sources for research, both academic and non-academic, increasingly require university/community partnerships as a prerequisite for the advancement of funds. Finally, and related to the third point, universities themselves face increasing calls for relevance from political actors and society at large – to serve as brain trusts. This becomes all the more compelling in the context of budgetary pressures and a more corporatist approach to government and tax spending, which demands clearer signals of accountability from universities that may narrow external interpretations of the value of research (Markey and Roseland 2001).

In each of these cases, the use of participatory research can help alleviate the pressure rising from demands for relevance, without necessarily sacrificing the more undefined, traditional goal of the pursuit of knowledge. Participatory research can further assist researchers and their institutions by helping to build the image and credibility of the institution in the public eye. Researchers will be seen to be playing active roles, as equal partners, in the production of knowledge and solution of real problems.

Coincident with these promotional factors for the use of participatory research, however, there are numerous academic critiques and institutional restrictions or expectations that question the validity of participatory research and complicate its ideal implementation. First, critiques of the participatory research process from within the university setting may limit the appeal of participatory models. Long-established standards for research and narrow parameters of objectivity do raise important questions challenging the use of participatory research in the university setting. The scientific method separates researcher from subject in order to ensure greater objectivity. Participatory research challenges the inherent objectivity of the traditional research process. Second, despite their participatory rhetoric, funding institutions often place demands on researchers that make it difficult to engage with individuals, organizations, or communities on a truly equal footing. Conflicts over the time line of the research and the control and distribution of funding represent two such complications that can arise from attempting to adopt a participatory research approach.

All of these social and institutional forces raise important questions and place great demands on researchers and community partners who are seeking to engage in participatory research.

The Role of Participatory Research in Rural British Columbia
As discussed in previous chapters, there has been extensive economic and political restructuring in rural resource communities in British Columbia over the past twenty years. Since the recession of 1981-82, communities have faced large-scale structural changes in the operation and productivity of the resource sector and fundamental shifts in the policies and attitudes

of governments. These changes have altered a traditionally paternalistic approach to land-use management and regional economic development (Barnes and Hayter 1994; Pierce 1998; Savoie 1992). The rapidity and scale of the changes leaves many communities ill-prepared to adjust to the transition within an effective time line. Added to the complex task of assuming more responsibility for their economic survival and prosperity, communities must also face a far more complex economic, social, and ecological setting in which to devise and implement development strategies than in the past. A depleted resource base, global pressures for sustainable development, and a greater number of competing and varied interests in the land base now define the parameters of the development process.

For Aboriginal communities, recent changes in the legal and political landscape have resulted in significant advances in the struggle for recognition of Aboriginal rights and title. The landmark *Delgamuukw* decision, which occurred just before the initiation of the Forest Communities project in 1997, granted legal recognition to Aboriginal title. Although the full implications of this decision are not yet known, the court decision provided a powerful and empowering backdrop for initiation of a CED relationship with the two Aboriginal communities in the project.

As a contextual backdrop, the uncertainty and complexity surrounding rural development issues in BC creates fertile ground within which to engage in participatory research relationships. There are numerous opportunities for combining the research and technical capacity of universities with the local knowledge and commitment of communities. The variability of the impacts of change, the need to foster new community development capacity, and the strong motivation to both understand change and explore new economic opportunities creates conditions for a mutually beneficial participatory research process.

Action Research by Demand?
In addition to forces operating at the university and community levels, a variety of project-specific details contributed to our decision to use participatory research. First, our conceptual and practical focus on CED necessarily demanded a collaborative approach to the project. It simply would not have been a CED process if the Simon Fraser University research team had been solely responsible for the project. As stated earlier, CED is a community-directed and driven process that relies upon the resources and skills found at the community-level. This does not rule out appropriate roles for outsiders, but the extent and determination of those roles is very much dependent upon a negotiated process with the community. In addition, the emphasis on community capacity in the research questions implies that the purpose of the project was to build skills and resources found at the community level. We did this in an effort to ensure that a continuation

of the CED process would be possible through community means upon formal project completion. As Elden and Chisholm note, the development of this "self-development capability" is central to action research (1993, 125): "Contemporary forms of action research also aim at making change and learning a self-generating and self-maintaining process in the systems in which the action researchers work. In addition to solving practical problems and contributing to general theory, the approach to action ... aims at helping systems to develop a higher degree of self-determination and self-development capability so that learning continues after the researcher leaves the system."

Second, the scope and realities of the research setting meant that community-based action was an absolute necessity in driving the process. The involvement of four diverse communities situated hundreds of kilometres from the university meant that (despite a generous travel budget and research positions at the university) action at the community level was highly dependent upon the community-based working groups.

Third, action research provided perhaps the only means through which the communities were willing to enter into the research relationship. The complementary relationship between action and research assured the communities that development activities would take place within the context of the project. However, communities were also gradually convinced of the necessity of the research process to evaluate development needs and opportunities. Community-based research provided an effective and appropriate information base upon which to develop or enhance CED initiatives.

Finally, in reference to the AR/PAR power debate raised earlier, two factors tied the project more closely to AR. First, the research team adopted a consensus-based approach to building community participation. This approach closely mirrors the principles of CED. Second, the project dealt directly with people and institutions in positions of recognized *formal* authority. At the local level, municipal councils and band councils facilitated the link between the research team and the communities. In addition, the fact that a Crown corporation provided the funding for the project influenced the definition of project objectives and shaped common perceptions of the project held by community members.

Despite the theoretical clarity of this self-definition of the AR approach by the research team, several factors cloud this interpretation. First, the Aboriginal communities in the project might not have viewed the larger implications of the project as consensus-based. Clearly, Aboriginal communities in BC meet the "oppressed" qualifications associated with developing-world conditions in which PAR originated. Additionally, given the struggles between Aboriginal communities and the provincial and federal governments, it is clear that Aboriginal communities do not necessarily view these governments (or Crown corporations for that matter) as holders of legitimate authority, particularly with regard to land use and title. Consequently, the consensus-based approach of the action research process may not be as applicable to the Aboriginal communities, despite our intentions and/or project limitations.

Second, a more structurally rich interpretation of CED must not overlook questions of power. While sharing in the economic benefits of timber harvesting, BC's forest communities have historically been dominated by corporate and government decision makers. In recent years, local economic benefits from resource extraction have declined. At the same time, despite increased consultation, communities have gained little in terms of real decision-making power. Working with resource-dependent communities to build greater degrees of self-reliance must ultimately confront or question the status quo of resource use and land-base control. In this sense, the process of retracing the patterns of development that have created conditions of economic instability, and highlighting opportunities for change and community control, may be interpreted as an empowering process more closely associated with PAR.

Each of these points highlights gaps in the theory/practice relationship of participatory research that is lacking in the literature. Questions regarding which criteria are more important to be able to clearly define or differentiate the research process require more discussion. From our perspective, the differentiation of the research process and intent is very much dependent upon the motivations of community or organizational partners. While the research team outlined a research strategy using AR, the use of the process by the communities both within and beyond the project varied. Some communities were more intent on challenging existing economic and power relationships than others; such is the nature of a collaborative research relationship where control is shared. While the distinction between AR and PAR may be clear in theory, in practice research activities may share characteristics of both, situated somewhere on a continuum between being embedded within and representing a challenge to status quo power relationships.

Lessons for Community-Based Research
Beyond the specific dynamics of the participatory research process, universities must grapple with basic questions and skills related to working with communities in a more interactive and action-oriented manner. The following section relays information from research gathered by the CED Centre concerning best practices in community-based research. The information is drawn from our experiences with the Forest Communities project and interviews with other community-based researchers from across the country. We divide community-based research practices into three categories: time and resources, community awareness, and the benefits of the research (see Table 9.1).

Table 9.1

Best practices in community-based research

Category	Best practices
Time and resources	Front-end negotiations
	Follow-up and dissemination
	Distance
	Community presence
Community awareness	Power dynamics
	Past research experience
	Conceptual differences
Benefits of research	Capacity transfer
	Community use of research
	Researcher training
	Theory/practice acceptance

Time and Resources

Community-based research can be very time-intensive. Because of this, it may require more resources than traditional research approaches in order to sustain an adequate research relationship and ensure community learning. Time needed in the front end for developing the research with community partners and in the follow-up stages to ensure quality dissemination adds time to the research process that is generally not adequately recognized in an institutional sense by universities or funding agencies. Particularly for rural researchers, the distance associated with linking universities (often in urban centres) with more remote communities intensifies resource demands.

In addition, resource demands may by heightened by the need to maintain a real presence in the community. The "research-and-run" approach is not conducive to building relationships or addressing complex issues at the community level. For example, assigning research assistants to liaise between the communities and the university in the Forest Communities project served an important function in the research process. Research assistants were able to maintain a more consistent community presence (supported by a generous travel budget) than would otherwise be possible for university professors.

Community Awareness

Community awareness here refers to the extent to which researchers are aware of their research context. First, our research indicates that community-based researchers tend not to pay enough attention to the power dynamics in the community. Again, time and the involvement of community participants can help inform the research process concerning both surface and subsurface power dynamics.

Second, understanding the research history of a community is important. Past research obviously represents an important source of information. It is also important, however, to recognize which research approach was used, who was involved, how recently the community was engaged in the research, and the attitudes of community members towards the research experience. For our project, we spent considerable time profiling the communities and meeting with the working groups to identify and understand previous community development efforts.

Third, it is useful to acknowledge the conceptual differences and different priorities that separate researchers from community members. These apply to a variety of components of the research process, including the use of jargon or technical language, the different values attached to the research process, and the priority that research will have for community members or research partners as they continue with the normal demands and pressures of their lives. In our case, community working group members reviewed all project reports. There was also an understanding at the community level that certain segments of our research were for more formal academic purposes. The communities understood our needs, provided that they were able to add tangible benefits to the community.

Benefits of Research

The benefits of community-based research are notoriously difficult to measure, particularly within the time frame of an individual research process. Having a clear idea of the benefits and goals of research from both a community and university perspective will facilitate more open relationships and enable greater mutual understanding in the research process. There are a number of techniques to address the question of who benefits from the research process.

First, as noted above, funding agencies often require that community partners be included in the research process. However, there is often a gap in community knowledge about how to best work with researchers. Communities don't necessarily define their own role, or understand how best to benefit from the research process and results. We witnessed this gap in certain communities, given their expectations that we would do the work and simply report back to the working group.

Second, the general suspicion that meets any insider/outsider relationship must be recognized. The division will always remain, but as participatory research becomes more acceptable in academic circles, and better training is provided to researchers seeking to employ the approach, communities will hopefully have more positive experiences to draw upon. As a result, communities will be better able to understand the research process from an academic perspective, even as researchers learn to better appreciate the community perspective.

Several researchers we interviewed mentioned the need for better training in participatory research techniques within programs and departments. As the use of participatory techniques increases, there will be a greater need to ensure that researchers are well prepared so as not to sour or burn out individuals and organizations at the local level. A phenomenon that is contributing to the empowerment of the community with respect to the research process is the creation of community-based research centres, such as the Inner Coast Natural Resource Centre in Alert Bay, BC, and the Nunavut Research Institute on a somewhat larger scale. These centres are playing proactive roles in defining research parameters, clarifying ethics on local terms, and ensuring that the community benefits from research taking place in the area.

Finally, making a conscious effort to include capacity building or capacity transfer in the research design will make the tangible and intangible transfer of specific information or technical expertise more explicit. The full extent of university resources remains relatively untapped with respect to the development needs of rural and small-town communities. The following section outlines the attempts within the project to ensure that capacity development was a critical component of the research process.

Building Community Capacity

There are two main strategic approaches in CED aimed at creating employment for individuals within a community. The first deals with the *supply side* of the market and focuses on activities that enhance the use or quality of local resources. The second deals with the *demand side,* focusing on responses to market forces or market opportunities (O'Neill 1994).

While business development strategies can be classified as labour demand side strategies, the supply side approach includes all of the activities and initiatives that build human resource capacity (i.e., the capacity of individual community members). These strategies nurture, enhance, and mobilize the human potential in a community to create the conditions necessary to support new community-based economic activity (Nozick 1999; Blakely 1989). Human capacity development is particularly important in the new knowledge-based economy, which brings urgent training requirements ranging from public education to developing specific skills in individuals (Frank 1994).

Human resource development options include providing vocational training to match employee skills with employer needs, employment readiness assistance, entrepreneurial training, and encouraging all levels and types of learning. Communities can also engage in an exercise of mapping community assets to discover, inventory, and mobilize the untapped traditionally non-economic gifts and skills of local people. A human resource development strategy might also attempt to work with difficult-to-employ citizens, offering skills upgrading, locating employers willing to place individuals, or creating ventures with their needs in mind. Finally, in reference to the success factors identified earlier, leadership development is an important human resource initiative.

Enhancing human resource capabilities was a strategy that overlapped with many others pursued by the communities. For example, community education was an important goal of the Lillooet heritage strategy. The Lillooet Tribal Council outlined the following strategies for community education:

- have St'at'imc people trained as resource management technicians
- increase involvement of elders and resource persons in teaching and passing on traditional practices and methods
- increase development of St'at'imc curriculum and use of St'at'imc teachers in formal settings and in language instruction

The principal strategic goal of the research team throughout the project was to build community capacity for CED, particularly among residents taking a leadership role in the CED process in their communities. In the following section, we will summarize and evaluate how we designed and implemented the training and education components of the Forest Communities project. Finally, we will share lessons for future CED training and education programs.

The capacity-building component of the project consisted of a series of community planning workshops, a bursary program sponsoring distance education participation in the CED program at the university, the design of an introductory web-based "Gateway" to the CED program, and technical assistance with CED research and the CED planning process. CED Centre students, instructors, and researchers also benefited from the practical learning experience, which in turn informed teaching, course development, and the publication of research findings.

Community Planning Workshops

Community workshops were an essential part of the capacity-building process. They allowed for ongoing input into the research process by community members, providing an opportunity for SFU researchers and community members to meet face to face and to share knowledge and experiences. We scheduled four workshops to facilitate the research and planning process (see Table 9.2). Members of the CED Centre research team facilitated each workshop in collaboration with the community-based working groups. In each case, we reviewed specific community-based research and discussed

Table 9.2

CED planning and capacity-building workshops

Workshop	Topics
Workshop 1	Introduction to the Forest Communities Project CED Planning and Capacity Assessment
Workshop 2	Capacity Assessment and Initiative Selection
Workshop 3	Review, Initiative Planning, and Design
Workshop 4	Community Collaborating: Sharing Ideas and Overcoming Barriers (Initiative Implementation)
Additional workshops	Introduction to CED, Bella Coola CED Summer Training Workshop, Lillooet

general information about CED and CED strategies. Workshop dialogue focused on the conditions of the community, opportunities and barriers to development, and how the specific theme of the workshop could be made contextually relevant to each community.

Participants generally considered the community workshops to be an effective format for learning and information sharing throughout the project. The workshops were useful for reinforcing the planning process, presenting research findings, and maintaining lines of communication between the CED Centre and the communities. Workshops provided an environment that was conducive to inter- and intra-community networking, skill development, and knowledge building. Perhaps most important, the workshops helped to build community trust and team building among community residents and the university-based research team.

An important characteristic of the workshop format was its flexibility. In theory, each community was to move through the workshop planning process at the same time. The reality of different community capacity levels and development aspirations meant that the workshops ultimately had to be individually tailored to meet community conditions. That said, balancing the CED process differences was a challenge to the CED Centre research team. In some cases, communities were moving further ahead and faster than the research process; in other cases, communities struggled to implement basic process steps in a timely fashion. We responded to the tension created by this process variability by fracturing the continuity of the CED process between communities. We then pieced together CED process reflections at the end of the project and through joint community-based workshops, where communities could learn from each other based upon their own experiences with similar process steps (albeit experienced at different times).

The workshops provided an avenue for sharing project ownership and responsibility with community members. One aspect of the research design that proved to be a barrier to fostering community-based participation in the early phases of the project was the communities' expectations of the university research team. The communities had previous experience working with outsiders in a more conventional consultant/client relationship, whereby the "expert" does the work and then reports to the community. Breaking through this expectation and nurturing community responsibility for the process required time and flexibility on the part of both the university research team and the project communities. Here again, the workshops facilitated negotiations and discussions regarding the respective roles of those involved in the project.

Our experience from the community workshops demonstrates the need for linking theory with practice. Most participants desired the opportunity to apply knowledge gained through the workshops to the problems affecting their communities. It proved important and highly effective to share recent and relevant CED books, journals, and case studies with the community working groups and then to facilitate discussion of how the theory and lessons contained in the resources were relevant or could be applied to the local community.

We also gained insights into workshop facilitation and instruction. Instructors must have hands-on experience with CED and understand how to transmit knowledge and to involve people in a participatory learning environment. Instructors must also be sensitive to, and employ strategies to address, cultural gaps. Our research team employed instructors with adult learning experience and strong theoretical and practical backgrounds, and we worked to gain an understanding of local cultural dynamics. Where specific knowledge or skill gaps existed, outside help was enlisted for specific community presentations. In addition, local partners were invaluable to the format and content of the workshops, working to bridge the cultural and knowledge gaps between the university and the community.

Finally, the efforts of those who participated in the project workshops provide evidence of their utility. For example, following a workshop experience, one participant decided to coordinate a CED conference in partnership with Community Futures and the Nuxalk Nation. The meeting was designed to bring together community groups to discuss potential funding sources for future skills and economic development initiatives. It was also an attempt to bring the various organizations and peoples in the Bella Coola valley and the Nuxalk to work together, contributing to the conflict resolution process presented in Chapter 8. In the South Cariboo, participants built on the skills and knowledge gained from the workshops to secure grants and partnership commitments for the development of the South Cariboo

Arts and Culture Centre. Finally, workshop participants have become mentors to their fellow community members. Relationships established at the local level through the research process, particularly community workshops, helped facilitate local initiatives.

The Bursary Program

We designed the CED bursary program to serve as an innovative approach to providing community members (particularly community leaders and decision makers) with formal CED training while also engaging in hands-on learning through participation in the research process. Community leaders were to enroll in CED classes at Simon Fraser University through distance education. The reality proved much more difficult to implement.

A number of students did complete the program. One Aboriginal participant was particularly enthusiastic about the opportunity to gain a university credential. Overall, however, the bursary program had limited success. We identified a number of problems with the program, offering insights into the challenges of distance education in a rural or small-town context:

- Many of the community members had only a basic education and had been out of formal learning for an extended period of time. Participants experienced difficulties in meeting the demands of distance learning.
- Many of the community candidates for the program did not have the necessary credentials to be admitted to the university through normal entrance procedures.
- People already in community planning and decision-making roles were overextended and were understandably unwilling to commit to a long-term distance education program.
- Some students did not have access to computers, modems, and the telephone/Internet connections required by the courses, representing technical limitations.
- The mobility and employment variability in rural areas made commitment to a multi-year distance education program difficult for some participants.

Given the importance of the bursary program as a capacity-building tool for the project and the clear difficulties associated with it, we decided to explore alternative approaches to formal distance education. First, we designed a self-taught, introductory course in CED called *Gateway: A Twelve-Week Introductory Course in CED* for bursary candidates and community members. We made the course available in print and electronic formats. The *Gateway* course presented community members with an opportunity to learn about CED on their own time, for free, and without the added pressures associated with formal coursework. A second strategy for bridging the educational divide was to invite community members to a joint summer workshop in CED.

The purpose of the Summer CED Workshop was to provide an intensive overview of the principles, techniques, and practical applications of CED. We designed the format to recognize the unique circumstances faced by rural communities and by community leaders pressed by local demands. We adopted a "train-the-trainers" approach, and encouraged participants to return to their communities and share their experiences with others in their organizations. The workshop brought representatives from each of the communities together and, in doing so, demonstrated the educational value of communities sharing their experiences.

In general, the bursary courses were based on distance learning and as a result failed to promote face-to-face interaction. The goal of the alternative course design, therefore, was to provide the participants with some form of structured learning while promoting a high degree of participation. The adoption of a case study approach, along with teaching aids and demonstration projects from other communities, enabled the presentation of the workshop material to be in a format that helped participants understand how the material related to initiatives in their own communities. We concluded that the case study approach helped participants diagnose their situation and prescribe contextually appropriate solutions to their problems.

Lessons for Capacity Building

The realities of implementing CED training and education programs at the community level posed a major challenge to the project, a challenge that varied with the dynamics in each of the four communities. Yet the design, implementation, and review of education, training, and capacity-building efforts in the research project provided valuable information with which to assess and make recommendations for future rural capacity-building endeavours:

1 *A Strong Need/Demand Exists for CED Training and Education:* Workshop participants and bursary students from the communities overwhelmingly indicated a need for continuing professional development and training. Research findings highlight the importance of building individual leadership capabilities. Three particular barriers impeded the need for training and education: 1) the cost of training and education, 2) access to specific skill training as close to home as possible, and 3) time to attend training classes or complete assignments.

2 *Geographic and Target Audience:* Training and education programs should target and be designed to suit the local audience. It is important to

consider distance and travel time when defining audience for program development. The preparedness of potential participants should also be carefully assessed before offering or proposing educational options.

3 *Scope:* CED is an emerging program for many organizations and communities. Training and education programs would be best positioned if they were to define CED as embracing social, economic, environment and cultural development. An emerging interest in an "internal" approach to traditional economic development activities presents opportunities for integrating CED with other disciplines and training programs.

4 *Credit Option:* Participants in the workshops showed significant interest in having a credit option available for their training efforts. CED must build upon experiential knowledge and recognize different ways of knowing. At the same time, however, there is a demand for receiving formal accreditation for training for personal and employment advancement.

5 *Funding Sources:* A fundraising strategy that attracts local sources of funding for training increases a sense of ownership. Commitment and accountability to bursaries and scholarships should be designed ahead of course registration with program communities and individuals.

6 *Learning Communities:* In a learning community, education and skills development can prepare its members for many roles, including, but not limited to, their future contribution to the workforce. Community members are independent and interdependent. (Ameyaw 1999)

Variable levels of educational experience, limited communications capacity, employment instability, and overextended leadership capacity in rural areas demand a more compact, intensive, and interpersonal approach to capacity building through training and education. The foundation of CED curriculum design should be the application of adult education principles. A flexible, adaptive curriculum that is responsive to challenges and growth in the CED education and training process is important. There is also a need for an interdisciplinary and entrepreneurial approach to designing CED courses. With these conditions in place, CED educators may play an important role in creating a generation of new planners who have the knowledge and skills to be effective CED leaders in their communities.

In response to the need to deliver flexible, practitioner-oriented training in CED, the CED Centre at Simon Fraser University launched a Certificate Program for CED Professionals in 2001. Our experiences in the Forest Communities project were instrumental in determining the format and content of the program.

Conclusion

The participatory/action research process facilitated a rich mutual learning process. Overall, a number of advantages and disadvantages of the action research process may be identified. We identified three advantages. First, action research offered flexibility in terms of research design, methods, and implementation. Through a process of cyclical reflection (facilitated primarily through project reporting to both the communities and the funding agency), the research process was able to respond to changing circumstances encountered as a result of working with communities facing complex issues in real time. Flexibility in the research process was particularly necessary given the diversity represented by the communities – each at different stages in the CED process and with varying capacities and resources allocated to do the work. Second, while action research reveals the limitations and barriers confronting participants in a given context, action is ultimately based upon the skills and resources of the local actors and organizations. This provides an opportunity to create asset-based action, rather than focusing on existing deficiencies. Concentrating the research and development process on existing resources enhances the degree of direct participation by community members (Whyte 1991). Third, and linked to the second point, action research is itself a capacity-building exercise. The direct involvement of participants increases experience with the process of generating research and applying the information to process and project development. This also creates the potential for a continuation of local development activity following the end of the formal research relationship.

Researchers must also be aware of the potential drawbacks associated with the action research approach. First, as mentioned earlier, action research can be very time-consuming. A collaborative approach to research and development ultimately depends upon the degree of trust generated between researchers and participants. Time is necessary to build relationships, clarify roles, and enable a gradual and comprehensive understanding of the specific context. Second, the participatory ideal presented in the action research/ participatory action research literature may be difficult to achieve in practice, particularly where volunteer efforts play a significant role in the research and evaluation process. A negotiated process is responsible for deciding the extent of participation and the responsibilities undertaken by the university research team and community representatives. Constantly evaluating the extent of participation and the reasons for either strong or weak levels of participation in the research process can assist with this potential barrier. Finally, and linked to the second point, local participation requirements in the research process may favour certain groups over others. The theoretical grounding of the project provided it with a strong commitment to building diverse representation and participation. However, formal levels of authority in each community (local councils) facilitated our original invitation to the community and the establishment of the research relationship. It was the responsibility of the research team to assess the representative balance of the community working groups and to encourage diverse participation; there were, however, both practical and political limits to fully realizing this participatory objective.

Throughout the course of the project, we identified a variety of knowledge and planning resources available to communities to assist them with their development objectives. However, a gap exists in the variety of resources, in their overall quality, and in their dissemination to the community level; further work needs to be done. As a result, participatory research and development planning are essential to support communities. Improving research practices at the university level and supporting community resources for outreach remain important goals in CED across the country.

10
Conclusion

In following the dictum that *analysis should precede strategy,* we have based both the foundation and execution of this book upon forging a strong link between, on the one hand, broad theoretical parameters that provide the backdrop for understanding economic dependency, transition, and ultimately resilience, and, on the other hand, empirical case studies at the local level that provide the insight for local context, practice, and policy development with respect to community economic development (CED). Our primary purpose has been to investigate the ability and role of CED to mediate the complex forces that are creating economic uncertainty in small towns and rural areas of BC and across Canada. Towards those ends we have tried to clarify and evaluate mechanisms and strategies for creating stronger, more self-reliant local/regional economies through local means. A tacit assumption throughout has been that the preservation of communities as viable and vibrant entities is a desirable goal that speaks to the need to rebalance our economic and social systems in order to recognize and uphold the importance of diversity in the lived worlds of rural and small-town places. As Rapaport reminds us, the "moral development of a civilization is measured by the breadth of its sense of community" (quoted in Homer-Dixon 2000, 396).

Local development initiatives can counteract the volatility caused by external forces by preparing the groundwork for more resilient and stable communities. The most recent shock waves impacting the forest industry in British Columbia provide, in our view, a compelling case for concerted action to reverse the tides of uneven development by elevating the importance of local action aimed at expanding social capital and community capacity through area-based planning. We have demonstrated that a maturation in thinking is beginning to emerge, away from dependency approaches towards a more balanced approach to CED – in short, a greater blending of internal and external initiatives.

This chapter will attempt to extend the previous analyses and strategies by considering some further ways in which community development initiatives can be strengthened through partnerships and cooperation between government, business, Native groups, and nongovernmental organization (NGO) interests, by building upon the experiences of other jurisdictions and by exploring the conditions that continue to disadvantage the welfare of communities. Before doing this, however, it is useful to reiterate some of the key parameters in the debate over the factors affecting the viability of resource-dependent communities generally, and more specifically in the forest sector of British Columbia. With respect to the latter what must be borne in mind is the fact that the industry is currently experiencing great uncertainty, in large measure due to several factors: the unresolved Canada-US softwood lumber dispute; proposed changes to forestry legislation that, among other things, will lead to greater concentration in processing; a growing potential for future uncompetitiveness vis-à-vis other producers because of the labour costs, inaccessibility of timber, and the rising value of the Canadian dollar; and the cumulative effects of damage from mountain pine beetle, increasing drought conditions, and forest fires.

The economic turbulence endemic to resource-based communities during the last quarter of the twentieth century in Canada has its origins in a number of significant transformations in trading/exchange relations, regulatory regimes, social norms, and environmental quality. While much is made of globalization of the economy and the neoliberal agenda, the fact remains that for some time, primary activities and sectors have been capturing a declining share of national income in all jurisdictions. It would be a major error, however, to suggest that we can do without these resources and the industries dependent upon them. This is true particularly in view of the significant place the resources occupy in terms of their share of exports and, of course, the basic human need for commodities as inputs to sustain the well-being of societies, both urban and rural.

Associated with the trend towards capital intensification of extraction and processing is a diminished demand for labour. From the 1950s to the 1970s, governments, conscious of core/periphery inequalities, responded, on the one hand, with large-scale capital-intensive resource development projects, as in the case of Northern British Columbia, and on the other, with measures that would both rationalize the respective industries and shelter weaker producers, particularly in agriculture. Ostensibly, governments made these interventions on equity and regional development grounds. In addition, in the last quarter of the twentieth century, the regulatory, trade, and competitive changes and the weakening in the demand for labour resulted in an out-migration of people, most often the very people who possessed the potential to fuel economic recovery. In summary, both demographic and attitudinal shifts further compromised community competitiveness.

The uncertainties facing communities can be further clarified with respect to three distinct sources, one old and two relatively new: (1) historical vagaries of the business cycle: resource industries are price takers not setters, and commodity prices for unfinished products are notoriously unstable in forestry, agriculture, fishing, and mining; (2) emerging constraints on supply due to declines in the availability of resource stocks in fishing and forestry, or what Clapp (1998) has referred to as the inevitability of the "resource cycle," as well as increasing insecurity in access to the land base due to Native land claims and new government regulations and land-use programs; and (3) increasing insecurity of access to traditional markets such as the United States and Europe because of tariff protection and/or consumer boycotting. Clearly the supply-based uncertainties, as outlined in (1) and (2), fly in the face of a historical legacy of resource abundance and plenitude. Demand-based uncertainties introduce the province to new and unpredictable trading relations. Coinciding with the rise of supply- and demand-based uncertainty has been the increasing role of stakeholder groups, which has forced a dramatic reinterpretation of the values associated with terrestrial and marine-based ecosystems, end uses, and rights to those uses (Markey et al. 2000). While our case studies did not deal extensively with these changing interpretations and the role of NGOs, there is no question that the landscape has been irrevocably transformed from one whose primary function was the provision of commodities to a far more complex mosaic of competing and complementary uses in both private and public domains.

Confronting Forest Dependencies
The phases of forest policy and development discussed earlier highlighted a transition from harvesting and production systems that were relatively decentralized and low-volume in the pre-1945 period to a centralized, high-volume, top-down industrial model with a focus on large-scale exports in the postwar period. Government planners based their policies on the premise that communities would benefit from the triadic relationship between government, business, and labour, anchored by the principle of sustained yield, expanded forest tenures, and new harvesting rules that collectively provided an integrated system tying mill requirements to minimum harvest levels. Community development became an appendage of forestry development and the principle of comparative advantage. In short, sector-based planning dominated the political agenda in most communities.

The health of communities became synonymous with a growth in incomes and jobs. The product of these policies was the highest level of dependency upon the forest resource of any province in Canada. At the same time, the number of jobs employed per unit volume of forest product was the lowest among OECD countries; and of course the economic multiplier from this export-oriented approach was also dismally low, the result of significant leakages to external regions. The very object of the new forest policy, community stability, became its casualty and could not be sustained over the long run due to excessively high harvesting/discount rates, well above the long-run sustained yield, the accompanying falldown effect, and competitive external pressures that accelerated capital intensification and job losses.

The forces of change were not limited to the mismanagement of a resource or new competitive pressures from abroad, however. Challenging the orthodoxy of the primacy of forests for industrial uses, environmentalists in BC and abroad became the harbingers of a shift in attitude about the need to re-evaluate our assumptions regarding the value of our forests. Similarly, First Nations groups and the protracted treaty talks added yet another dimension to the disputes over access to and the value of the forest base. New government initiatives during the 1990s designed to improve the management of the industrial side of forest management, combined with withdrawals of land from the harvesting base with the introduction of the Forest Practices Code, the Protected Areas Strategy, and Special Management Zones, further impacted communities and their employment bases. At the same time, the introduction of the Commission on Resources and the Environment (CORE) and Local Resource Management Planning (LRMP) processes brought with them a need for public consultation and the articulation of community/stakeholder values. Arguably this experience along with Human Resources Canada and regional development agencies such as Western Economic Diversification assisted communities in becoming more proactive in local development initiatives.

If communities are to move forward to become key participants in planning their futures, the errors and limitations of past practices and policies must be understood. This book began with an analysis of the characteristics of staples development. Issues such as lack of reinvestment, foreign control, limited research and development, lack of manufacturing, high staples export levels, and resource exhaustion typify such development patterns and form the context and baseline in attempts to reverse the economic fortunes of communities throughout the province. In retrospect, the lack of economic diversity has condemned communities to certain instability and a future of missed opportunities.

Implications for the Unevenness of Development

In addressing questions of economic diversification from the local level, we must be mindful of the potential social and economic impacts (unintended or not) from an uneven development perspective. When uneven development, and not simply local development, is introduced into our planning processes, the turn towards the local becomes rife with both broad and localized risks. Let us elaborate on this.

At a broad level, an increasing emphasis on local development carries with it the risk of perpetuating, if not exacerbating, the unevenness of development. The variability of the local response, determined by the impact of macroeconomic conditions, local capacity, the availability of human and natural resources, and so on, challenges the ingrained legacies of regional development in Canada (and in other industrialized nations). Such legacies stress the importance of maintaining the parity and universalization of development across national space.

Some critics of local development or new regional approaches warn of broader ideological dangers and manipulations associated with the localist cause. Specifically, there is a danger of unknowingly or cynically perpetuating a neoliberal agenda in the name of community and regional development: "Unwittingly, the New Regionalism assists the use of geography to dismantle national redistributive structures and hollow out the democratic content of economic governance, not least under the guise of constructing new regional structures" (Lovering 1999, 392).

Bryant (1999) offers hints of a solution to balancing decentralized local control with the preservation of equity and constructive public interest. He argues that it is possible for the state to recognize and support the capacity of communities to pursue their own development objectives while at the same time protecting the broader public interest. Amin and Thrift reinforce the sentiments of Bryant in stating that the role of government must change and not be rendered obsolete in an era of globalization (1997, 157):

> Nothing short of state and societal reform in the direction of decentralization, democratization and participation seems to be called for, thus moving beyond the call for the construction of networks of association that maximize learning and adaptation. These are lofty goals to aim for and ones which are easily sacrificed in a contemporary policy culture driven by formal and quick-fix solutions. In the main, public policy is troubled by arguments which appeal to long-term, holistic, evolutionary and processural discourses. Yet it is becoming increasingly clear that these are the discourses of the real economy. Thus, imagining the parameters of a dialogic policy rationality is the next challenge, one that ought to be taken up to get us out of the cul-de-sac of contemporary debate on whether, in an era of globalization, the state matters and at what spatial scale.

The principles of CED, in terms of seeking mutually beneficial local and extra-local relationships, serve as a guide for a more dialogic policy approach. Principles alone do not guarantee compliance, however; thus, reinforcing a role for the state is essential in protecting and outlining substantive rules for each spatial domain. This is particularly true for smaller communities, which may not be able to amass the necessary local capacity or resources to construct an effective local development response. Communities must not become perpetual wards of the state by continuing to exist despite the lack of any internal commitment to or prospects for development prosperity. However, communities merit a sincere effort to construct local opportunities and to build local capacity to take advantage of those opportunities over a realistic time frame. This requires a more patient and thoughtful approach to restructuring than the delivery of random programs wielded from the top down, or simple abandonment and thoughtless centralization. In this context, the role of the state is twofold: on the one hand, it must temper raw market forces while a community or region reinvents itself; on the other hand, it must protect broader public interests concerning the use of state resources and the protection of broader public values. Where the line is drawn should be a by-product of a meaningful (i.e., dialogical) local development process.

CED: Scaling Up

Scaling up the activity and reach of CED represents one approach to addressing questions of uneven development from a CED perspective. CED, in a Canadian non-metropolitan context, in part grew out of the uncertainties associated with staples dependency. More specifically, both market and policy failures have acted as catalysts for the animation of a broadly defined "third sector." The post-Fordist era, with its renegotiated relations among government, big business, and labour, tilted the playing field in such a way as to further weaken the competitiveness of communities dependent upon relatively unprocessed resources. Most notably, the reality of the rootedness of place had to confront not only the new flexible accumulation regimes (a signature of globalization) but frequently a declining resource base. Although initially a reactive exercise, a do-or-die phenomenon, the collective experience of researchers and practitioners has ushered in a new era for local development, as illustrated in this book. A key issue that we will explore shortly are the strategies and support mechanisms available to governments to "scale up" CED initiatives to make them a more integrated and prominent feature of the political, economic, and social landscapes of communities. While there are numerous challenges facing the expansion, if not overall legitimacy, of CED, none in our view is greater than encouraging government to act as an agent influencing the necessary conditions for change in such areas as community resource management.

Even though little can be done to shape exogenous market-based forces, changes in government regulation have the potential to significantly alter the opportunities for CED in this province. Community resource management (CRM), while not a panacea for community instability, is an important building block towards that goal. Since CRM cuts across a number of CED approaches, it is useful to explore, in more detail, its promise and its limitations for forest-based communities. As evidence of the potential for CRM, it served as a dominant strategic focus in three of four case communities.

In a paper on community-based management of the forest resource, M'Gonigle (1996, 3) characterized "both existing and alternative forest tenures along a spectrum." At one end is the traditional productionist/corporate tenure model, which dominates the industry today. Associated with this are certain labour and production relations, profit motives, harvest strategies, and stewardship practices. At the other end of the spectrum is situated an alternative community-based model with a tenure system that would maintain ecosystem values by allowing harvesting and production but within the limits of the ecosystem.

M'Gonigle maintains that a community forest must have three characteristics: (1) it must be rooted in an ecosystem perspective; (2) there must be a high degree of local control and decision making; and (3) there must be local control of economic institutions for production and marketing purposes. More recent work by M'Gonigle and colleagues (2001) extends this paradigm by proposing the formation of a Community Ecosystem Trust. Under this proposed new legal framework and accompanying charter, the Crown and First Nations would allow their resources to be held in trust without forfeiting sovereignty or title. In effect, a new intermediary land status is created in which "two co-existent legal orders can come together without compromising the integrity of either" (5). Democratically elected trustees would manage the resources, based upon charter principles and local management plans. The beneficiaries would be the community members at large through retention of jobs and income locally. This model would differ from the "stakeholder consensus" model used in CORE and LRMP in that it would emphasize cooperation over competition. Moreover, it would be performance-based and would require communities to opt into this formal arrangement. Given that the legislation would be enabling, it would not necessitate participation but provide for voluntary applications.

This trust model further extends the "spectrum of forest tenures." Between the extremes are of course a variety of other possible tenure arrangements and mixes of resource management regimes that place varying importance on nonproduction values and alternative uses and decentralized decision making. We must acknowledge that this trust model or other forms of community resource management require some devolution of powers and, in other cases, giving up of powers. Do governments wish to continue to be the handmaidens of the traditional resource sector or do they wish to move forward in new and innovative ways to empower individuals to improve community access to resources and to develop strategies for value-added processing and integrated CED strategies? A prime objective of this strategy would be improved stewardship of both terrestrial and aquatic ecosystems. From a decision-making perspective, there is much that can be learned from devolution of powers in the European Union (EU). In area-based planning initiatives, for example, the doctrine of subsidiarity is employed. In principle, central governments perform a subsidiary function, restricting their activities to those that cannot be performed locally or regionally (Buttimer 2001). This principle is clearly in its infancy in British Columbia.

The previously outlined possibilities for community resource management highlight both the challenges and opportunities with respect to the necessary ingredients and pathways for economic and social development. If one accepts the premise that development is the product of varying mixes of capital, it is possible, conceptually, to map out the changing importance of those forms of capital within the context of CED. Traditional development in resource dependent communities has favoured the use of natural and physical capital as the key catalyst for income and employment growth and community stability. Sustainable community development, while recognizing the importance of these forms of capital, would place more emphasis upon human/financial and social/cultural capital. While the former is relatively well understood, the latter is not. Roseland (1999, 193) notes that "social capital refers to the organizations, structures and social relations that people build up independently of the state or large corporations." Roseland goes on to cite Putnam's work (1993) indicating that social capital, while a public good, greatly enhances a society's productive potential and return on investment. Similarly, Daly and Cobb (1994) refer to the importance of moral capital as an essential ingredient for the success of capitalist economies and recognize that its creation is independent of the market.

Community capacity is the sum total of the individual forms of capital. All are necessary but none is sufficient. Social capital provides the moral compass and momentum in a CED context, through the complex networking, trust, and common goals alluded to earlier. Direct financial investment is a critical complement to social capital and a building block to enlarge community capacity. As previously noted, however, this development paradigm is faced with a Catch-22 situation in that community capacity is needed to raise financial capital and that capital is needed to raise capacity. The bottom line in all of this, as pointed out in Chapter 5, is that the higher the capacity, the greater the ability to be proactive in a strategic planning sense, and to creatively exploit the proper balance between localist and linking approaches to CED.

If capacity enhancement is the touchstone of successful CED, the means of its achievement are diverse but often complementary. It was argued in

Chapter 5 that there is a continuum of circumstances within which CED may be applied. A community's location on that continuum is a function of the capacity of the community to engage in CED and the existing or potential economic circumstances. Within this context, we identified two sources of confusion about the role and efficacy of CED in our discussion of a CED framework. One referred to the notion that CED is really appropriate for marginalized communities only, and the other to the notion that CED should be more localist in its strategic orientation. We have argued that CED is appropriate in both marginal and mainstream contexts. Indeed, proactivity can be a powerful mediating force in the face of possible restructuring. Equally important is the necessity to strike a balance between strategies that strengthen, on the one hand, local products and services and, on the other hand, strategies that promote stronger ties to the regional, national, and international economies. The applicability of each approach is a function of a complex set of conditions relating to community assets, leadership strength, social dynamics, and a variety of market-driven and policy forces.

The choices or options potentially available to communities can be better evaluated when placed against the context of a community's dependency on the natural resource base. Horne's detailed analysis (1999) of local area dependencies and impact ratios provides a fine-grained breakdown of a community's share of income derived from forestry operations. From this he calculates diversity and vulnerability measures. This information provides us with another spectrum or continuum ranging from high income dependency, low diversity, and high vulnerability (to changes in the industry) to the opposite situation of low dependency, high diversity, and low vulnerability. Parenthetically, all of the previously outlined CED approaches have as an end goal the shifting of communities to a low-vulnerability status.

We can now derive a better sense of scenarios available to communities through the intersection of the two continuums, one representing degrees of forest dependency and the other representing management options and control of the forest harvesting base (Figure 10.1). Through this schematic representation, we can better appreciate the strong correlation between medium and strong dependency (and hence high vulnerability) on the one dimension and a corporate tenure model on the other. To improve their stability, communities must, as a first step, enlarge their economic bases through diversification, and also seek greater autonomy, that is, shifting to the lower right by assuming greater control of and responsibility for the management and marketing of the resource. Some communities may choose the extreme lower right, as outlined by M'Gonigle in his conditions for Community Forests (1996). This, of course, does not guarantee a decline in vulnerability.

Figure 10.1

Community dependency and forest management options

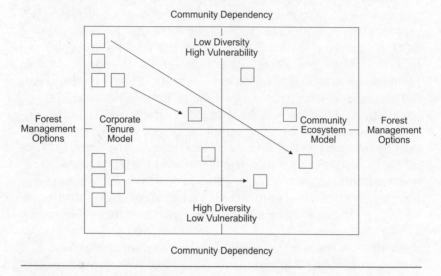

Challenges and Opportunities

A community's assets and its choice of strategies to expand capacity through CED will heavily influence the transition to a more community-based, more diverse, and less vulnerable economic system. The challenges facing the expansion of the role of CED alluded to in Chapter 5 are not only market- and policy-driven but very much informational, organizational, and behavioural in nature. Further insight into the nature and scope of these barriers to CED and opportunities for improvement (depending upon the degree to which they were present) were addressed in Chapter 8. These barriers and opportunities that were based upon responses from participants in a final workshop included individual capacity, access to capital, community education and awareness, community organizing, policy and the role of government, and resource management.

We believe that communities must articulate and respond to these challenges to mitigate their negative impact. In some cases, this will be done on an individual basis; in others, it will require lobbying and partnerships with other communities. The power and influence of these collective efforts should not be underestimated. For example, research on the growth in importance of NGOs has demonstrated that, during the past decade, some of the effects of globalization and environmental deterioration have been successfully counteracted by the emergence of transnational NGOs and lobbying groups (Soyez 2001). Could equivalent organizational groups emerge for CED? In other words, how can communities respond individually and collectively to mitigate the negative impacts of globalization and environmental degradation, and how can research promote our understanding of these phenomena?

Given the close overlap among the challenges identified in the literature (Chapter 5) and by the workshop participants, we can combine them to provide a juncture for explaining prescriptive or remedial actions. We have already dealt with specific proposals for improving access to resource management in the preceding section, so this issue will be addressed only tangentially under "Policy and Access" below.

Measurement and Recognition

CED and its benefits continue to be undervalued by decision makers partly because of the difficulties in measuring certain non-remunerative activities but also perhaps in setting the standard too high. To some degree, these failings are part of a more general process of undervaluation that occurs for the informal sector. We believe this to be less the case in communities with strong social entrepreneurs and/or community development corporations whose communication and organizational skills provide important legitimacy to these activities. Encouragingly, from a third-sector perspective, increasing attention and research is being devoted to understanding CED's role and importance in national economies (Johnston et al. 1995; Rifkin 1995). A sea change in attitudes has already occurred in the last twenty years with respect to the importance of developing human and social capital, but the focus has been mostly on developing countries. The arguments by M'Gonigle and colleagues (2001) that we need to move from a "liquidation" to a "restoration" economy in a first-world context is part of an ongoing debate about the praxis of sustainable development. In all likelihood, these will gain currency in time.

Capacity Constraints

A number of factors influence the capacity/capital catch-22 dynamic noted earlier, including size and wealth of a community, proximity to urban areas, and a legacy, or lack thereof, of government largesse in the development of community infrastructure. The tendency for participants in CED organizations to be overtaxed in terms of demands on time is endemic to most communities (Mitchell et al. 2001). Three important policy priorities to mitigate these problems are the establishment of special infrastructure investment funds provincially and nationally, continued efforts to improve the educational and skill levels of the future 15 to 25 age group, and the dissemination of best practice knowledge about CED from current practitioners.

Market Relationships

While exports have been the lifeblood of many BC communities, this dependency is not without significant uncertainty and instability. The question is then whether the source of the problem is the level of exports per se or whether it is the structure of the exports and the underlying relationships. BC forest-based communities, as well as the forest sector more generally, have been wedded to a low-value and high-volume industrial strategy. As previously illustrated, the number of jobs generated per unit volume of wood has been among the lowest in Canada, reflecting low multipliers or spin-offs from the export of wood products, which in turn reflects significant leakages out of the local economy (poorly integrated forward, backward, and final demand linkages). Perhaps most symptomatic of this is the lack of emphasis on value-added and diversification strategies. The horizontal integration of the industry leading to larger and more concentrated but specialized producers further threatens competition. Where processing and value-added manufacturing occur, it is increasingly taking place in the Lower Mainland of BC. Thus, the dependency upon exports is really only the proximate cause of the instability. The ultimate cause consists of the poorly articulated production linkages, low-value-added strategies for the province generally, and high degrees of concentration in the Lower Mainland. Making local and regional economies more integrative and competitive will increase the multiplier effect. It will require, however, a combination of top-down and bottom-up strategies that draw their inspiration from the community through CED but require enabling legislation and policies to facilitate access to the resources and significant structural and spatial shifts in the forest economy.

Regulatory/Policy Environment

Governments have fashioned a complex regulatory environment to control access to the forest resource and to promote sustained yield and alternative uses such as tourism, recreation and amenity values, and social services. Conceptually speaking, governments, as regulatory agents, have attempted to counteract the negative effects, spatially and temporally, stemming from accumulation regimes of modern and post-modern capitalism. Unfortunately, the theoretical justification for regulation has run into the harsh realities of the space economy, not to mention the problems of resourcism as identified by Clapp (1998) and the current mantra of deregulation of the economy. Despite the fact that "new" knowledge-based economies are premised upon space/time convergence, the reality is that "old" economies such as forestry are still very much place-based and locality-driven. Also symptomatic of the problem of local dependency are the poor or nonexistent markets for many services in these areas, which of course further undermines capacity.

While there exist examples of contextually sensitive and appropriate attempts at intervention by senior governments – such as through the Community Forest Pilot program, select programs of Human Resources Development Canada, and Community Futures Development Corporations – these are the exception. More commonly, there has been a long list of negative influences ranging from urban bias and rigid program designs to offloading of services. Even though local development initiatives and CED have captured the attention of government ministries, the responses have been for the most part inconsistent, uncoordinated, and weak. As previously noted, governments cannot do CED but they can play an important facilitating role. Without doubt, a large gap exists between government capacity to exercise this role and specific action plans; for example, the BC provincial government eliminated regional development officers in 1996. Part of the confusion and lack of direction arises from a continued outmoded model of large income transfers, either for large capital-intensive investments or for bailouts (e.g., Skeena Cellulose), or a preoccupation with a particular community-based model, such as cooperatives. Instead of big government working with big business, there must be a better match between needs at the local level and responses from above.

Local Politics
CED is often an intensely political process for three principal reasons: it must vie for resources in an environment of acute resource scarcity; it must often challenge the status quo, particularly in overcoming outmoded approaches to development; and it must operate within the prevailing social dynamics, and so it must forge consensus and cooperation with potentially conflicting groups, including government. The work by Cox and Mair (1988) on "local dependence" and Gill and Reed (1999) on promoting tourism, recreation, and amenity values is instructive of the formidable barriers to reaching consensus that exist in most communities. The success stories of many communities, however, point to the role of leadership in transcending the divisions and providing an important bridge to historically adversarial relationships.

Of course, local leadership includes political leadership. It follows that there is a need not only for a rethinking and redesign of senior government policy towards local development initiatives but also for a reassessment of the role of local government in facilitating CED. As we have seen, there are different models of engagement for local government. Arguably, there is justification for an arm's-length relationship between local government and community-based economic development organizations (CEDOs). At the same time, there is the very real risk of local elites dominating the development agenda and in the process short-circuiting what ought to be a democratic process. In the case of First Nations communities, there is very little separation, if any, between the governance structure of band councils on the one hand and local development initiatives on the other. In many cases, band councils do not have the capacity or continuity to sustain larger-scale development initiatives. We will return to the appropriate scale for government involvement in the final sections of this chapter.

Access Issues

Finally, the challenge for CED to achieve broader relevancy and impact will, in our view, be a function of the willingness of government to recast the regulatory landscape to improve access to the resource base and enable power sharing. The treaty process and other negotiations with First Nations have the potential to radically transform historical relationships, as do the proposed changes to the Forest Act that allow for up to 20 percent of harvested timber to be auctioned on the open log market. As previously argued, changes in access to the forest resource could produce significant benefits for forest-based communities without sacrificing Crown title, sovereignty, or other constitutional prerogatives of the nation-state. The willingness to experiment and to foster structural change will lay the essential groundwork for a more diverse and contextually responsive partnership with government. The proposal by the provincial government to create a Community Charter for the so-called heartland regions of British Columbia promises greater autonomy for local government. What is unclear is the degree to which this may be yet another offloading of service responsibilities, an orphaning, if not an abandonment, of traditional provincial responsibilities. In both forest policy and Community Charter cases, the challenge will be to find the right balance, previously noted by Bryant (1999), between the move towards decentralized local control on the one hand and preservation of equity and constructive public interests on the other. The reforms to forest policy may ultimately tip the balance in favour of the broader public interests and economic efficiency at the expense of local development prospects. Ideally, these interests should be complementary and, with the right mix of public policy, capable of achieving greater net benefits in social welfare.

Sharing the Knowledge

In Chapter 1, we introduced five research questions that proposed to address issues relating to identifying and expanding capacity, linking capacity to specific CED initiatives, and ultimately sharing these experiences with other communities. Despite the diversity of development issues facing communities across BC, the large corpus of existing research on success factors and the in-depth case studies informing this research make it possible to identify common themes that are transferable and have broad relevance in terms of planning process and successful action.

Research

To ensure that communities were active members of and participants in this research, participatory/action research (P/AR) methods were chosen. For academic researchers, this affords the possibility of combining traditional pursuit of knowledge with opportunities for effecting change. Without question, this research method, while in many ways experimental, furthered our goals far more effectively than if we had restricted ourselves to a more arm's-length and detached mode of inquiry. As previously mentioned, P/AR represented a collaborative process linking university researchers with practitioners in the joint pursuit of better theory and practice. While the university acted as a catalyst in initiating the research, community-based working groups formed the nuclei of the local representation, becoming vital and reliable sources of information in terms of capacity assessment and community aspirations.

We placed a very heavy emphasis on incorporating local knowledge. We saw P/AR as containing an important didactic or, more precisely, an autodidactic function in which the potential for further learning in CED was enhanced, both theoretically and practically. The planning process was multifaceted, beginning with capacity assessment, which was then linked to the success factor framework; these approaches were then integrated to determine which was the most appropriate action plan or CED strategy. Just as P/AR was seen as fostering an improved environment for ongoing learning, so the planning process was meant to be dynamic, open-ended, and ongoing.

To determine whether communities were indeed expanding capacity, we identified various outcomes that served as convenient benchmarks for measuring progress. At the core of these interpretations is the notion that as community capacity is enlarged, communities become more resilient and flexible. While something of a simplification, two governance models were identified: directed and facilitated CED. Clearly there is room for more research on the relative strengths of each approach. Having said this, the directed model is likely a better organizational model for dealing with provincial governments and their attempts to enable community-based development efforts.

An important by-product of the research process was the highlighting of shortcomings of the action research approach, including heavy time commitments, the failure to be inclusive of all groups and stakeholders, and, related to this, the challenge of meeting the participatory ideal. From a broader perspective, there are important lessons to be learned about the role and potential of universities through the research process, not just to generate knowledge but to become active agents of progressive change. Universities as brain trusts can and should serve the common good.

Planning Process

It was argued in Chapter 5 that the successful integration and modification of the strategic planning model in CED serves to promote and standardize the CED process. Strategic planning is, of course, a means to realize a community's development potential. Strategic planning, as Bryant (1999) reminds us, must, however, take account of the dynamic and uncertain environment and position communities accordingly. Understanding success factors and placing them within the dimensions of a success factor framework served as a creative and comparative base for assessing development prospects. Two important issues need to be addressed with respect to the application of such a framework. In a sense, these issues are the bookends to the general question of why some communities are more likely to succeed. At the one end is the issue of the relative weight or importance to be attached to each of the major groupings. There is very little research to provide clarification, in part because of the contextually contingent nature of these success factors. These difficulties are analogous to the ongoing debate over the differential importance to be attached to the principal dimensions or imperatives of sustainable development: economy, society, and ecology. Further complicating this issue is the role and the nature of the interaction among endogenous and exogenous or external factors. In the next section, we will briefly explore this factor as it relates to changes in government policy in the forest products industry.

The other issue is equally messy and complex, and deals with the minimum information standards or requirements necessary to proceed with a CED strategy. There are really two parts to this, one qualitative and the other quantitative. Having high-quality or high-resolution information but low-quantity information may be highly preferable to the opposite situation. Again, this will be contextually contingent and very difficult to make generalizations about. What can be proffered more generally, however, is that communities should not be blinded by the exercise into thinking that they cannot proceed without a complete spreadsheet of information and a complement of success factors. Trial and error, while painful and at times demoralizing, is very much a part of development and a learning process in its own right.

It is important to appreciate the fact that every community contains what Bryant refers to as orientations (1999, 71): "Each orientation represents a bundle of initiatives, decisions, and actions; together the observed orientations define a community's development patterns." Equally important, however, are the less tangible latent orientations, latent because "the problems or opportunities associated with them have not yet been recognized as important to a community's development" (Bryant 1999, 72).

Ultimately, however, it is the strategic orientations that will drive the CED process and the specific needs of a community. The identification and evaluation processes can be improved by ongoing research on success factors and best practices in CED. Programs for sharing knowledge through the Internet and through university/government-sponsored research are a low-cost yet effective method for disseminating up-to-date data and information on community experiences. While recognizing that these experiences are placed-based and contextually contingent, sufficient common ground exists for unravelling the complex code of community development.

In Chapter 8, we identified two main points that summarize the general lessons for the implementation of local development strategies. To reiterate, the case studies reinforce the importance of starting small and building up to larger initiatives as organizational capacity and community support increases. Second, the case studies point to the value of pursuing a balanced approach to CED through both localist and linking initiatives. In other words, local development is a product of both internal and external sources for building economic capacity.

Towards a Community Charter

As the "new economy" weakens the traditional foundations and effectiveness of the nation-state, what are the opportunities for fashioning new relationships between the core and periphery and between the local and national/provincial levels of decision making? Are there principles and action plans that can be agreed upon that will better protect the interests of those living in resource-dependent communities? Is there, in short, a willingness to explore a social contract, a community charter if you like, that is sensitive to the special development problems of these communities?

To begin with, Massam and Dickinson note (1999, 227): "A civil society is not comprised of citizens pitted against the state. Rather, it is a civic state that promotes the interconnectedness of social groups and the state apparatus. It is a celebration of human linkages that share in the responsibility for the fair distribution of the necessary goods that ensure for each person a life of dignity within the sustainable limits of his or her environment."

The CED "lever" can be considerably lengthened for maximum purchase through the recognition of important synergisms and development principles sensitive to scale, context, and social involvement. Recent research in Europe and in British Columbia underscores the necessity of recognizing civic engagement and cooperation among groups at various spatial scales to promote sustainable development. In Figure 10.2, for example, Smith's research (2002) on the health of the Fraser Valley agro-ecosystem situates communities according to their degree of civic engagement and the extent to which the stakeholders in the system are actively involved in working together towards common solutions. Many communities lacked both of these attributes, with an attendant weakening in control over negative environmental development. We would argue that this same model is applicable to

Figure 10.2

Civic engagement

Active civic engagement
with diverse regional representation

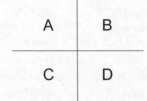

Cooperation integration
of policy actors, NGOs,
non-profit organizations,
and community leaders

Competition and autonomy
of policy actors, NGOs,
non-profit organizations,
and community leaders

Poor civic engagement
with low regional representation

A Active civic engagement with a diverse and high number of actors present in the region.
   A high level of cooperation and integration of effort for a sustainable ecosystem.
B Active civic engagement with a diverse and high number of actors present in the region.
   A high level of competition and autonomous effort among the different groups.
C A few civic organizations and policy actors. Cooperation on key issues may not be representative or participatory.
D Few civic organizations, poor regional representation, and limited cooperation among potential policy actors.
Source: Adapted from Smith 2002.

---

the complex and difficult development aspirations of forest-based communities. Moving to the top left quadrant has the potential to realize important synergisms and capitalize on what Bryant (1999) referred to as latent orientations. It also has the potential to bring about a better balance between local needs and broader public interests. In terms of our four study communities, Salmon Arm and 100 Mile House ranked much higher than Bella Colla or Lillooet in terms of cooperation, participation, regional representation, and active civic engagement.

From a complementary perspective, Buttimer (2001), in a study of the changing scale of European agricultural development (which has been both market- and policy-driven) and the accompanying landscape, environmental, and social transformations, advances a number of principles for better understanding the phenomena and safeguarding the rights and aspirations of local communities. These principles include subsidiarity, horizons of discretionary reach, and appropriate scales of development.

Subsidiarity, to reiterate, refers to the subsidiary function of a central authority – the state – performing only those tasks that cannot be effectively carried out at a local or regional level. Buttimer adds (2001, xxii): "In practice, it should take full account of the traditions and sensitivities of different regions of the community and the cost-effectiveness of various actions, while improving the choice of actions and appropriate mixes of instruments at community and/or other levels." This principle is practically nonexistent in British Columbia (other than in urban planning), in part because so much of the development context has been circumscribed by sector-based as opposed to area-based approaches. Area-based approaches would by definition recognize and enshrine multiple use of a forest resource and alternative approaches to development, such as tourism, recreation, and amenity activities. The LRMP process has attempted to do this but it has been characterized by competition, factionalism, and, in many cases, lack of alternatives to continued dependency on the forest resource.

Horizons of discretionary reach refer to "the realms – both spatial and institutional – within which access to resources, information and decision-making about landscape and life can be negotiated" (Buttimer 2001). This can be viewed from the bottom up, in which individuals and communities exert varying degrees of control over their social, economic, and political lives, particularly with respect to the dominant sectors and functional spaces within which they operate, or from a top-down perspective involving state, semi-state, and EU policies, regulations, and decision making. In the context of forest-based communities and CED initiatives, the horizons of discretionary reach are limited, if not severely truncated by a high degree of concentration in the industry, limited access to the resource base, and low value-added possibilities. The ability of communities to share CED experiences and to join together to promote economic and social opportunities of mutual benefit is one of the little explored yet potentially rewarding examples of community reaches. In this connection, the Internet and electronic access to information have provided critical "virtual access" to the larger world, extending a community's knowledge base to augment present and future negotiations.

The third principle, appropriate scales of development, cuts across the previous two. It refers to a scale for action and interaction defined spatially as well as functionally. An important element of judgment permeates the criteria of appropriateness, influenced by sector, context, and aesthetic and moral preferences (Buttimer 2001). An interesting question is where top-down and bottom-up approaches to planning meet. Is it possible for the region to become the most suitable or appropriate level for decision making? Is there a regional level of CED that should be promoted? Some experimentation in regional land-use planning has occurred in BC in the LRMP process. Regional districts have of course exerted considerable influence in rural areas, but not with respect to working with CED groups. Research by Linning (1999) on the impacts of reduction in the size of the harvestable forest base as well as a shift to long-run sustained yield harvest levels clearly illustrated the differential and variable nature of the employment and income impacts for forest-based communities. Clearly, context matters, and therefore planning with respect to these sensitivities becomes all the more important. This underscores the importance of clearly identifying strategic orientations of communities, and of understanding and articulating the spatial scale of development planning (localist or linking); it also underscores the important facilitating role of government programs and policy, and the need for communities to devise their own economic plans before addressing regional collaborative possibilities.

Whether we call this a charter, contract, or principles for survival in a post-productivist period, the urgency to examine relations between core and periphery has never been greater. The subtext for this rebalancing, to facilitate greater community input and participation in the economic affairs of a region, is part of an emerging zeitgeist that demands a rebalancing in our relations with government and the political economy alike, a strategy that calls into question either/or solutions: the socialist/welfare state or unfettered free enterprise systems. Complexity in problems and diversity of needs must be answered with a complexity and diversity of responses that are contextually sensitive and that acknowledge the legitimate rights and aspirations of people to become more self-reliant. Most communities will survive in spite of deregulation and the offloading of service provision, but all of this will come at a greater social cost than if we were to more imaginatively envision the potential for local actions to influence the resilience of our peoples and places.

Appendix
Success Factors Framework

The following tables are intended to assist communities in selecting indicators and data sources for each success factor. We have provided a range of sample indicators and information sources so that communities may select those that are most appropriate for their individual situations. There are many other possible indicators and sources of information.

We highly recommend initiating a community dialogue about appropriate indicators and sources of information. Community meetings, surveys, and focus groups, for example, can yield both opinions on which indicators are most relevant and data on specific indicators. Taking time to select appropriate indicators is important: quality information leads to quality and appropriate development decisions.

Table A1

Human resource factors

Factor	Measure/indicator	Sample data sources
Skills	• Informal individual and community attributes • Traditional knowledge • Apprenticeship programs (presence of and participation in) • Requirement for outside hiring by local employers • Training, education, experience	• Skills inventory • Asset mapping • Employer interviews • Records of training institutions, employment centres • Census statistics (e.g., experience by industry)
Education and training	• Educational levels • Literacy rates • Access to education/training facilities • Participation in continuing education programs • Computer ownership • Internet accounts/servers • Library usage	• Census information • Inventory of community facilities • Records of educational institutions • Internet server and library records
Leadership	• Identification • Qualities (*see* Table 6.3)	• Profile of community leaders according to selected characteristics • Qualitative research techniques (interviews, observation, etc.)
Civic engagement	• Voter participation rates • Community meeting attendance • Trust/neighbourliness • Attitudes (e.g., optimism, focus on future, unity, diversity) • Out-migration • Local newspaper readership • Volunteerism (% who volunteer eight hours or more per month) • Membership base of community organizations • Community centre/facility usage • Stewardship: recycling, water, energy use • Local spending and investment	• Meeting, membership, voting, and community facility records • Interviews • Census information • Newspaper subscription information • Leakage studies • Utility, waste management companies

▶

◄ *Table A1*

Factor	Measure/indicator	Sample data sources
Entrepreneurial spirit	• Sectoral specialization • Number of new business start-ups • Existence of and enrollment in entrepreneurial training programs • Demand for business development services • Local ownership of local firms and resources • Policy and regulatory framework • Leadership attitude towards entrepreneurship • Local examples of successful entrepreneurs • Number of community associations	• Business licence information (municipal) • Start-up and bankruptcy statistics • Census (employment by industry, self-employment statistics) • Inventory/profile of community services • Records of business development organizations • Interviews
Labour force readiness	• Labour force participation • Incidence of suicide, drug and alcohol abuse • Life expectancy • Infant mortality • Incidence of disease • Demographics (18-44, 65+) • Presence of healing centres or addiction programs • Access to medical services • Incidence of poverty • Social assistance levels	• Inventory/profile of community services • Census data • Health and social assistance statistics • Qualitative methods (interviews, observation, etc.)

Table A2

Social factors

Factor	Measure/indicator	Sample data sources
Sense of community	*See* "Civic engagement" in Table A1. Also: • Levels of informal economic activity • Crime rates • Community celebrations/events • Poverty levels, meeting of basic needs • Internal fundraising capacity	• Interviews • Documentation • Community newspapers • Statistics (census, provincial, agencies)
Community-based organizations	• Number of community associations • Issue range of organizations: social, cultural, economic, ecological • Provision of local services • Health of community organizations • Financial sustainability • Management and proposal-writing capability • Long-term vision • Clear mandate	• Database/inventory of community organizations • Organizational documentation (minutes, annual reports, newsletters) • Interviews, observation
Community participation, planning, and cooperation	• Broad-based participation in organizations/initiatives • Avenues for information sharing (e.g., newsletters) • Volunteer programs, coordination, and support • Monitoring processes for development activities • Existence of land-use plan/planning process • Existence of CED plan/planning process • Local involvement in resource management • Presence of coalitions/partnership initiatives • Radius of trust	• Resident surveys, interviews re satisfaction with participation opportunities • Documentation (community newspapers, minutes, reports, etc.) • Documented land-use and resource management policies and associated public/stakeholder involvement processes • Relationship/network diagrams created in small groups

Table A3

Economic factors

Factor	Measure/indicator	Sample data sources
Economic health	• Strong export base/trade relationships • Employment/unemployment • Income and income distribution • In-/out-migration levels • Social assistance levels • Economic multiplier • Office vacancy rates • Building permits	• Statistics Canada (Labour Force Survey, Census) • Travel surveys and statistics • Local qualitative information
Diversity	• Employment by sector • Income by sector (including retirement and social assistance) • Variety in size of local businesses (home-based, SME, large corporate)	• Statistics • Local firms (surveys, interviews, annual reports, etc.) • Business licence information
Adaptability	• Research and development • New product development • Staff training programs • Compliance with new industry standards and regulations • Access to information: Internet, resource centres, postsecondary institutions, networks with external agencies and other communities	• Firms (interviews, observation, documentation) • Inventory of services • Internet service providers • Evidence of linkages with external organizations
Health of local businesses	• Diversity and security of markets • Local purchasing, hiring, investing/leakage • Supply and demand linkages among local businesses • Availability of financing for growth and transition • Personnel turnover • Profit margins/costs of production • Price stability	• Firms, business organizations • Leakage surveys • Market information (e.g., lumber, fish price trends)

▶

◄ *Table A3*

Factor	Measure/indicator	Sample data sources
Sustainability	• Impact of current economic activity on opportunities for future generations • Presence of integrated resource management • Perception of fairness in resource allocation from a diversity of local actors and economic interests • Harvest rates • Value added • Restoration activities	• Ecological indicators (*see* Table A4) • Qualitative data (interviews, surveys, focus groups, etc.) • Resource and waste management agencies • Profile of local resource and environmental management activities
Informal economic activity	• Elder and child care by friends and family • Gathering/harvesting for food and/or fuel • Number of community organizations/volunteerism	• Diaries, surveys, interviews, etc. • Census information *See also* "Community-based organizations" in Table A2.
Local control	• Number and range of locally owned enterprises • Total employment in local enterprises • Evidence of local buying/hiring, leakage, multiplier • Community currency • Local access to, and control of, land and natural resources • Dependency on government revenues and outside markets	• Firms • Leakage surveys • Municipal finance statistics • Statistics Canada • Resource management agencies
Access to capital	• Ability to obtain grant funding from external sources (e.g., government, foundations, or private donors) • Local sources of capital or credit (e.g., local credit unions, community loan funds or foundations, local investors) • Investor confidence • Tax base • Evidence that the community is willing and able to invest in a CED process or initiative	• Organization documentation • Interviews (e.g., CED and business organizations, financial institutions) • Inventory of available services • Municipal finance statistics

►

◄ *Table A3*

Factor	Measure/indicator	Sample data sources
Location/ infrastructure	• Proximity to urban/larger centre • Transportation routes/options • Communication network • Catchment area population • Economic analysis (e.g., trade capture, pull factor) • Quality of local infrastructure: power and water, sewage treatment, transportation, communication/information services, local buildings (condition, availability), heritage sites	• Qualitative assessments of locational conditions • Sales tax information, retail sales/expenditure, income and population statistics • Road distances
Service amenities	• Cultural programs and services • Educational facilities • Health care services • Recreational programs and services • Community festivals • Arts programs and events • Range of retail and service businesses	• Inventory of services • Qualitative assessments • Visitor/resident surveys

Table A4

Ecological factors

Factor	Measure/indicator	Sample data sources
Ecosystem health	• Soil erosion • Waste production/disposal • Habitat degradation/preservation • Species diversity • Threatened/endangered species (e.g., indicator species) • Water and air quality	• Resource and environmental management agencies • Studies by industry, academics, and NGOs • Qualitative assessments (e.g., resident opinion)
Natural resources	• Political/legal and physical availability of resource stocks: forest (timber and non-timber products), fish/aquatic, wildlife, minerals • Agricultural capability	*See* "Ecosystem health" above
Commercial and subsistence harvesting	• Harvesting rates (stage in the resource cycle) • Harvesting methods and practices • Value-added activities (optimum use)	• Business organizations, directories, inventories, and publications • Statistics re value-added and harvest levels
Ecological amenities	• Distinct or unique natural features • Scenic beauty • Integrity/health of the surrounding ecosystem • Recreational linkages: trails, beaches, interpretation, etc. • Clean air and water • Level of outdoor/ecologically related tourism activity	• Tourism studies, inventories • Tourism/visitor statistics
Stewardship	• Transportation (pedestrian, bicycle, public transport) • Recycling, composting programs • Pollution prevention/clean-up • Energy conservation • Habitat and species restoration • Harvesting practices • Local involvement in resource management • Land-use planning processes/ ecosystem protection	• Utilities (usage rates) • Inventories of activities and services • Census (transportation) *Also see* "Civic engagement" in Table A1 and "Sustainability" in Table A3.

Notes

Foreword
1 New Economics Foundation, *Ghost Town Britain* (London: New Economics Foundation, 2003).
2 C. Hines, *A Global Look to the Local: Replacing Economic Globalisation with Democratic Localisation* (London: International Institute for Environment and Development [IEED], 2004). Hines argues that the world needs a radically new approach – "localisation," which has the potential to radically increase all aspects of democratic participation and is a necessary precondition for improvements in our food systems, environment, and society worldwide.

Chapter 2: Context and Communities
1 Fordism describes an economic paradigm defined by the standardization of the production process (through highly organized and specialized labour practices) in order to generate high volumes and stimulate high consumption patterns. The system was maintained through a trilateral relationship between large companies, large unions, and a large, interventionist state (Peet 1997; Hayter 2000).
2 Location Quotients (LQ) provide a measure of the intensity of employment in the different industry groups in the rural and small-town (RST) areas, relative to employment in the same group in Canada as a whole. An LQ of 100 indicates an equal degree of intensity; a value above 100 indicates a higher intensity and an associated industry specialization; a value below 100 indicates a lower intensity.

Chapter 3: Forest Dependency and Local Development in British Columbia
1 *Calder v. the Attorney General of British Columbia* (1973) 34 D.L.R. (3d) 145 (S.C.C.).
2 "Forest lands are allocated to timber companies and cutting rights are distributed through various leasing arrangements. The arrangements undertaken by the government to transfer rights to harvest timber or manage forest lands to private companies, while retaining title to the land, are collectively referred to as the 'forest tenure system'" (Haley and Luckert 1990, 2). The Ministry of Forests (MoF) in BC defines the province's forest tenure system as "the collective legislation, regulations, contractual agreements, permits and government policies that define and constrain a person's right to harvest the province's timber." Ministry of Forests, Timber Tenure System in British Columbia (Victoria: Ministry of Forests, n.d.), 1.
3 Williamson and Annamraju employ a methodology similar to that of Horne and Powell (1995). The unit of measurement for estimating the contribution of forestry to the community's economic base is employment income for all CSDs (Census Sub Divisions) larger than 250 persons. For communities smaller than 250 persons, income data are not available in the Census, and so employment (the number of people employed) is the unit of measurement.

4   Other studies have produced results similar to the Williamson report. For example, a Forestry Canada Information Report produced in 1989 stated: "Outside of the major southwestern urban centres, 30% of all communities and regions are dependent solely on the forest sector for their economic well-being, and another 40% rely on the forest industry as one of their top three employers. During times of economic growth, this dependency has been a boon for rural BC as the forest industry has consistently paid high wages and salaries. However, this dependency has left much of the province vulnerable to economic downturns, such as the recession of the early 80s."

Chapter 4: Transition in BC's Forest Economy

1   In 1999, the BC forest industry reported net earnings of $923 million, generating a return on capital employed of 7.6 percent, below a rate of 9.6 percent for the rest of Canada and far below the industry's minimum return on capital employed threshold of 12 percent.
2   *Delgamuukw v. British Columbia* (1997) 3 S.C.R. 1010.
3   *R. v. Sparrow,* [1990] 1 S.C.R. 1075.
4   BC Stats defines small businesses as those with under fifty employees.

Chapter 7: The Community Economic Development Process

1   The Strategic Plan was developed with assistance from Marie Barney and Victor Cumming, Southern Interior Forest Extension and Research Partnership (SIFERP).
2   The following provides excerpts only from the Heritage Strategic Plan. In the original, each goal is accompanied by various strategies, which are then accompanied by the following workplan information: Responsibility, How?, and Time Frame.
3   Other research methods include: (1) *Asset mapping:* The purpose of asset mapping is to build collaborative relationships and to direct them towards community development projects (Kretzman and McKnight 1993). The asset mapping process produces a visual representation and inventory of the resources, talents, and strengths of a community. The process identifies and records the capacity of each community member, association, and institution through a capacity study. Researchers may then explore the relationships between individuals, groups, and institutions to create innovative solutions to development challenges or opportunities. (2) *Focus groups:* Focus groups can be particularly useful in assessing community perceptions related to specific development issues. Development organizations may randomly assemble groups or target specific sectors (e.g., by gender, age, employment status, etc.). Focus groups help to create a safe environment for open discussion and tend to provide a more thorough examination of development issues than a survey. Group sizes may vary, as may the interviewing time and location. A modified version of the focus group is the "living room" or "kitchen table" meeting, which creates a non-intimidating environment that combines research, information sharing, and socializing (Gill 1996). (3) *Community interviewing:* Blakely (1994) suggests that it is important to tap the local personal knowledge of community residents. Community-wide interviewing (interviewing of a wide range of community members) can be a time-consuming process, but it may yield the most comprehensive data about the community. Community interviewing facilitates broader participation in the planning process and can be structured to inform the development process about both subjective issues, such as community visioning, and more tangible development opportunities.

Chapter 8: Community Economic Development Strategies

1   We conducted research in three phases. First, a community forum was held to launch the initiative and to gather input from the local construction industry into how a local networking organization could contribute to the industry. Second, we conducted a survey of construction value in the Shuswap region to better assess the value and potential value of the industry. Finally, we conducted a household needs assessment to further identify construction values.
2   In this section, Jennifer Gunter, a research assistant with the Forest Communities project, provides a closer look at the prospects for community forestry success. For more information, see Gunter 2000.

Chapter 9: The Community/University Relationship

1 Greenwood et al. (1993) state that the addition of "participation" to action research is necessary because of the many cases of nonparticipatory action research they have observed in the US.

Bibliography

Aglietta, M. 1979. *A Theory of Capitalist Regulation: The US Experience.* London: NLB.

Aguinis, H. 1993. Action research and scientific method: Presumed discrepancies and actual similarities. *Journal of Applied Behavioural Science* 29 (4): 417-31.

Ameyaw, S. 1999. Assessing training and education needs: Lessons from SFU/FRBC CEDC research project. Working paper. Burnaby, BC: CED Centre, Simon Fraser University.

Amin, A., and N. Thrift. 1997. Globalization, socio-economics, territoriality. In *Geographies of Economies,* ed. R. Lee and J. Wills. New York: Arnold.

Argyris, C. 1980. Making the undiscussable and its undiscussability discussable. *Public Administration Review* 40 (3): 205-13.

Argyris, C., and D.A. Schön. 1974. *Theory in Practice: Increasing Professional Effectiveness.* San Francisco: Jossey-Bass.

–. 1978. *Organizational Learning: A Theory of Action Perspective.* Reading, MA: Addison-Wesley.

–. 1996. *Organizational Learning II: Theory, Method and Practice.* Reading, MA: Addison-Wesley.

Armstrong, H.W., B. Kehrer, and A.M. Wood. 2002. The evaluation of community economic development initiatives. *Urban Studies* 39 (2): 457-81.

Arnstein, S.R. 1969. A ladder of citizen participation. *Journal of American Institute of Planners* (July): 216-24.

Aspen Institute. 1996. *Measuring Community Capacity Building.* Washington, DC: BR Publications.

Auty, R.M. 1994. Industrial policy reform in six large newly industrializing countries: The resource curse thesis. *World Development* 22 (1): 11-26.

–. 1995. Industrial policy, sectoral maturation, and postwar economic growth in Brazil: The resource curse thesis. *Economic Geography* 71 (3): 257-72.

Barnes, T.J. 1996. External shocks: Regional implications of an open staple economy. In *Canada and the Global Economy: The Geography of Structural and Technological Change,* ed. J. Britton. Montreal: McGill-Queen's University Press.

Barnes, T.J., and R. Hayter. 1992. The little town that did: Flexible accumulation and community response in Chemainus, British Columbia. *Regional Studies* 26 (7): 647-63.

–. 1994. Economic restructuring, local development and resource towns: Forest communities in coastal British Columbia. *Canadian Journal of Regional Science* 17 (3): 289-310.

–. 1997. *Trouble in the Rainforest: British Columbia's Forest Economy in Transition.* Victoria: Western Geographical Press.

Barnes, T.J., J. Britton, W. Coffey, D. Edgington, M. Gertler, and G. Norcliffe. 2000. Canadian economic geography at the millennium. *Canadian Geographer* 44 (1): 4-24.

Bar-On, D. 1999. *The Indescribable and the Undiscussable: Reconstructing Human Discourse After Trauma.* Budapest: CEU Press.

Baxter, D., and A. Ramlo. 2002. *Resource Dependency: The Spatial Origins of British Columbia's Economic Base.* Vancouver: Urban Futures Institute.

BC Stats. 1998. Forty years later, forestry exports as important as ever. *Bulletin,* January 1998.

–. 1999a. What drives the economies of BC's rural communities? Victoria: Ministry of Finance and Corporate Relations.

–. 1999b. Business indicators: December 1999. Victoria: Ministry of Finance and Corporate Relations.

–. 2000. Value added wood exports grow fast in British Columbia, but faster in rest of Canada. Victoria: Ministry of Finance and Corporate Relations.

–. 2001a. Tourism industry monitor – Annual 2000. <http://www.bcstats.gov.bc.ca>.

–. 2001b. After much economic diversification, BC exports are still mainly resource based. Victoria: Ministry of Finance and Corporate Relations.

–. 2001c. Business indicators, April 2001. Victoria: Ministry of Finance and Corporate Relations.

–. 2001d. Guide to the BC economy. Victoria: Ministry of Finance and Corporate Relations.

–. 2003a. Business indicators: BC's tourism sector struggles through 2001. Victoria: Ministry of Management Services.

–. 2003b. Profile of the British Columbia high technology sector. Victoria: BC Ministry of Competition, Science and Enterprise; BC Treaty Commission.

–. 2003c. British Columbia regional index. <http://www.regionalindex.gov.bc.ca/>.

BC Wild. 1998. *Overcut: British Columbia Forest Policy and the Liquidation of Old-Growth Forests.* Vancouver: BC Wild.

Beatty, J., and G. Hamilton. 1998. Forest industry crisis escalates amid closures. *Vancouver Sun,* 3 October, A3.

Beckley, T., and T. Burkosky. 1997. *Social Indicator Approaches to Assessing and Monitoring Forest Community Sustainability.* Ottawa: Canadian Forest Service, Northern Forestry Centre.

Bellan, S. 1995. *Small Business and the Big Banks.* Toronto: James Lorimer.

Bendavid-Val, A. 1991. *Regional and Local Economic Analysis for Practitioners.* London: Praeger.

Berck, P., D. Burton, G. Golfman, and J. Geoghegan. 1992. Instability in forestry and forest communities. In *Emerging Issues in Forest Policy,* ed. P.N. Nemetz. Vancouver: UBC Press.

Berkhofer, R. 1978. *The White Man's Indian: Images of the American Indian from Columbus to the Present.* New York: Knopf.

Betts, M., and D. Coon. 1996. *Working with the Woods.* Fredericton: Conservation Council of New Brunswick.

Birner, R., and H. Wittmer. 2001. Converting social capital into political capital: How do local communities gain political influence? Paper submitted to the Eighth Annual Conference of the International Association for the Study of Common Property.

Blakely, E.J. 1989. *Planning Economic Development: Theory and Practice.* Thousand Oaks, CA: Sage Publications.

–. 1994. *Planning Local Economic Development: Theory and Practice.* London: Sage Publications.

Blomley, N. 1996. Shut the province down: First Nations blockades in BC, 1984-1995. *BC Studies* 3: 8-9.

Boelscher, M. 1988. *The Curtain Within: Haida Social and Mythical Discourse.* Vancouver: UBC Press.

Bollman, R. 1992. *Rural and Small Town Canada.* Toronto: Supply and Services Canada.

–. 2001a. Measuring economic well-being or rural Canadians using income indicators. *Rural and Small Town Canada: Analysis Bulletin* 2 (5).

–. 2001b. Employment structure in rural and small town Canada: An overview. *Rural and Small Town Canada: Analysis Bulletin* 2 (6).

–. 2001c. Employment structure and small town Canada: The primary sector. *Rural and Small Town Canada: Analysis Bulletin* 2 (7).

–, ed. 2001d. Definitions of rural. *Rural and Small Town Canada: Analysis Bulletin* 3 (3).

–. 2001e. Employment in rural and small town Canada: An update to 2000. *Rural and Small Town Canada: Analysis Bulletin* 3 (4).

Boothroyd, P., and C. Davis. 1991. *The Meaning of Community Economic Development.* Vancouver: School of Community and Regional Planning, University of British Columbia.

British Columbia. 1995. Social and Economic Impacts of Aboriginal Land Claims Settlements: A Case Study Analysis. Victoria: Ministry of Aboriginal Affairs.

–. 1998a. Backgrounder: Community Forest Pilot project. Victoria: Ministry of Forests.

–. 1998b. News release: Legislation enables community forest agreements. Victoria: Ministry of Forests.

–. 1999a. Ministry of Environment, Lands and Parks. <http://www.elp.gov.bc.ca>.

–. 1999b. Ministry of Forests. <http://www.for.gov.bc.ca>.

–. 2003. The BC Heartlands Strategy. <http://www2.news.gov.bc.ca/nrm_news_releases/2003OTP0009-000153.htm>.

British Columbia Treaty Commission. 2003. <http://www.bctreaty.net/files_2/updates.html>.

Britton, J., ed. 1996. *Canada and the Global Economy: The Geography of Structural and Technological Change.* Montreal: McGill-Queen's University Press.

Brodie, J. 1990. *The Political Economy of Canadian Regionalism.* Toronto: Harcourt Brace Jovanovich.

Brohman, J. 1995. Economism and critical silences in development studies: A theoretical critique of neoliberalism. *Third World Quarterly* 16 (2): 297318.

Brown, D., and R. Tandon. 1983. Ideology and political economics in inquiry: Action research and participatory research. *Journal of Applied Behavioural Science* 19 (3): 277-94.

Brundtland, G.H. 1987. *Our Common Future: The World Commission on Environment and Development.* Oxford: Oxford University Press.

Bryant, C.R. 1994. The locational dynamics of community economic development. In *Community Economic Development in Canada, Volume 1,* ed. D. Douglas, 203-36. Toronto: McGraw-Hill Ryerson.

–. 1995a. The role of local actors in transforming the urban fringe. *Journal of Rural Studies* 11 (3): 255-67.

–. 1995b. *Sustainable community analysis workbook 1-4.* Waterloo, ON: University of Waterloo.

–. 1999. Community change in context. In *Communities, Development, and Sustainability across Canada,* ed. J. Pierce and A. Dale. Vancouver: UBC Press.

Bryant, C.R., and A.E. Joseph. 2001. Canada's rural population: Trends in space and implications in place. *Canadian Geographer* 45 (1): 132-37.

Bryant, C.R., and R.E. Preston. 1989. Towards a framework of local initiatives and community economic development. In *Papers in Canadian Economic Development, Volume 2,* ed. C.R. Bryant and B. Buck. Waterloo, ON: University of Waterloo.

Bryant, C.R., L. Allie, et al. 2000. Linking community to the external environment: The role and effectiveness of local actors and their networks in shaping sustainable community development. In *Reshaping of Rural Ecologies, Economies and Communities,* ed. J.T. Pierce, S.D. Prager, and R.A. Smith. Vancouver: IGU.

Bryden, J., and J. Hart. 2003. *Why Do Local Economies Differ? The Dynamics of Rural Areas in the European Union.* Lampeter: The Edwin Mellen Press.

Burda, C. 1999. Ecosystem-based community forestry in British Columbia: An examination of the need and opportunity for policy reform, integrating lessons from around the world. MA thesis, University of Victoria.

Burda, C., D. Curran, F. Gale, and M. M'Gonigle. 1997. *Forests in Trust: Reforming British Columbia's Forest Tenure System for Ecosystem and Community Health.* Victoria: Eco-Research Chair of Environmental Law and Policy, Faculty of Law and Environmental Studies Program, University of Victoria.

Buttimer, A., ed. 2001. *Sustainable Landscapes and Lifeways.* Cork, Ireland: Cork University Press.

Canadian Association of Single-Industry Towns (CASIT). 1989. The vulnerability checklist: A tool for community self-assessment. Local Development Series paper no. 10. Ottawa: Economic Council of Canada.

Canadian CED Network (CCEDNet). 2001. National policy forum. Vancouver, 22-24 March.

Canadian Forest Service (CFS). 2001. *The State of Canada's Forests: 1999-2000.* Ottawa: Natural Resources Canada.

Canadian Rural Secretariat. 1998. Rural dialogue: Rural Canadians speak out. <http://www.rural.gc.ca/discpaper_e.html>.

Cardinal, D., R. Holt, et al. 2003. *Ecosystem-based Management Planning Handbook*. Vancouver: Coast Information Team Secretariat.

Cashore, B., G. Hoberg, M. Howlett, J. Rayner, and J. Wilson. 2001. *In Search of Sustainability: British Columbia Forest Policy in the 1990s*. Vancouver: UBC Press.

Chambers, R. 1994. The origins and practice of participatory rural appraisal. *World Development* 22 (7): 953-69.

Chaskin, R., S. Venkatesh, A. Vidal, P. Brown. 2001. *Building Community Capacity*. New York: Walter de Gruyter.

Chesler, M. 1991. Participatory action research with self-help groups: An alternative paradigm for inquiry and action. *American Journal of Community Psychology* 19 (5): 757-68.

Chisholm, R., and M. Elden. 1993. Features of emerging action research. *Human Relations* 46 (2): 275-97.

Clapp, R.A. 1998. The resource cycle in forestry and fishing. *Canadian Geographer* 42 (2): 129-44.

–. 1999. Response to C. Millar and G.M. Winder. *Canadian Geographer* 43 (3): 327-30.

Clarke, G., I. Bowler, J. Darrall, D. Heaney, and B. Ilbery. 2000. Quality and identify in rural development. In *Claiming Rural Identities*, ed. T. Haartsen, P. Groote, and P. Huigen. Assen, Netherlands: Van Gorcum and Company.

Clogg, J. 1999. Tenure background paper. Vancouver: West Coast Environmental Law.

Cloke, P. 1977. An index of rurality for England and Wales. *Regional Studies* 11: 31-46.

Coffey, W.J. 1996. The role and location of service activities in the Canadian space economy. In *Canada and the Global Economy: The Geography of Structural and Technological Change*, ed. J.N.H. Britton. Montreal: McGill-Queen's University Press.

Coffey, W.J., and M. Polese. 1984. The concept of local development: A stages model of endogenous regional growth. *Papers of the Regional Science Association* 35: 1-12.

–. 1985. Local development: Conceptual bases and policy implications. *Regional Studies* 19: 85-93.

Colussi, M., and P. Rowcliffe. 1999. *The Community Resilience Manual: A Resource for Rural Recovery and Renewal*. Port Alberni: Centre for Community Enterprise.

Commission on Employment and Unemployment in Newfoundland (CEUN). 1986. Building on our strengths. Report of the Commission on Employment and Unemployment in Newfoundland. St. John's: CEUN.

Consilium. 1997. Community economic development: A toolkit for economic development officers. Ottawa: Arviat Business Training Centre.

Coopers and Lybrand Consulting. 1996. Current and future economic benefits of British Columbia parks. Report for the BC Ministry of Environment, Lands and Parks. Vancouver: Coopers and Lybrand.

Coppack, P. 1988. Reflections on the role of amenity in the evolution of the urban field. *Geografiska Annaler* 70: 353-61.

Courant, P., E. Niemi, and E. Whitlaw, ed. 1997. The ecosystem-economy relationship: Insights from six forested LTER sites. Report to the National Science Foundation, Grant No. DEB-9416809.

Cox, K.R., and A. Mair. 1988. Locality and community in the politics of local development. *Annals of the Association of American Geographers* 78: 307-25.

Crihfield, J. 1991. Education and rural development: Lessons for the rural Midwest. In *Rural Community Economic Development*, ed. N. Walzer. New York: Praeger.

Cummings, H.F. 1989. Rural development and planning in Canada: Some perspectives on federal and provincial roles. *Plan Canada* 29 (2): 8-18.

Dale, A. 2001. *At the Edge: Sustainable Development in the 21st Century*. Vancouver: UBC Press.

Daly, H., and J. Cobb. 1994. *For the Common Good*. Boston: Beacon Press.

Dauncey, G. 1988. *After the Crash: The Emergence of a Rainbow Economy*. Basingstoke, UK: Green Print.

Davis, H.C., and T. Hutton. 1992. Structural change in the British Columbia economy: Regional diversification and metropolitan transition. Victoria: BC Round Table on the Environment and the Economy.

De Wolf, J. 2002. Growth drivers in British Columbia. Vancouver: BC Progress Board.

Denman Island Community Forest Cooperative. 1998. Denman Island Community Forest Cooperative. <http://www.denmanis.bc.ca/forestry.htm>.

Deva Heritage Consulting. 1998. Stl'atl'imx/Hydro community research project: Final report. Vancouver: Deva Consulting.

District of 100 Mile House. 1999. Community Forest Application. 100 Mile House: District of 100 Mile House.

Douglas, D., ed. 1994. *Community Economic Development in Canada*. Toronto: McGraw-Hill Ryerson.

Drache, D. 1976. Rediscovering Canadian political economy. *Journal of Canadian Studies* 11: 3-18.

Drushka, K. 1993. Forest tenure: Forest ownership and the case for diversification. In *Touch Wood: BC Forests at the Crossroads*, ed. K. Drushka, B. Nixon, and R. Travers. Madeira Park, BC: Harbour Publishing.

–. 1999. A case of stunted growth. *Vancouver Sun*, 31 March, D1, D19.

Drushka, K., B. Nixon, and R. Travers, eds. 1993. *Touch Wood: BC Forests at the Crossroads*. Madeira Park, BC: Harbour Publishing.

Du Plessis, V., R. Beshiri, R. Bollman, and H. Clemenson. 2002. Definitions of rural. Ottawa: Minister of Industry, Statistics Canada.

Dubnick, M.J. 1996. Public service ethics and the cultures of blame. Paper presented at the *Fifth International Conference of Ethics in the Public Service*, Brisbane, Australia, 5-9 August.

Dufour, G., F. Eichgruen, M. Eversfield, S. Miller, D. Sekyer. 1998. Small business profile '98. Western Economic Diversification Canada; BC Ministry of Small Business, Tourism and Culture; BC Stats; and BC Ministry of Finance and Corporate Relations.

Dyck, N. 1991. *What Is the Indian "Problem"? Tutelage and Resistance in Canadian Indian Administration*. St. John's: Institute of Social and Economic Research, Memorial University.

Dykeman, F.E. 1990. Entrepreneurial and sustainable rural communities. Sackville, NB: Rural and Small Town Research Programme, Mount Allison University.

Economic Council of Canada. 1990. *From the Bottom Up: The Community Economic-Development Approach*. Ottawa: Economic Council of Canada.

Edwards, G. 1994. Actions speak louder than words. Ottawa: National Round Table Review, Spring.

Elden, M., and R. Chisholm. 1993. Emerging varieties of action research: Introduction to the special issue. *Human Relations* 46 (2): 121-41.

Etzioni, A. 1968. *Active Society: A Theory of Societal and Political Processes*. New York: Free Press.

Fairbairn, B. 1998. A preliminary history of rural development policy and programmes in Canada, 1945-1995. Saskatoon: University of Saskatchewan, New Rural Economy Program.

Fallows, J. 1989. *More Like Us: Making America Great Again*. Boston: Houghton Mifflin.

Federation of Canadian Municipalities (FCM). 1999. The FCM quality of life reporting system. Ottawa: FCM.

Filion, P. 1988. Potentials and weaknesses of strategic community development planning: A Sudbury case study. *Canadian Journal of Regional Science* 11: 307-411.

–. 1991. Local economic development as a response to economic transition. *Canadian Journal of Regional Science* 14: 347-70.

–. 1998. Potential and limitations of community economic development: Individual initiative and collective action in a post-Fordist context. *Environment and Planning A* 30: 1101-23.

Flora, J., and C. Flora. 1991. Local economic development projects: Key factors. In *Rural Community Economic Development*, ed. N. Walzer. New York: Praeger.

Forest Resources Commission. 1991. *Background Papers, Volume 3*. Victoria: Government of BC.

Frank, F. 1994. Training – An urgent community economic development need. In *Community Economic Development: Perspectives on Research and Policy*, ed. B. Galaway and J. Hudson, 237-48. Toronto: Thompson Educational Publishing.

Frank, F., and A. Smith. 1999. *The Community Development Handbook*. Hull, QC: Labour Market Learning and Development Canada.

Freire, P. 1970. *Pedagogy of the Oppressed*. New York: Continuum Publishing.

Freudenburg, W. 1992. Addictive economies: Extractive industries and vulnerable localities in a changing world economy. *Rural Sociology* 57: 305-32.

Friedmann, J. 1988. *Life Space and Economic Space*. New Brunswick, NJ: Transaction.

–. 1992. *Empowerment: The Politics of an Alternative Development*. Oxford: Blackwell.

G.E. Bridges and Associates. 1994. Socio-economic assessment of timber supply scenarios: Mid coast TSA. Prepared for Economics and Trade Branch, Ministry of Forests.

Galaway, B., and J. Hudson. 1994. *Community Economic Development: Perspectives on Research and Policy*. Toronto: Thompson Educational Publishing.

Gale, R., F. Gale, and T. Green. 1999. Accounting for the forests: A methodological critique of Price Waterhouse's report *The Forest Industry in British Columbia, 1997*. Victoria: Sierra Club of British Columbia.

Gale, S. 1996. Community based planning and management processes. Prepared for the British Columbia Fisheries Secretariat.

Gallaugher, P., C. Knight, and K. Vodden, eds. 1996. Coastal communities taking action: A year of dialogue along the British Columbia coast. Forum proceedings. Simon Fraser University at Harbour Centre, Vancouver, 25 April.

Gibbs, C., and D. Bromley. 1989. Institutional arrangements for management of rural resources: Common-property regimes. In *Common Property Resources: Ecology and Community-based Sustainable Development*, ed. F. Berkes. London: Belhaven Press.

Gibbs, D. 1996. Integrating sustainable development and economic restructuring: A role for regulation theory. *Geoforum* 27 (1): 1-10.

Gill, A. 1996. Rooms with a view: Informal settings for public dialogue. *Society and Natural Resources* 9: 633-45.

Gill, A., and M. Reed. 1997. The re-imagining of a Canadian resource town: Post productivism in a North American context. *Journal of Applied Geographical Studies* 1 (2): 129-47.

–. 1999. Incorporating post-productivist values into sustainable community processes. In *Communities, Development, and Sustainability across Canada*, ed. J. Pierce and A. Dale. Vancouver: UBC Press.

Government of BC. 1991. In fairness to all: Moving towards treaty settlements in BC. Victoria: Government of British Columbia.

Greenwood, D., W.F. Whyte, and I. Harkavy. 1993. Participatory action research as a process and as a goal. *Human Relations* 46 (2): 175-91.

Grenier, L. 1998. *Working with Indigenous Knowledge: A Guide for Researchers*. Ottawa: International Development Research Centre.

Gunter, J. 2000. Creating the conditions for sustainable community forestry in British Columbia: A case study of the Kaslo Community Forest. MA thesis, Simon Fraser University. <http://www.sfu.ca/cedc>.

Hala'w Group. 2000. The Hala'w initiative. Lillooet: Hala'w Group.

Haley, D. 1997. Community forests: From dream to reality. Unpublished paper prepared for the Rossland Conference on Community Forestry, Rossland, BC, 29-31 January.

Halseth, G. 1998. Community economic development strategies on resource communities under stress – Illustrations from British Columbia. Paper presented at the Canadian Association of Geographers meeting, University of Ottawa.

Halseth, G., and D. Arnold. 1997. Community (Internet) access groups: Case studies from rural and small town British Columbia, Canada. Prepared for the Community Economic Development Centre, Simon Fraser University.

Hamilton, G. 1998. Forestry reaching into guts and feathers. *Vancouver Sun*, 12 March, D1, D18.

–. 2003. US demands sweeping changes to forest policy. *Vancouver Sun*, 21 July.

Hammond, H. 1991. *Seeing the Forest Among the Trees*. Vancouver: Polestar Press.

Harden, W. 1960. Social and economic effects of community size. *Rural Sociology* 25 (Summer): 204-11.

Harris, C. 2001. Post-modern patriotism: Canadian reflections. *Canadian Geographer* 45 (1): 193-207.

Hayter, R. 2000. *Flexible Crossroads: The Restructuring of British Columbia's Forest Economy.* Vancouver: UBC Press.

Hayter, R., and T. Barnes. 1990. Innis' staple theory, exports, and recession: British Columbia, 1981-1986. *Economic Geography* 66: 156-73.

Health Canada. 1998. Community action resources for Inuit, Métis and First Nations: Toolbox. Ottawa: Minister of Public Works and Services Canada.

Henderson, H. 1994. Paths to sustainable development. *Futures* 26 (2): 125-37.

Higgins, B., and D. Savoie. 1995. *Regional Development Theories and their Application.* London: Transaction Publishers.

Hirschman, A.O. 1958. *The Strategy of Economic Development.* New Haven: Yale University Press.

Hoberg, G. 2002. The BC Liberals' "new era of sustainable forestry": A progress report. <http://www.policy.forestry.ubc.ca/campbell.html>.

Hoggart, K., and H. Buller. 1987. *Rural Development: A Geographical Perspective.* London: Croom Helm.

Homer-Dixon, T. 2000. *The Ingenuity Gap.* New York: Knopf.

Horne, G. 1999. British Columbia local area economic dependencies and impact ratios – 1996. Victoria: BC Ministry of Finance and Corporate Relations.

Horne, G., and C. Powell. 1995. British Columbia local area economic dependencies and impact ratios – 1991. BC Ministry of Finance and Corporate Relations, February 1995.

–. 1999. British Columbia local area economic dependencies and impact ratios – 1996. BC Ministry of Finance and Corporate Relations, May 1999.

House, J.D., and K. McGrath. 2004. Innovative governance and development in the New Ireland: Social partnership and the integrated approach. *Governance* 17 (1) [in press].

Howlett, M. 2001. Policy venues, policy spillovers, and policy changes: The courts, Aboriginal rights, and British Columbia forest policy. In *In Search of Sustainability: British Columbia Forest Policy in the 1990s,* ed. B. Cashore, G. Hoberg, M. Howlett, J. Rayner, and J. Wilson, 120-39. Vancouver: UBC Press.

Howlett, M., and A. Netherton. 1999. *The Political Economy of Canada.* Toronto: Oxford University Press.

Hume, S. 1999. Leaked memo shows stewardship barely exists. *Vancouver Sun,* J1 17, B3.

Hussmann, M. 1993. Small town revitalization through the Main Street approach. In *Community-based Approaches to Rural Development: Principles and Practice,* ed. D. Bruce and M. Whitla. Sackville, NB: Mount Allison University.

Hustedde, R.J. 1991. Developing leadership to address rural problems. In *Rural Community Economic Development,* ed. N. Walzer. New York: Praeger.

Hutton, T. 1994. Visions of a "post-staples" economy: Structural change and adjustment issues in British Columbia. Vancouver: Centre for Human Settlements, University of British Columbia.

Hymes, D. 1962. The ethnography of speaking. In *Anthropology and Human Behavior,* ed. T. Gladwin and W.C. Sturtevant. Washington, DC: Anthropological Society of Washington.

IMPAX. 1996. Shuswap clusters – Economic profiles: Shuswap Region of the Columbia Shuswap Regional District. Vancouver: IMPAX Policy Services International.

Indian and Northern Affairs Canada (INAC). 2003. Crown and First Nations roles in reserve land management. Ottawa: INAC. <http://www.ainc-inac.gc.ca/pr/pub/matr/clm_e.html>.

Innis, H. 1933. *Problems of Staple Production in Canada.* Toronto: Ryerson Press.

–. 1956. *The Fur Trade in Canada: An Introduction to Canadian Economic History.* Toronto: University of Toronto Press.

Jackson, E., and J. Pierce. 1990. Mobilizing capital for regional development. Local Development Series paper no. 21. Ottawa: Economic Council of Canada.

Jacobs, P. 1989. Foreword. In *Common Property Resources: Ecology and Community-Based Sustainable Development,* ed. F. Berkes. London: Belhaven Press.

Johansen, H., and G. Fuguitt. 1973. Changing retail activity in Wisconsin villages: 1939-1954-1970. *Rural Sociology* 38 (Summer): 207-18.

John, D., S. Batie, and K. Norris. 1989. A brighter future for rural America? Washington, DC: National Governors Association, Centre for Policy Research.

Johnston, R., P. Taylor, and M. Watts. 1995. *Geographies of Global Change: Remapping the World in the Late Twentieth Century.* Oxford: Blackwell.

Kaner, S. 1996. *Facilitator's Guide to Participatory Decision-making.* Gabriola, BC: New Society Publishers.

Kaufman, H., and L. Kaufman. 1990. Toward the stabilization and enrichment of a forest community. In *Community and Forestry,* ed. R. Lee, D. Field, and W. Burch. San Francisco: Westview Press.

Kootenay Conference on Forest Alternatives (KCFA). 1999. Forest tenure reform: A path to community prosperity? Proceedings of the conference, 4-6 November, Nelson, BC.

Kretzmann, J., and J. McKnight. 1993. Building communities from the inside out. Evanston, IL: Neighbourhood Innovations Network, Northwestern University.

Kusel, J. 1996. Well-being in forest dependent communities, part 1: A new approach. In Sierra Nevada Ecosystem Project: Final report to Congress, vol. 2, Assessments and scientific basis for management options, 361-73. Davis: Centers for Water and Wildland Resources, University of California.

Lamontagne, F. 1994. Development indicators and development planning: A case study. In *Community Economic Development: Perspectives on Research and Policy,* ed. B. Galaway and J. Hudson. Toronto: Thompson Educational Publishing.

Laxer, G. 1989. *Open for Business.* Toronto: Oxford University Press.

Lee, R., D. Field, and W. Burch, eds. 1990. *Community and Forestry: Continuities in the Sociology of Natural Resources.* San Francisco: Westview Press.

Levitt, K. 1970. *Silent Surrender: The Multinational Corporation in Canada.* Toronto: Macmillan of Canada.

Lewin, K. 1946. Action research and minority problems. *Journal of Social Issues* 2 (4): 34-46.

Lewis, M. 1994. The scope and characteristics of community economic development in Canada. In *Community Economic Development: Perspectives on Research and Policy,* ed. B. Galaway and J. Hudson. Toronto: Thompson Educational Publishing.

Lewis, M., and F. Green. 1992. *Strategic Planning for the CED Practitioner.* Vancouver: West Coast Development Group.

Linning, I. 1999. A regional analysis of British Columbia forest policy and land use initiatives on employment and income. MA thesis, Department of Geography, Simon Fraser University.

Lipietz, A. 1994. Post-Fordism and democracy. In *Post-Fordism,* ed. A. Amin, 338-57. Oxford: Blackwell.

–. 2001. The fortunes and misfortunes of post-Fordism. In *Phases of Capitalist Development: Booms, Crises and Globalizations,* ed. R. Albritton, M. Itoh, R. Westra, and A. Zuege. New York: Palgrave.

Little, B. 2002. BC's decades of "genteel decline." *Globe and Mail,* 20 April, B1, B4.

Lloyd, P. 1996. Social and economic inclusion through regional development: The community economic development priority in European Structural Funds programmes in Great Britain. Luxembourg: Regional Policy and Cohesion, European Union.

Longo, J. 1998. What do you mean by social capital anyway? A social capital literature review and conceptual framework. Working paper. Victoria: Centre for Public Sector Studies.

Lovering, J. 1999. Theory led by policy: The inadequacies of the "new regionalism." *International Journal of Urban and Regional Research* 23: 379-85.

Machlis, G.E., and J.E. Force. 1990. Community stability and timber-dependent communities: Future research. In *Community and Forestry: Continuities in the Sociology of Natural Resources,* ed. R.G. Lee, D.R. Field, and W.R. Burch, Jr. San Francisco: Westview Press.

Mackintosh, W.A. 1969. Economic factors in Canadian history. In *Approaches to Canadian Economic History,* ed. W.T. Easterbrook and M. H. Watkins. Toronto: McClelland and Stewart.

MacLeod, G. 2001. Beyond soft institutionalism: Accumulation, regulation, and their geographical fixes. *Environment and Planning A* 33 (7): 1145-67.

MacNeil, T. 1994. Governments as partners in community economic development. In *Community Economic Development: Perspectives on Research and Policy,* ed. B. Galaway and J. Hudson, 178-86. Toronto: Thompson Educational Publishing.

–. 1997. Assessing the gap between community development practice and regional development policy. In *Community Organizing: Canadian Experiences,* ed. B. Wharf and M. Clague. Toronto: Oxford University Press.

MacNeil, T., and R. Williams. 1995. Evaluation framework for community economic development. Ottawa: National Welfare Grants.

Maki, T., G. Walter, and S. Hutcheson. 1993. Community sustainability and forest resource use: Discussions with community leaders in the Alberni-Clayoquot and the Cowichan Valley Regional Districts. Prepared by Sustainable Communities Initiative Component Three Working Group. Victoria: University of Victoria Centre for Sustainable Regional Development.

Marchak, P.G. 1983. *Green Gold: The Forest Industry in British Columbia.* Vancouver: UBC Press.

Marchak, P., S. Aycock, and D. Herbert. 1999. *Falldown: Forest Policy in British Columbia.* Vancouver: The David Suzuki Foundation and Ecotrust Canada.

Markey, S., and M. Roseland. 2001. Reaching across the divide: The role of universities in building capacity for community economic development. Burnaby: CED Centre, Simon Fraser University.

Markey, S., and K. Vodden. 2003. Concepts, techniques and principles for CED practice. Burnaby: CED Centre and Centre for Distance Education, Simon Fraser University.

Markey, S., J.T. Pierce, and K. Vodden. 2000. Resources, people and the environment: A regional analysis of the evolution of resource policy in Canada. *Canadian Journal of Regional Science* 23 (3): 427-54.

Marshall, A., B. Shepard, and J. Roberts. 2001. Career counseling for youth affected by social and economic restructuring. Proceedings of the World Congress of the International Association for Educational and Vocational Guidance, Paris, France.

Martin, R., and P. Sunley. 1998. The post-Keynesian state and the space economy. In *Geographies of Economies,* ed. R. Lee and J. Wills. New York: Arnold.

Martinussen, J. 1997. *Society, State and Market: A Guide to Competing Theories of Development.* Halifax: Fernwood Publishing.

Massam, B., and J. Dickinson. 1999. The civic state, civil society and the promotion of sustainable development. In *Communities, Development, and Sustainability across Canada,* ed. J.T. Pierce and A. Dale, 208-42. Vancouver: UBC Press.

Massey, D. 1995. *Spatial Divisions of Labour.* London: Macmillan.

McInnes, C. 2002. BC's equalization cheque on the way. *Vancouver Sun,* 28 February, A2.

McKnight, J. 1995. *The Careless Society.* New York: Basic Books.

Meeker-Lowry, S. 1988. *Economics as if the Earth Really Mattered: A Catalyst Guide to Socially Conscious Investing.* Gabriola, BC: New Society Publishers.

M'Gonigle, M. 1996. Living communities in a living forest: Towards an ecosystem-based structure of local tenure and management. Victoria: Eco-Research Chair of Environmental Law and Policy, Faculty of Law and Environmental Studies Program, University of Victoria.

–. 1997. Reinventing British Columbia: Towards a new political economy in the forest. In *Trouble in the Rainforest: British Columbia's Forest Economy in Transition,* ed. T.J. Barnes and R. Hayter, 37-50. Victoria: Western Geographical Press.

M'Gonigle, M., and B. Parfitt. 1994. *Forestopia: A Practical Guide to the New Forest Economy.* Madeira Park, BC: Harbour Publishing.

M'Gonigle, M., B. Egan, and L. Ambus. 2001. The Community Ecosystem Trust: A new model for developing sustainability. Victoria: POLIS Project on Ecological Governance.

M'Gonigle, M., and D. Curran. 1997. Co-management discussion paper. Victoria: Faculty of Law and School of Environmental Studies, University of Victoria.

Midgley, J. 1986. *Community Participation, Social Development and the State*. New York: Methuen.

Miller, L., B. Rossing, and S. Steele. 1990. *Partnerships: Shared Leadership among Stakeholders*. Madison, WI: University of Wisconsin Press.

Millerd, D., and J. Nichol. 1994. Building a sustainable fishing industry: A sectoral strategy for prosperity and resource health. Ottawa: Fish Processing Strategic Task Force.

Mitchell, B.E. 1995. *Resources and Environmental Management in Canada*. Toronto: Oxford University Press.

Ministry of Community, Aboriginal and Women's Services. 2002. The Community Charter: A new legislative framework for local government. Victoria: The Ministry.

Mitchell, D., J. Longo, and K. Vodden. 2001. Building capacity or straining resources? The changing role of non-profit sector in threatened coastal economies. In *The Nonprofit Sector and Government in a New Century*, ed. K. Brock and K. Banting, 147-88. Kingston, ON: School of Policy Studies, Queen's University.

Monet, D., and Skanu'u (A. Wilson). 1992. *Colonialism on Trial: Indigenous Land Rights and the Gitksan and Wet'suwet'en Sovereignty Case*. Gabriola, BC: New Society Publishers.

Murdoch, J., and T. Marsden. 1995. The spatialization of politics: local and national actor-spaces in environmental conflict. *Transactions of the Institute of British Geographers* 20: 368-80.

Murray, S., and D. Bartoszewski. 1998. Profits or plunder: Mismanagement of BC's forests. Vancouver: Sierra Legal Defence Fund.

Neil, C., and M. Tykkylainen, eds. 1998. *Local Economic Development: A Geographical Comparison of Rural Community Restructuring*. New York: United Nations University Press.

New Economics Foundation (NEF). 2002. *The Money Trail*. London: New Economics Foundation and the Countryside Agency.

Newby, L. 1999. Sustainable local economic development: A new agenda for action? *Local Environment* 4 (1): 67-72.

Nixon, B. 1993. Changing the way we make forest decisions. In *Touch Wood: BC Forests at the Crossroads*, ed. K. Drushka, B. Nixon, and R. Travers. Madeira Park, BC: Harbour Publishing.

Notzke, C. 1994. *Aboriginal People and Natural Resources in Canada*. Toronto: York University Press.

Nozick, M. 1992. *No Place Like Home: Building Sustainable Communities*. Ottawa: Canadian Council on Social Development.

–. 1999. Strategies, models, case examples for CED in forest communities. Draft working paper. Burnaby: CED Centre, Simon Fraser University.

Nutt, R. 2000. Forest sector slams government's take. *Vancouver Sun*, 4 August, F1, F5.

Nutter, R., and M. McKnight. 1994. Scope and characteristics of CED: Summary, policy implications and research needs. In *Community Economic Development: Perspectives on Research and Policy*, ed. B. Galaway and J. Hudson, 92-96. Toronto: Thompson Educational Publishing.

O'Neill, T. 1994. Regional, local and community-based economic development. In *Community Economic Development: Perspectives on Research and Policy*, ed. B. Galaway and J. Hudson, 59-72. Toronto: Thompson Educational Publishing.

Ommer, R., and P. Sinclair. 1996. Systemic crisis in rural Newfoundland: Can the outports survive? St. John's: Eco-research Program.

Palmer, V. 1999. The grandest jobs-timber accord that never was. *Vancouver Sun*, 12 June, A22.

–. 2001. Forestry cuts face some unintended results. *Vancouver Sun*, 28 November, A22.

Peet, R. 1997. *Theories of Development*. New York: Guilford Press.

Pell, D. 1994. The third sector, sustainable development and community empowerment. In *Community Economic Development in Canada*, ed. D. Douglas, 161-86. Toronto: McGraw-Hill Ryerson.

Peters, E.J. 2000. Aboriginal people and Canadian geography: A review of the recent literature. *Canadian Geographer* 44 (1): 44-55.

–. 2001. Geographies of Aboriginal people in Canada. *Canadian Geographer* 45 (1): 138-44.

Picot, G., and J. Heath. 1992. Small communities in Atlantic Canada: Their industrial structure and labour market conditions in the early 1980s. In *Rural and Small Town Canada*, ed. R. Bollman, 167-92. Toronto: Thompson Educational Publishing.

Pierce, J.T. 1990. *The Food Resource*. New York: John Wiley and Sons.

–. 1992. Progress and the biosphere: The dialectics of sustainable development. *Canadian Geographer* 36 (4): 306-20.

–. 1998. Sustaining rural environments: Widening communities of knowledge. In *Dimensions of Sustainable Rural Systems*, ed. I.R. Bowler, C.R. Bryant, and P.P. Huigen. Utrecht/Groningen: Netherlands Geographical Studies.

–. 1999. Communities as the strong link in sustainable development. In *Communities, Development, and Sustainability across Canada*, ed. J.T. Pierce and A. Dale, 277-90. Vancouver: UBC Press.

–. 2000. Introduction: Reshaping of rural ecologies, economies, and communities – An overview of the BC scene. In *Reshaping of Rural Ecologies, Economies and Communities*, ed. J.T. Pierce, S.D. Prager, and R.A. Smith. Vancouver: IGU.

Pierce, J.T., and A. Dale, eds. 1999. *Communities, Development, and Sustainability across Canada*. Vancouver: UBC Press.

Pierce, J.T., S.D. Prager, and R.A. Smith. 2000. *Reshaping of Rural Ecologies, Economies and Communities*. Vancouver: IGU.

Pinkerton, E., ed. 1989. *Co-operative Management of Local Fisheries: New Directions for Improved Management and Community Development*. Vancouver: UBC Press.

–. 1993. Co-management efforts as social movements: The Tin Wis coalition and the drive for forest practices legislation in BC. *Alternatives* 19 (3): 34-38.

Polese, M., and R. Shearmur. 2002. The periphery in the knowledge economy. The spatial dynamics of the Canadian economy and the future of non-metropolitan regions in Quebec and the Atlantic provinces. Montreal: Institut national de la recherche scientifique/INRS-Urbanisation, Culture et Societe.

Poncelet, E. 2001. A kiss here and a kiss there: Conflict and collaboration in environmental partnerships. *Environmental Management* 27 (1): 13-26.

Power, T.M. 1996a. *Lost Landscapes and Failed Economies: The Search for a Value of Place*. Washington, DC: Island Press.

–. 1996b. *Environmental Protection and Economic Well-being: The Economic Pursuit of Quality*. New York: M.E. Sharpe.

Price Waterhouse. 1999. *The Forest Industry in British Columbia, 1997*. Vancouver: Price Waterhouse.

Putnam, R.D. 1993. *Making Democracy Work: Civic Traditions in Modern Italy*. Princeton, NJ: Princeton University Press.

–. 1995. Bowling alone. *Journal of Democracy* 6 (1): 65-78.

Quarter, J. 1992. *Canada's Social Economy: Cooperatives, Non-profits and other Community Enterprises*. Toronto: J. Lorimer.

Randall, J., and G. Ironside. 1996. Communities on the edge: An economic geography of resource-dependent communities in Canada. *Canadian Geographer* 40: 17-35.

Rapaport, R. 1970. Three dilemmas in action research. *Human Relations* 23: 499-513.

Rasker, R., and B. Alexander. 1997. *The New Challenge: People, Commerce and the Environment in the Yellowstone to Yukon Region*. Washington, DC: The Wilderness Society.

Reason, P. 1994. *Participation in Human Inquiry*. London: Sage.

Reed, B.J., and D. Paulson. 1990. Small towns lack the capacity for successful development efforts. *Rural Development Perspectives* 6 (June/September): 26-30.

Reed, M.G. 1990. *Managing for Sustainable Development: A Case Study of a Hinterland Community, Ignace, Ontario, Canada*. Waterloo, ON: University of Waterloo.

–. 1995a. Cooperative management of environmental resources: A case study from Northern Ontario, Canada. *Journal of Economic Geography* 71 (2): 132-49.

–. 1995b. Implementing sustainable development in hinterland regions. In *Resources and Environmental Management in Canada*, ed. B. Mitchell. Toronto: Oxford University Press.

Reed, M.G., and A. Gill. 1997. Community economic development in a rapid growth setting: A case study of Squamish, BC. In *Troubles in the Rainforest*, ed. T. Barnes and R. Hayter. Victoria: Western Geographical Series, University of Victoria.

Reimer, B. 1999. Building community capacity in the new rural economy. Canadian Rural Restructuring Foundation, <http://nre.concordia.ca/project_overview.htm>.

Remedios, P. 2001. Cultural tourism and indigenous knowledge: Towards sustainable community economic development. <http://www.sfu.ca/cedc>.

Rifkin, J. 1995. *The End of Work: The Decline of the Global Labour Force and the Dawn of the Post-market Era*. New York: G.P. Putnam's Sons.

Robinson, G.M. 1990. *Conflict and Change in the Countryside: Rural Society, Economy, and Planning in the Developed World*. London: Belhaven Press.

Roseland, M. 1998. *Toward Sustainable Communities*. Gabriola, BC: New Society Publishers.

–. 1999. Natural capital and social capital; implications for sustainable community development. In *Communities, Development, and Sustainability across Canada*, ed. J.T. Pierce and A. Dale, 190-207. Vancouver: UBC Press.

Ross, D., and P. Usher. 1987. *From the Roots Up*. Toronto: James Lorimer.

Ross, D., and G. McRobie. 1989. A feasibility study for a Centre for Community Economic Development at Simon Fraser University. <http://www2.sfu.ca/cedc/resources/online/cedconline/mcrobie.htm#ced>.

Rostow, W.W. 1960. *The Stages of Economic Growth: A Non-communist Manifesto*. London: Cambridge University Press.

Sale, K. 1985. *Dwellers in the Land: The Bioregional Vision*. San Francisco: Sierra Club Books.

Salmon Arm Economic Development Corporation (SAEDC). 1997. Salmon Arm, British Columbia: Economic Development Challenges. Salmon Arm: SAEDC.

–. 1999. Salmon Arm Community Development Strategy. Salmon Arm: SAEDC.

–. 2000. Salmon Arm Business Expansion and Retention Program "BEaR" Final Report – Phase One. <http://www.salmonarmedc.com>.

–. 2001. Salmon Arm: Economic Development Strategy. Salmon Arm: SAEDC.

Salway Black, S. 1994. Redefining success in community development: A new approach for determining and measuring the impact of development. Richard Schramm Paper on Community Development. Boston: Lincoln Filene Center, Tufts University.

Sanjan, M.A., and M.E. Soulé. 1997. Moving beyond Brundtland: The conservation value of British Columbia's 12 percent protected areas strategy. Vancouver: Greenpeace Canada.

Savoie, D. 1992. *Regional Economic Development: Canada's Search for Solutions*. Toronto: University of Toronto Press.

–. 1997. *Rethinking Canada's Regional Development Policy: An Atlantic Perspective*. Ottawa: Canadian Institute for Research on Regional Development.

–. 2000. *Community Economic Development in Atlantic Canada: False Hope or Panacea*. Ottawa: National Library of Canada.

Schaller, D. 1996. Indigenous ecotourism and sustainable development: The case of Rio Blanco, Ecuador. <http://www.eduweb.com/schaller/Section2RioBlanco.html>.

Schlager, E., and E. Ostrom. 1993. Property rights regimes and coastal fisheries: An empirical analysis. In *The Political Economy of Customs and Culture: Informal Solutions to the Commons Problem*, ed. T. Anderson and R. Simmons, 13-41. Lanham, MD: Rowman and Littlefield Publishers.

Schoonmaker, P., and B. von Hagen. 1995. Willipa indicators for a sustainable community. Portland, OR: The Willipa Alliance and Ecotrust.

Schroeder K. 1997. Participatory action research in a traditional academic setting: Lessons from the Canada-Asia partnership. *Convergence* 30 (4): 41-49.

Schumacher, E.F. 1973. *Small is Beautiful: Economics as if People Mattered*. New York: Harper and Row.

Schwindt, R., and T. Heaps. 1996. *Chopping Up the Money Tree: Distributing Wealth from British Columbia's Forests*. Vancouver: The David Suzuki Foundation.

Scott, A. 1997. *The Promise of Paradise: Utopian Communities in BC*. Vancouver: Whitecap Books.

Senge, P., A. Kleiner, C. Roberts, R.B. Ross, and B.J. Smith. 1994. *The Fifth Discipline Fieldbook.* New York: Doubleday.

Sierra Business Council. 1996. Sierra Nevada Wealth Index: Understanding and tracking our region's wealth. Sacramento: Sierra Business Council.

Sloan, G. 1945. *Report of the Honourable Gordon McG. Sloan, Chief Justice of British Columbia relating to the forest resources of British Columbia.* Victoria: C.F. Banfield King's Printer.

Smith, R. 1999. Strategies, initiatives and models for community economic development. Working paper. Burnaby: CED Centre, Simon Fraser University. <http://www.sfu.ca/cedc>.

–. 2002. The role of community in agroecosystem health: A study of the Fraser Valley of British Columbia. MA thesis, Department of Geography, Simon Fraser University.

Solomon, L. 2003. Rural separatism. *National Post,* 30 May.

Soyez, D. 2001. Bottom-up globalization: Trans-national lobbies and industrial change. In *Sustainable Landscapes and Lifeways,* ed. A. Buttimer, 59-78. Cork, Ireland: Cork University Press.

Spruill, V. 1989. On blaming: An entry to the question of values. Presented for the symposium in honor of Hans Loewald, MD, New Haven, CT, 17 October 1987. *Psychoanalytic Study of the Child* 44: 241-63.

Stacey, C., and R. Needham. 1993. Heritage: A catalyst for innovative community development. In *Community-based Approaches to Rural Development: Principles and Practice,* ed. D. Bruce and M. Whitla. Sackville, NB: Mount Allison University.

Stringer, E.T. 1996. *Action Research: A Handbook for Practitioners.* Thousand Oaks, CA: Sage Publications.

Stohr, W.B., and F. Taylor. 1981. *Development from Above or Below?* Toronto: John Wiley and Sons.

Sustainable Seattle. 1998. Indicators of sustainable community. A status report for Seattle/King County. Seattle: Sustainable Seattle.

Tennant, P. 1989. *Aboriginal Peoples and Politics in BC.* Vancouver: UBC Press.

Terluin, I., and J. Post. 2003. Differences in economic development in rural regions of advanced countries: A review of theories. Paper presented at the Regional Studies Association International Conference, Pisa, Italy.

Tester, F. 1992. Reflections on Tin Wis: Environmentalism and the evolution of citizen participation in Canada. *Alternatives* 19 (1): 34-41.

Troughton, M. 1995. Presidential address: Rural Canada and Canadian rural geography – An appraisal. *Canadian Geographer* 39 (4): 290-305.

Union of BC Municipalities (UBCM). 1997. *Creative Connections: Arts and Culture in British Columbia Communities.* Richmond: UBCM.

Van Gils, P. 2000. Fundamentals of CED finance. *Making Waves* 11 (4): 2-9.

Vodden, K. 1997. Working together for a green economy. In *Eco-city Dimensions: Healthy Communities, Healthy Planet,* ed. M. Roseland. Gabriola, BC: New Society Publishers.

–. 1999. Co-management and sustainable community economic development in a BC fishing community. MA thesis, Department of Geography, Simon Fraser University.

Vodden, K., and J. Gunter. 1999. Ecological restoration and sustainable community economic development in British Columbia fish and forest dependent communities. In *Helping the Land Heal: Ecological Restoration in British Columbia. Conference Proceeding,* ed. B. Egan. Vancouver: BC Environmental Network Educational Foundation.

Vodden, K., A. Miller, and J. McBride. 2001. Assessing the business information needs of Aboriginal entrepreneurs in British Columbia – Final report. Prepared for Western Economic Diversification Canada and BC Ministry of Small Business, Tourism and Culture.

Walter, G.R. 1996. Sustainable communities initiative. <http://castle.uvic.ca/sci>.

Walzer, N., ed. 1991. *Rural Community Economic Development.* New York: Praeger.

Watkins, M.H. 1963. A staple theory of economic growth. *Canadian Journal of Economics and Political Science* 29 (2): 141-58.

–. 1981. The staple theory revisited. In *Culture, Communication, and Dependency: The Tradition of H.A. Innis,* ed. W.H. Melody, L. Salter, and P. Heyer, 53-71. Norwood, NJ: Ablex Publishing.

–. 1982. The Innis tradition in Canadian political economy. *Canadian Journal of Political Science and Social Theory* 6 (1-2): 12-34.

Watkinson, C. 2001. Community forestry for the Nuxalk Nation. Presentation to Community Forestry Forum, 27 November 2002, Bella Coola, BC.

Weaver, C., and T. Gunton. 1982. From drought assistance to megaprojects: Fifty years of regional theory and policy in Canada. *Canadian Journal of Regional Science* 5 (1): 5-37.

Whyte, W.F. 1991. *Participatory Action Research*. London: Sage.

Williamson, T., and S. Annamraju. 1996. Analysis of the contributions of the forest industry to the economic base of rural communities in Canada. Working paper no. 43, Industry, Economics and Programs Branch, Natural Resources Canada – Canadian Forest Service.

Wilson, F. 1999. Cutting costs: The politics of trees and fees in BC. Canadian Centre for Policy Alternatives, BC Office.

Wilson, P. 1997. Building social capital: A learning agenda for the 21st century. *Urban Studies* 34 (5-6): 745-60.

Wismer, S., and D. Pell. 1981. *Community Profit: Community-based Economic Development in Canada*. Toronto: Five Press.

Woolcock, M. 2001. The place of social capital in understanding social and economic outcomes. *ISUMA: Canadian Journal of Policy Research* 2 (1): 11-17.

World Resources Institute. 2001. Canada's forests at a crossroads: An assessment in the year 2000. Washington, DC: World Resources Institute.

Young, D., and J. Charland. 1992. *Successful Local Economic Development Initiatives*. Toronto: ICURR Press.

Index

Printed and bound in Canada by Friesens
Set in Stone by Artegraphica Design Co. Ltd.
Text design: Irma Rodriguez
Copy editor: Francis Chow
Proofreader: Lenore Hietkamp
Indexer: Patricia Buchanan
Cartographer: John Ng